We are going to fall in love.

3

最終兵器彼女

SAIKANO

THE LAST LOVE SONG ON THIS LITTLE PLANET. ™

Story & Art by Shin Takahashi

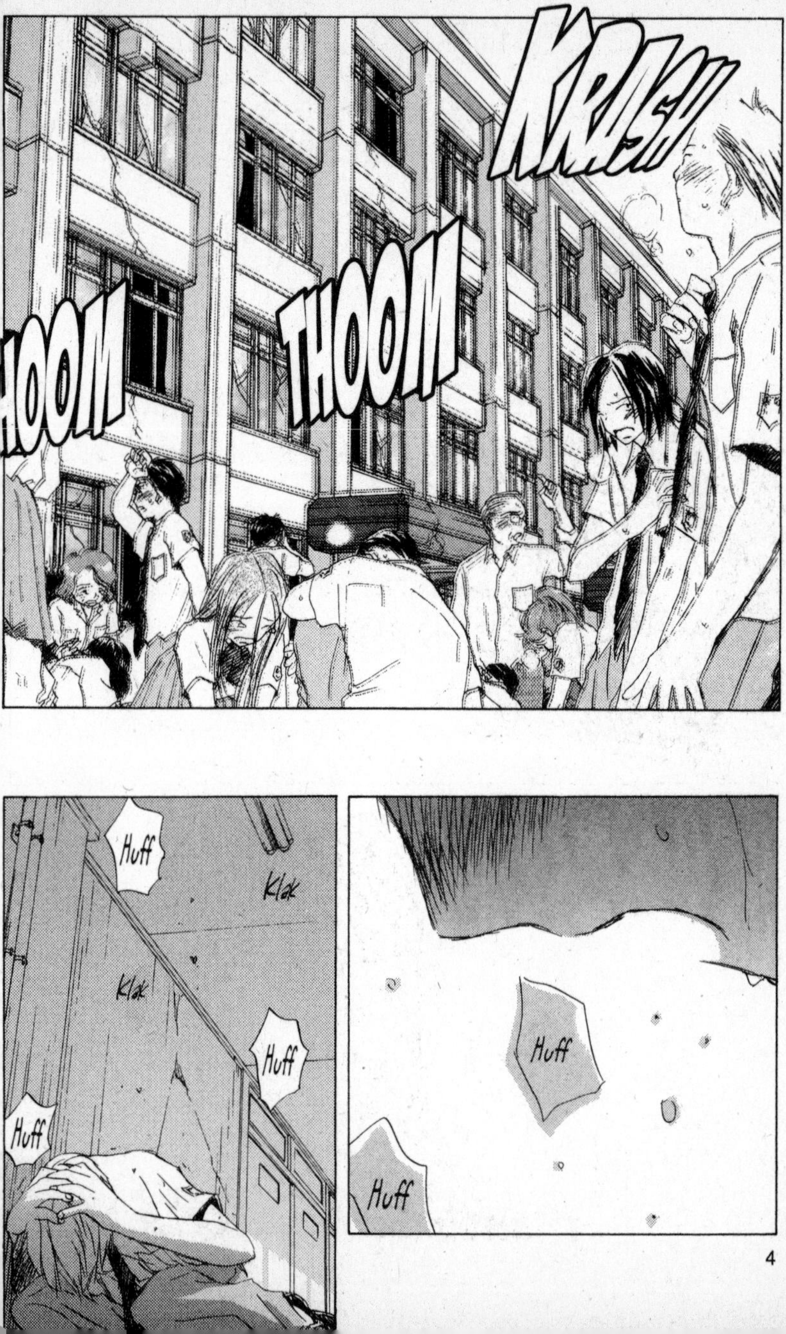
KRASH
THOOM
HOOM
Huff
Huff
Huff
Klak
Klak
Huff
Huff

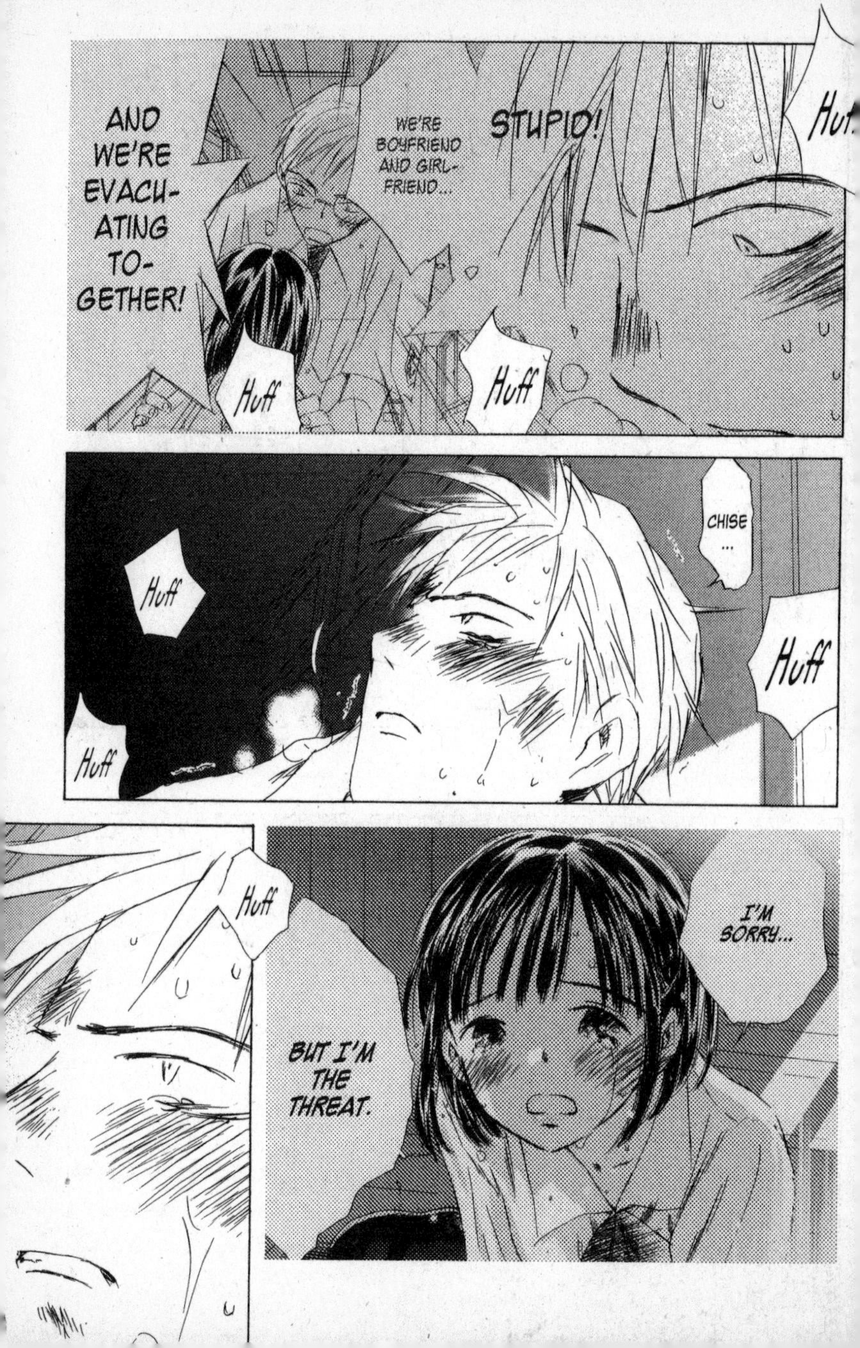
Huf
STUPID!
WE'RE BOYFRIEND AND GIRL-FRIEND...
AND WE'RE EVACU-ATING TO-GETHER!
Huff
Huff
CHISE ...
Huff
Huff
Huff
I'M SORRY...
BUT I'M THE THREAT.
Huff

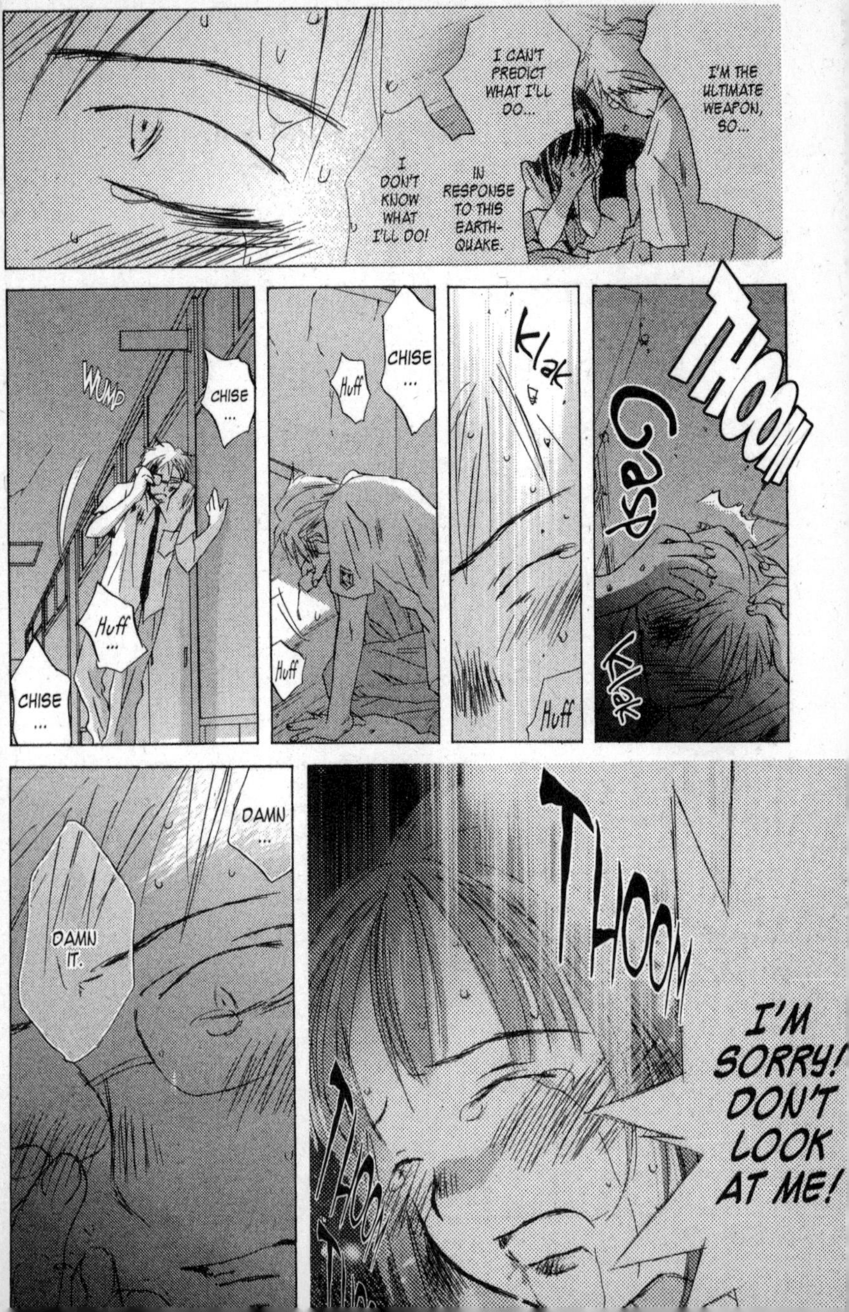
I'M THE ULTIMATE WEAPON, SO...
I CAN'T PREDICT WHAT I'LL DO...
IN RESPONSE TO THIS EARTHQUAKE.
I DON'T KNOW WHAT I'LL DO!
THOOM
Gasp
klak
klak
Huff
CHISE ...
Huff
Huff
WUMP
CHISE ...
Huff ...
CHISE ...
THOOM
I'M SORRY! DON'T LOOK AT ME!
THOOM
DAMN ...
DAMN IT.

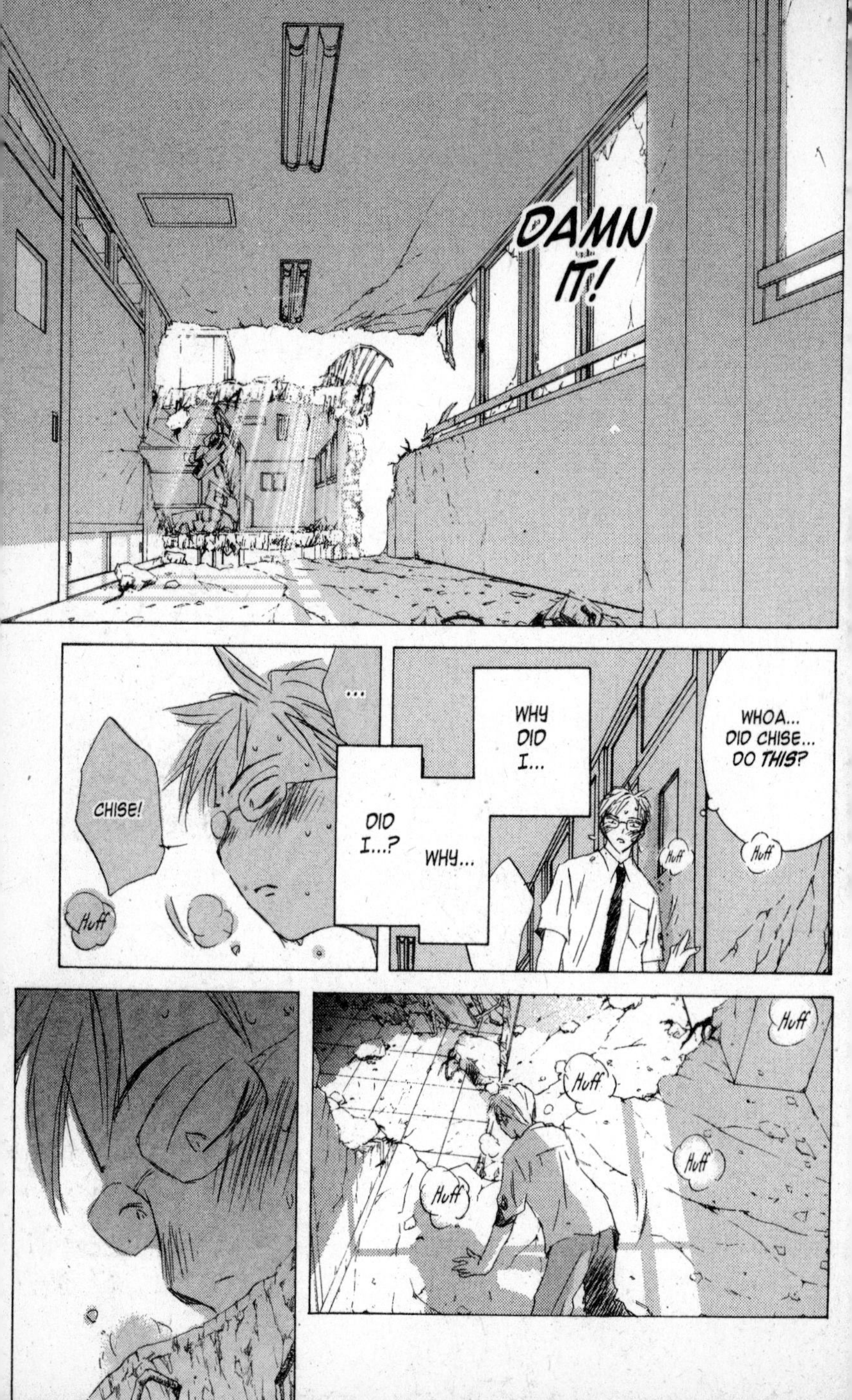
DAMN IT!
WHOA... DID CHISE... DO THIS?
Huff
Huff
WHY DID I...
WHY...
DID I...?
...
CHISE!
Huff
Huff
Huff
Huff
Huff
Huff

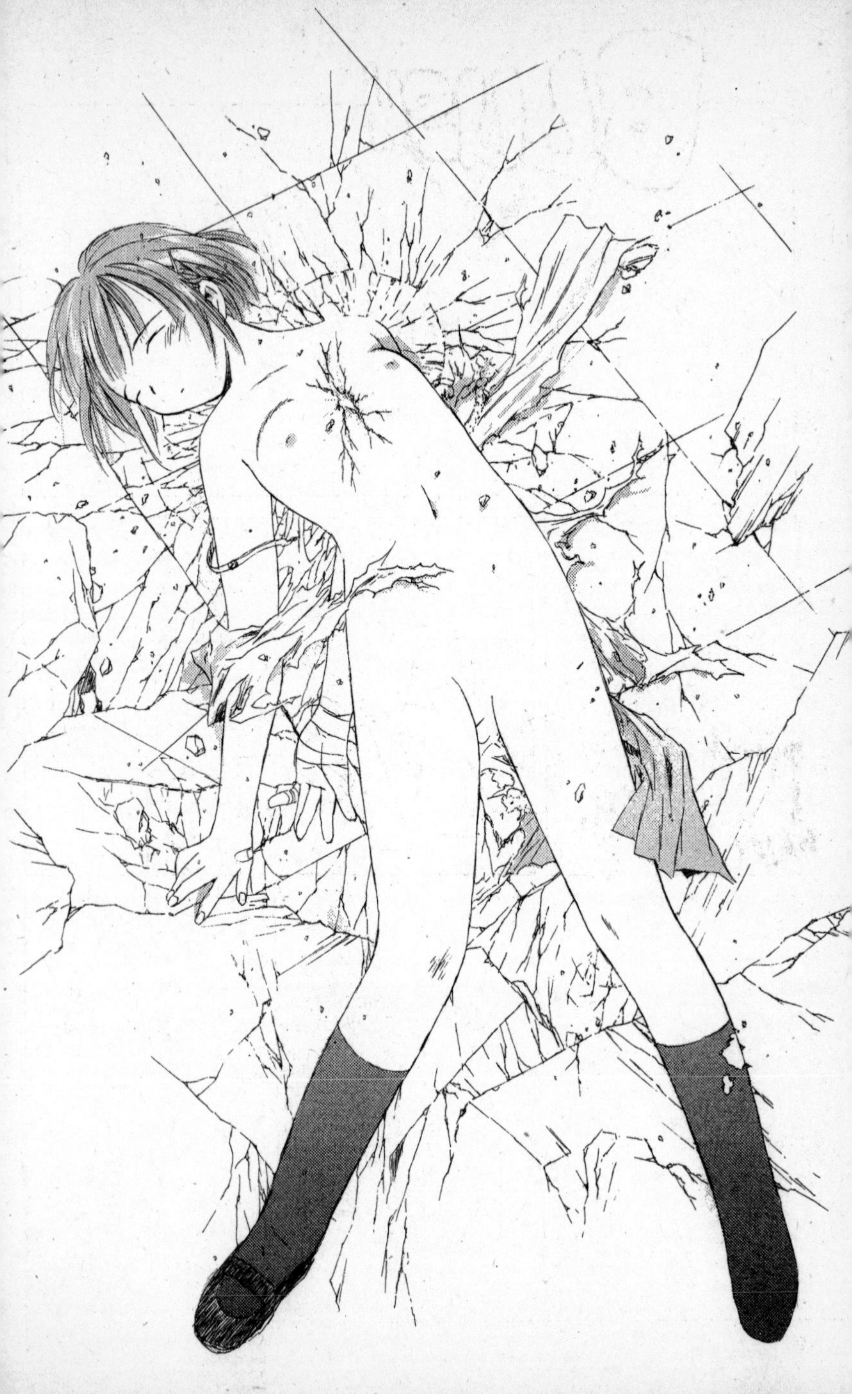

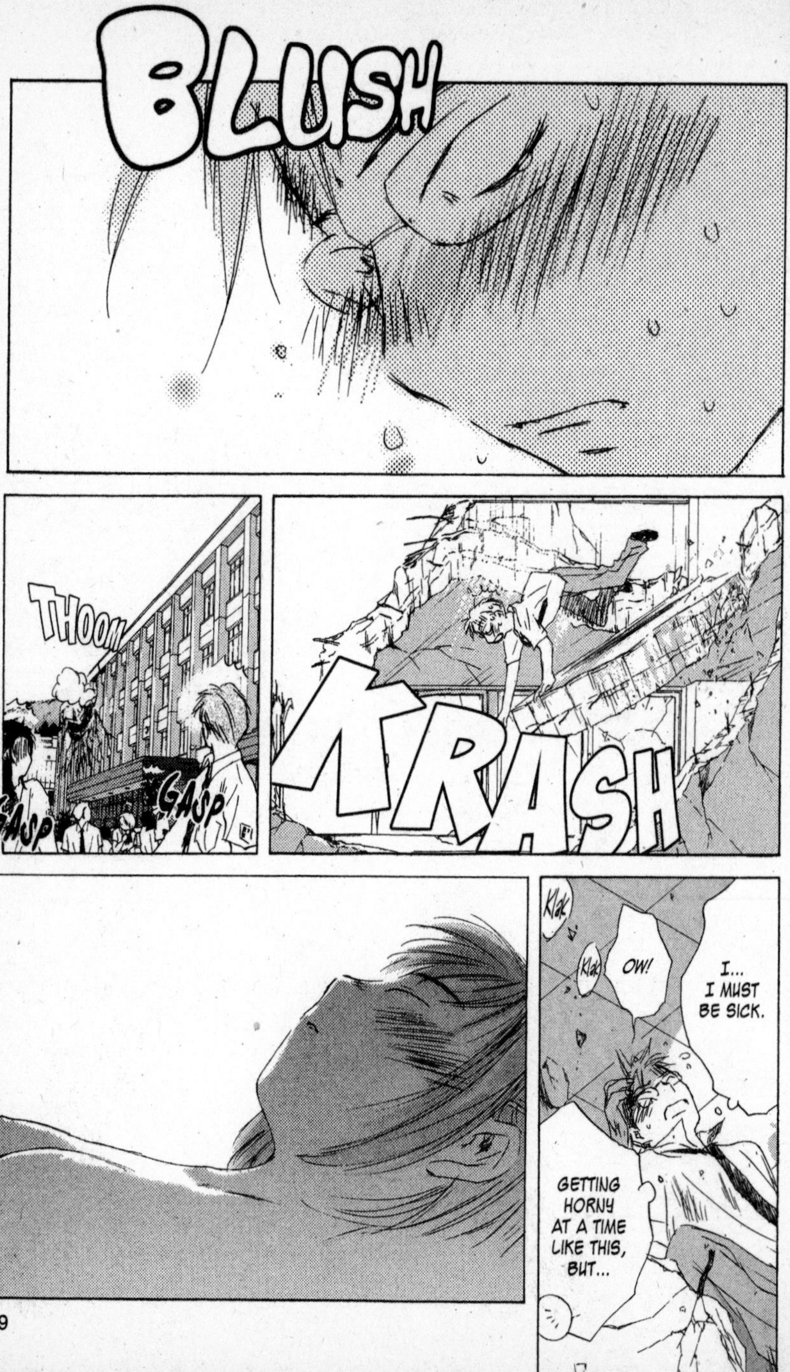

BLUSH
KRASH
THOOM
GASP
GASP
Klak
Klak
OW!
I... I MUST BE SICK.
GETTING HORNY AT A TIME LIKE THIS, BUT...

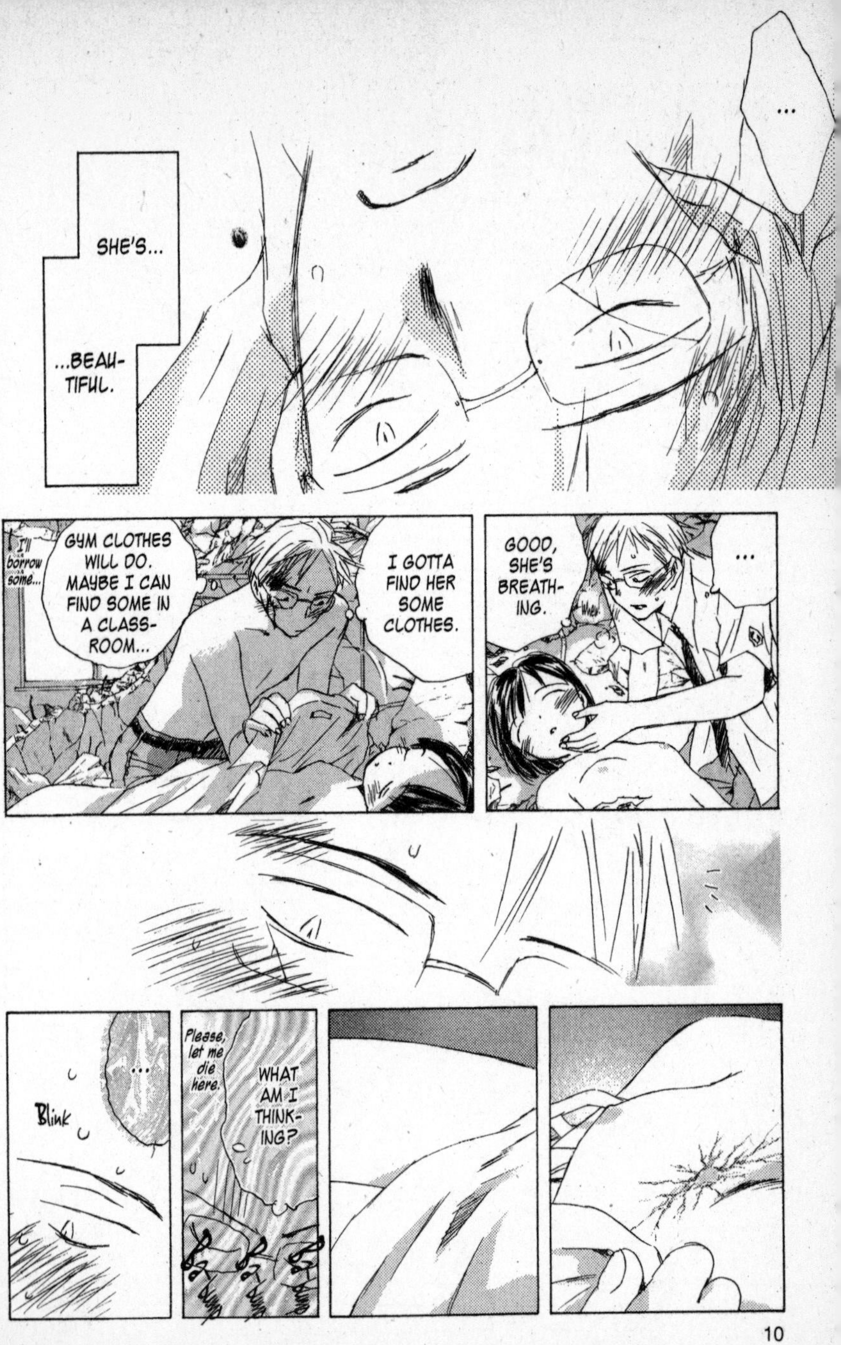
...
SHE'S...
...BEAU-TIFUL.
...
GOOD, SHE'S BREATH-ING.
I GOTTA FIND HER SOME CLOTHES.
GYM CLOTHES WILL DO. MAYBE I CAN FIND SOME IN A CLASS-ROOM...
I'll borrow some...
WHAT AM I THINK-ING?
Please, let me die here.
...
Blink

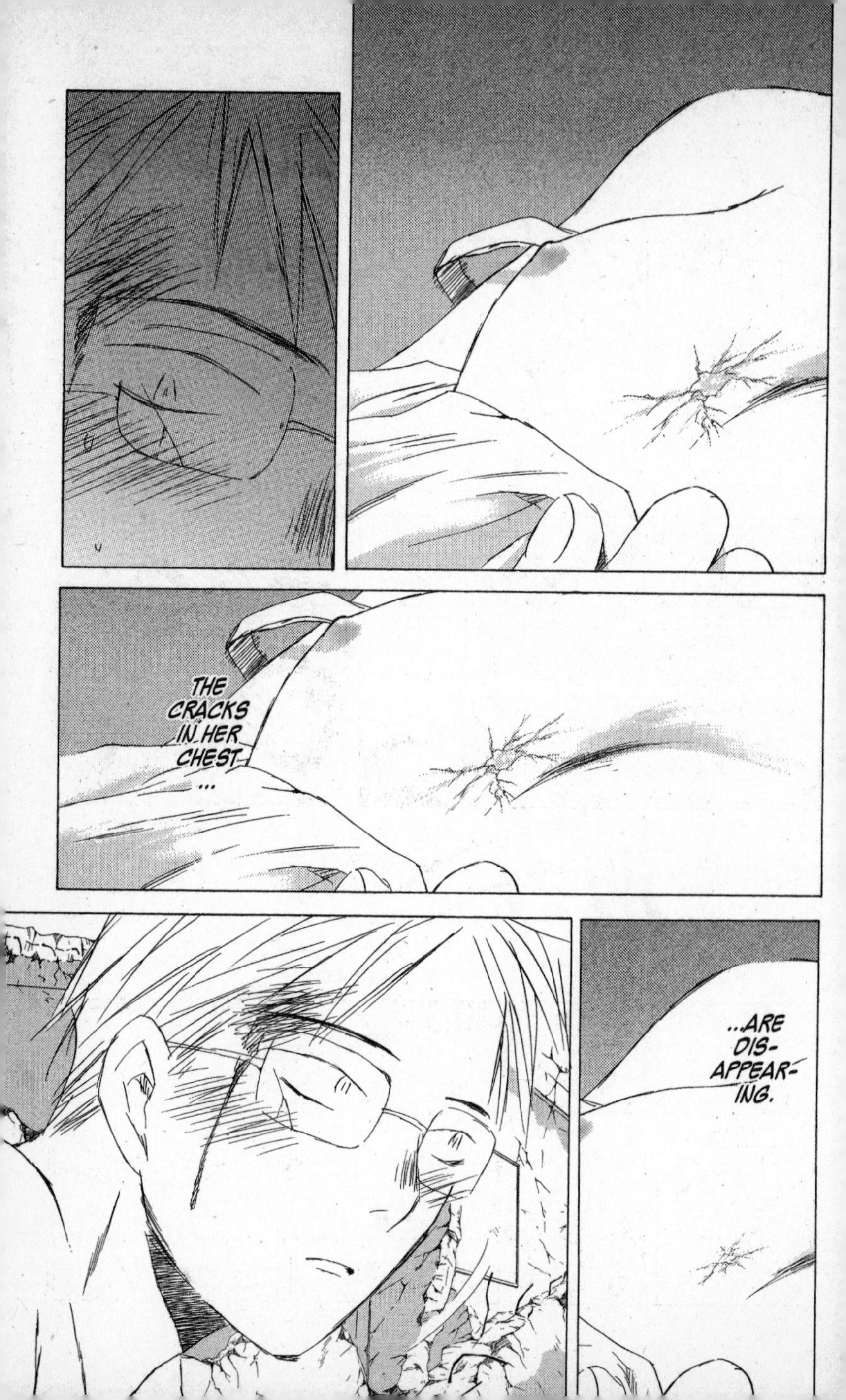
THE CRACKS IN HER CHEST ...
...ARE DIS-APPEAR-ING.

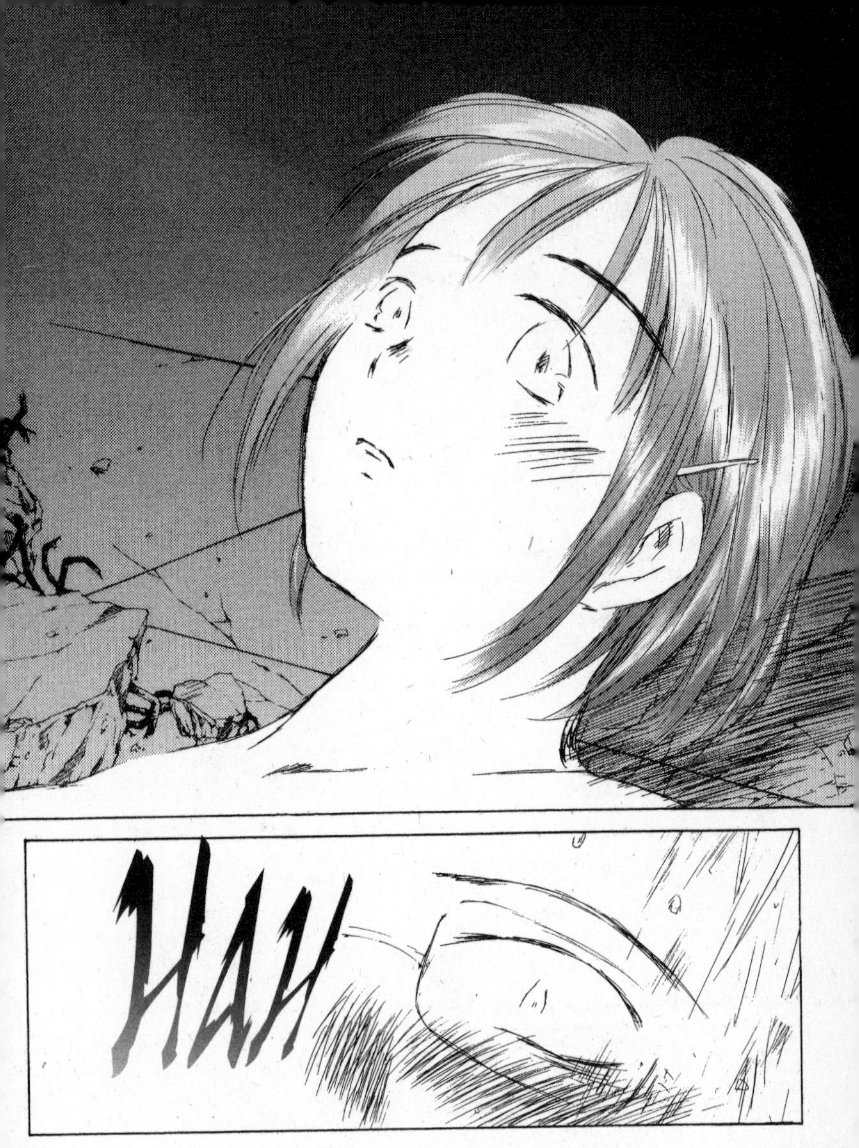
HAH

Even
I don't
know
what I
might
do...

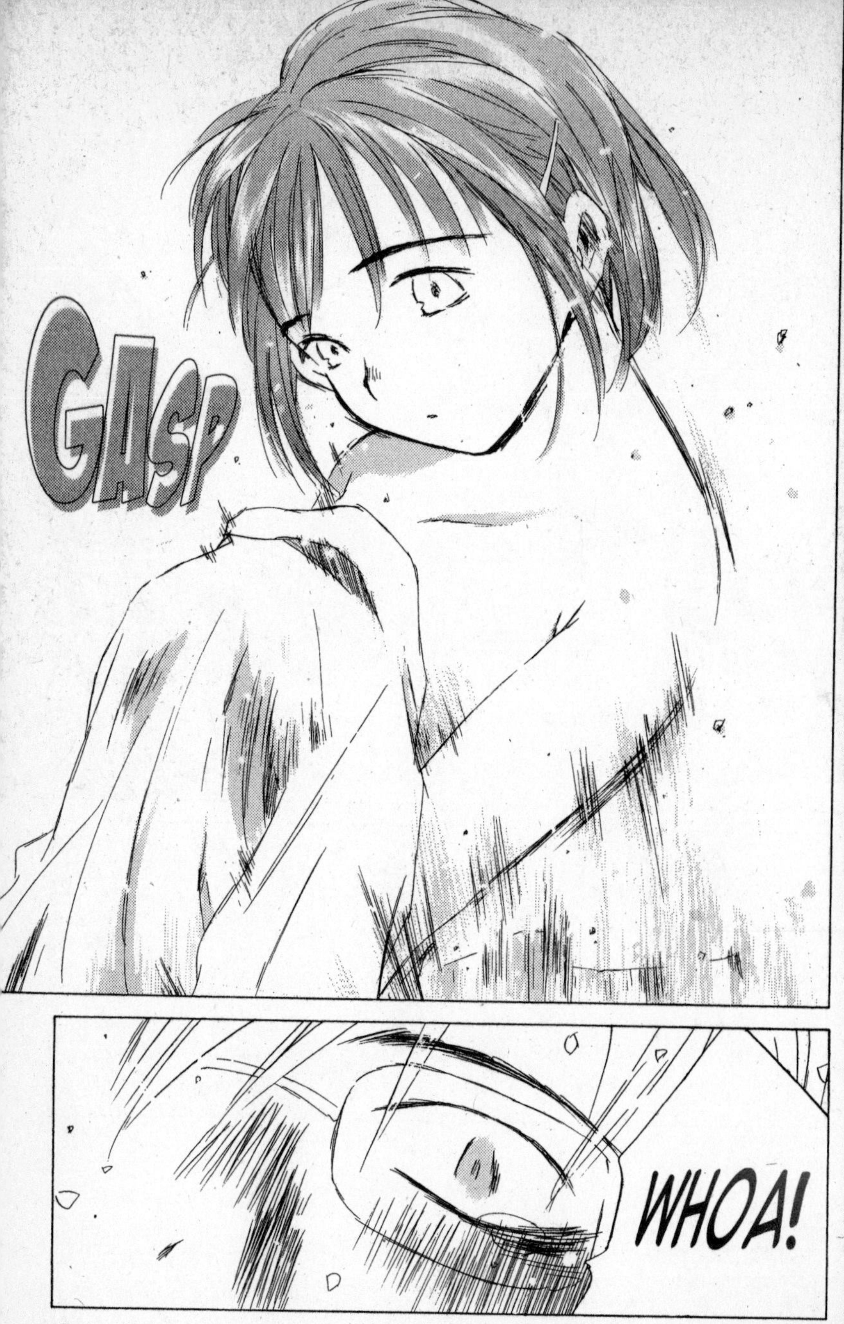
GASP
WHOA!

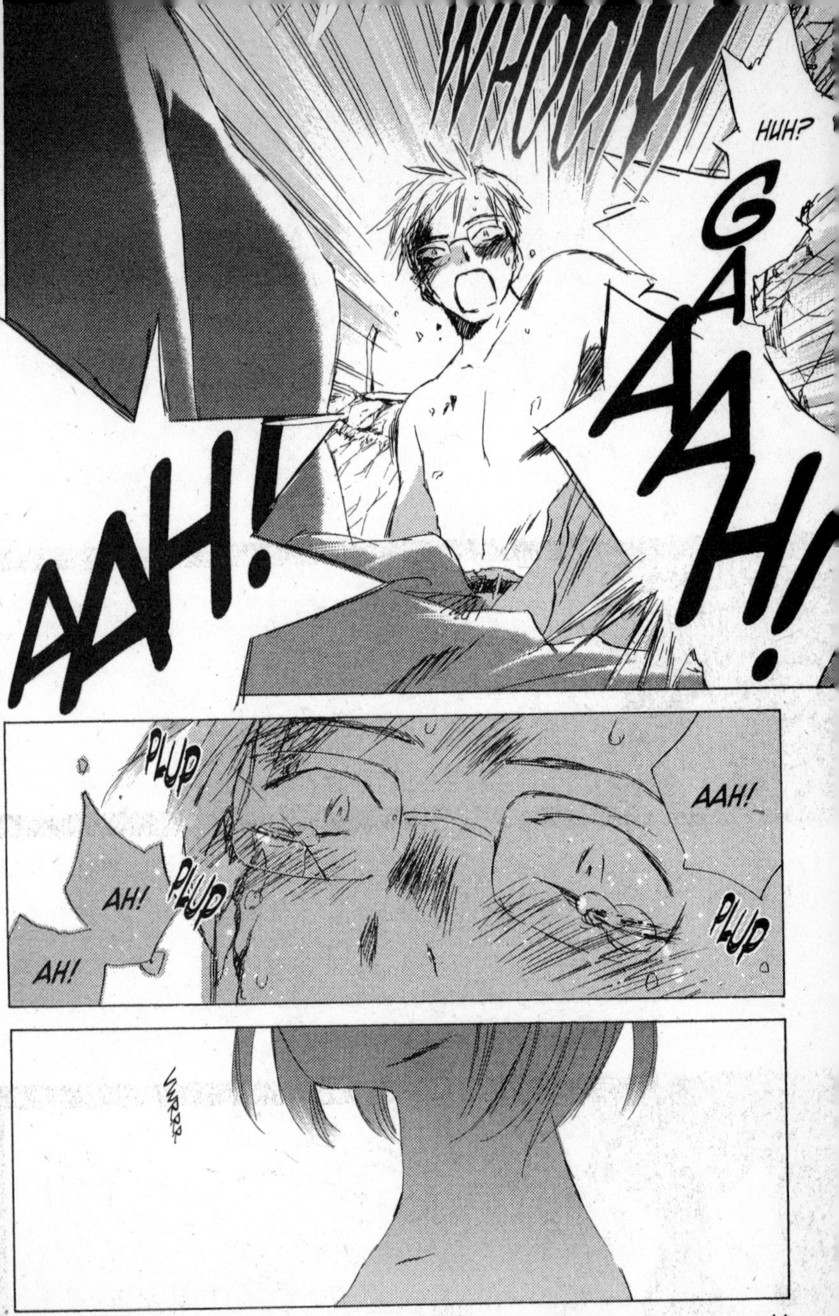
WHOOM
HUH?
GAAAH!
AAH!
AAH!
PLUP
PLUP
PLUP
AH!
AH!
VVRRR

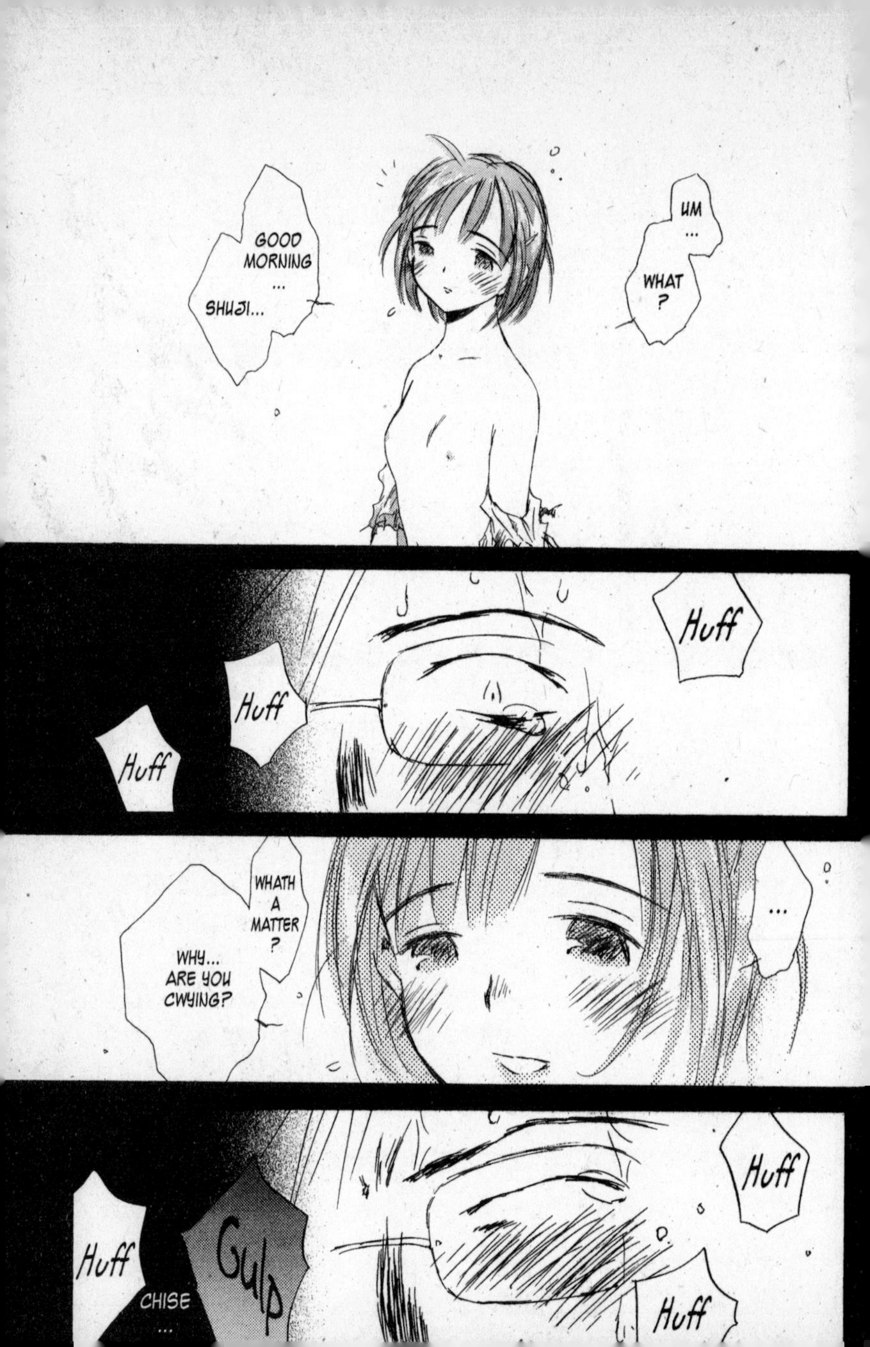
UM ... WHAT ?
GOOD MORNING ... SHUJI...
Huff
Huff
Huff
...
WHATH A MATTER ?
WHY... ARE YOU CWYING?
Huff
Huff
Gulp
Huff
CHISE ...

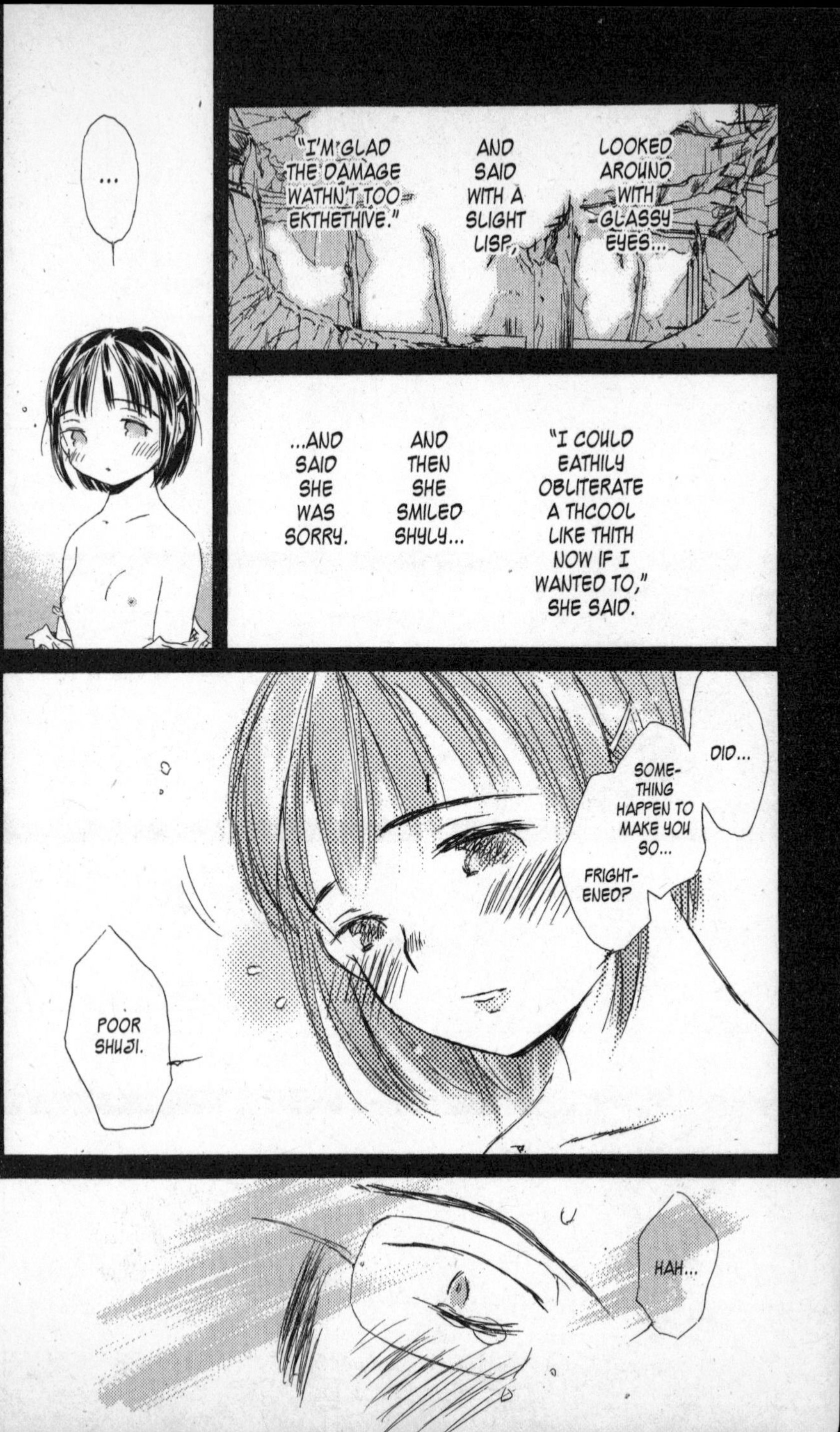
LOOKED AROUND WITH GLASSY EYES...
AND SAID WITH A SLIGHT LISP,
"I'M GLAD THE DAMAGE WATHN'T TOO EKTHETHIVE."
"I COULD EATHILY OBLITERATE A THCOOL LIKE THITH NOW IF I WANTED TO," SHE SAID.
AND THEN SHE SMILED SHYLY...
...AND SAID SHE WAS SORRY.
...
DID...
SOME-THING HAPPEN TO MAKE YOU SO...
FRIGHT-ENED?
POOR SHUJI.
HAH...

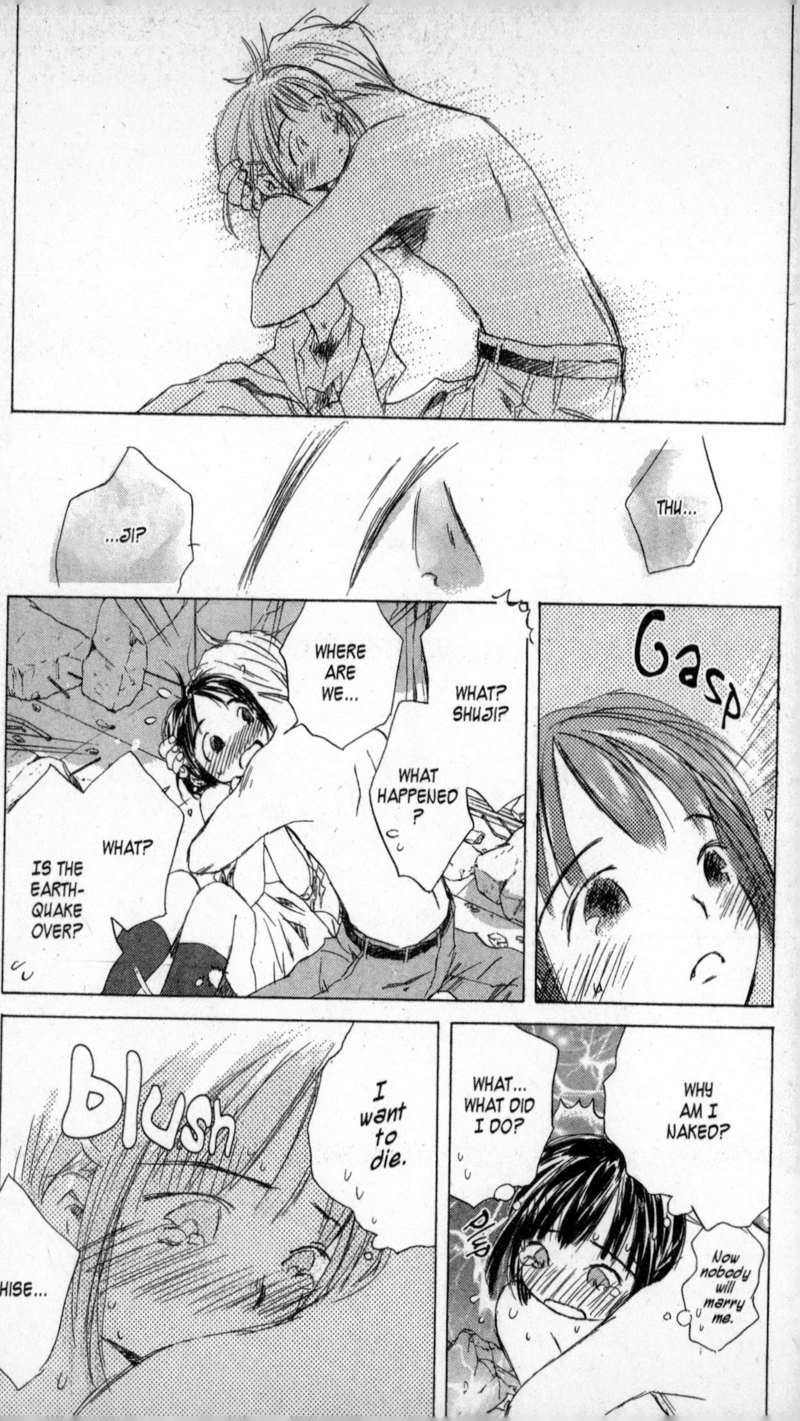
THU...
...JI?
Gasp
WHAT? SHUJI?
WHERE ARE WE...
WHAT HAPPENED?
WHAT?
IS THE EARTH-QUAKE OVER?
WHY AM I NAKED?
WHAT... WHAT DID I DO?
Plup
Now nobody will marry me.
I want to die.
blush
CHISE...

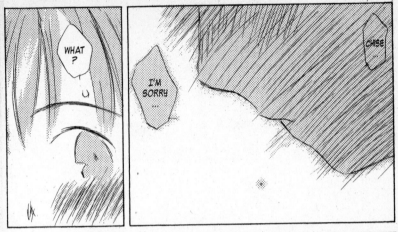

WHAT
?

I'M
SORRY
...

CHISE

I'M
SORRY,
CHISE...

I'M
SORRY!

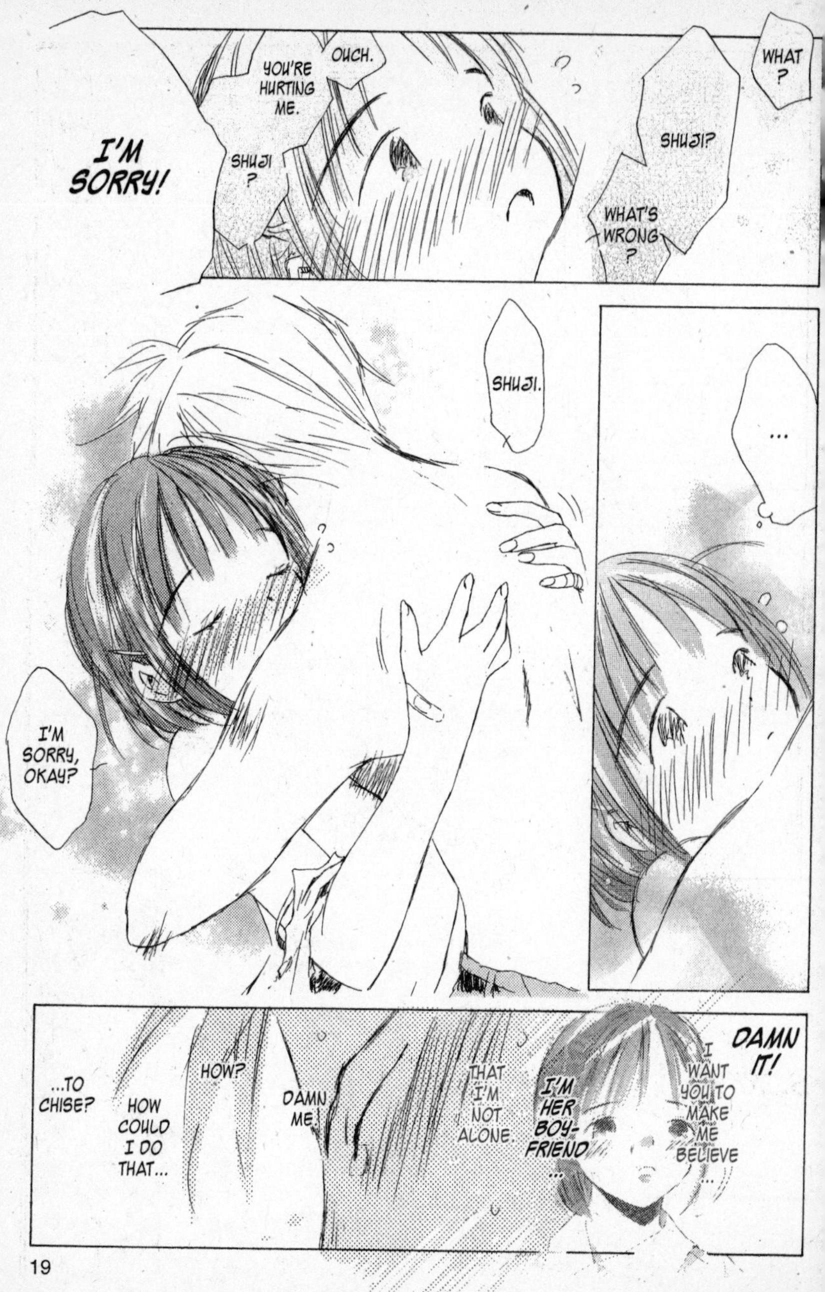
WHAT ?
SHUJI?
WHAT'S WRONG ?
OUCH.
YOU'RE HURTING ME.
SHUJI ?
I'M SORRY!
...
SHUJI.
I'M SORRY, OKAY?
DAMN IT!
I WANT YOU TO MAKE ME BELIEVE ...
I'M HER BOY-FRIEND ...
THAT I'M NOT ALONE.
DAMN ME.
HOW?
HOW COULD I DO THAT...
...TO CHISE?

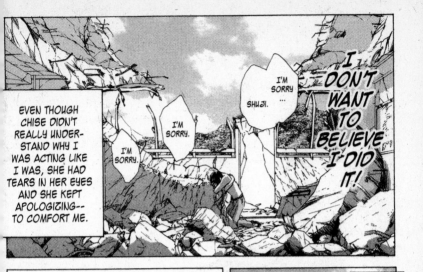

I DON'T WANT TO BELIEVE I DID IT!
I'M SORRY... SHUJI.
I'M SORRY.
I'M SORRY.
EVEN THOUGH CHISE DIDN'T REALLY UNDER-STAND WHY I WAS ACTING LIKE I WAS, SHE HAD TEARS IN HER EYES AND SHE KEPT APOLOGIZING-- TO COMFORT ME.
OR MAYBE SHE APOLO-GIZED...
BECAUSE SHE ALWAYS THINKS SHE'S TO BLAME FOR EVERY BAD THING THAT HAPPENS IN THE WORLD.
WHEN THIS THOUGHT HIT ME, I BEGAN TO FEEL HER PAIN.
I LOOKED UP TO STOP MY OWN TEARS, AND I SNEEZED.
CHISE JUST LOOKED AT ME FOR A MOMENT, AND THEN SHE LAUGHED.

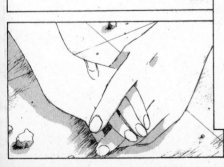

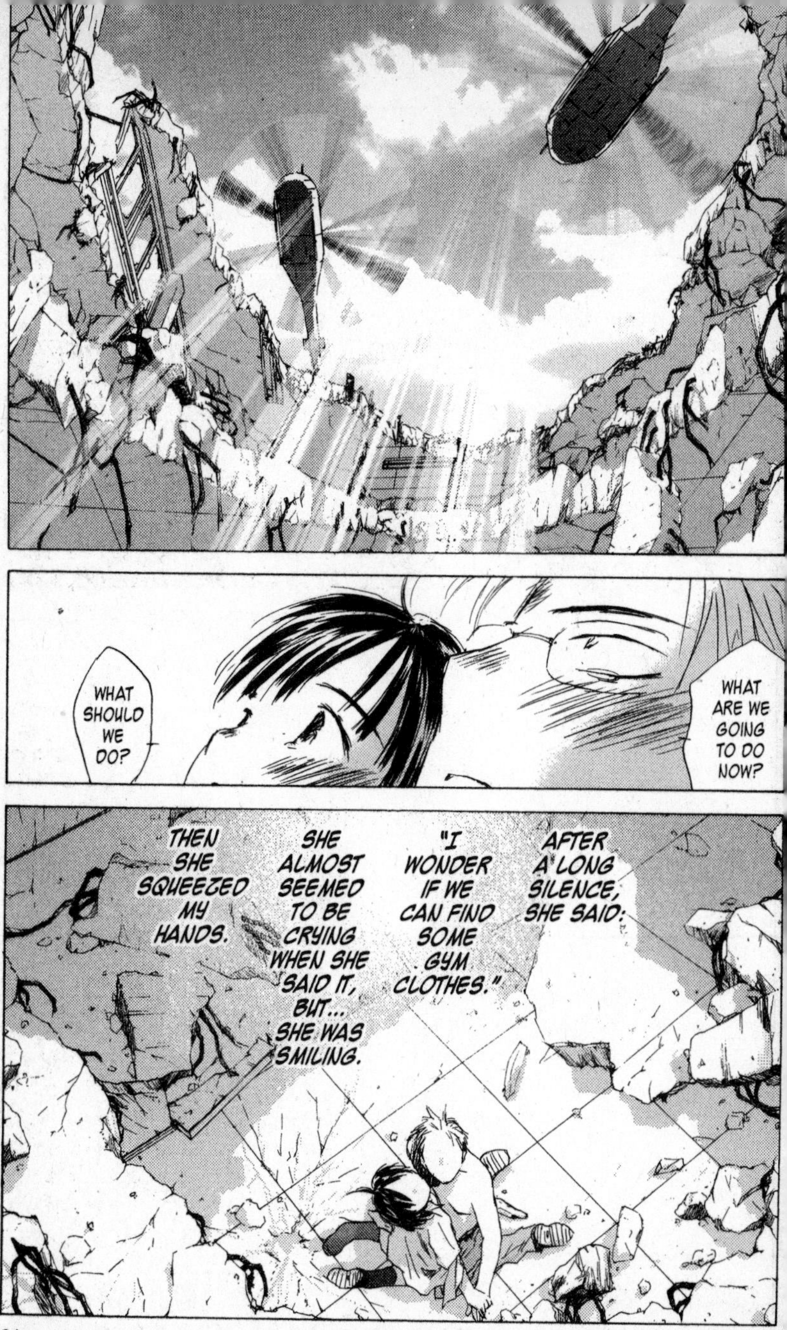
WHAT ARE WE GOING TO DO NOW?
WHAT SHOULD WE DO?
AFTER A LONG SILENCE, SHE SAID:
"I WONDER IF WE CAN FIND SOME GYM CLOTHES."
SHE ALMOST SEEMED TO BE CRYING WHEN SHE SAID IT, BUT... SHE WAS SMILING.
THEN SHE SQUEEZED MY HANDS.

Table of Contents

最終兵器彼女 SAIKANO™

3

Chapter 4

Fuyumi (6) —————————— 3

Fuyumi (7) —————————— 47

Fuyumi (8) —————————— 65

Chapter 5

On This Planet (1) —————————— 87

On This Planet (1) —————————— 105

On This Planet (1) —————————— 125

On This Planet (1) —————————— 145

Intermission

Just Friends–Shuji —————————— 191

Intermission

Just Friends–Chise —————————— 211

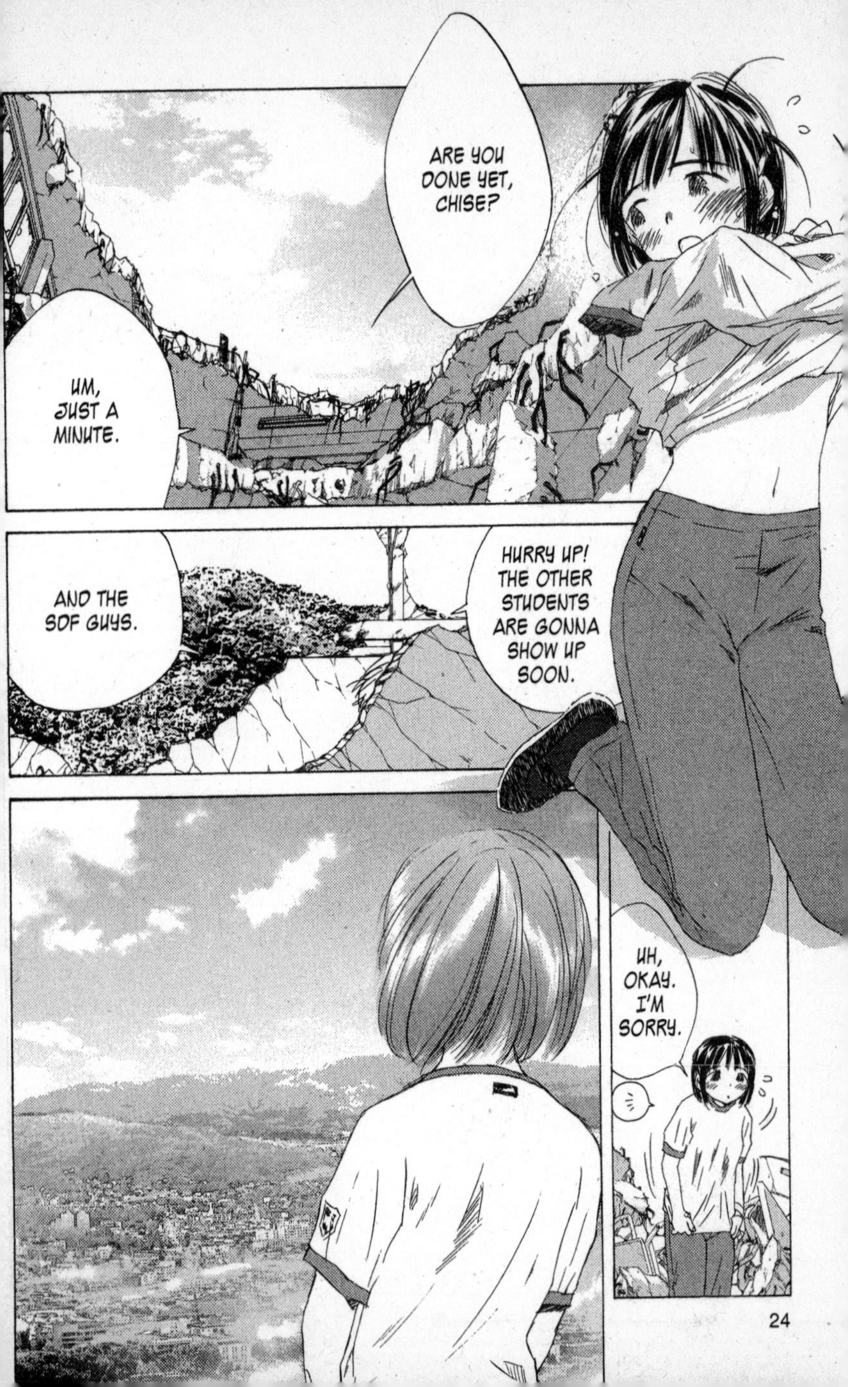
ARE YOU DONE YET, CHISE?
UM, JUST A MINUTE.
HURRY UP! THE OTHER STUDENTS ARE GONNA SHOW UP SOON.
AND THE SDF GUYS.
UH, OKAY. I'M SORRY.

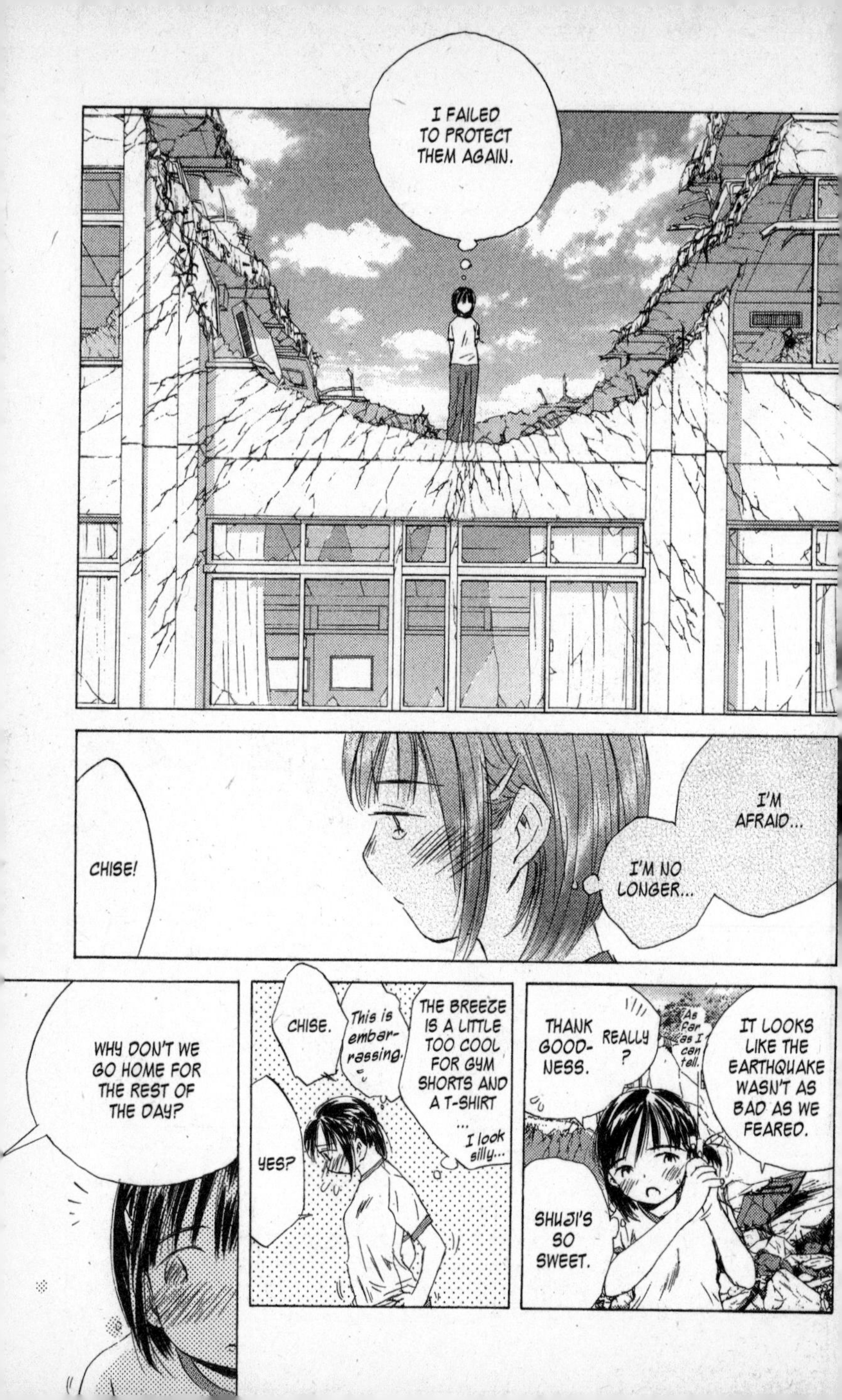
I FAILED TO PROTECT THEM AGAIN.
I'M AFRAID...
I'M NO LONGER...
CHISE!
IT LOOKS LIKE THE EARTHQUAKE WASN'T AS BAD AS WE FEARED.
As far as I can tell.
REALLY?
THANK GOODNESS.
SHUJI'S SO SWEET.
THE BREEZE IS A LITTLE TOO COOL FOR GYM SHORTS AND A T-SHIRT ...
I look silly...
This is embarrassing.
CHISE.
YES?
WHY DON'T WE GO HOME FOR THE REST OF THE DAY?

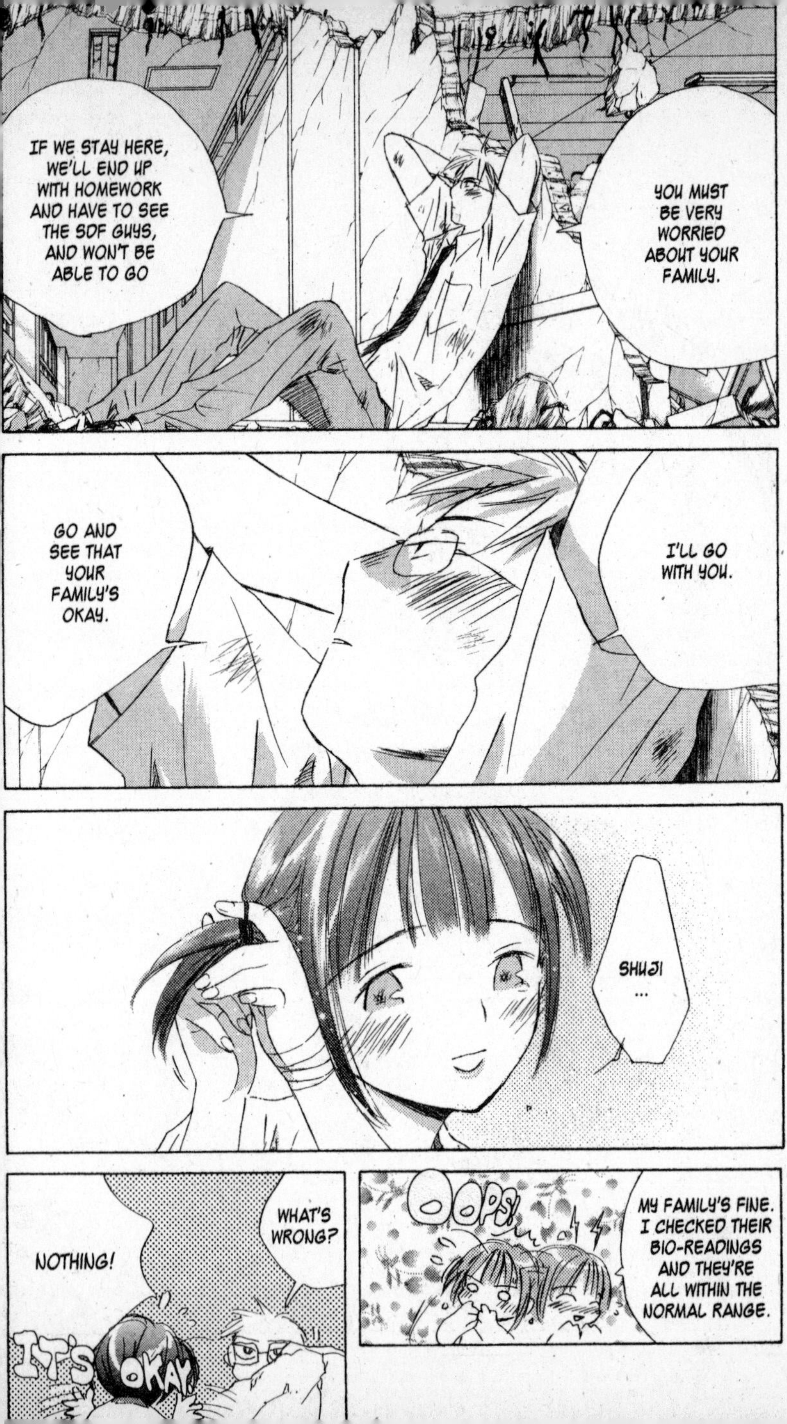
YOU MUST BE VERY WORRIED ABOUT YOUR FAMILY.
IF WE STAY HERE, WE'LL END UP WITH HOMEWORK AND HAVE TO SEE THE SDF GUYS, AND WON'T BE ABLE TO GO
I'LL GO WITH YOU.
GO AND SEE THAT YOUR FAMILY'S OKAY.
SHUJI ...
MY FAMILY'S FINE. I CHECKED THEIR BIO-READINGS AND THEY'RE ALL WITHIN THE NORMAL RANGE.
OOPS!
WHAT'S WRONG?
NOTHING!
IT'S OKAY

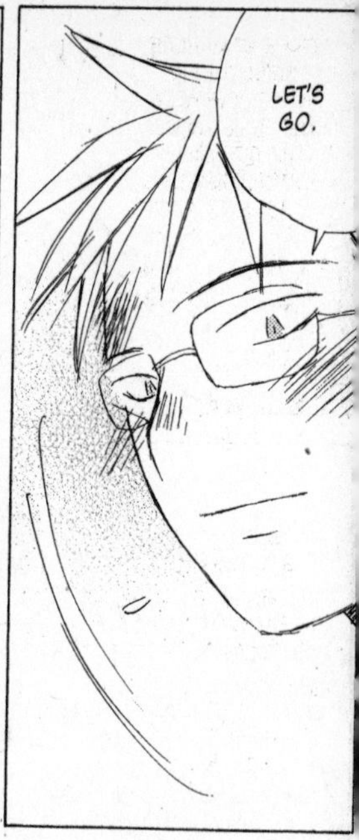
LET'S GO.

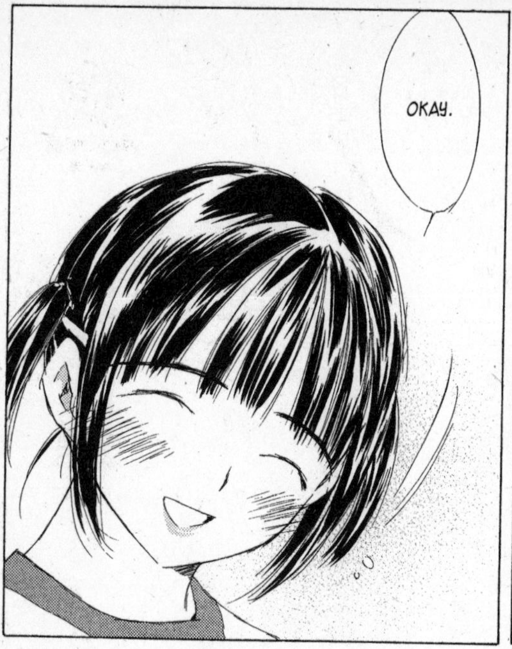
OKAY.

THE LAST LOVE SONG ON THIS LITTLE PLANET.

Chapter 4: Fuyumi (6)

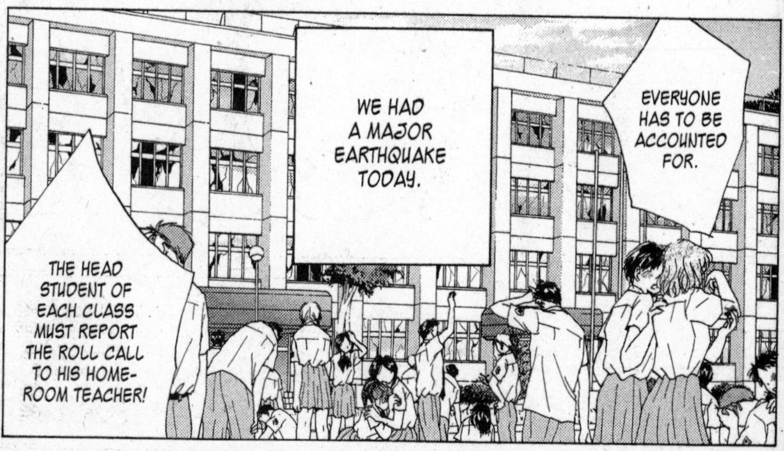
EVERYONE HAS TO BE ACCOUNTED FOR.
WE HAD A MAJOR EARTHQUAKE TODAY.
THE HEAD STUDENT OF EACH CLASS MUST REPORT THE ROLL CALL TO HIS HOME-ROOM TEACHER!

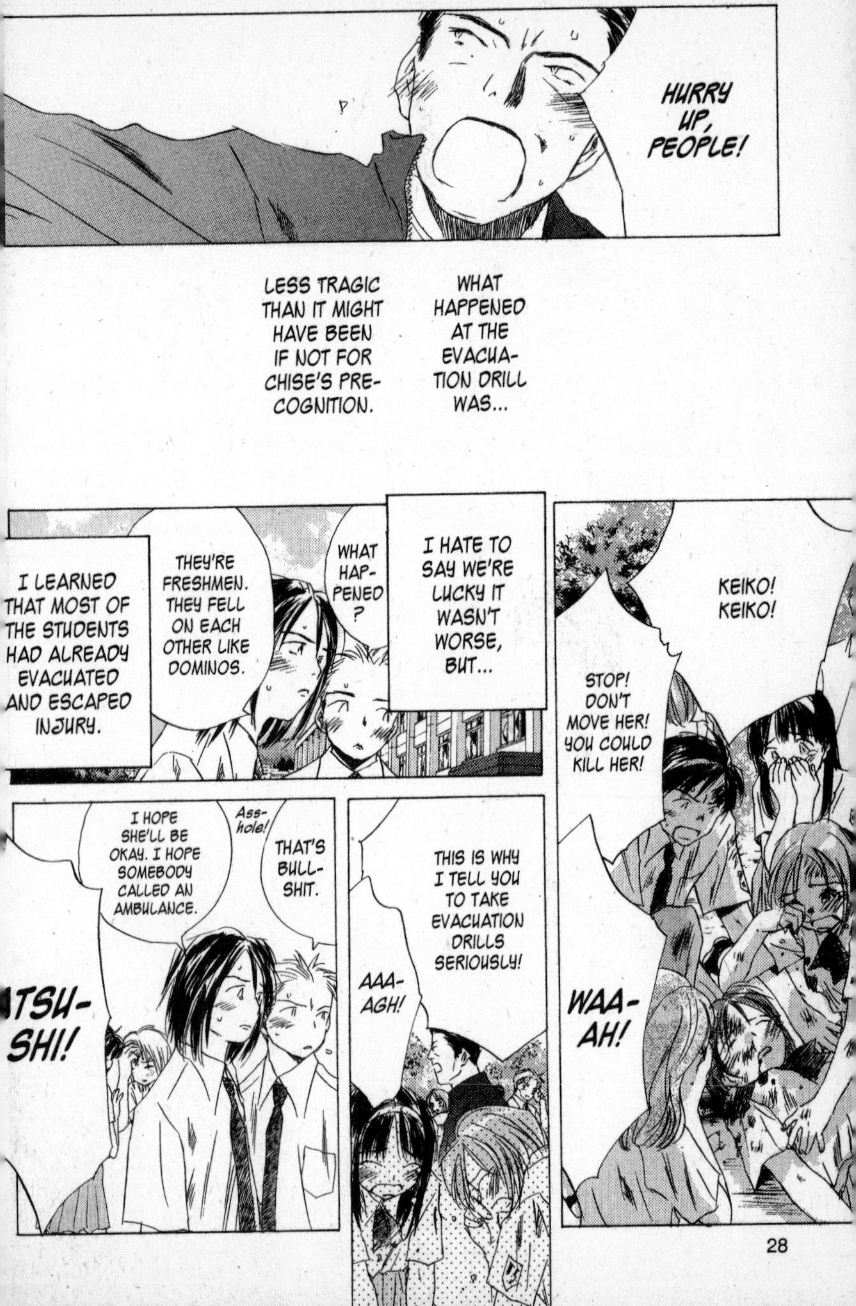
HURRY UP, PEOPLE!
WHAT HAPPENED AT THE EVACUATION DRILL WAS...
LESS TRAGIC THAN IT MIGHT HAVE BEEN IF NOT FOR CHISE'S PRECOGNITION.
KEIKO! KEIKO!
STOP! DON'T MOVE HER! YOU COULD KILL HER!
WAA-AH!
I HATE TO SAY WE'RE LUCKY IT WASN'T WORSE, BUT...
WHAT HAPPENED?
THEY'RE FRESHMEN. THEY FELL ON EACH OTHER LIKE DOMINOS.
I LEARNED THAT MOST OF THE STUDENTS HAD ALREADY EVACUATED AND ESCAPED INJURY.
THIS IS WHY I TELL YOU TO TAKE EVACUATION DRILLS SERIOUSLY!
AAA-AGH!
THAT'S BULLSHIT.
Asshole!
I HOPE SHE'LL BE OKAY. I HOPE SOMEBODY CALLED AN AMBULANCE.
ATSU-SHI!

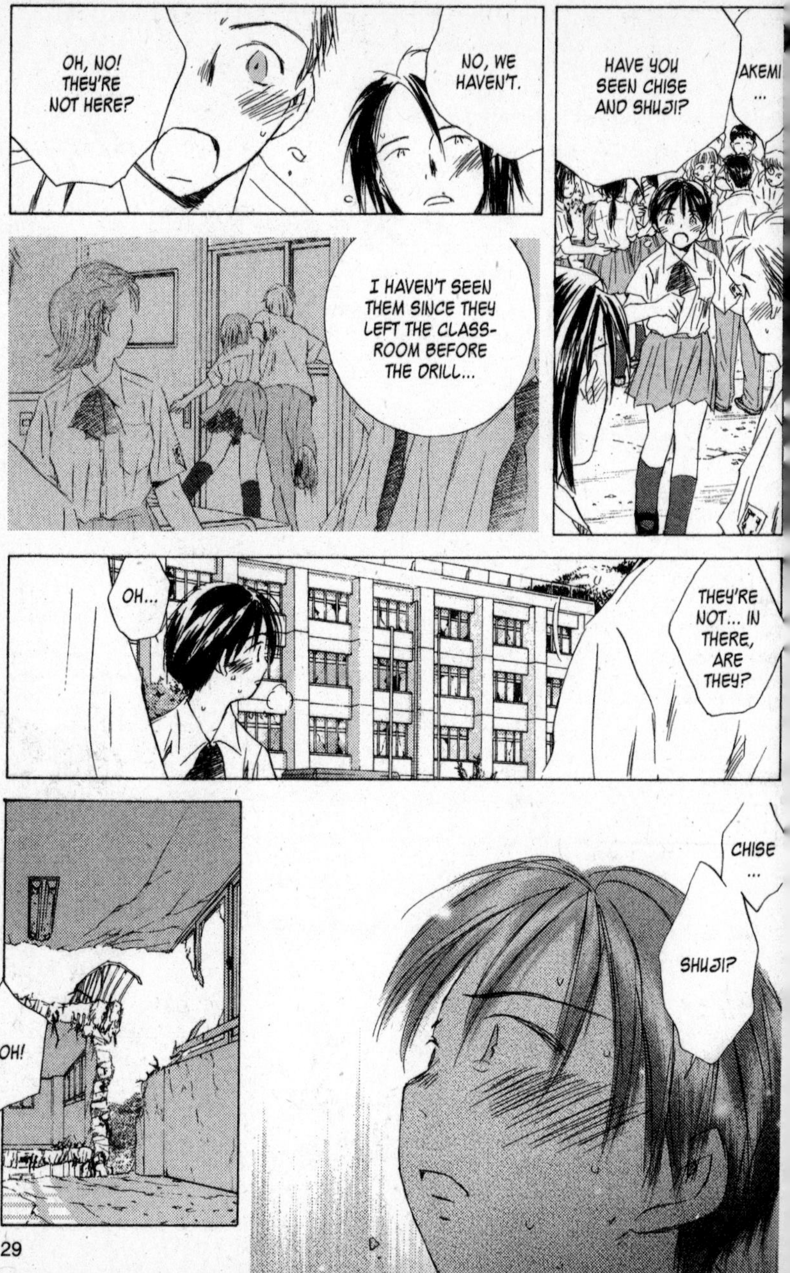
AKEMI ...
HAVE YOU SEEN CHISE AND SHUJI?
NO, WE HAVEN'T.
OH, NO! THEY'RE NOT HERE?
I HAVEN'T SEEN THEM SINCE THEY LEFT THE CLASS-ROOM BEFORE THE DRILL...
THEY'RE NOT... IN THERE, ARE THEY?
OH...
CHISE ...
SHUJI?
OH!

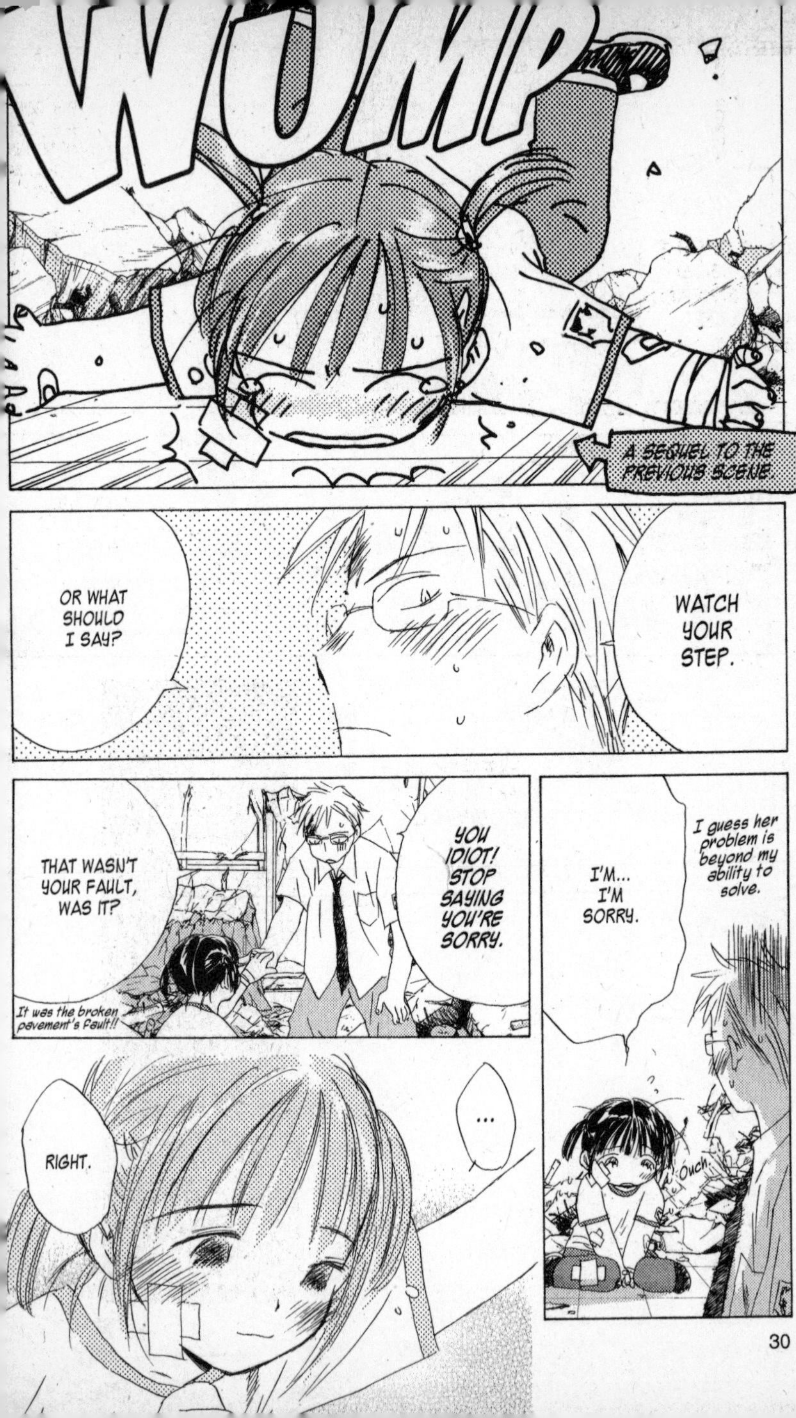
WOMP
A SEQUEL TO THE PREVIOUS SCENE.
WATCH YOUR STEP.
OR WHAT SHOULD I SAY?
I guess her problem is beyond my ability to solve.
I'M... I'M SORRY.
Ouch.
YOU IDIOT! STOP SAYING YOU'RE SORRY.
THAT WASN'T YOUR FAULT, WAS IT?
It was the broken pavement's fault!!
...
RIGHT.

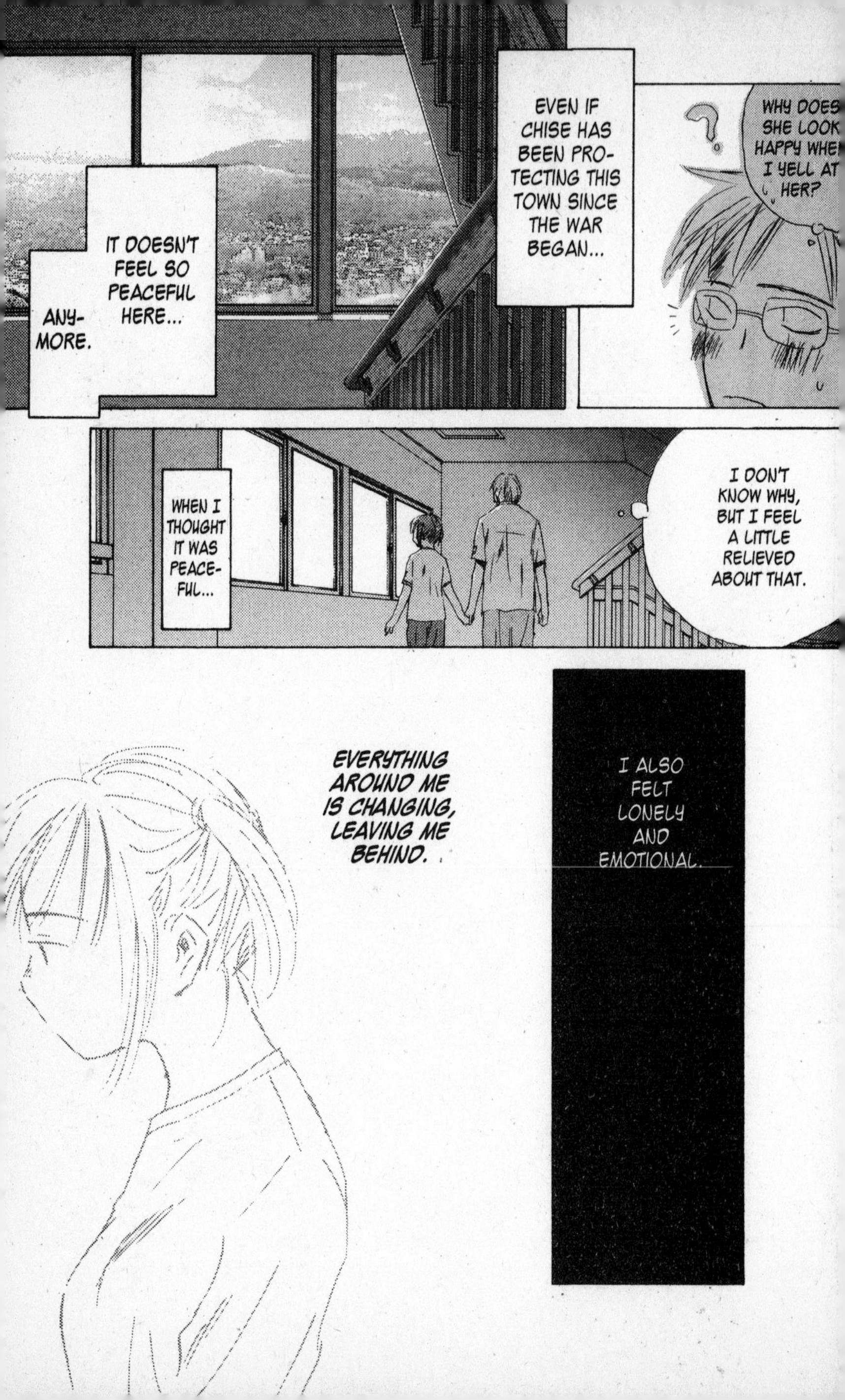
WHY DOES SHE LOOK HAPPY WHE I YELL AT HER?
EVEN IF CHISE HAS BEEN PROTECTING THIS TOWN SINCE THE WAR BEGAN...
IT DOESN'T FEEL SO PEACEFUL HERE...
ANYMORE.
I DON'T KNOW WHY, BUT I FEEL A LITTLE RELIEVED ABOUT THAT.
WHEN I THOUGHT IT WAS PEACEFUL...
I ALSO FELT LONELY AND EMOTIONAL.
EVERYTHING AROUND ME IS CHANGING, LEAVING ME BEHIND.

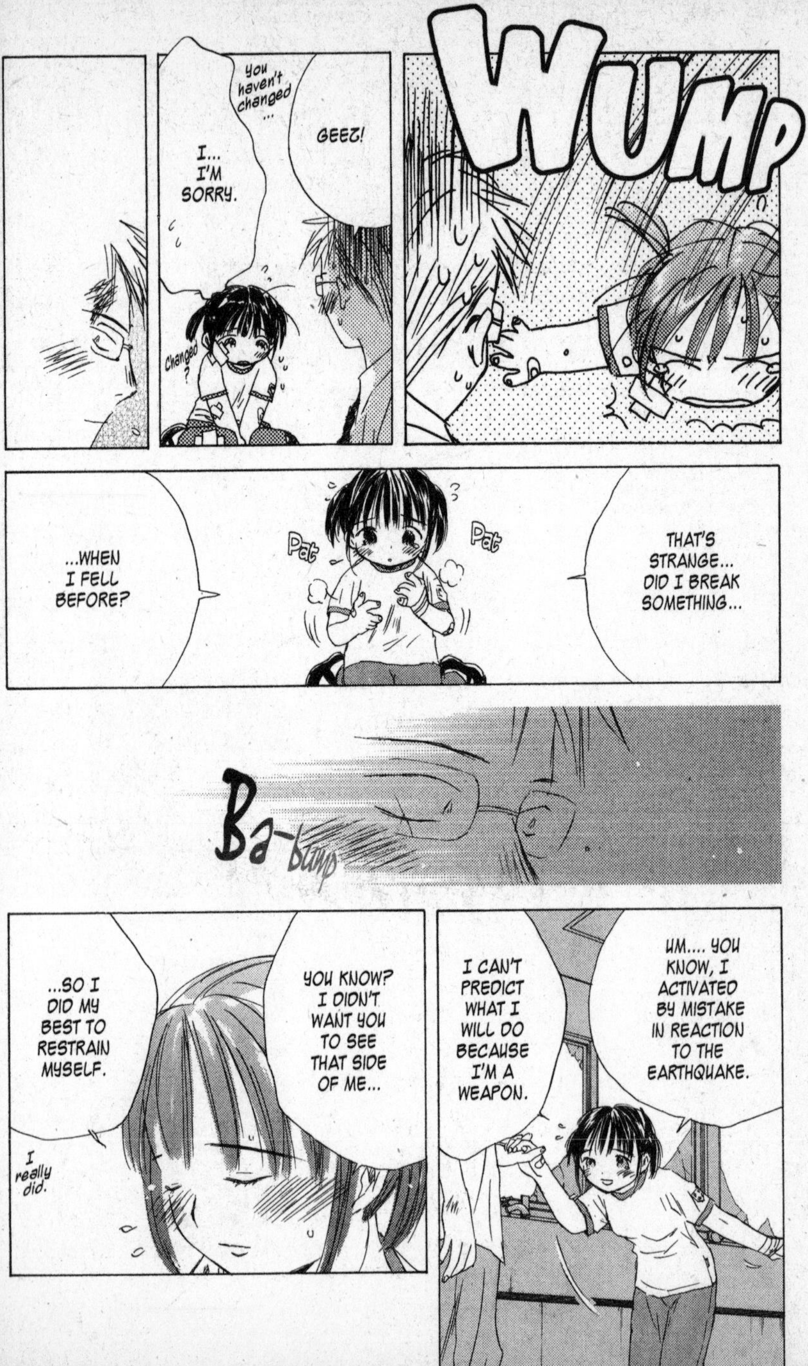
WUMP
GEEZ!
You haven't changed...
I... I'M SORRY.
Changed?
THAT'S STRANGE... DID I BREAK SOMETHING...
Pat
Pat
...WHEN I FELL BEFORE?
Ba-bump
UM.... YOU KNOW, I ACTIVATED BY MISTAKE IN REACTION TO THE EARTHQUAKE.
I CAN'T PREDICT WHAT I WILL DO BECAUSE I'M A WEAPON.
YOU KNOW? I DIDN'T WANT YOU TO SEE THAT SIDE OF ME...
...SO I DID MY BEST TO RESTRAIN MYSELF.
I really did.

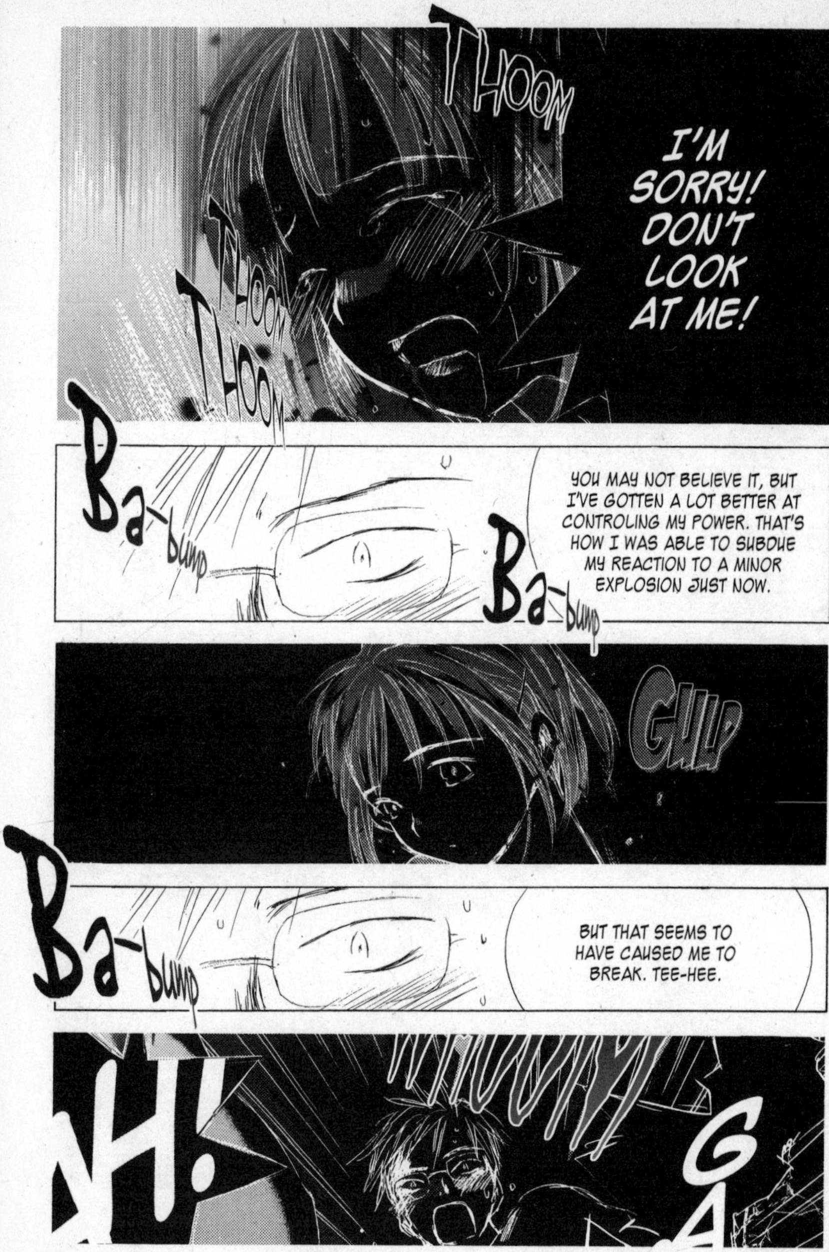
THOOM
I'M SORRY! DON'T LOOK AT ME!
THOOM
THOOM
YOU MAY NOT BELIEVE IT, BUT I'VE GOTTEN A LOT BETTER AT CONTROLING MY POWER. THAT'S HOW I WAS ABLE TO SUBDUE MY REACTION TO A MINOR EXPLOSION JUST NOW.
Ba-bump
Ba-bump
GULP
BUT THAT SEEMS TO HAVE CAUSED ME TO BREAK. TEE-HEE.
Ba-bump

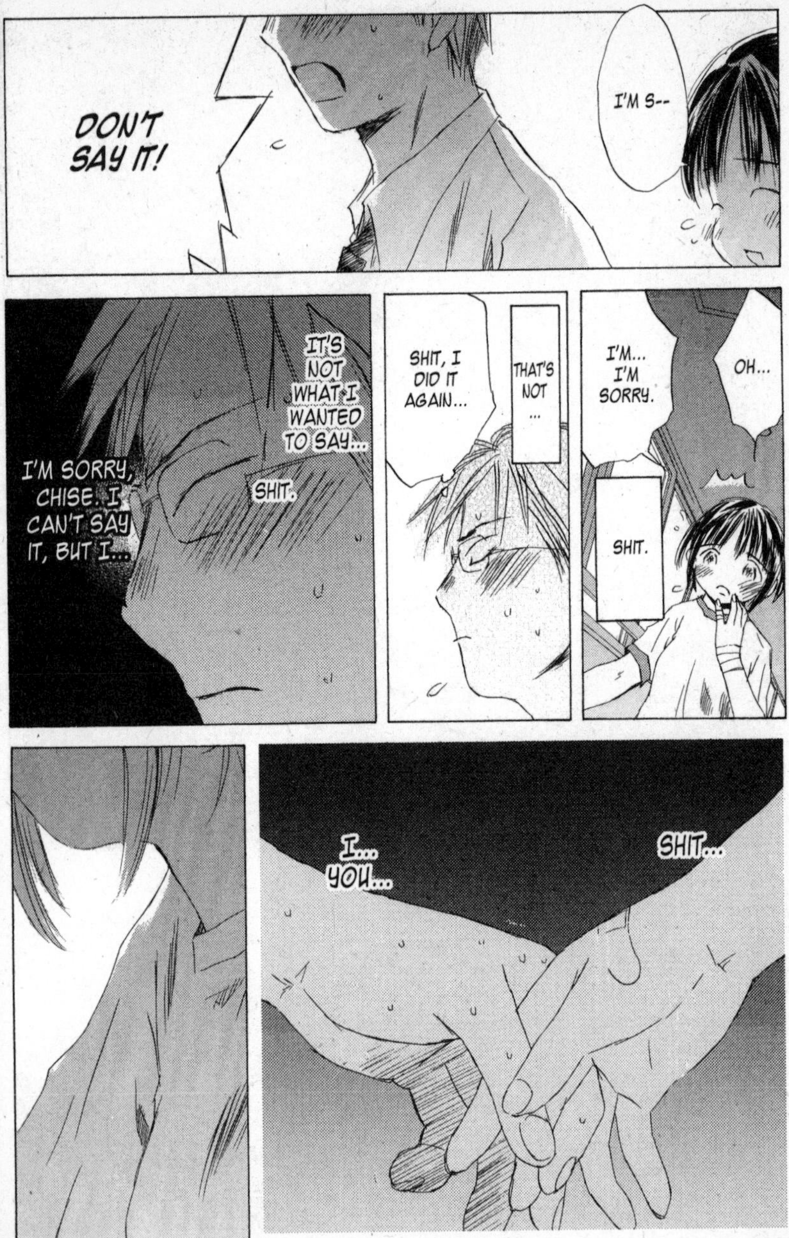
I'M S--
DON'T SAY IT!
OH...
I'M... I'M SORRY.
SHIT.
THAT'S NOT ...
SHIT, I DID IT AGAIN...
IT'S NOT WHAT I WANTED TO SAY...
SHIT.
I'M SORRY, CHISE. I CAN'T SAY IT, BUT I...
SHIT...
I... YOU...

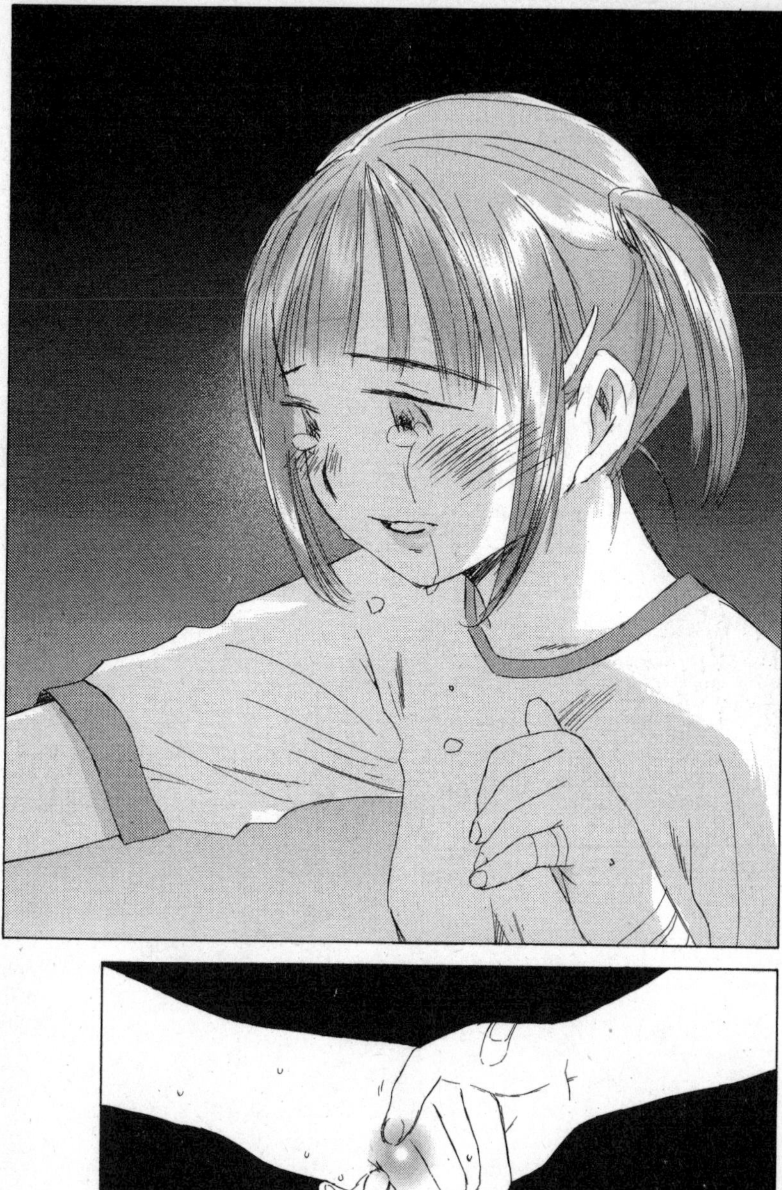

WE CAN'T WALK THROUGH THE COURTYARD. THERE ARE A LOT OF SDF GUYS THERE.

I'M SORRY, SHUJI.

I'M SORRY.

DON'T BE SORRY. OKAY, WE'LL GO OUT THE HALLWAY THAT LEADS TO THE GYM.

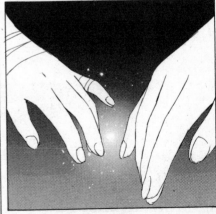

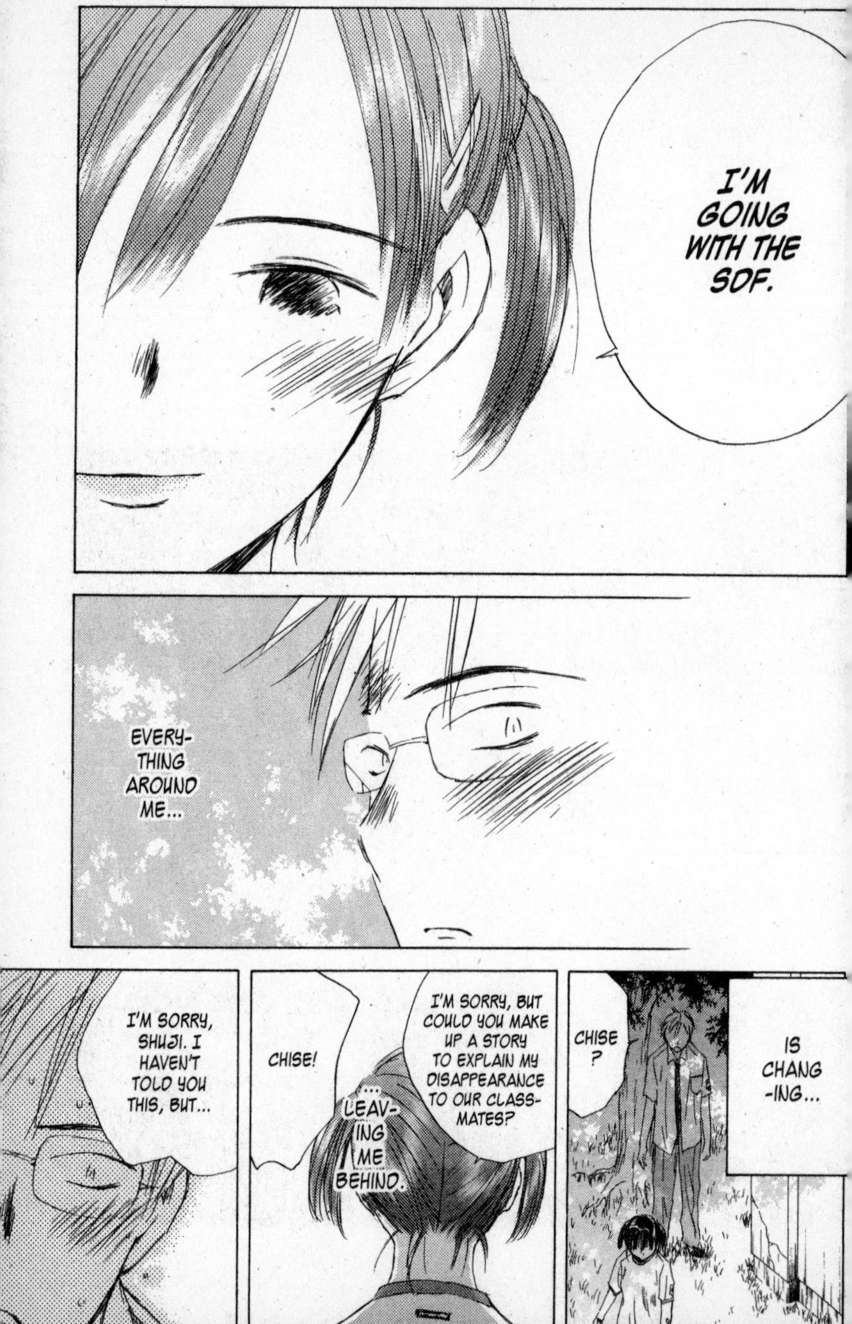
I'M GOING WITH THE SDF.
EVERYTHING AROUND ME...
IS CHANG-ING...
CHISE?
I'M SORRY, BUT COULD YOU MAKE UP A STORY TO EXPLAIN MY DISAPPEARANCE TO OUR CLASS-MATES?
CHISE!
...LEAV-ING ME BEHIND.
I'M SORRY, SHUJI. I HAVEN'T TOLD YOU THIS, BUT...

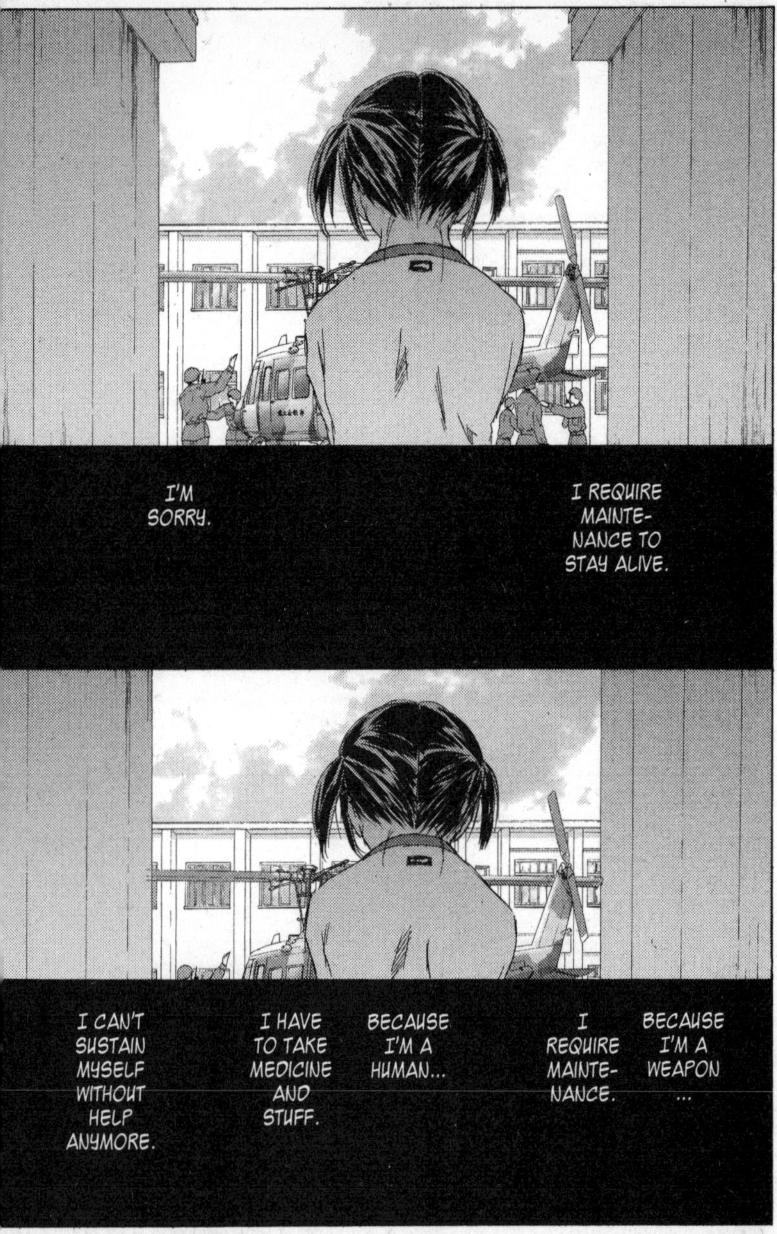
I REQUIRE MAINTE-NANCE TO STAY ALIVE.
I'M SORRY.
BECAUSE I'M A WEAPON ...
I REQUIRE MAINTE-NANCE.
BECAUSE I'M A HUMAN...
I HAVE TO TAKE MEDICINE AND STUFF.
I CAN'T SUSTAIN MYSELF WITHOUT HELP ANYMORE.

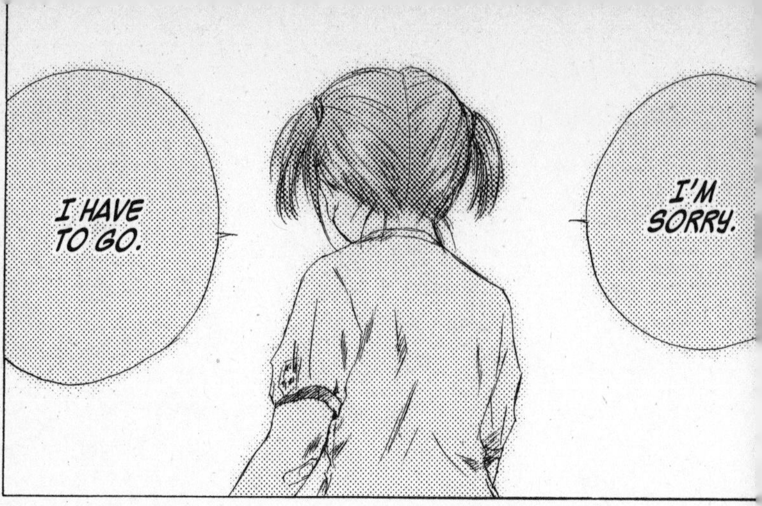
I'M SORRY.
I HAVE TO GO.

CHISE.

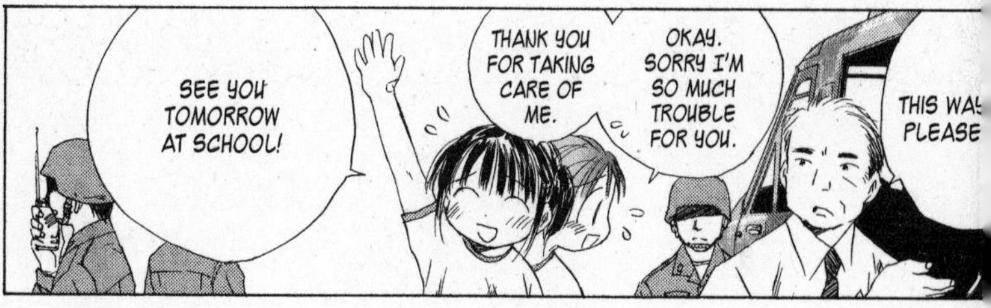
THIS WAY PLEASE
OKAY. SORRY I'M SO MUCH TROUBLE FOR YOU.
THANK YOU FOR TAKING CARE OF ME.
SEE YOU TOMORROW AT SCHOOL!

CHISE.

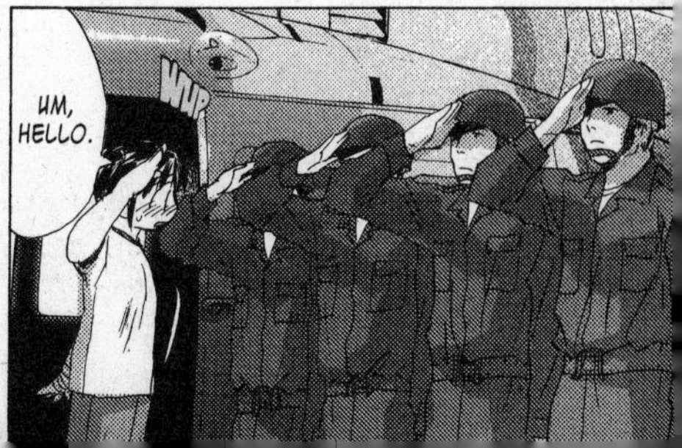
UM, HELLO.

CHISE ...

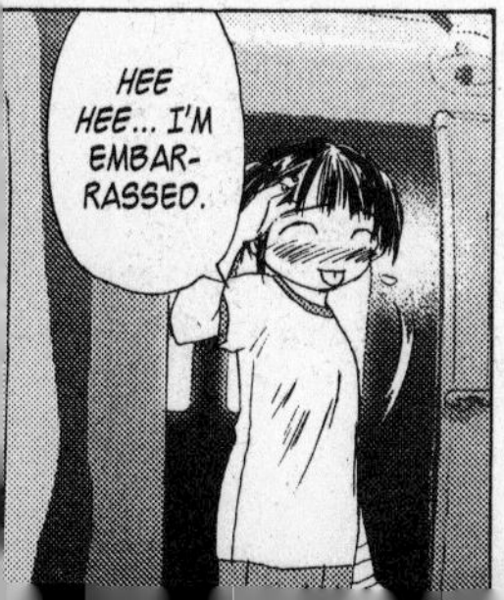
HEE HEE... I'M EMBAR-RASSED.

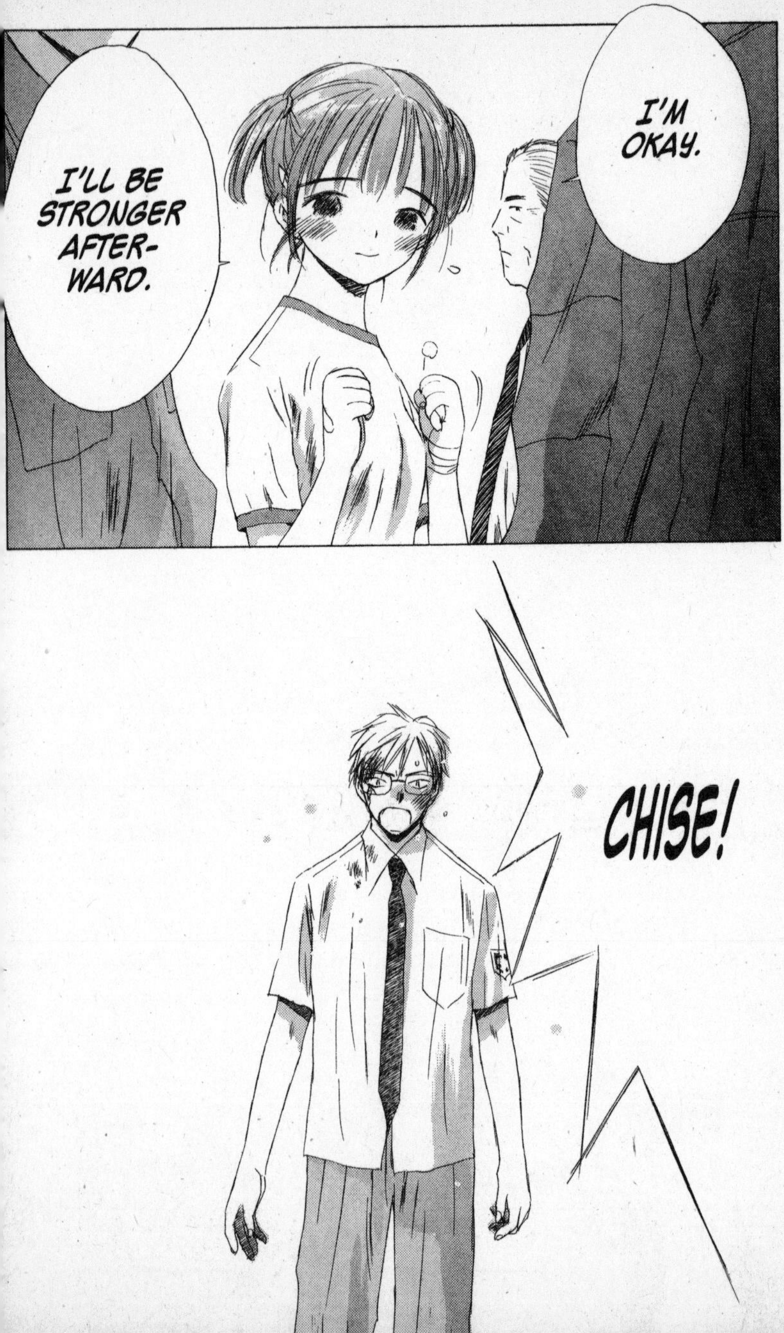
I'M OKAY.
I'LL BE STRONGER AFTER-WARD.
CHISE!

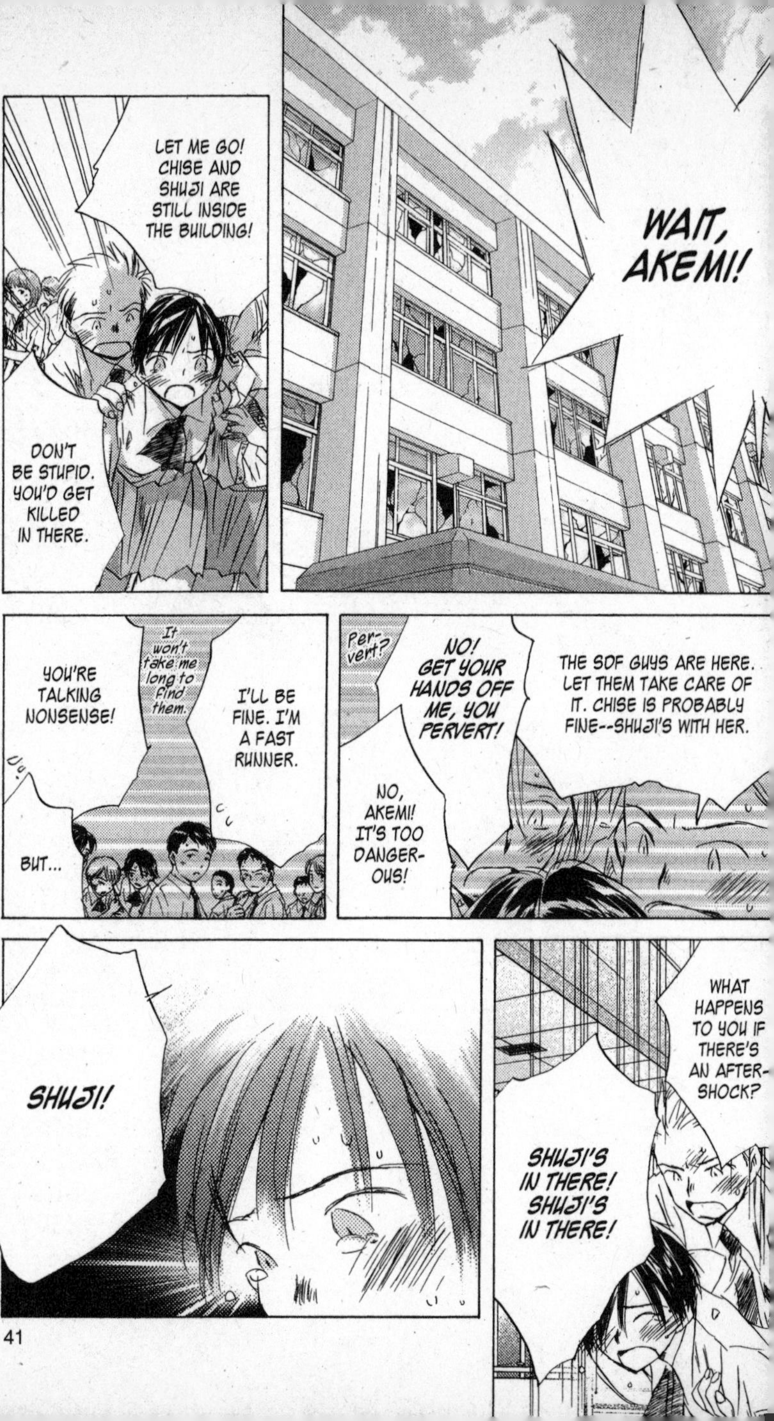
WAIT, AKEMI!
LET ME GO! CHISE AND SHUJI ARE STILL INSIDE THE BUILDING!
DON'T BE STUPID. YOU'D GET KILLED IN THERE.
THE SDF GUYS ARE HERE. LET THEM TAKE CARE OF IT. CHISE IS PROBABLY FINE--SHUJI'S WITH HER.
NO! GET YOUR HANDS OFF ME, YOU PERVERT!
Per-vert?
NO, AKEMI! IT'S TOO DANGER-OUS!
I'LL BE FINE. I'M A FAST RUNNER.
It won't take me long to find them.
YOU'RE TALKING NONSENSE!
BUT...
WHAT HAPPENS TO YOU IF THERE'S AN AFTER-SHOCK?
SHUJI'S IN THERE! SHUJI'S IN THERE!
SHUJI!

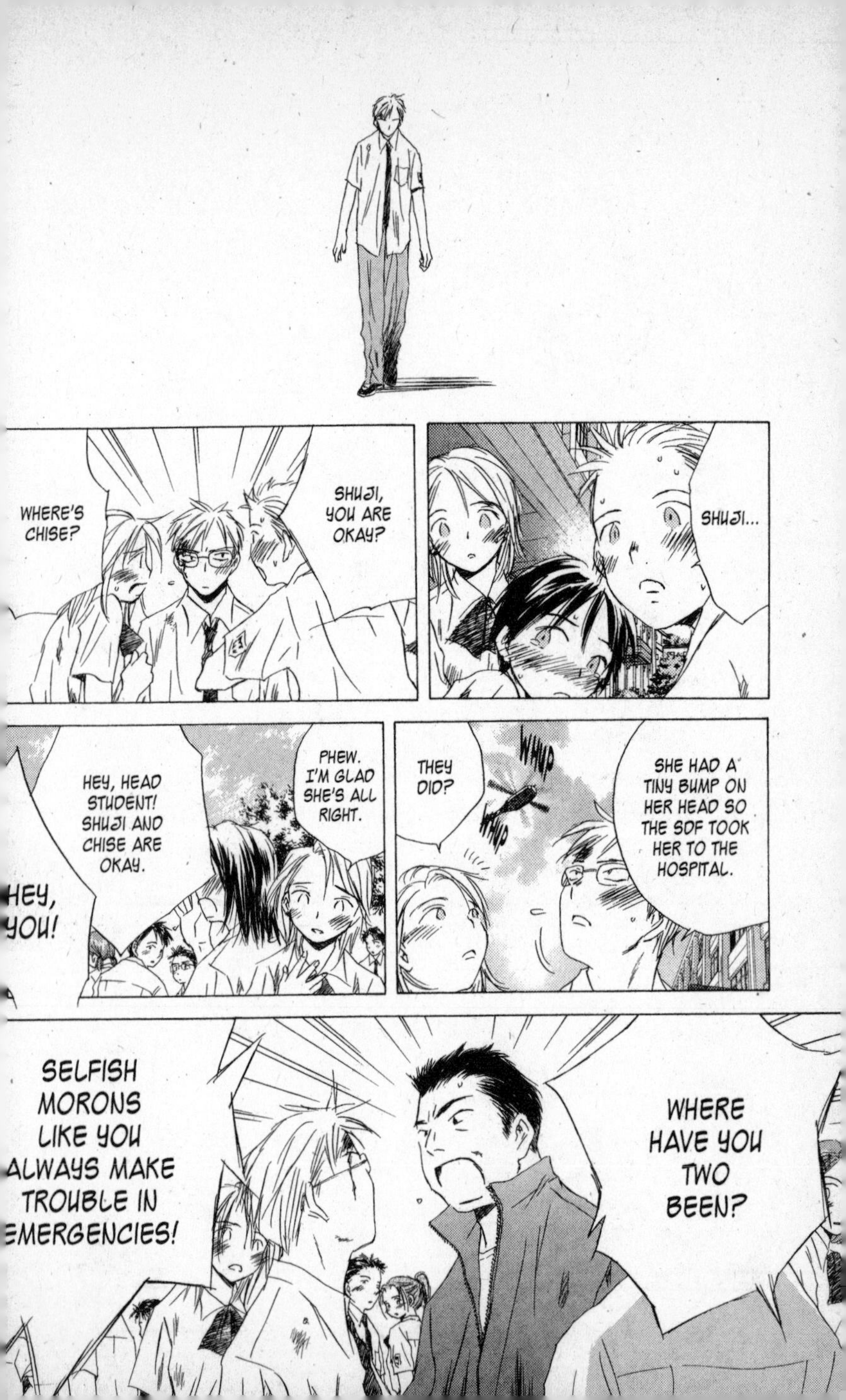
SHUJI...
SHUJI, YOU ARE OKAY?
WHERE'S CHISE?
SHE HAD A TINY BUMP ON HER HEAD SO THE SDF TOOK HER TO THE HOSPITAL.
WHIP
WHIP
THEY DID?
PHEW. I'M GLAD SHE'S ALL RIGHT.
HEY, HEAD STUDENT! SHUJI AND CHISE ARE OKAY.
HEY, YOU!
WHERE HAVE YOU TWO BEEN?
SELFISH MORONS LIKE YOU ALWAYS MAKE TROUBLE IN EMERGENCIES!

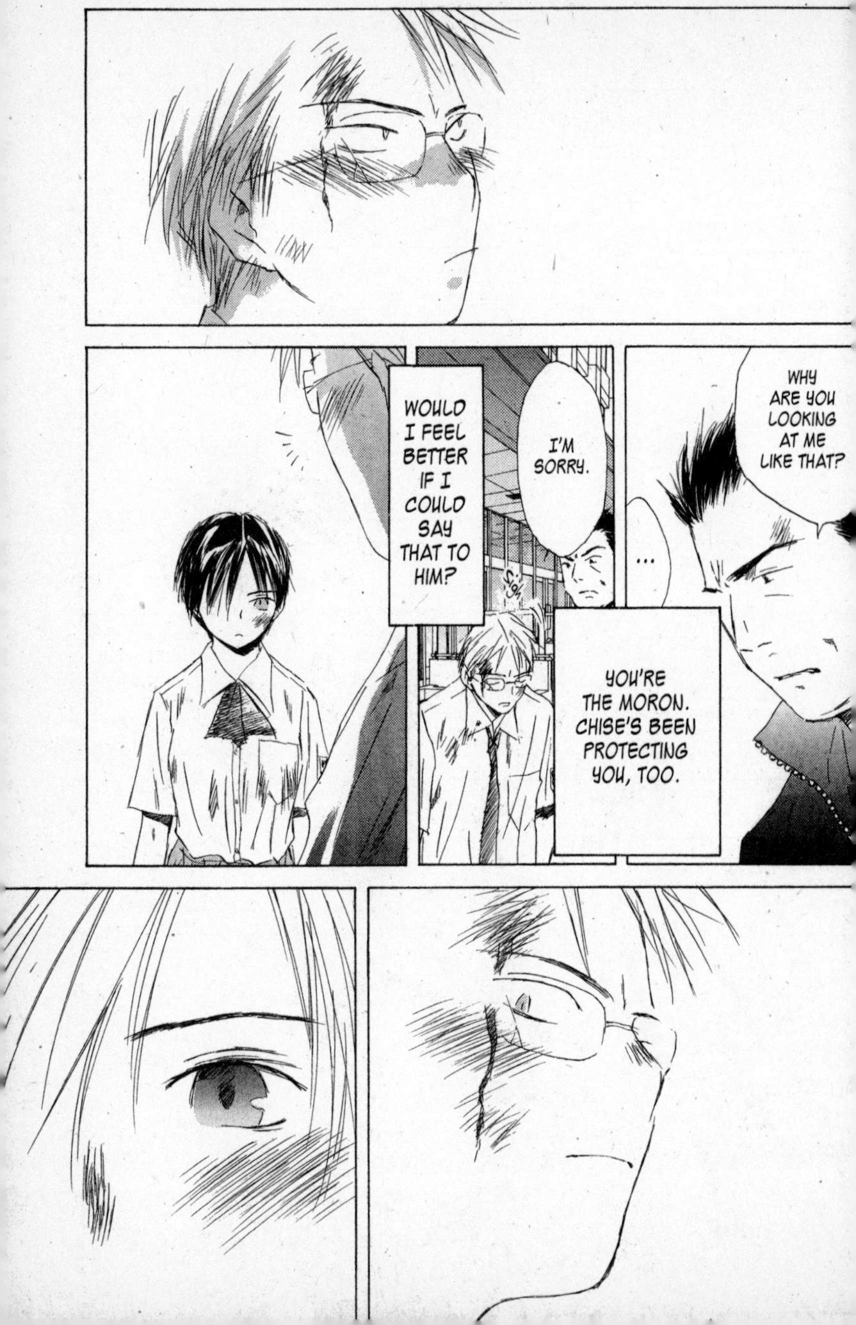
WHY ARE YOU LOOKING AT ME LIKE THAT?
...
YOU'RE THE MORON. CHISE'S BEEN PROTECTING YOU, TOO.
I'M SORRY.
SIGH
WOULD I FEEL BETTER IF I COULD SAY THAT TO HIM?

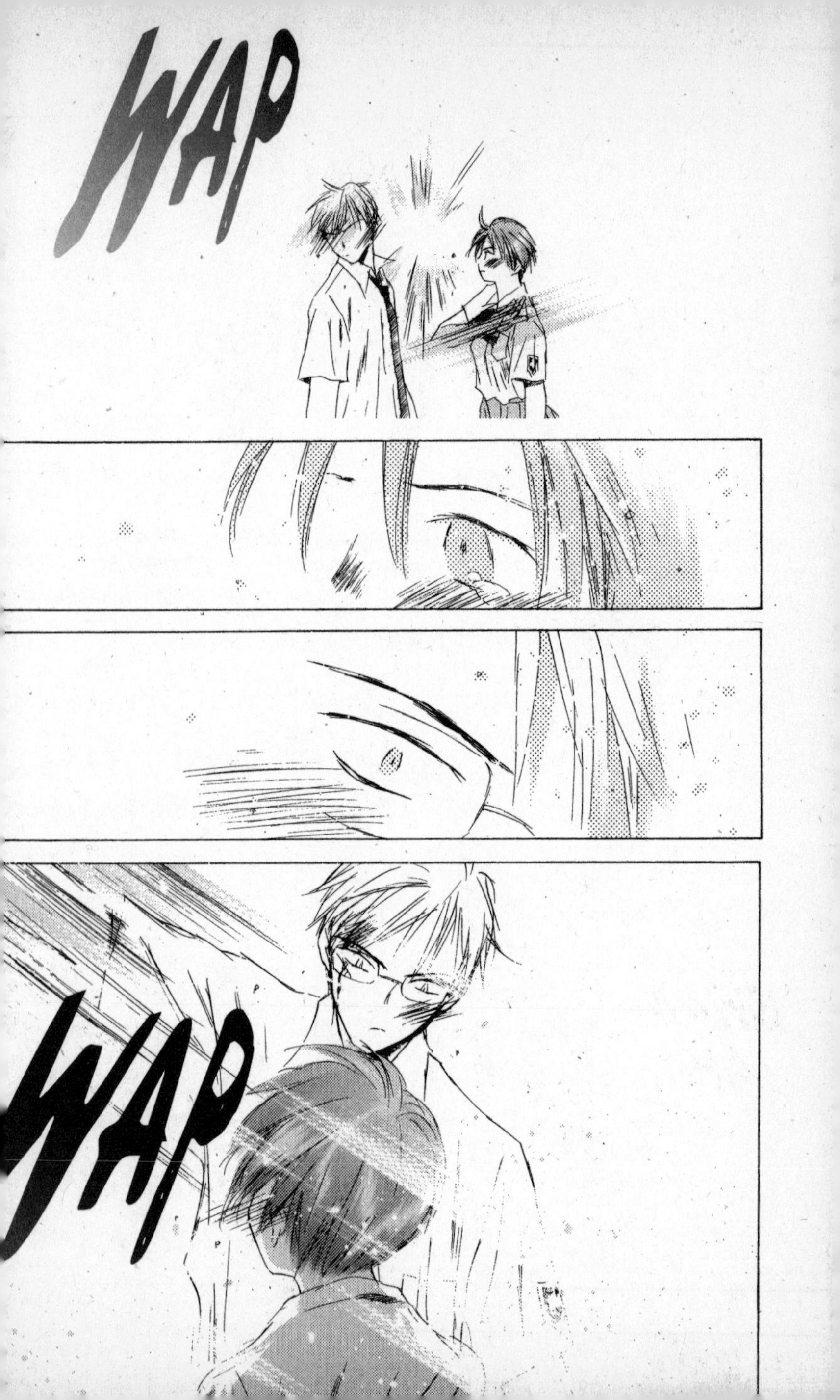
WAP
WAP

I'M SORRY.

...

BWAA-AH...

WAA-AAH!

SOB ...

SNIFF ...

PLIP PLIP

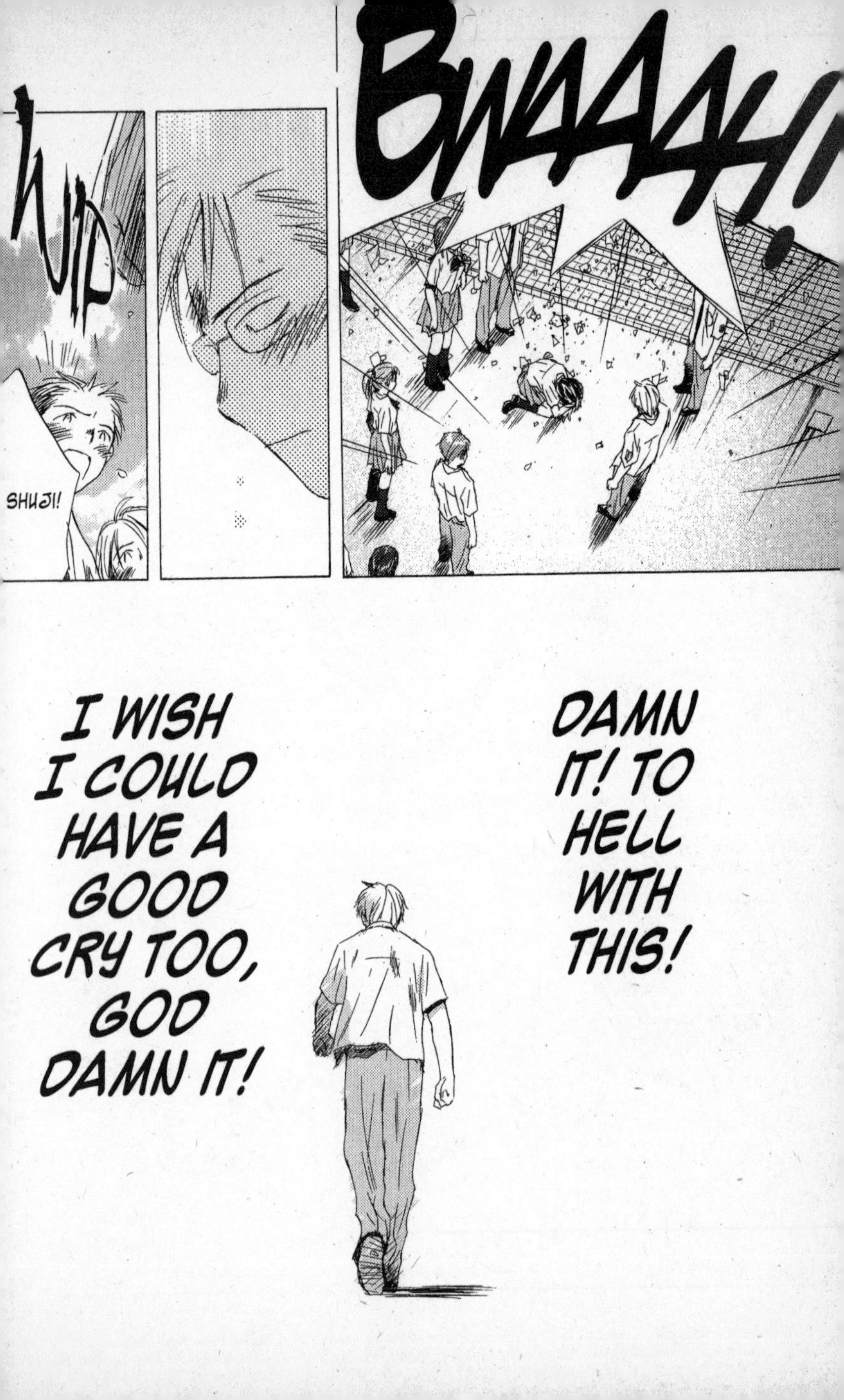
BWAAAH!!
WHIP
SHUJI!
DAMN IT! TO HELL WITH THIS!
I WISH I COULD HAVE A GOOD CRY TOO, GOD DAMN IT!

THE LAST LOVE SONG ON THIS LITTLE PLANET.

Chapter 4: Fuyumi (7)

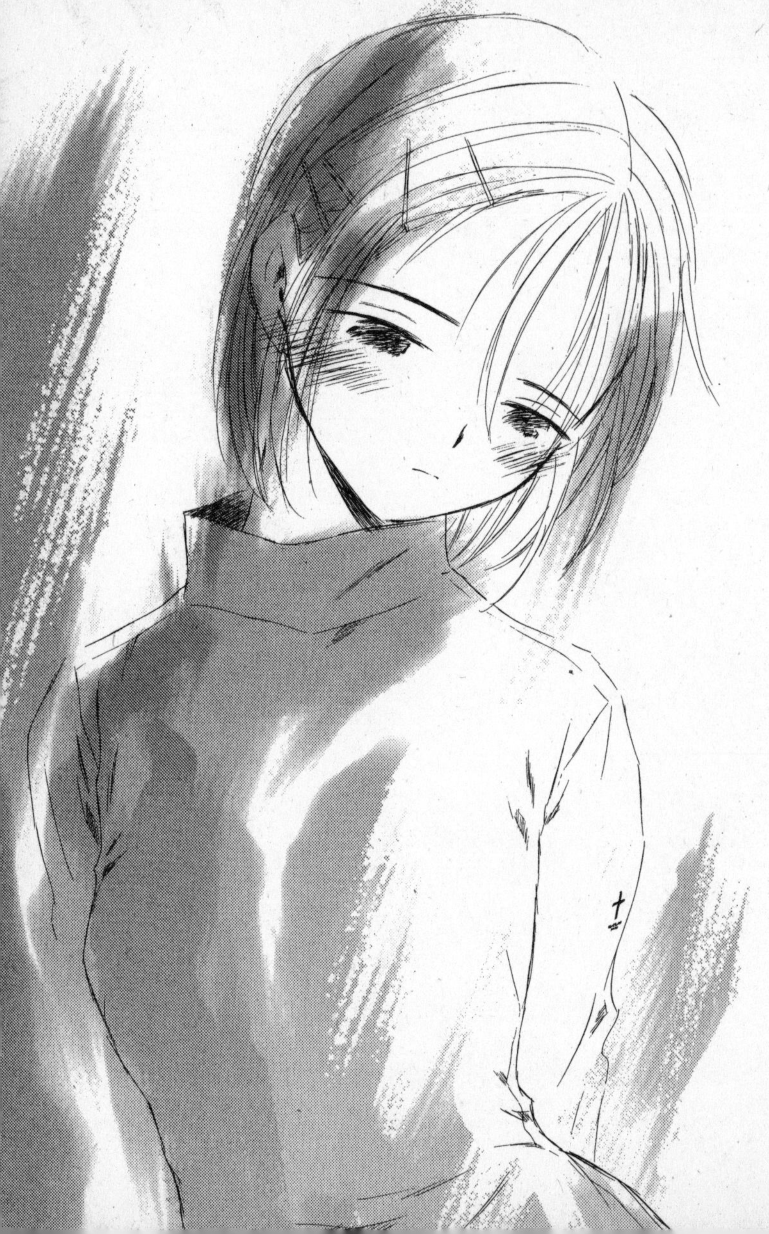

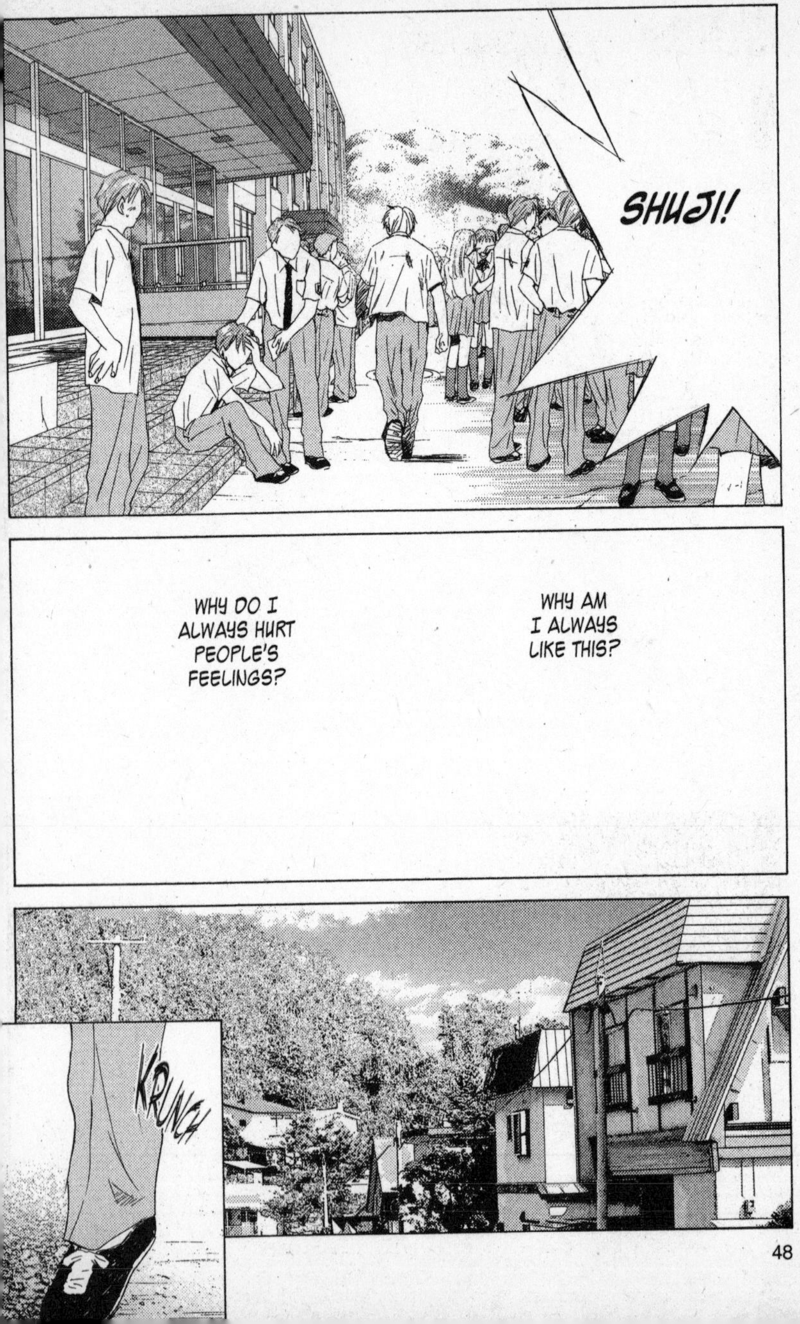
SHUJI!
WHY AM I ALWAYS LIKE THIS?
WHY DO I ALWAYS HURT PEOPLE'S FEELINGS?
KRUNCH

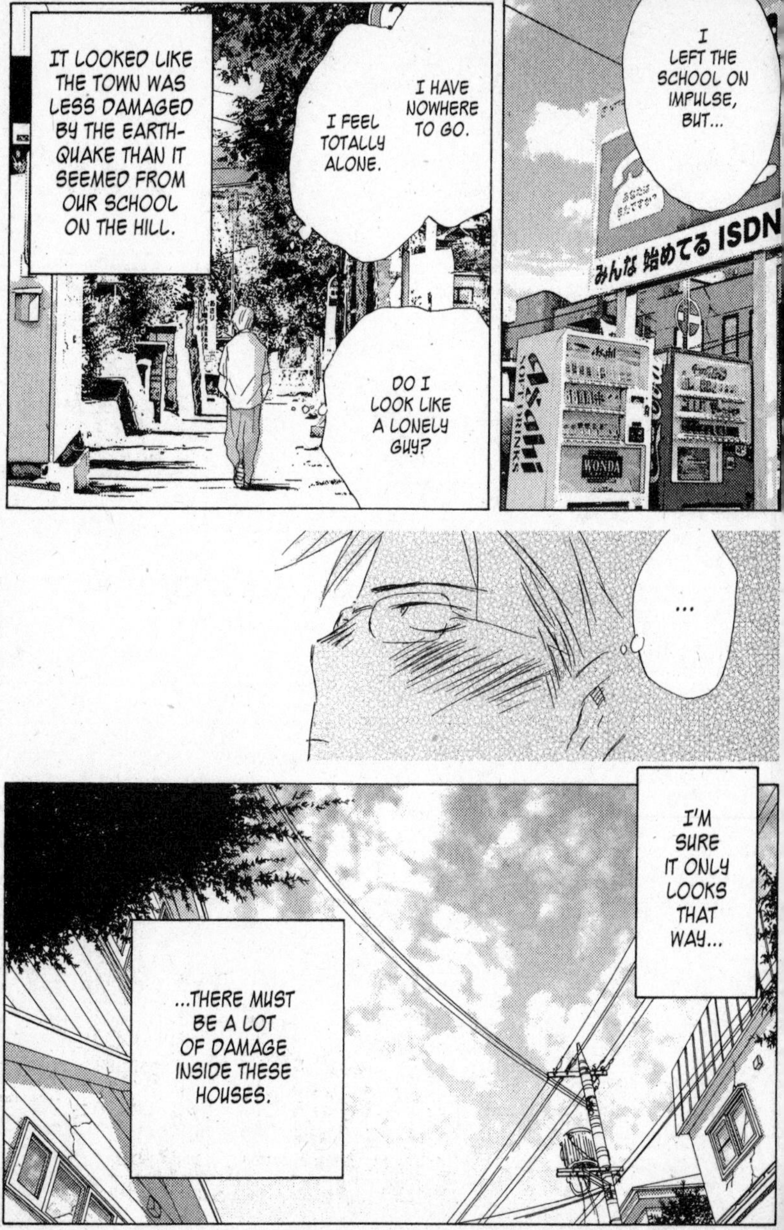

I LEFT THE SCHOOL ON IMPULSE, BUT...
みんな 始めてる ISDN
WONDA
I HAVE NOWHERE TO GO.
I FEEL TOTALLY ALONE.
IT LOOKED LIKE THE TOWN WAS LESS DAMAGED BY THE EARTH-QUAKE THAN IT SEEMED FROM OUR SCHOOL ON THE HILL.
DO I LOOK LIKE A LONELY GUY?
...
I'M SURE IT ONLY LOOKS THAT WAY...
...THERE MUST BE A LOT OF DAMAGE INSIDE THESE HOUSES.

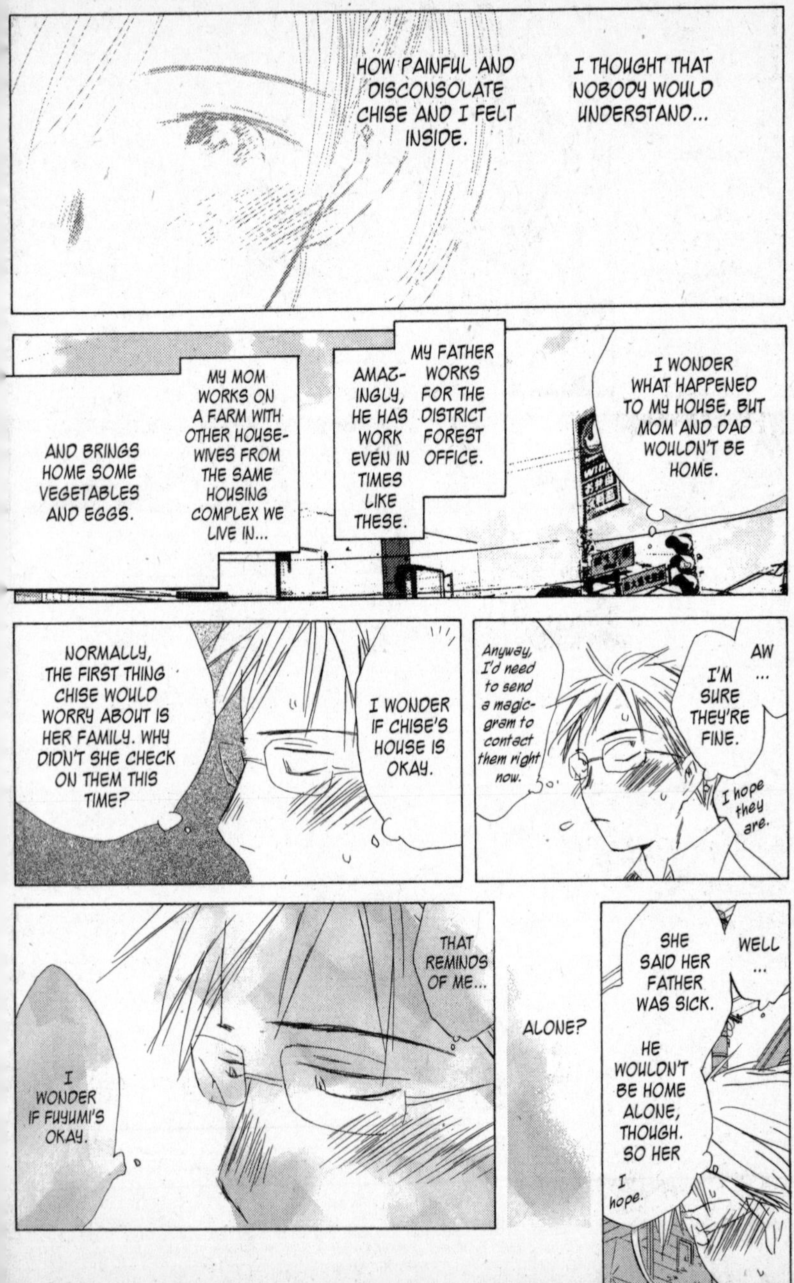
I THOUGHT THAT NOBODY WOULD UNDERSTAND...
HOW PAINFUL AND DISCONSOLATE CHISE AND I FELT INSIDE.
I WONDER WHAT HAPPENED TO MY HOUSE, BUT MOM AND DAD WOULDN'T BE HOME.
MY FATHER WORKS FOR THE DISTRICT FOREST OFFICE.
AMAZINGLY, HE HAS WORK EVEN IN TIMES LIKE THESE.
MY MOM WORKS ON A FARM WITH OTHER HOUSEWIVES FROM THE SAME HOUSING COMPLEX WE LIVE IN...
AND BRINGS HOME SOME VEGETABLES AND EGGS.
AW ...
I'M SURE THEY'RE FINE.
I hope they are.
Anyway, I'd need to send a magic-gram to contact them right now.
I WONDER IF CHISE'S HOUSE IS OKAY.
NORMALLY, THE FIRST THING CHISE WOULD WORRY ABOUT IS HER FAMILY. WHY DIDN'T SHE CHECK ON THEM THIS TIME?
WELL ...
SHE SAID HER FATHER WAS SICK.
HE WOULDN'T BE HOME ALONE, THOUGH. SO HER
I hope.
ALONE?
THAT REMINDS OF ME...
I WONDER IF FUYUMI'S OKAY.

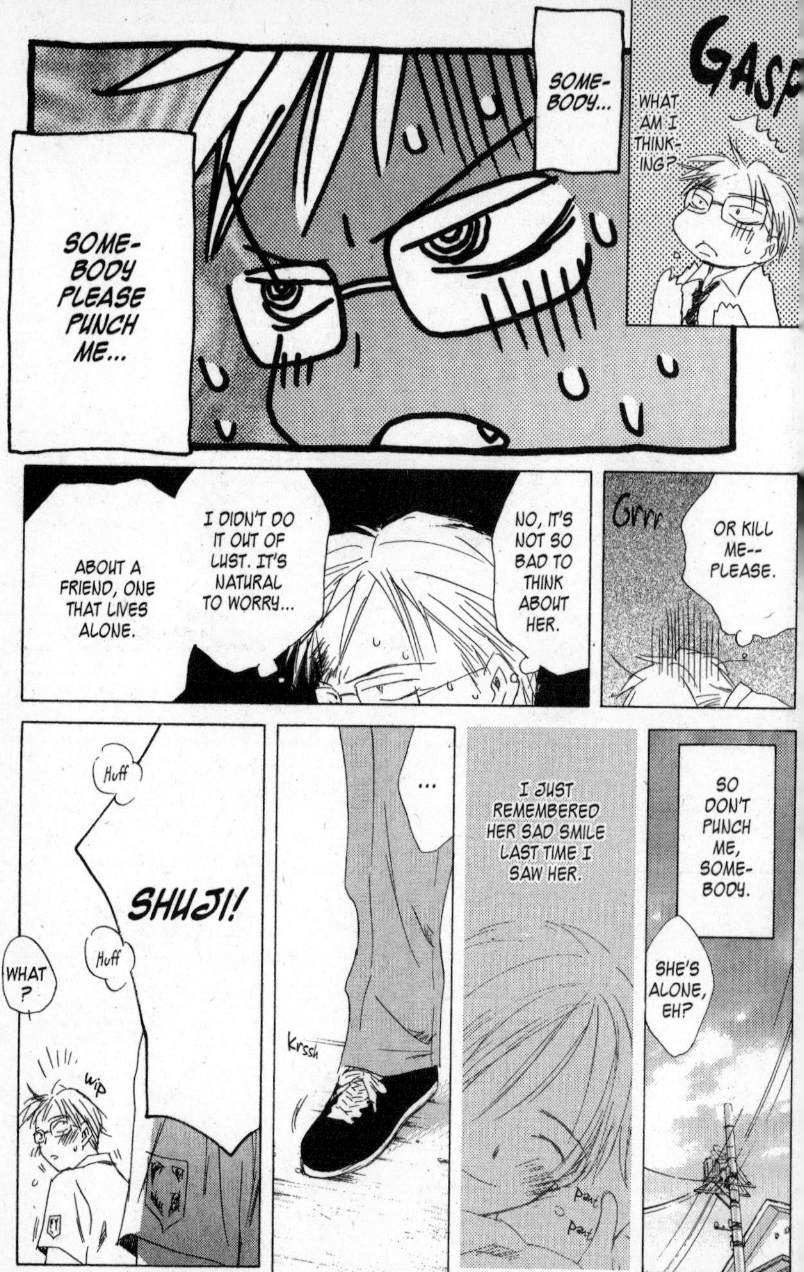
GASP
WHAT AM I THINKING?
SOME-BODY...
SOME-BODY PLEASE PUNCH ME...
Grrr
OR KILL ME-- PLEASE.
NO, IT'S NOT SO BAD TO THINK ABOUT HER.
I DIDN'T DO IT OUT OF LUST. IT'S NATURAL TO WORRY...
ABOUT A FRIEND, ONE THAT LIVES ALONE.
SO DON'T PUNCH ME, SOME-BODY.
SHE'S ALONE, EH?
I JUST REMEMBERED HER SAD SMILE LAST TIME I SAW HER.
Pant
Pant
...
Krssh
Huff
SHUJI!
Huff
WHAT?
wip

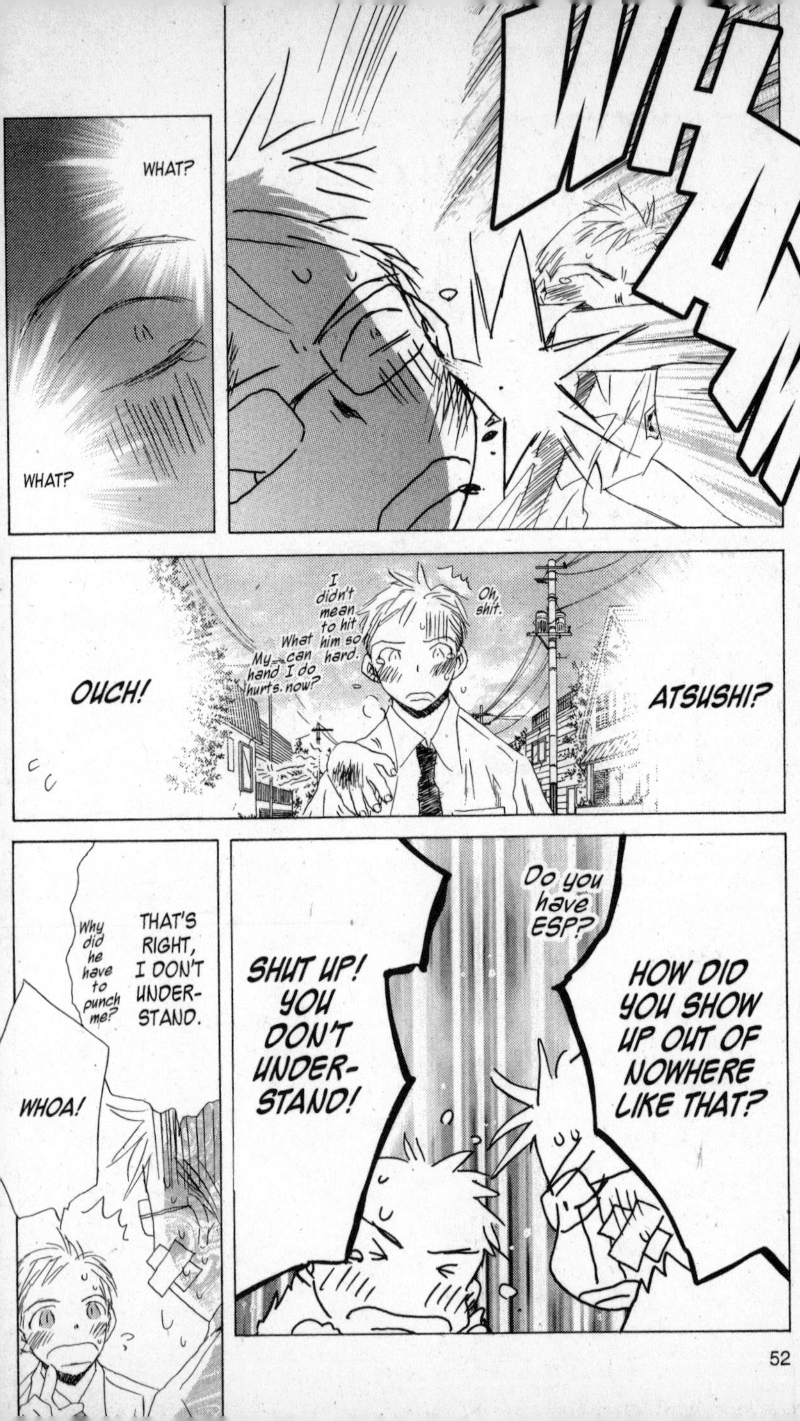

WHAM
WHAT?
WHAT?
Oh, shit.
I didn't mean to hit him so hard.
What can I do now?
My hand hurts.
ATSUSHI?
OUCH!
HOW DID YOU SHOW UP OUT OF NOWHERE LIKE THAT?
Do you have ESP?
SHUT UP! YOU DON'T UNDERSTAND!
THAT'S RIGHT, I DON'T UNDERSTAND.
Why did he have to punch me?
WHOA!

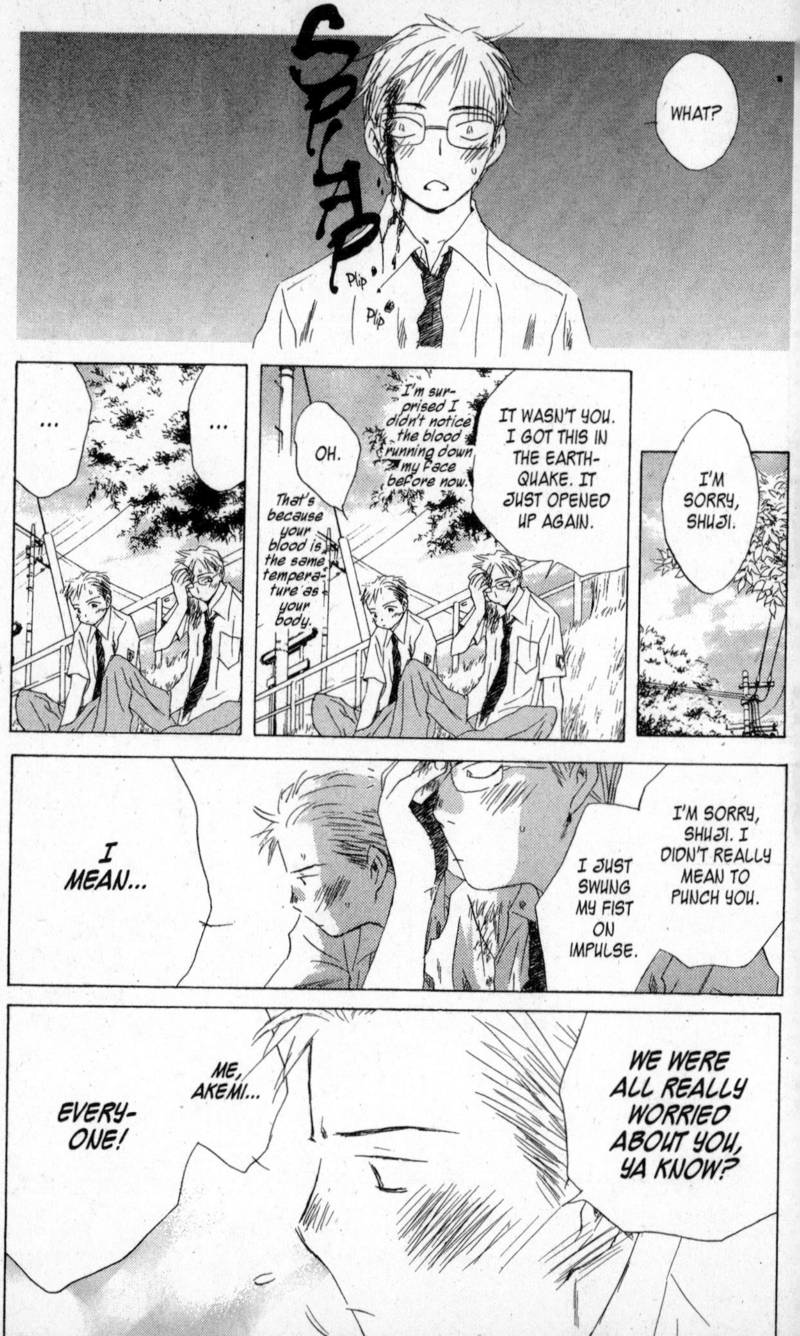
WHAT?
SPLAP
Plip
Plip
I'M SORRY, SHUJI.
IT WASN'T YOU. I GOT THIS IN THE EARTH-QUAKE. IT JUST OPENED UP AGAIN.
I'm sur-prised I didn't notice the blood running down my face before now.
OH.
That's because your blood is the same tempera-ture as your body.
...
...
I'M SORRY, SHUJI. I DIDN'T REALLY MEAN TO PUNCH YOU.
I JUST SWUNG MY FIST ON IMPULSE.
I MEAN...
WE WERE ALL REALLY WORRIED ABOUT YOU, YA KNOW?
ME, AKEMI...
EVERY-ONE!

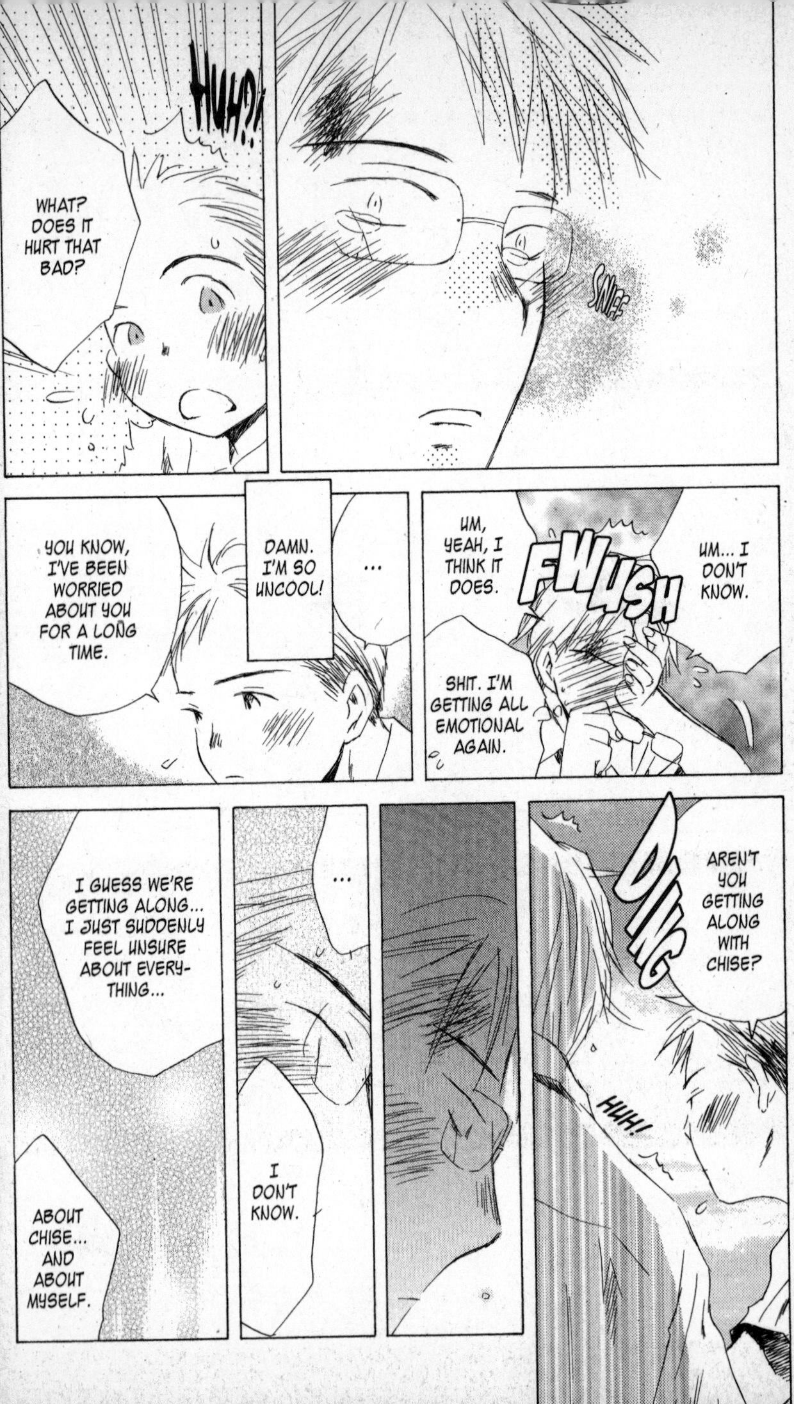
SNIFF
HUH?!
WHAT? DOES IT HURT THAT BAD?
UM... I DON'T KNOW.
FWUSH
UM, YEAH, I THINK IT DOES.
SHIT. I'M GETTING ALL EMOTIONAL AGAIN.
DAMN. I'M SO UNCOOL!
...
YOU KNOW, I'VE BEEN WORRIED ABOUT YOU FOR A LONG TIME.
DING
AREN'T YOU GETTING ALONG WITH CHISE?
HUH!
...
I DON'T KNOW.
I GUESS WE'RE GETTING ALONG... I JUST SUDDENLY FEEL UNSURE ABOUT EVERYTHING...
ABOUT CHISE... AND ABOUT MYSELF.

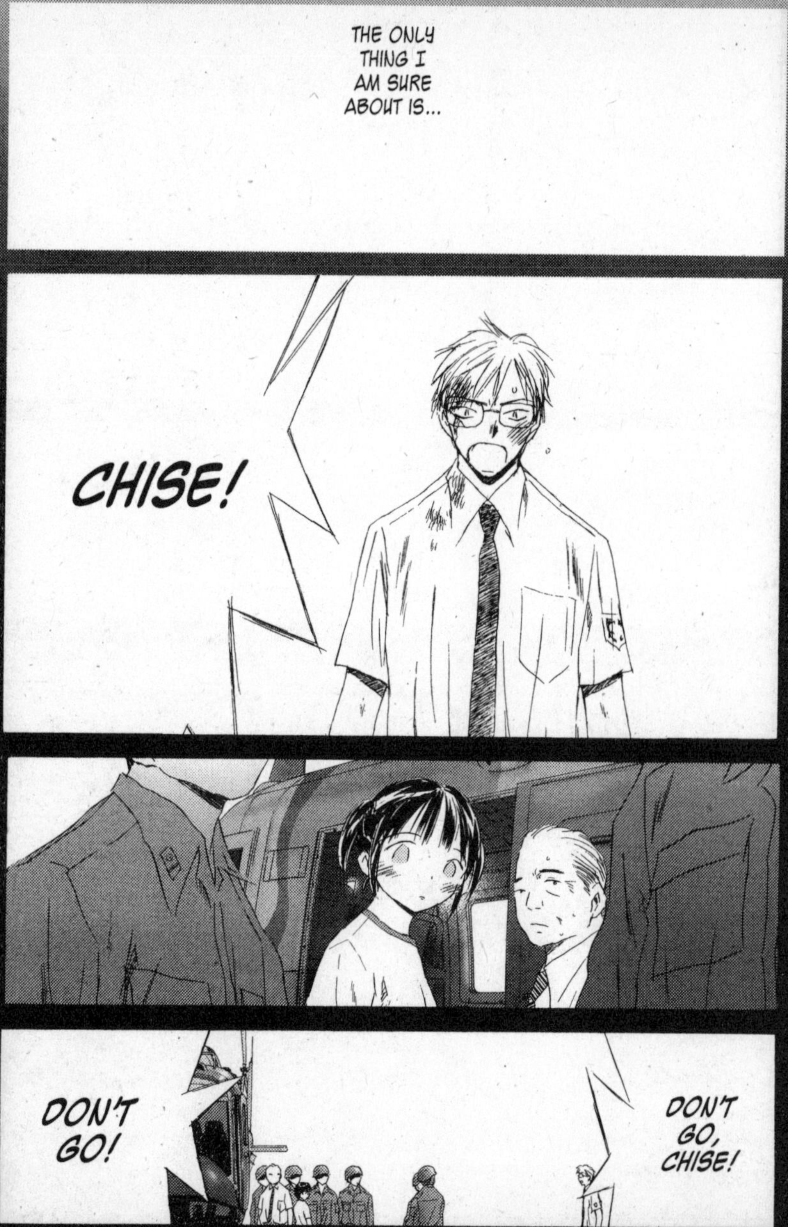
THE ONLY THING I AM SURE ABOUT IS...
CHISE!
DON'T GO, CHISE!
DON'T GO!

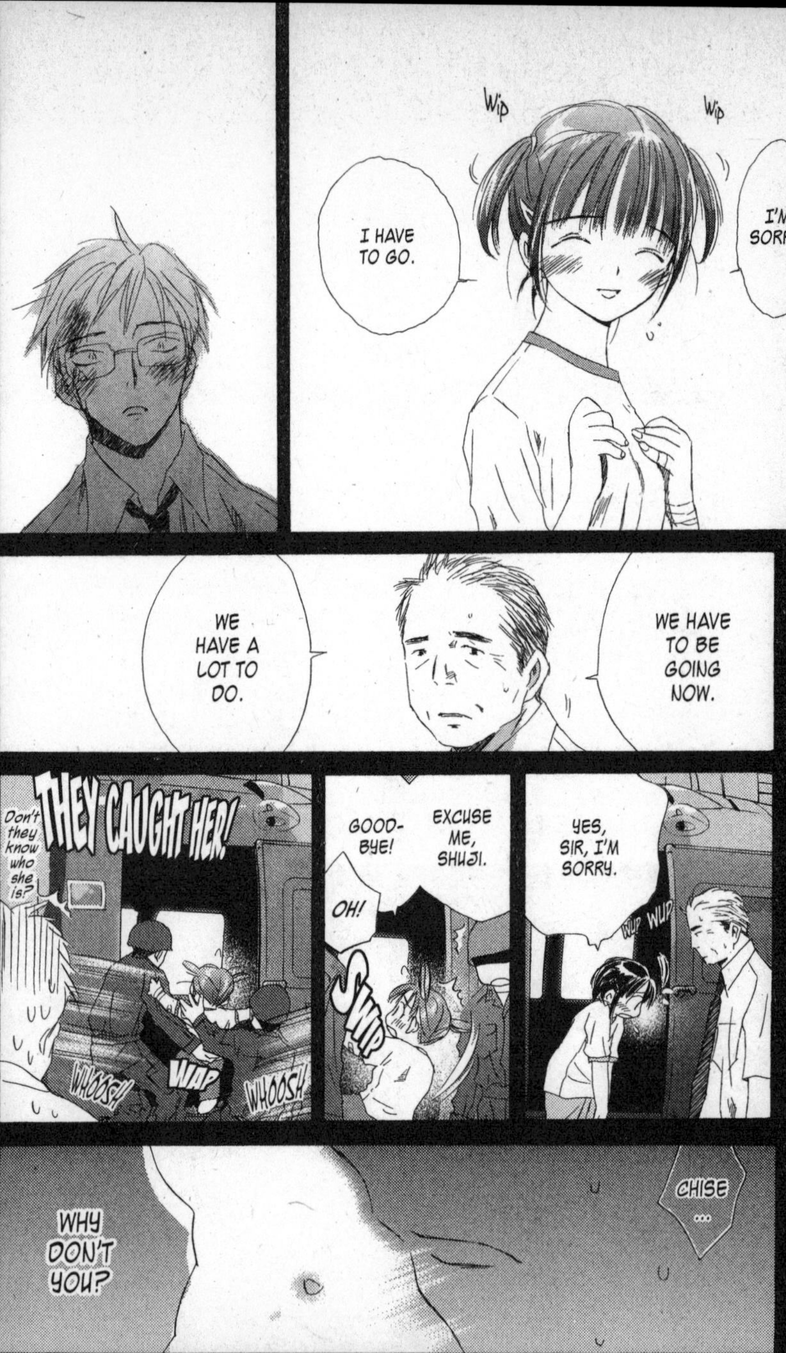
Wip
Wip
I'M SORRY.
I HAVE TO GO.
WE HAVE TO BE GOING NOW.
WE HAVE A LOT TO DO.
YES, SIR, I'M SORRY.
WUP WUP
EXCUSE ME, SHUJI.
GOOD-BYE!
OH!
SWIP
THEY CAUGHT HER!
Don't they know who she is?
WHOOSH
WAP
WHOOSH
CHISE...
WHY DON'T YOU?

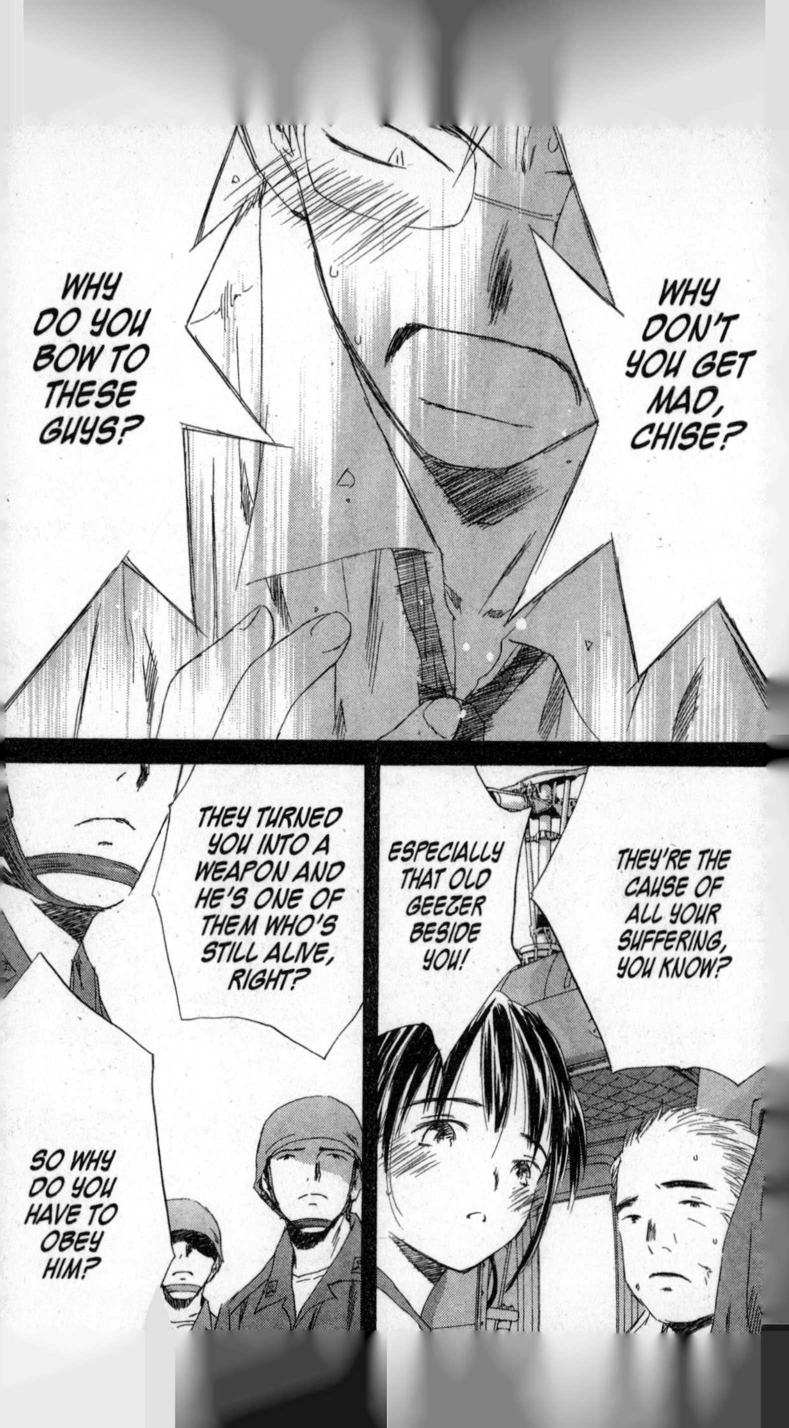
WHY DON'T YOU GET MAD, CHISE?
WHY DO YOU BOW TO THESE GUYS?
THEY'RE THE CAUSE OF ALL YOUR SUFFERING, YOU KNOW?
ESPECIALLY THAT OLD GEEZER BESIDE YOU!
THEY TURNED YOU INTO A WEAPON AND HE'S ONE OF THEM WHO'S STILL ALIVE, RIGHT?
SO WHY DO YOU HAVE TO OBEY HIM?

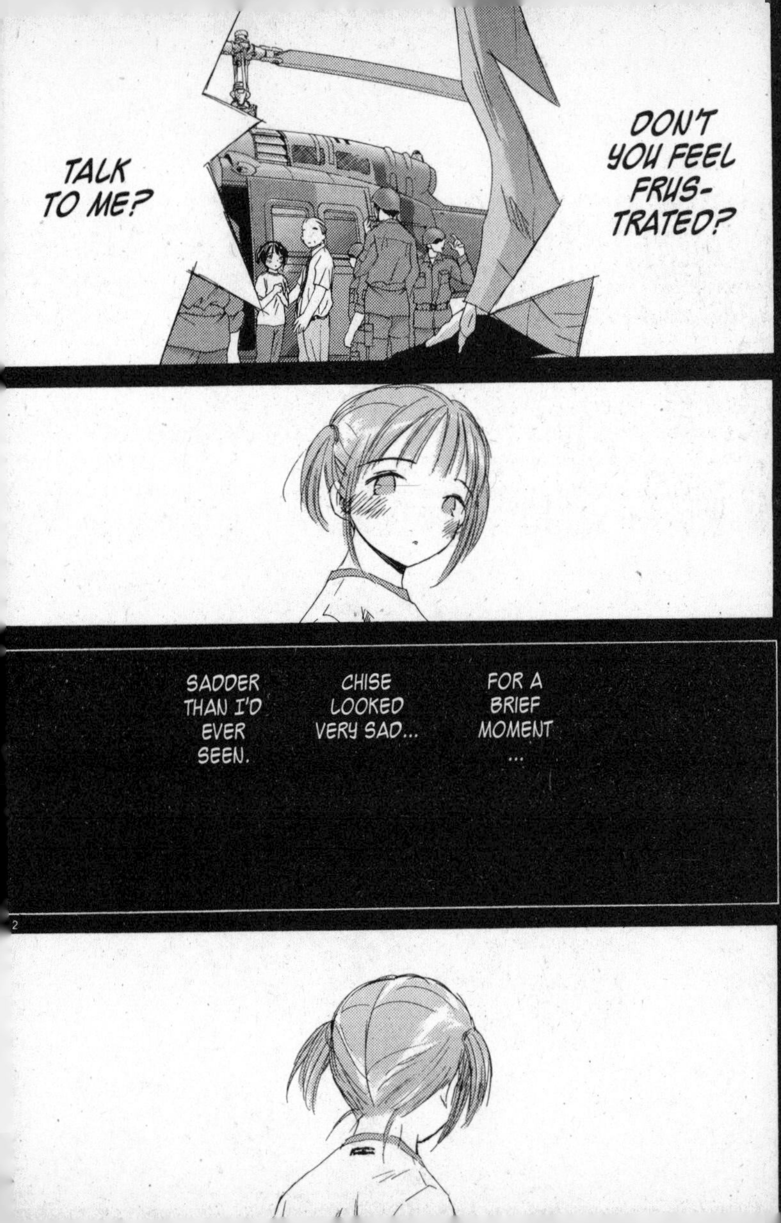
DON'T YOU FEEL FRUS-TRATED?
TALK TO ME?
FOR A BRIEF MOMENT ...
CHISE LOOKED VERY SAD...
SADDER THAN I'D EVER SEEN.

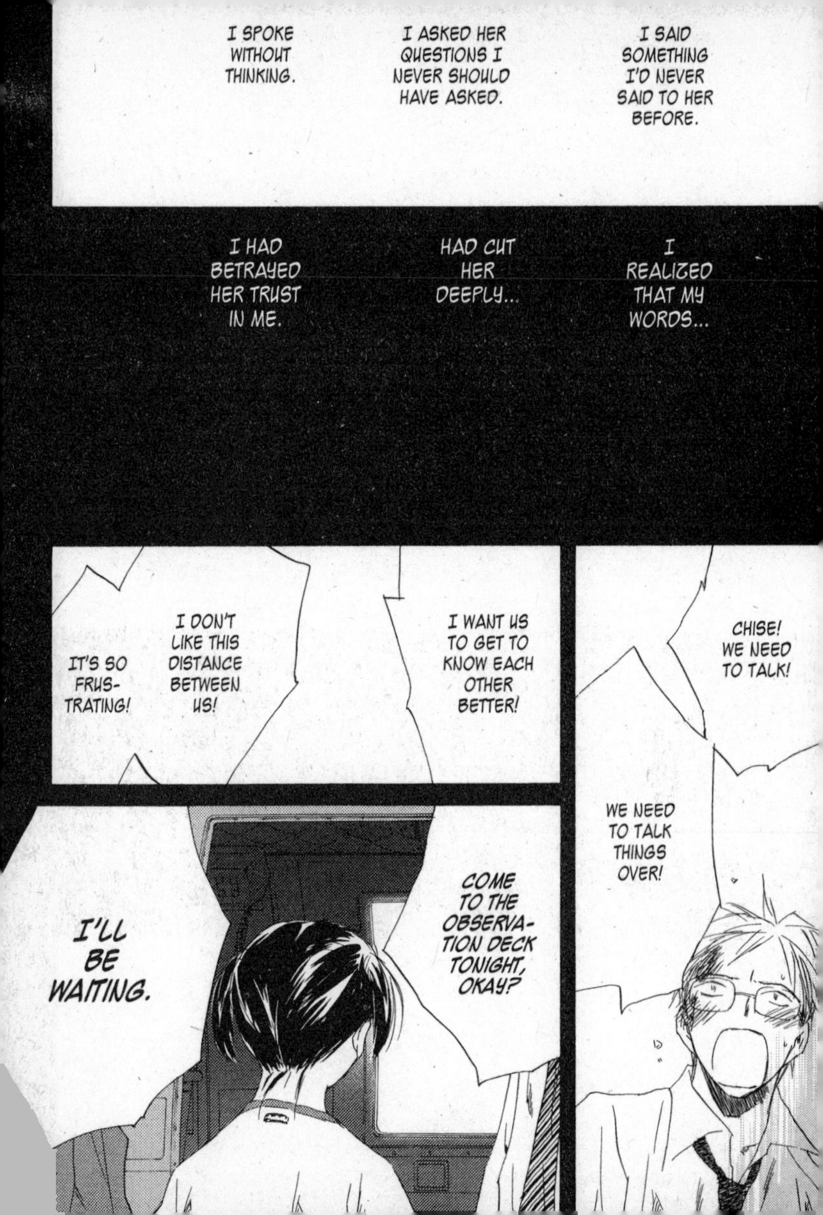
I SAID SOMETHING I'D NEVER SAID TO HER BEFORE.
I ASKED HER QUESTIONS I NEVER SHOULD HAVE ASKED.
I SPOKE WITHOUT THINKING.
I REALIZED THAT MY WORDS...
HAD CUT HER DEEPLY...
I HAD BETRAYED HER TRUST IN ME.
CHISE! WE NEED TO TALK!
WE NEED TO TALK THINGS OVER!
I WANT US TO GET TO KNOW EACH OTHER BETTER!
I DON'T LIKE THIS DISTANCE BETWEEN US!
IT'S SO FRUS-TRATING!
COME TO THE OBSERVA-TION DECK TONIGHT, OKAY?
I'LL BE WAITING.

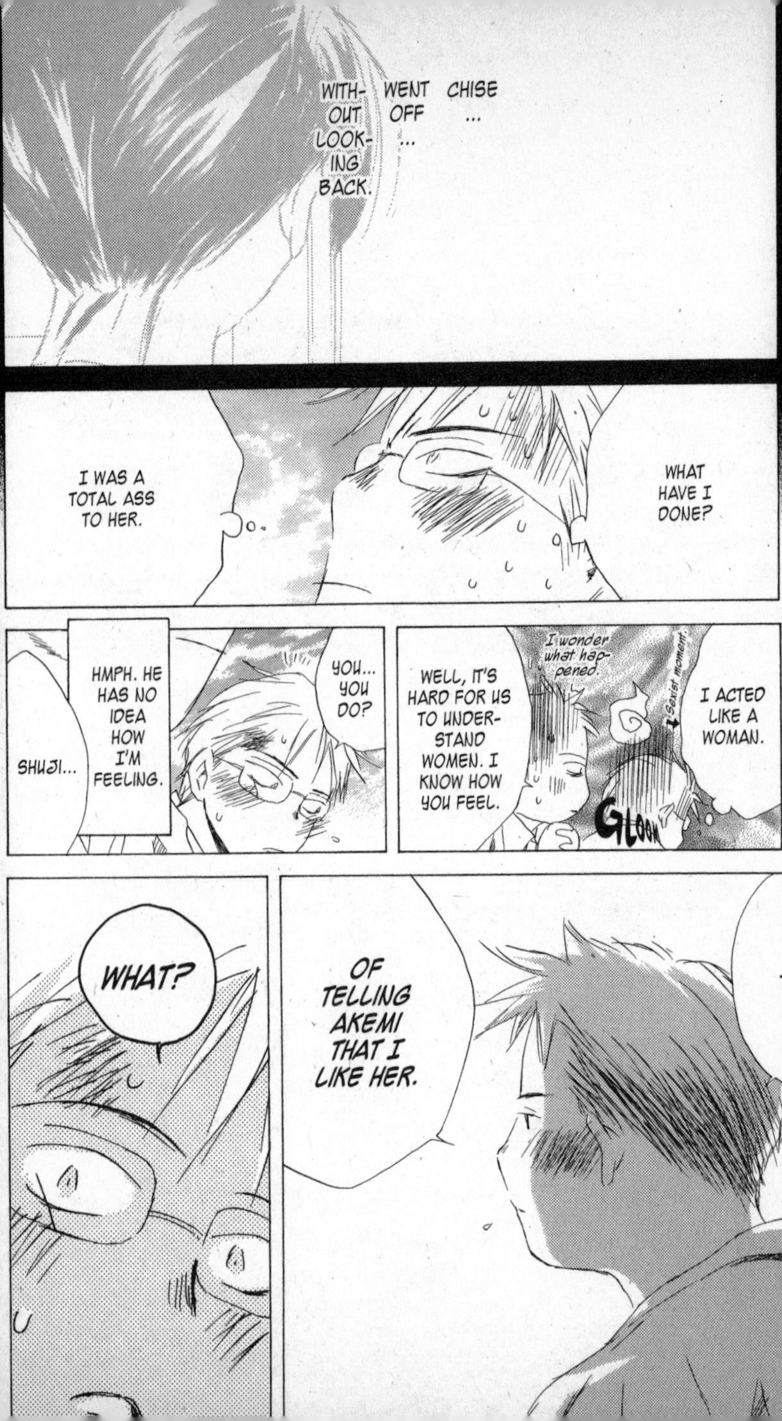
CHISE ...
WENT OFF ...
WITHOUT LOOKING BACK.
WHAT HAVE I DONE?
I WAS A TOTAL ASS TO HER.
I ACTED LIKE A WOMAN.
Sexist moment.
I wonder what happened.
WELL, IT'S HARD FOR US TO UNDERSTAND WOMEN. I KNOW HOW YOU FEEL.
GLOOM
YOU... YOU DO?
HMPH. HE HAS NO IDEA HOW I'M FEELING.
SHUJI...
I'M THINKING...
OF TELLING AKEMI THAT I LIKE HER.
WHAT?

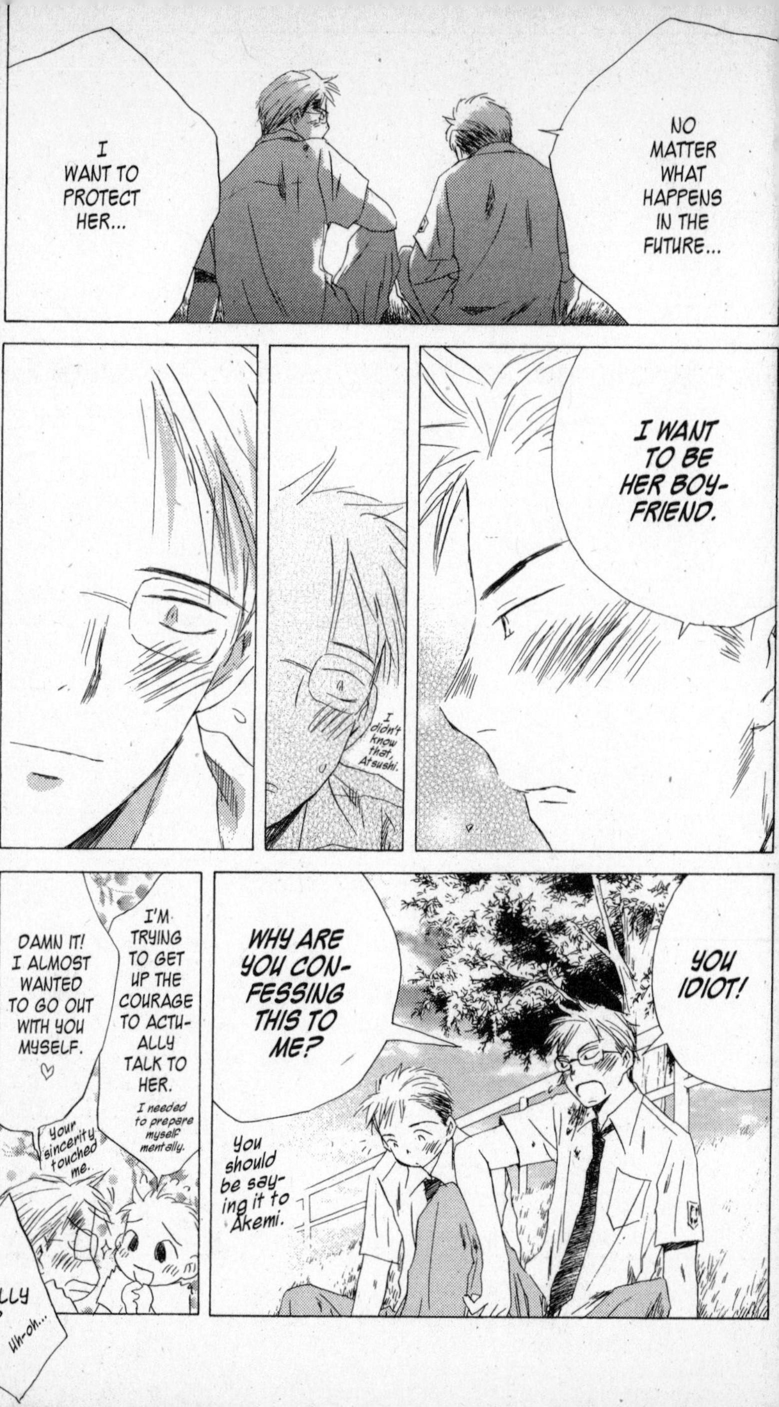
NO MATTER WHAT HAPPENS IN THE FUTURE...
I WANT TO PROTECT HER...
I WANT TO BE HER BOY-FRIEND.
I didn't know that, Atsushi.
YOU IDIOT!
WHY ARE YOU CON-FESSING THIS TO ME?
You should be say-ing it to Akemi.
I'M TRYING TO GET UP THE COURAGE TO ACTU-ALLY TALK TO HER.
I needed to prepare myself mentally.
DAMN IT! I ALMOST WANTED TO GO OUT WITH YOU MYSELF. ♡
Your sincerity touched me.
REALLY?
Uh-oh...

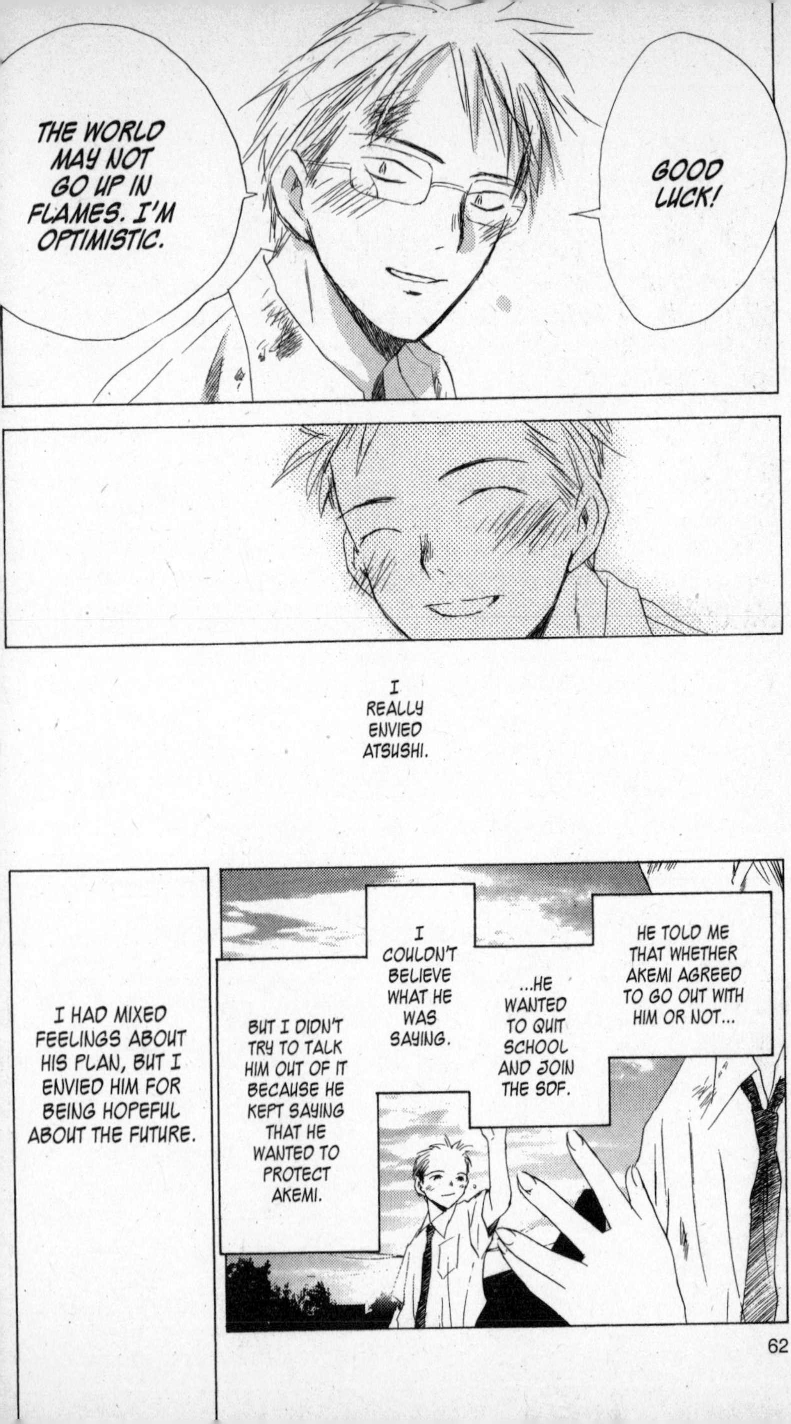
GOOD LUCK!
THE WORLD MAY NOT GO UP IN FLAMES. I'M OPTIMISTIC.
I REALLY ENVIED ATSUSHI.
HE TOLD ME THAT WHETHER AKEMI AGREED TO GO OUT WITH HIM OR NOT...
...HE WANTED TO QUIT SCHOOL AND JOIN THE SDF.
I COULDN'T BELIEVE WHAT HE WAS SAYING.
BUT I DIDN'T TRY TO TALK HIM OUT OF IT BECAUSE HE KEPT SAYING THAT HE WANTED TO PROTECT AKEMI.
I HAD MIXED FEELINGS ABOUT HIS PLAN, BUT I ENVIED HIM FOR BEING HOPEFUL ABOUT THE FUTURE.

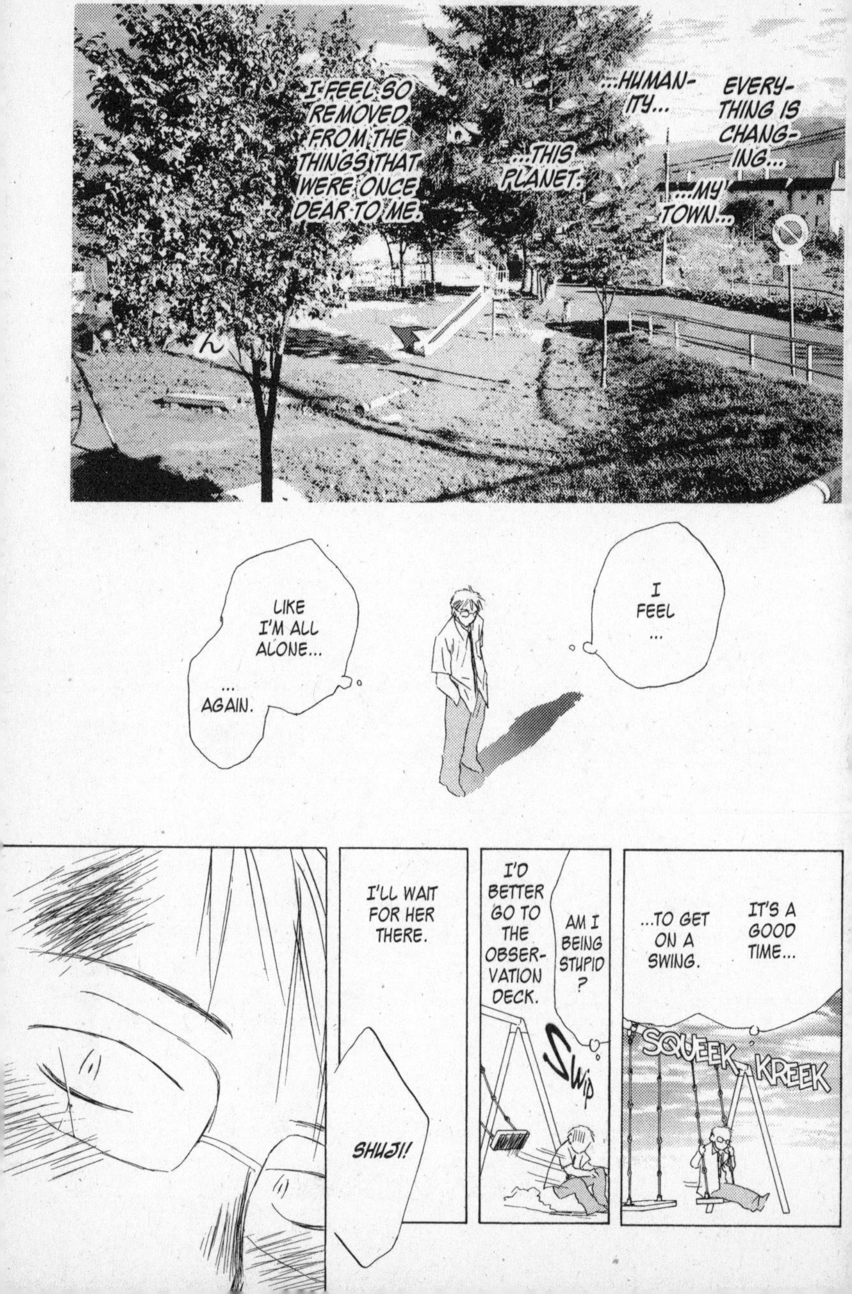
EVERY-THING IS CHANGING...
...MY TOWN...
...HUMANITY...
...THIS PLANET.
I FEEL SO REMOVED FROM THE THINGS THAT WERE ONCE DEAR TO ME.
I FEEL ...
LIKE I'M ALL ALONE... ... AGAIN.
IT'S A GOOD TIME...
...TO GET ON A SWING.
SQUEEK
KREEK
AM I BEING STUPID ?
I'D BETTER GO TO THE OBSERVATION DECK.
SWIP
I'LL WAIT FOR HER THERE.
SHUJI!

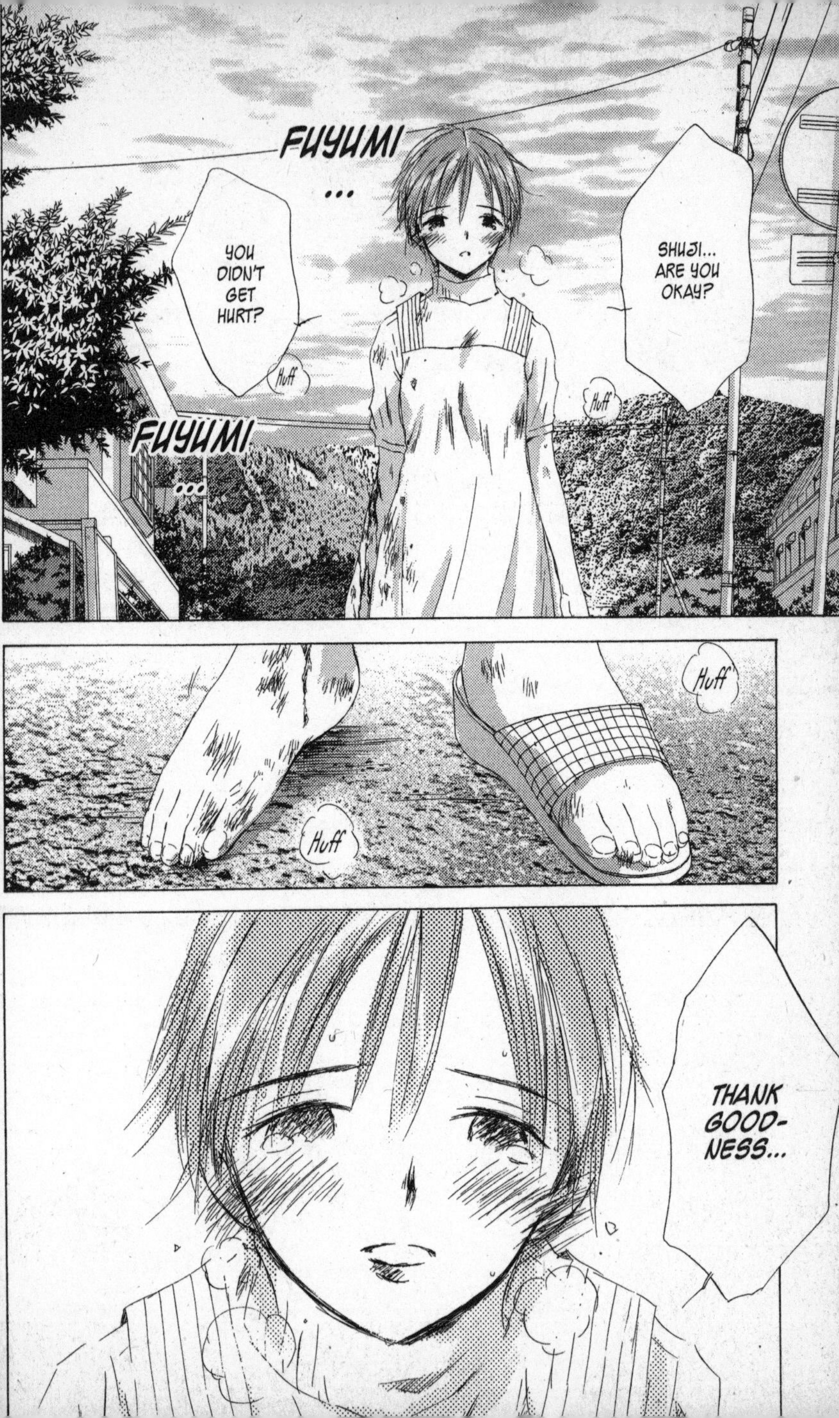
SHUJI... ARE YOU OKAY?
Huff
FUYUMI ...
YOU DIDN'T GET HURT?
Huff
FUYUMI ...
Huff
Huff
THANK GOOD-NESS...

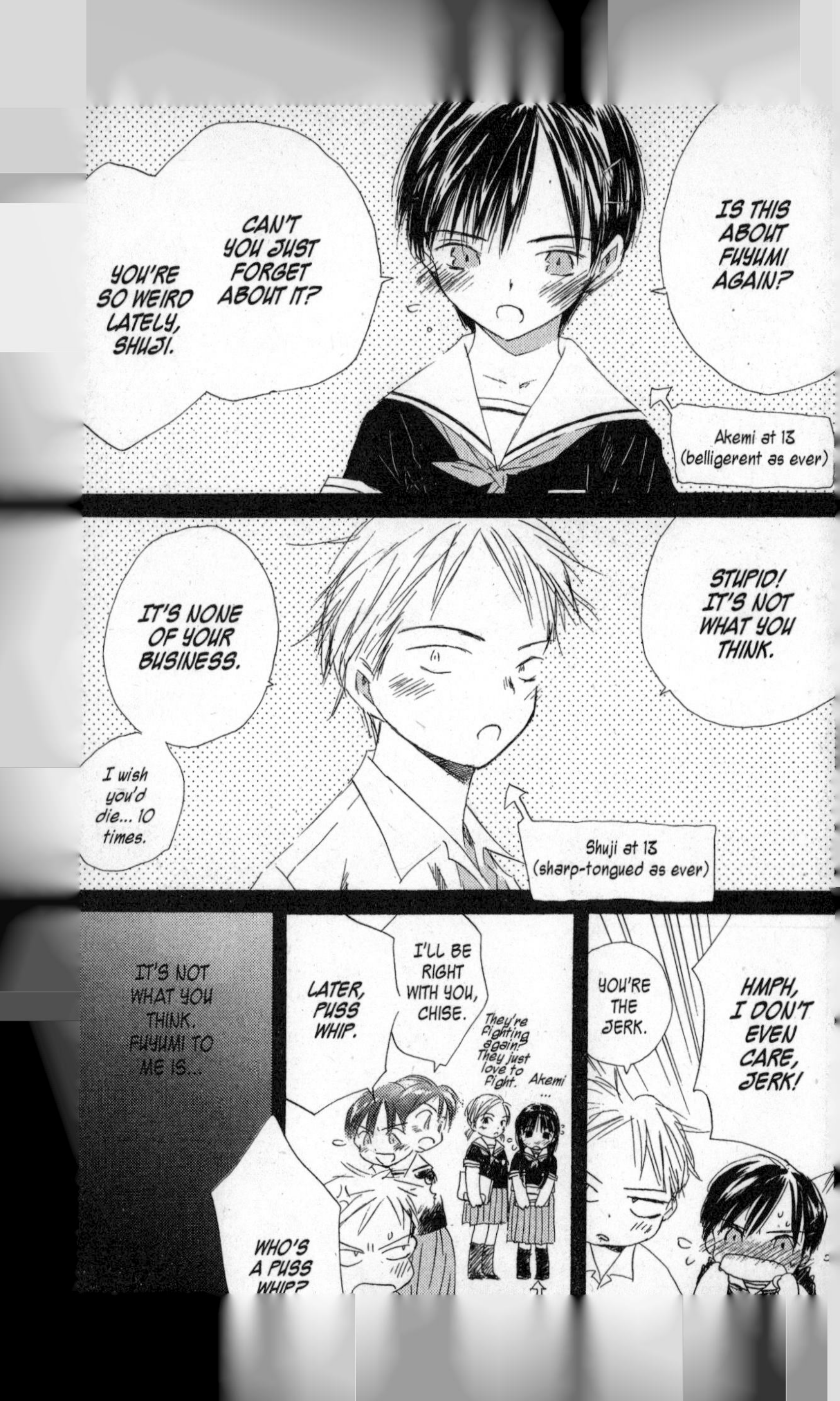
IS THIS ABOUT FUYUMI AGAIN?
Akemi at 13 (belligerent as ever)
CAN'T YOU JUST FORGET ABOUT IT?
YOU'RE SO WEIRD LATELY, SHUJI.
STUPID! IT'S NOT WHAT YOU THINK.
Shuji at 13 (sharp-tongued as ever)
IT'S NONE OF YOUR BUSINESS.
I wish you'd die... 10 times.
HMPH, I DON'T EVEN CARE, JERK!
YOU'RE THE JERK.
I'LL BE RIGHT WITH YOU, CHISE.
LATER, PUSS WHIP.
They're fighting again! They just love to fight.
Akemi ...
WHO'S A PUSS WHIP?
IT'S NOT WHAT YOU THINK. FUYUMI TO ME IS...

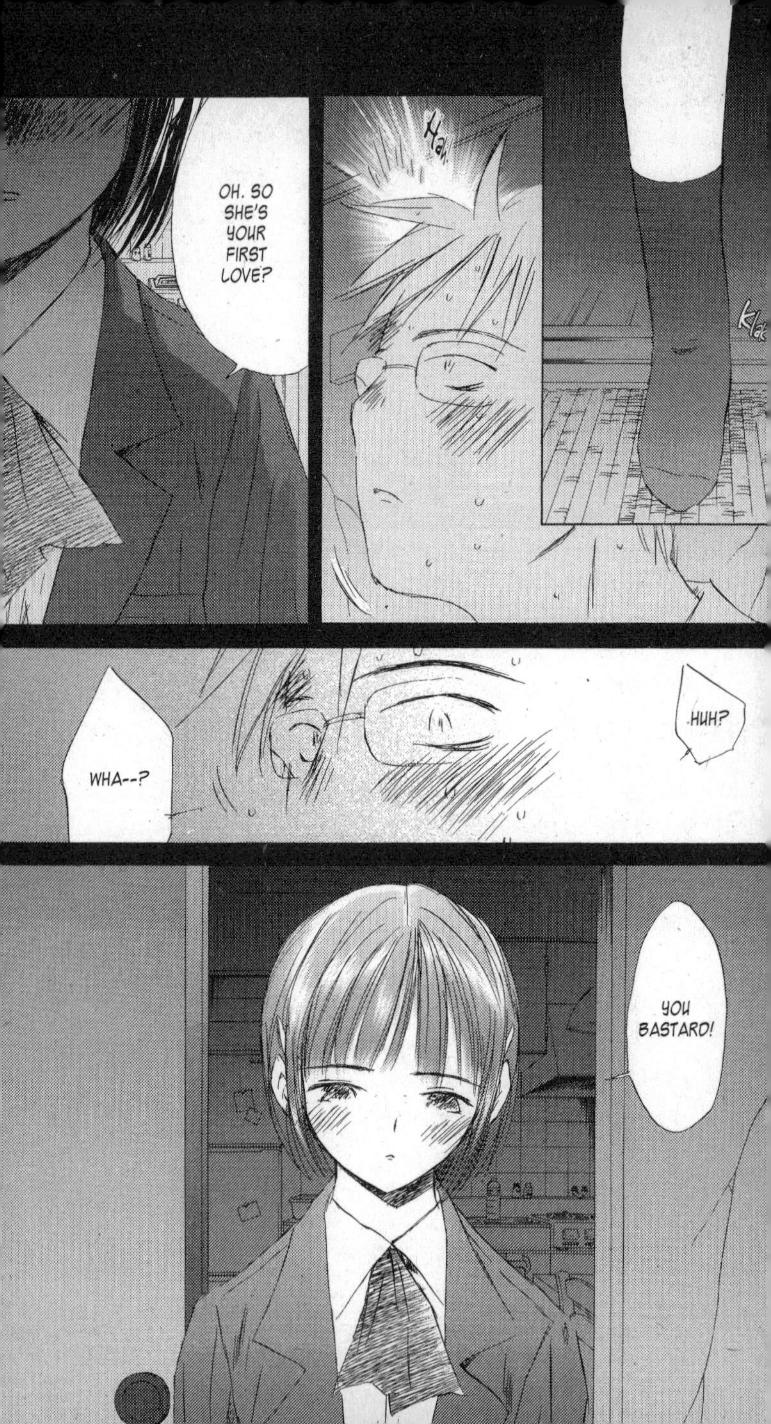

Klak
Hah.
OH. SO SHE'S YOUR FIRST LOVE?
HUH?
WHA--?
YOU BASTARD!

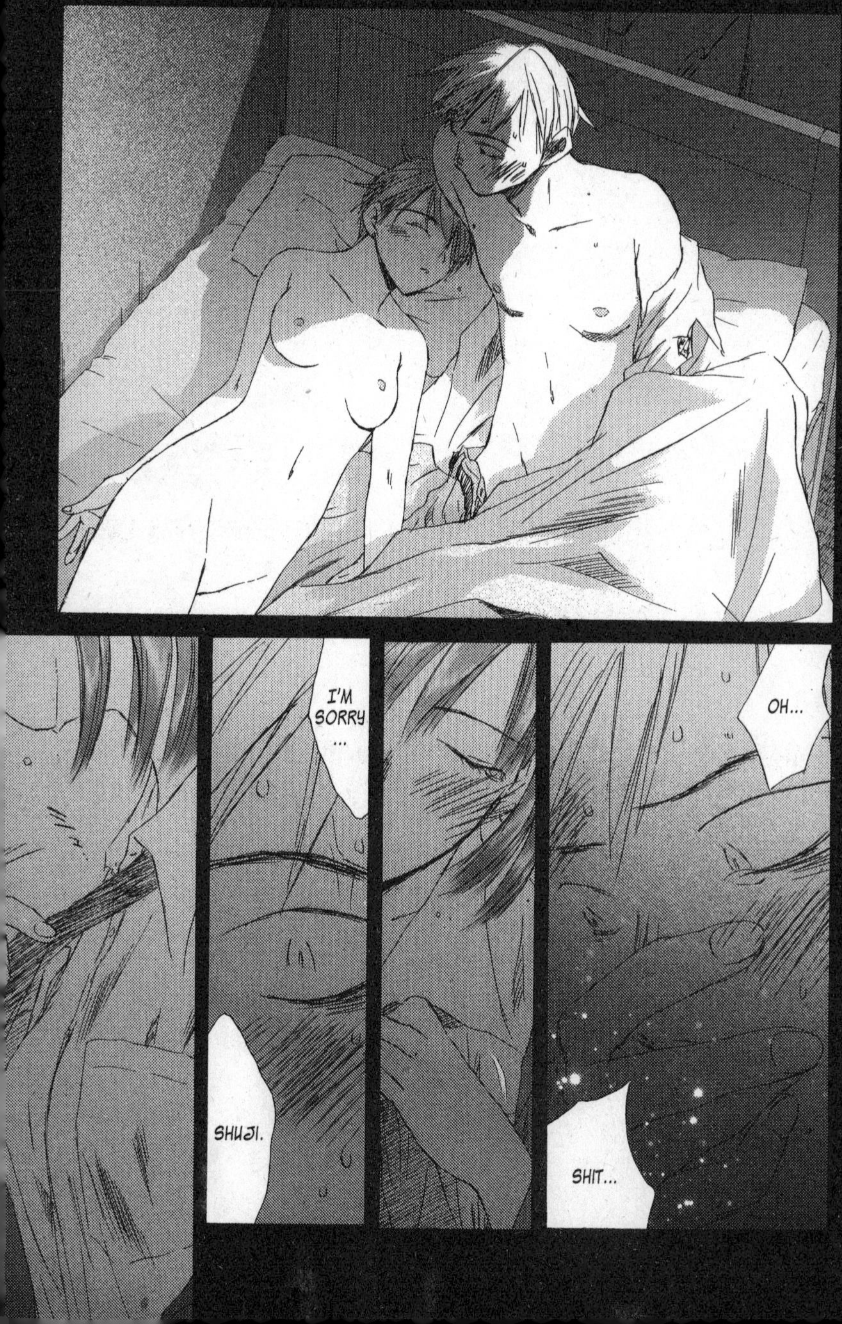
OH...
SHIT...
I'M SORRY ...
SHUJI.

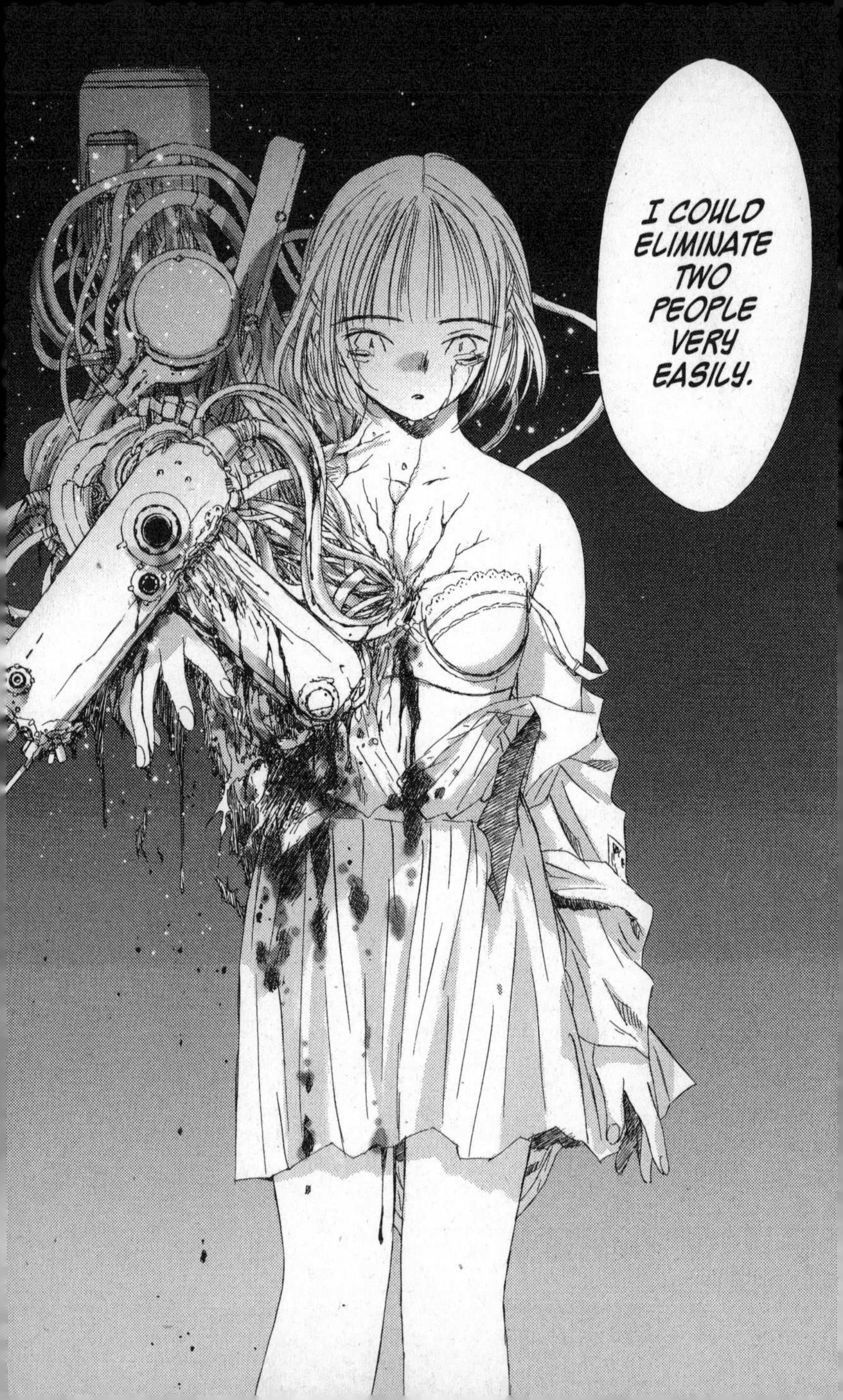
I COULD ELIMINATE TWO PEOPLE VERY EASILY.

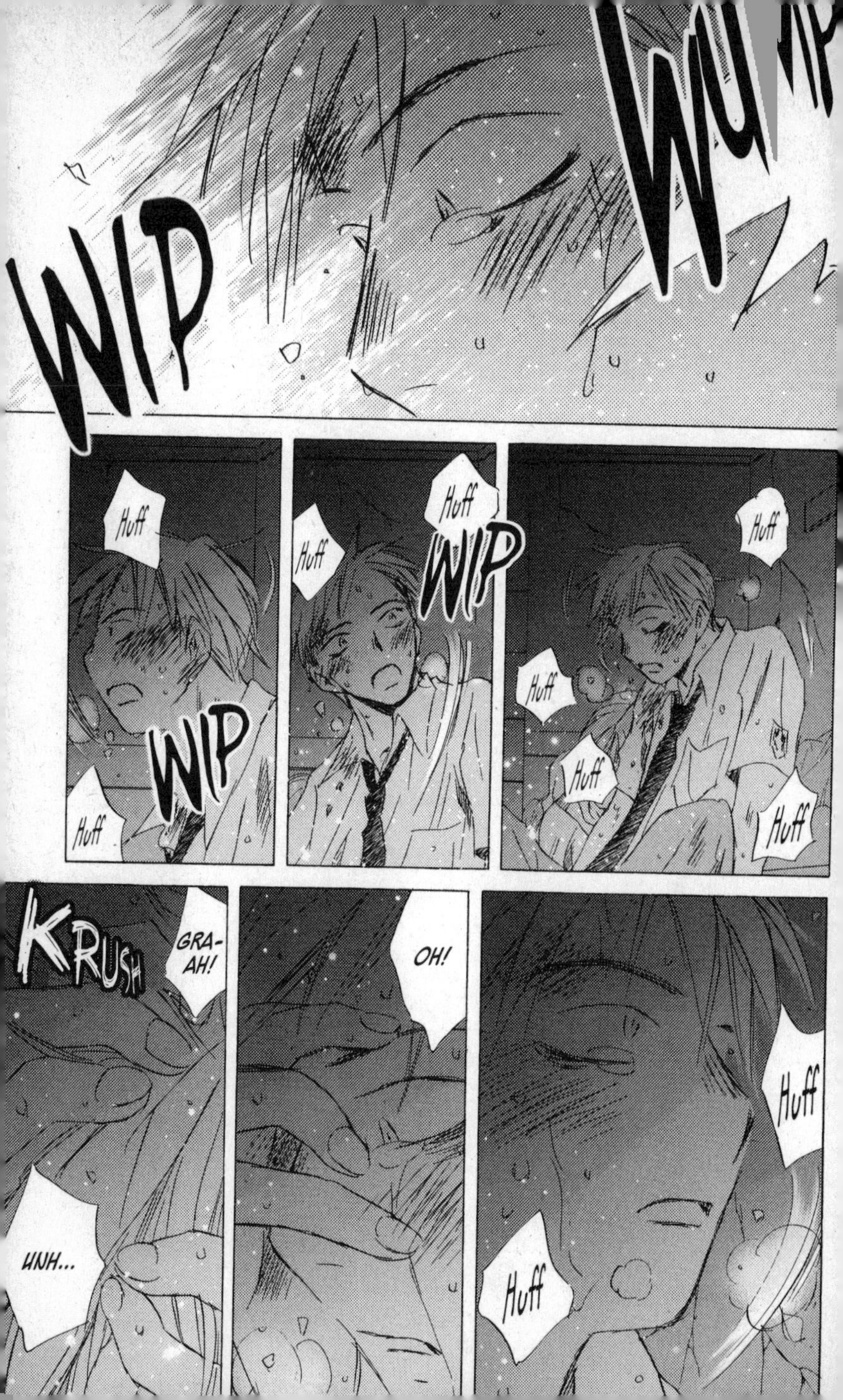
WIP
Huff
Huff
Huff
Huff
Huff
WIP
Huff
Huff
WIP
Huff
Huff
Huff
OH!
GRA-AH!
KRUSH
UNH...

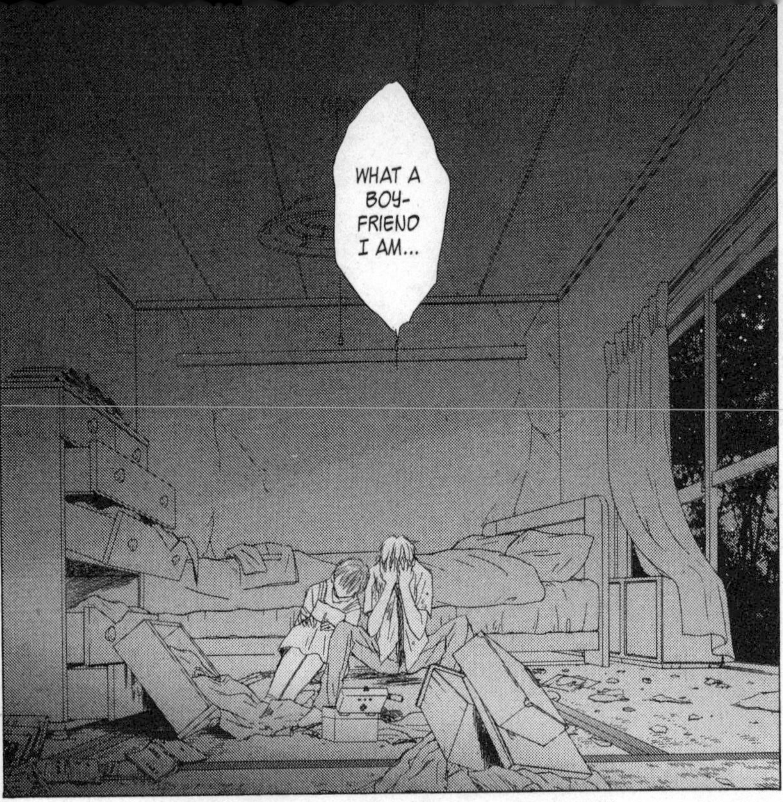
WHAT A BOY-FRIEND I AM...

THE LAST LOVE SONG ON THIS LITTLE PLANET.

Chapter 4: Fuyumi (8)

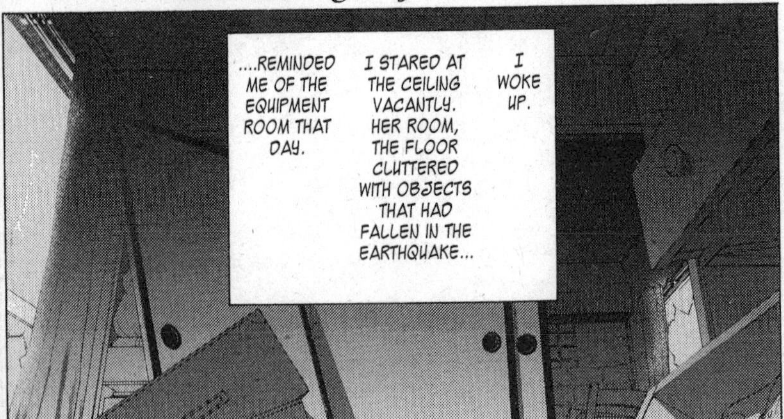
I WOKE UP.
I STARED AT THE CEILING VACANTLY. HER ROOM, THE FLOOR CLUTTERED WITH OBJECTS THAT HAD FALLEN IN THE EARTHQUAKE...
....REMINDED ME OF THE EQUIPMENT ROOM THAT DAY.

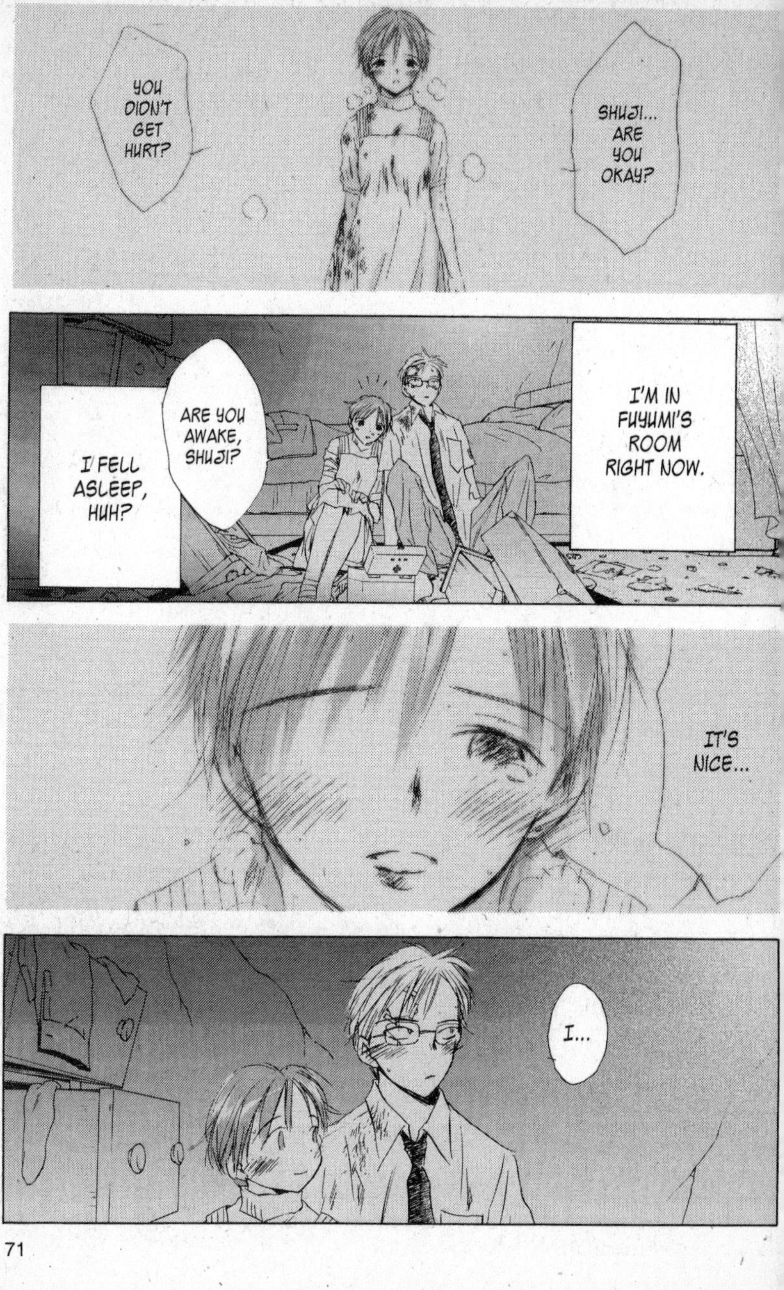
SHUJI... ARE YOU OKAY?
YOU DIDN'T GET HURT?
I'M IN FUYUMI'S ROOM RIGHT NOW.
ARE YOU AWAKE, SHUJI?
I FELL ASLEEP, HUH?
IT'S NICE...
I...

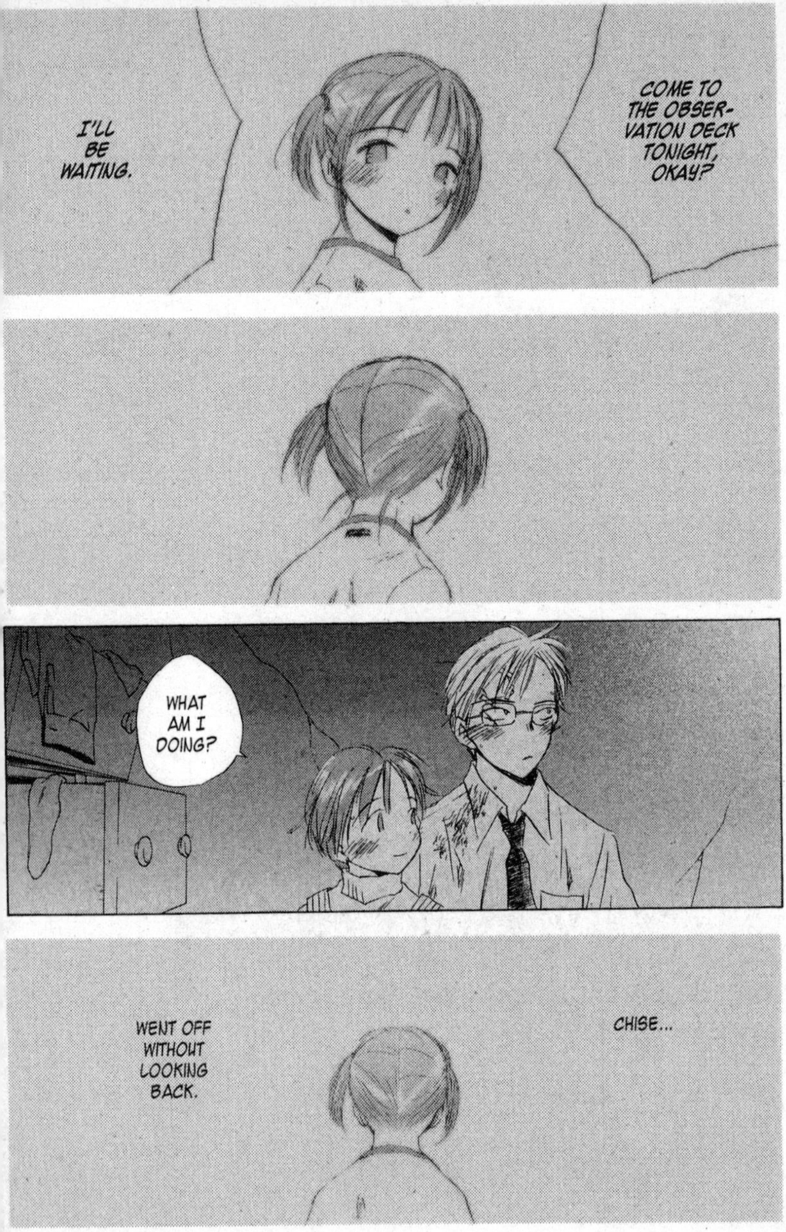
COME TO THE OBSERVATION DECK TONIGHT, OKAY?
I'LL BE WAITING.
WHAT AM I DOING?
CHISE...
WENT OFF WITHOUT LOOKING BACK.

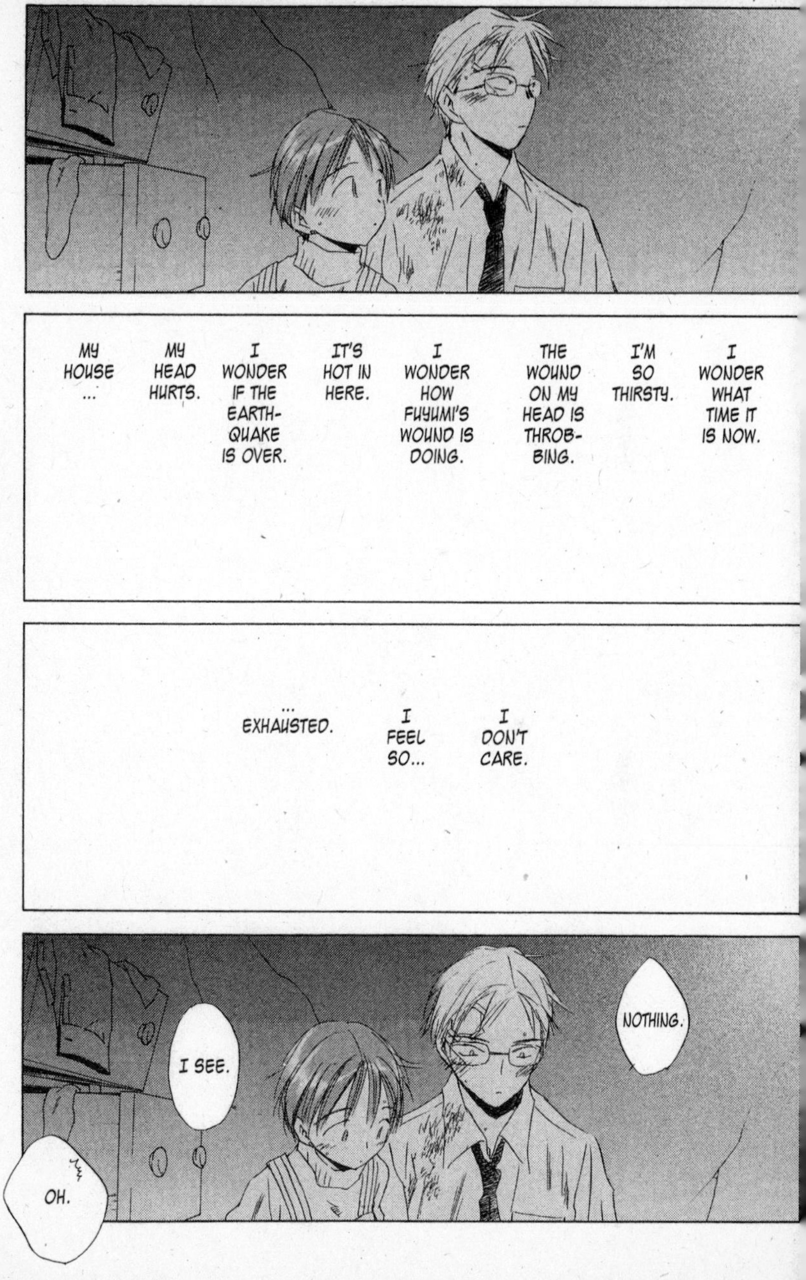
I WONDER WHAT TIME IT IS NOW.
I'M SO THIRSTY.
THE WOUND ON MY HEAD IS THROBBING.
I WONDER HOW FUYUMI'S WOUND IS DOING.
IT'S HOT IN HERE.
I WONDER IF THE EARTHQUAKE IS OVER.
MY HEAD HURTS.
MY HOUSE ...
I DON'T CARE.
I FEEL SO...
...EXHAUSTED.
NOTHING.
I SEE.
OH.

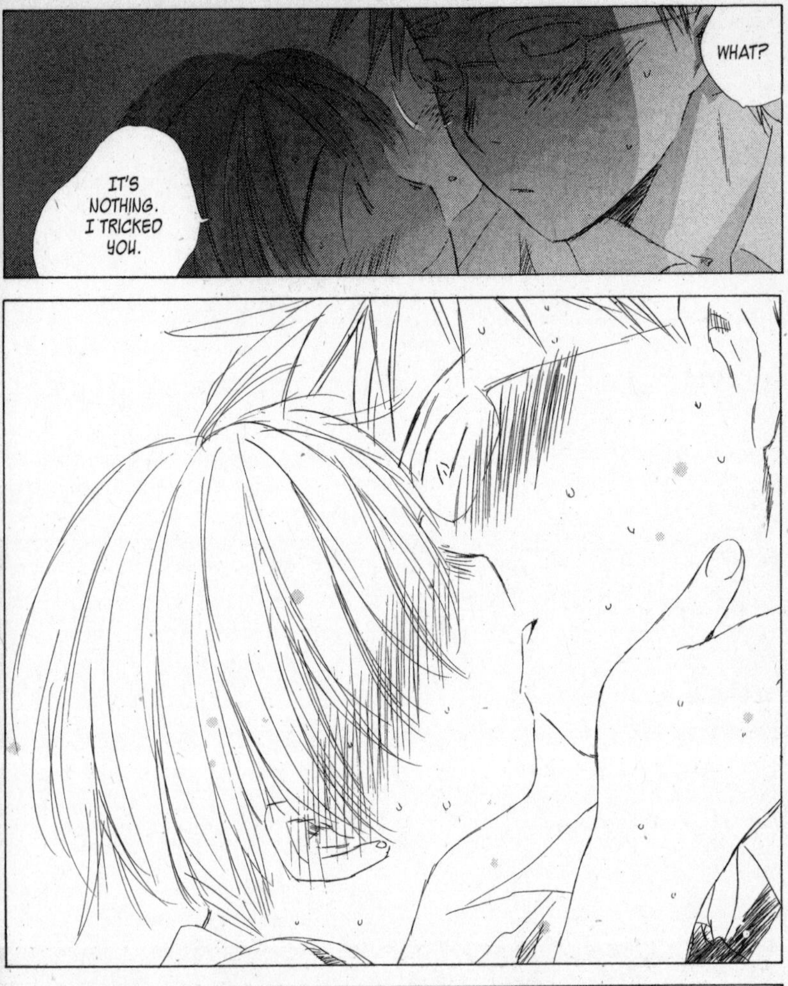
WHAT?
IT'S NOTHING. I TRICKED YOU.
FOR SOME REASON ...
I DIDN'T TRY TO PUSH HER AWAY...
OR YELL AT HER.
I JUST GAVE MYSELF OVER...
TO THAT SOFT-NESS.

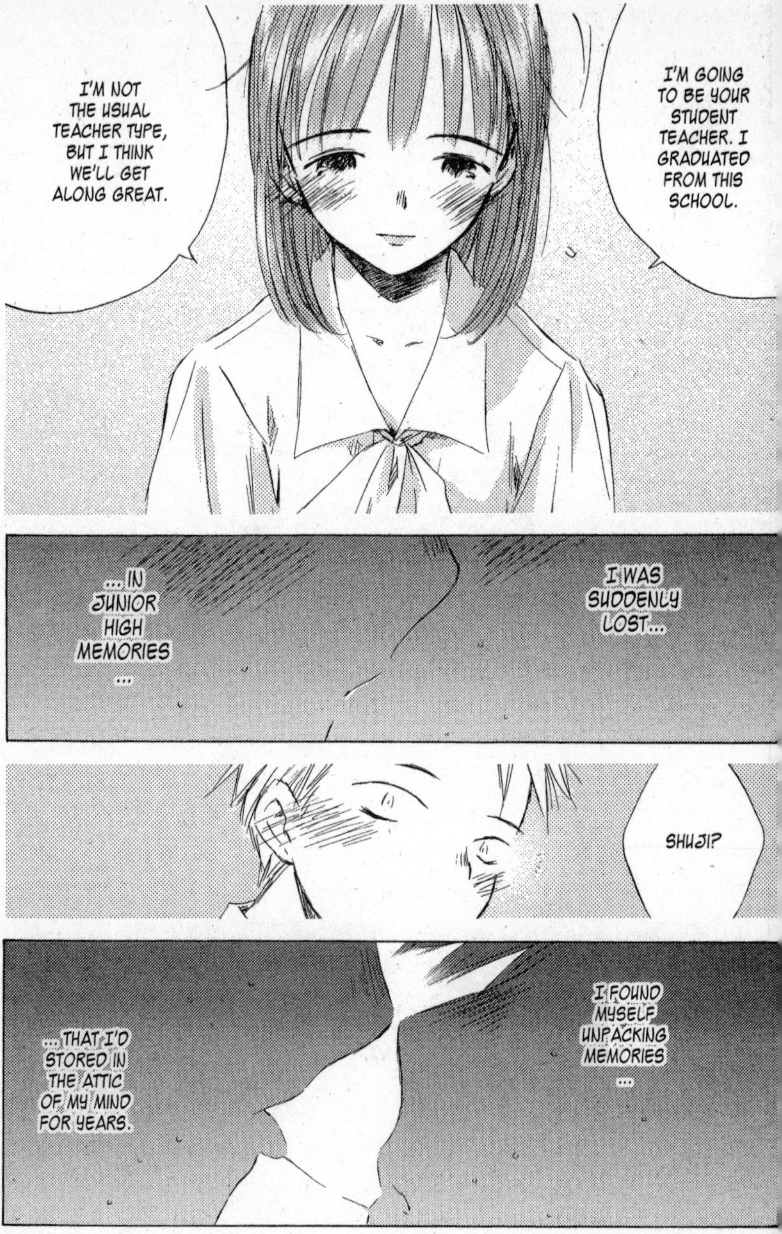

I'M GOING TO BE YOUR STUDENT TEACHER. I GRADUATED FROM THIS SCHOOL.
I'M NOT THE USUAL TEACHER TYPE, BUT I THINK WE'LL GET ALONG GREAT.
I WAS SUDDENLY LOST...
...IN JUNIOR HIGH MEMORIES ...
SHUJI?
I FOUND MYSELF UNPACKING MEMORIES ...
...THAT I'D STORED IN THE ATTIC OF MY MIND FOR YEARS.

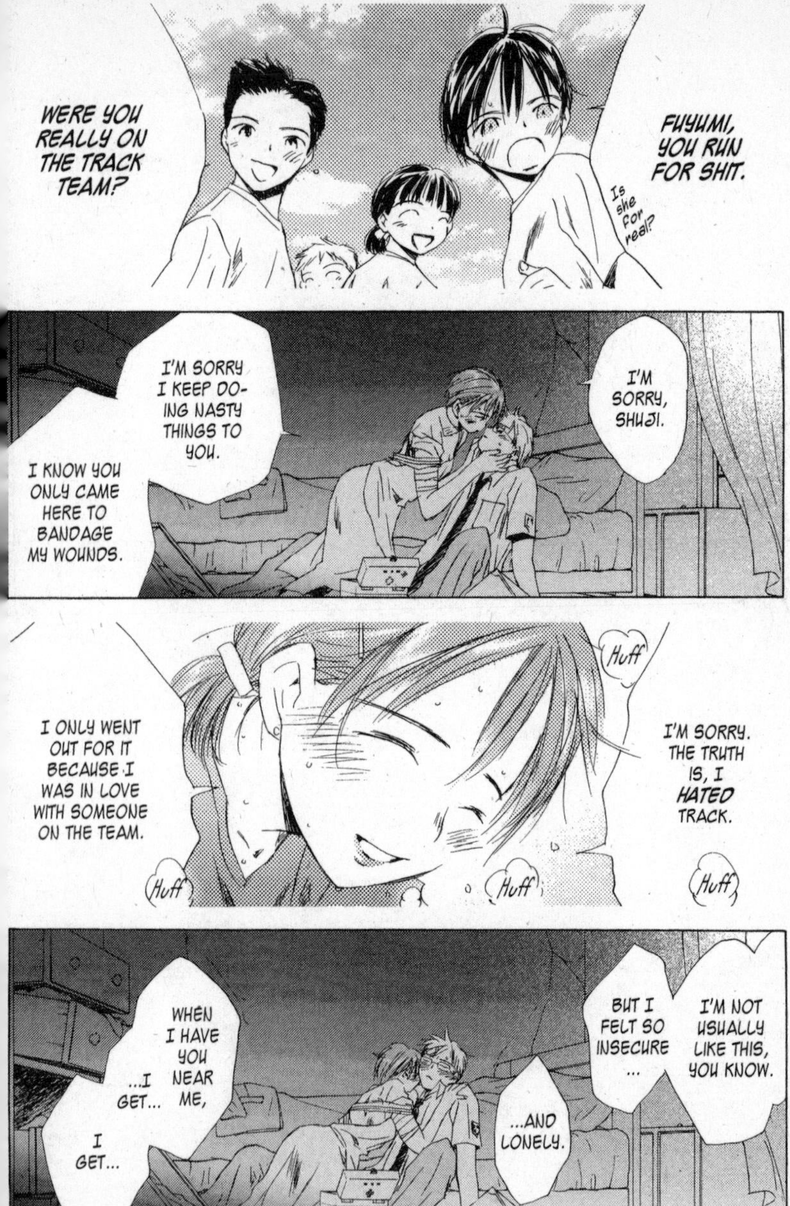

FUYUMI, YOU RUN FOR SHIT.
Is she for real?
WERE YOU REALLY ON THE TRACK TEAM?
I'M SORRY, SHUJI.
I'M SORRY I KEEP DO-ING NASTY THINGS TO YOU.
I KNOW YOU ONLY CAME HERE TO BANDAGE MY WOUNDS.
Huff
I'M SORRY. THE TRUTH IS, I HATED TRACK.
I ONLY WENT OUT FOR IT BECAUSE I WAS IN LOVE WITH SOMEONE ON THE TEAM.
Huff
Huff
Huff
I'M NOT USUALLY LIKE THIS, YOU KNOW.
BUT I FELT SO INSECURE ...
...AND LONELY.
WHEN I HAVE YOU NEAR ME,
...I GET...
I GET...

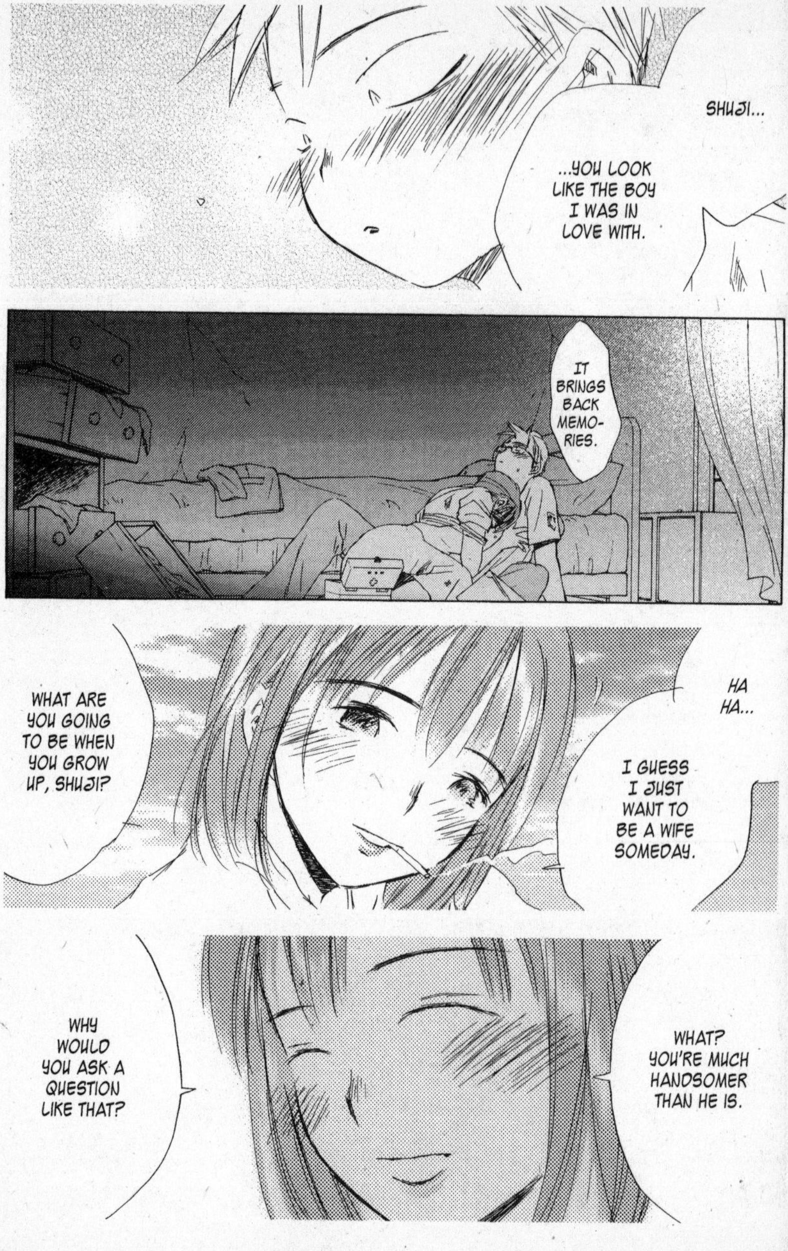
SHUJI...
...YOU LOOK LIKE THE BOY I WAS IN LOVE WITH.
IT BRINGS BACK MEMO-RIES.
HA HA...
I GUESS I JUST WANT TO BE A WIFE SOMEDAY.
WHAT ARE YOU GOING TO BE WHEN YOU GROW UP, SHUJI?
WHAT? YOU'RE MUCH HANDSOMER THAN HE IS.
WHY WOULD YOU ASK A QUESTION LIKE THAT?

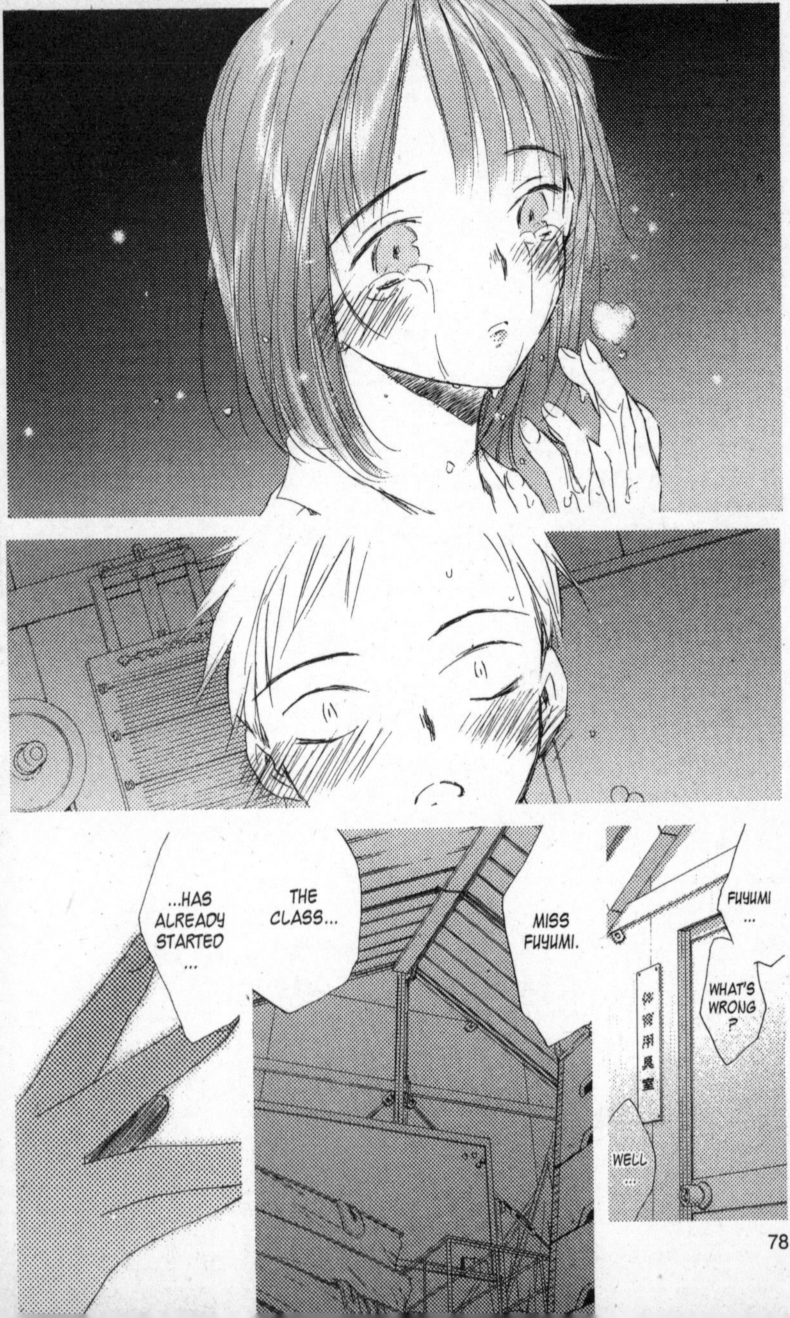
FUYUMI ...
WHAT'S WRONG ?
WELL ...
MISS FUYUMI.
THE CLASS...
...HAS ALREADY STARTED ...

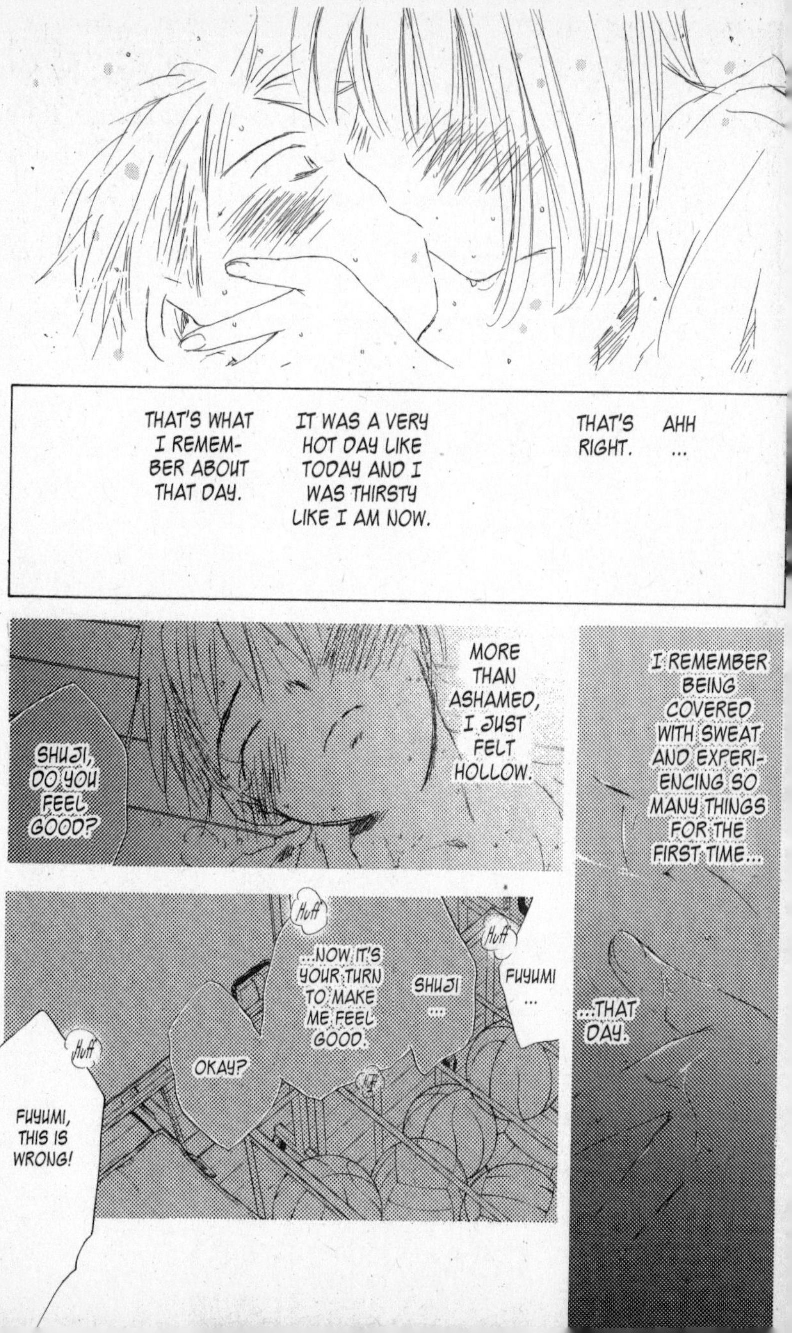
AHH ...
THAT'S RIGHT.
IT WAS A VERY HOT DAY LIKE TODAY AND I WAS THIRSTY LIKE I AM NOW.
THAT'S WHAT I REMEMBER ABOUT THAT DAY.
I REMEMBER BEING COVERED WITH SWEAT AND EXPERIENCING SO MANY THINGS FOR THE FIRST TIME...
...THAT DAY.
MORE THAN ASHAMED, I JUST FELT HOLLOW.
SHUJI, DO YOU FEEL GOOD?
Huff
FUYUMI ...
Huff
SHUJI ...
...NOW IT'S YOUR TURN TO MAKE ME FEEL GOOD.
OKAY?
Huff
FUYUMI, THIS IS WRONG!

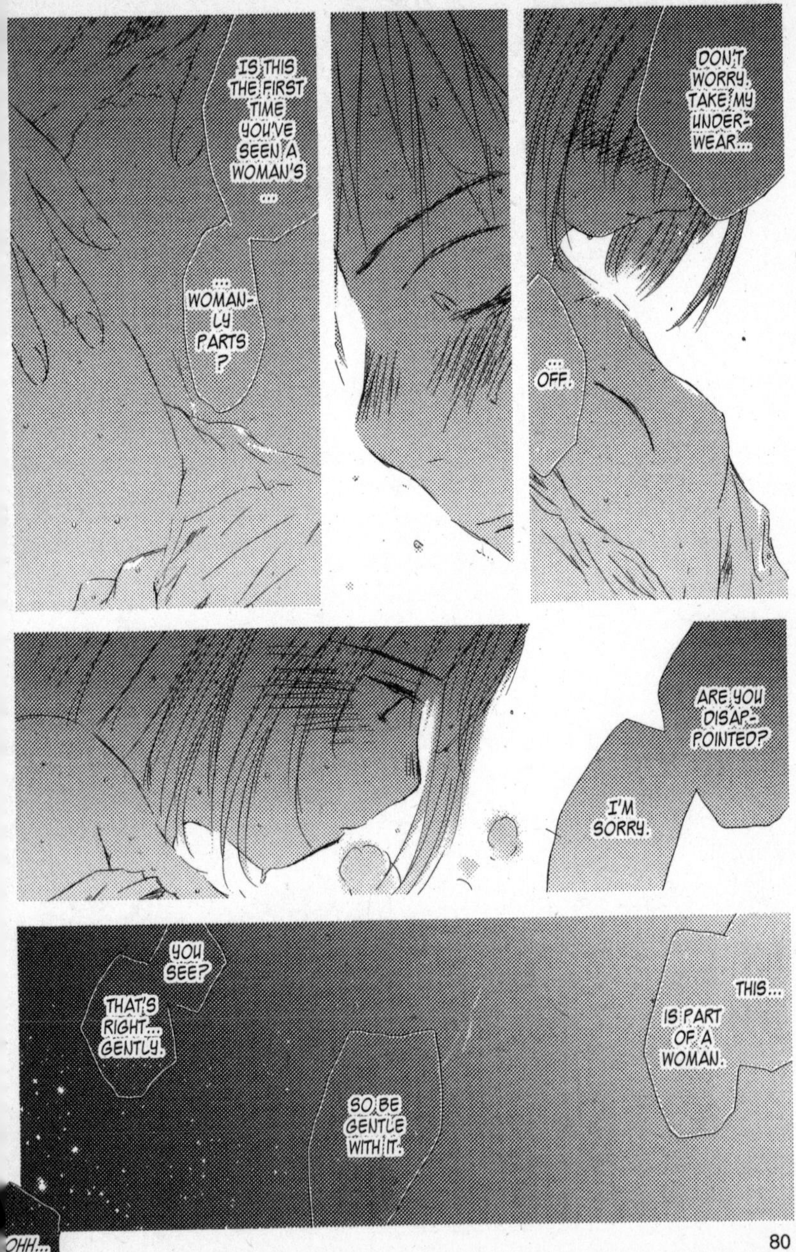
DON'T WORRY. TAKE MY UNDER-WEAR...
...OFF.
IS THIS THE FIRST TIME YOU'VE SEEN A WOMAN'S ...
...WOMAN-LY PARTS?
ARE YOU DISAP-POINTED?
I'M SORRY.
THIS...
IS PART OF A WOMAN.
SO BE GENTLE WITH IT.
YOU SEE?
THAT'S RIGHT... GENTLY.
OHH...

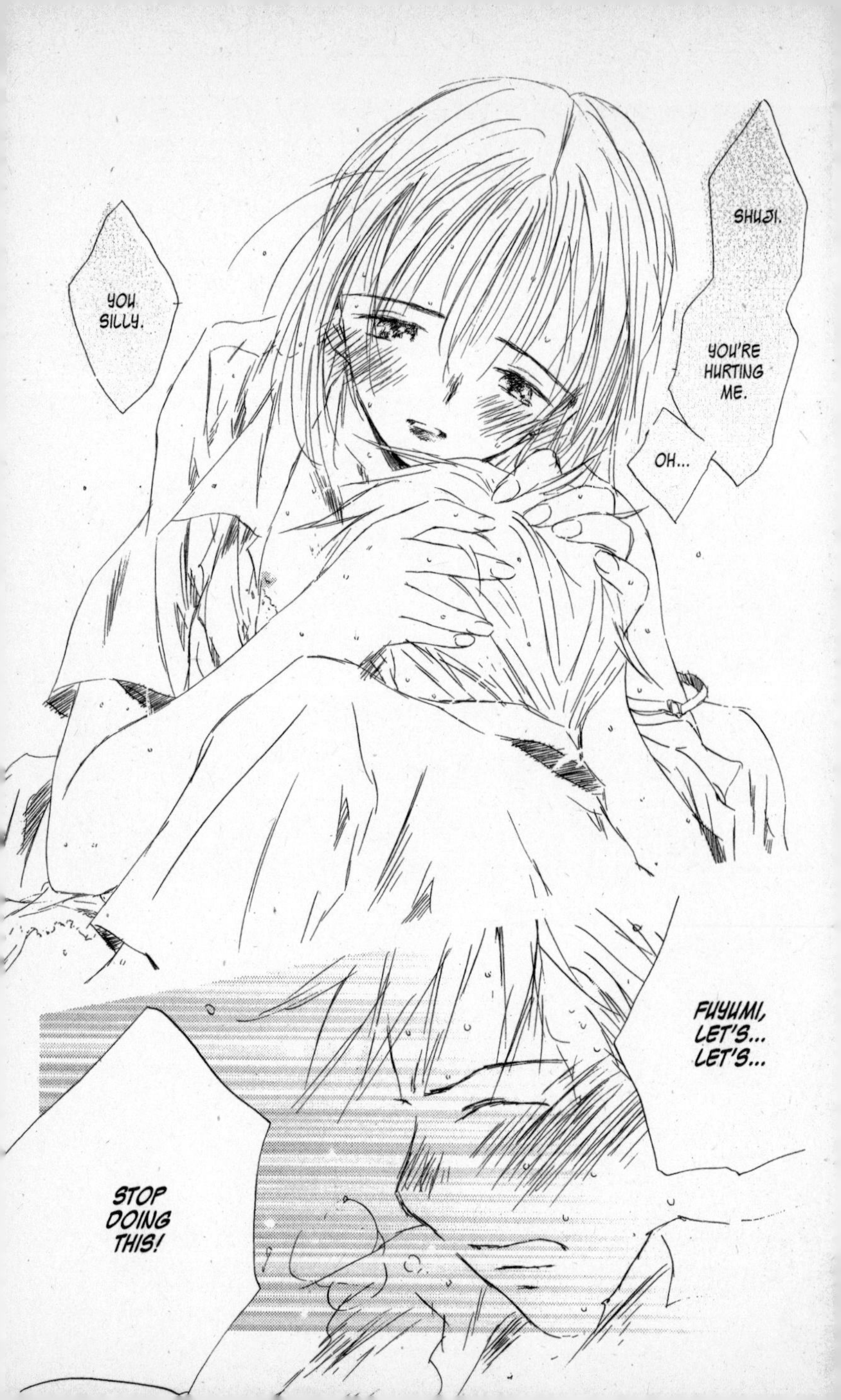
SHUJI.
YOU'RE HURTING ME.
OH...
YOU SILLY.
FUYUMI, LET'S... LET'S...
STOP DOING THIS!

WHAT IS FUYUMI...

FUYUMI...

TO ME AFTER ALL?

WHOA

OH.

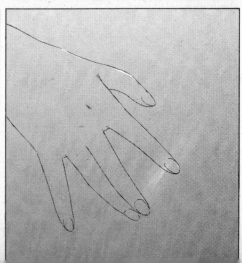

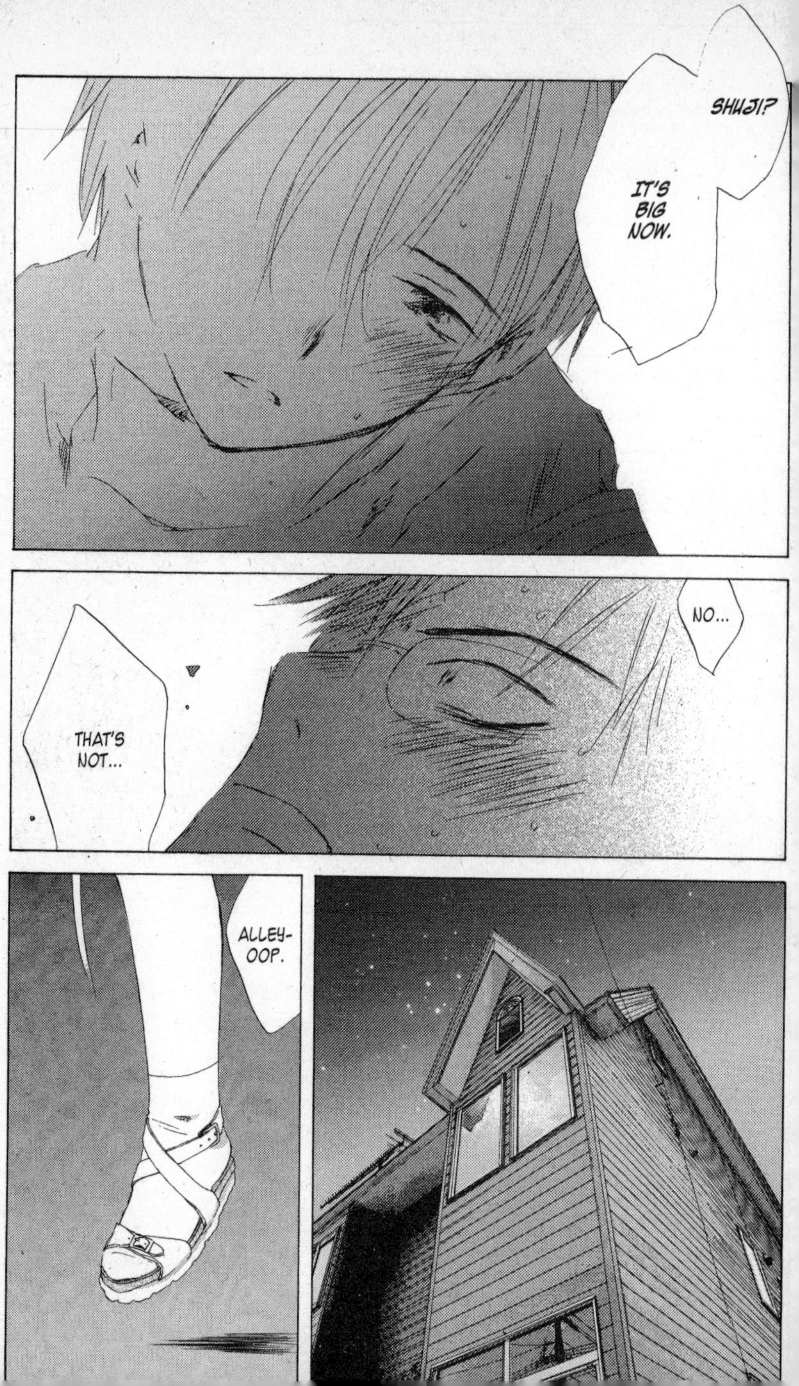
SHUJI?
IT'S BIG NOW.
NO...
THAT'S NOT...
ALLEY-OOP.

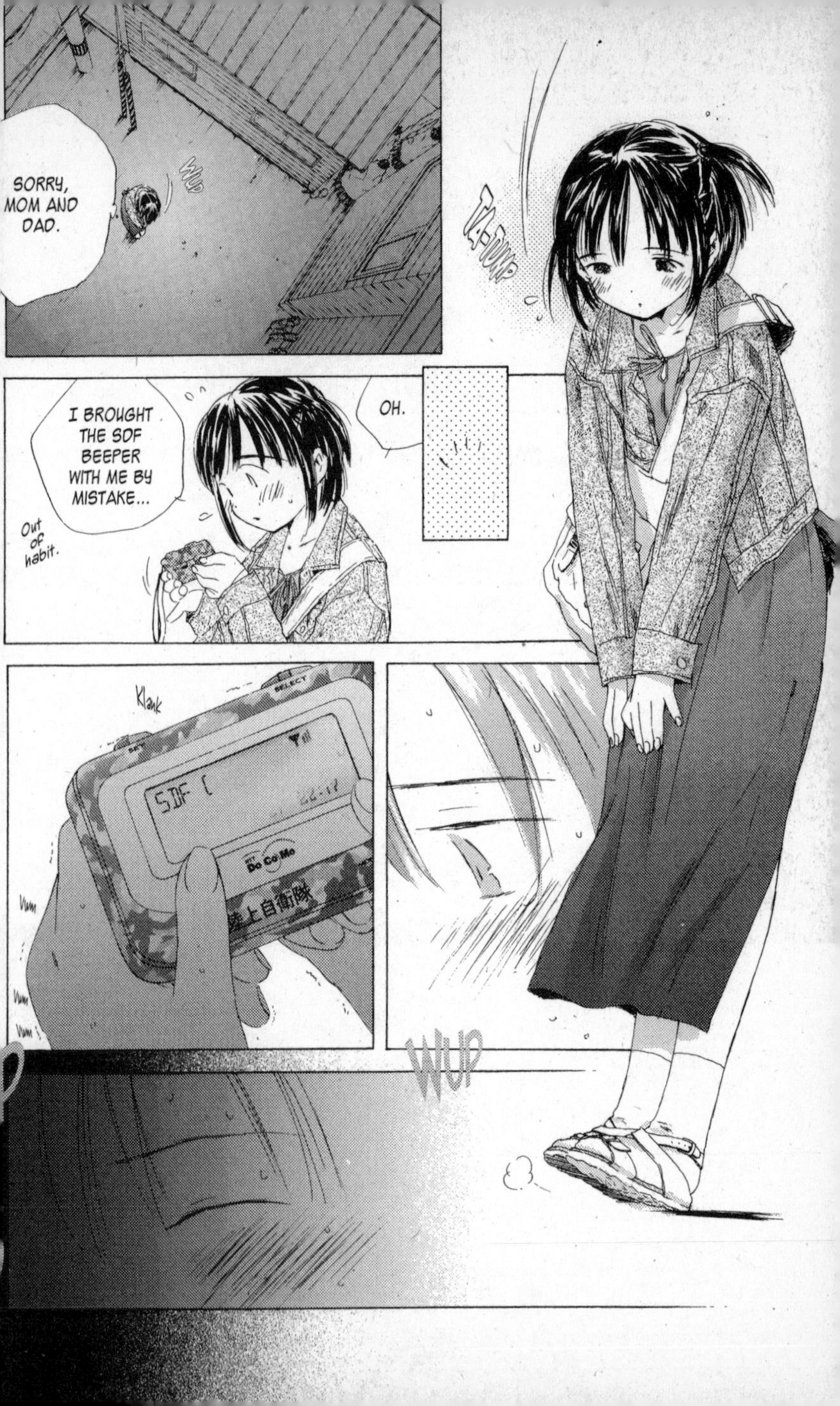
TA-TUMP
SORRY, MOM AND DAD.
WUP
OH.
I BROUGHT THE SDF BEEPER WITH ME BY MISTAKE...
Out of habit.
Klank
SELECT
SDF (
DoCoMo
上自衛隊
Vum
Vum
Vum
WUP

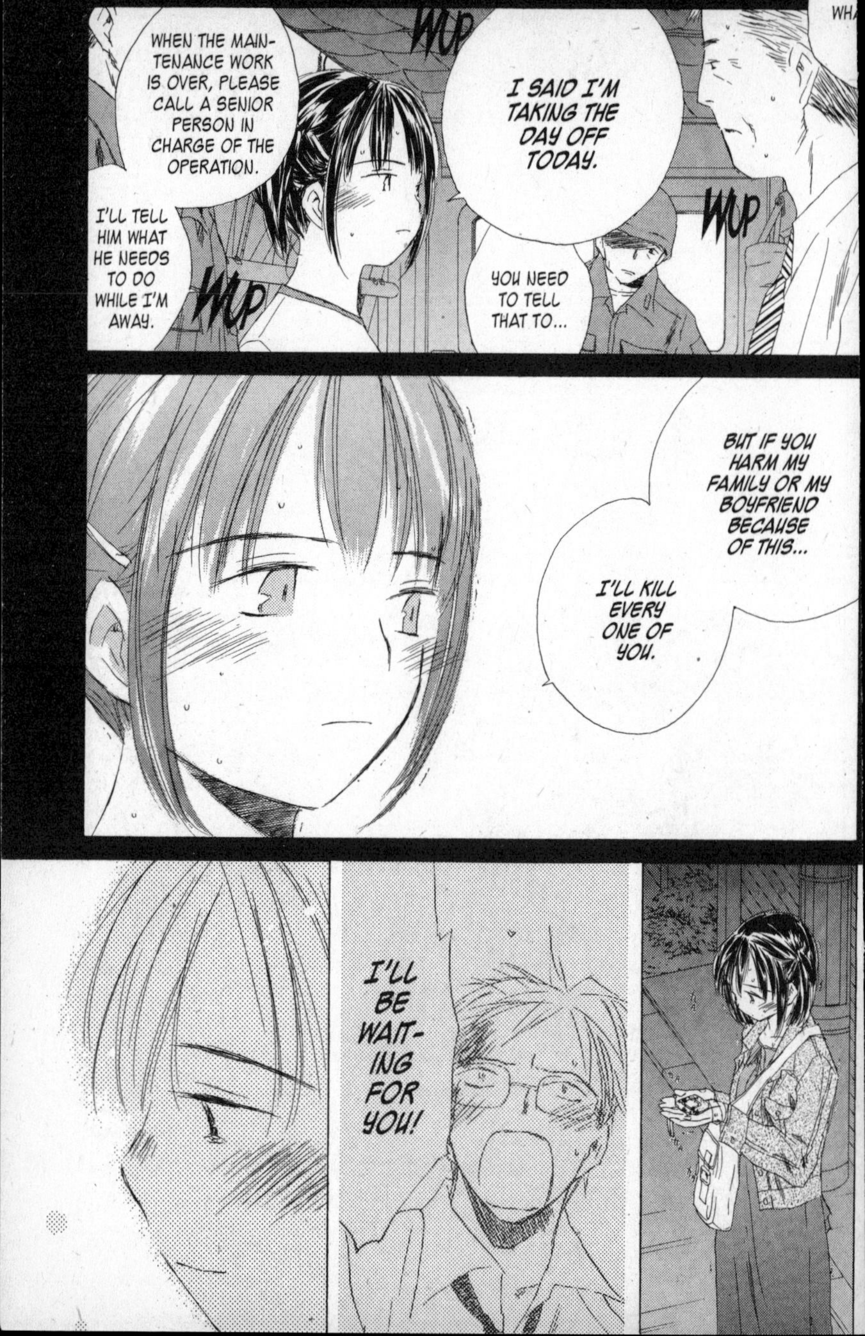
WUP
I SAID I'M TAKING THE DAY OFF TODAY.
WUP
YOU NEED TO TELL THAT TO...
WHEN THE MAINTENANCE WORK IS OVER, PLEASE CALL A SENIOR PERSON IN CHARGE OF THE OPERATION.
I'LL TELL HIM WHAT HE NEEDS TO DO WHILE I'M AWAY.
WUP
BUT IF YOU HARM MY FAMILY OR MY BOYFRIEND BECAUSE OF THIS...
I'LL KILL EVERY ONE OF YOU.
I'LL BE WAITING FOR YOU!

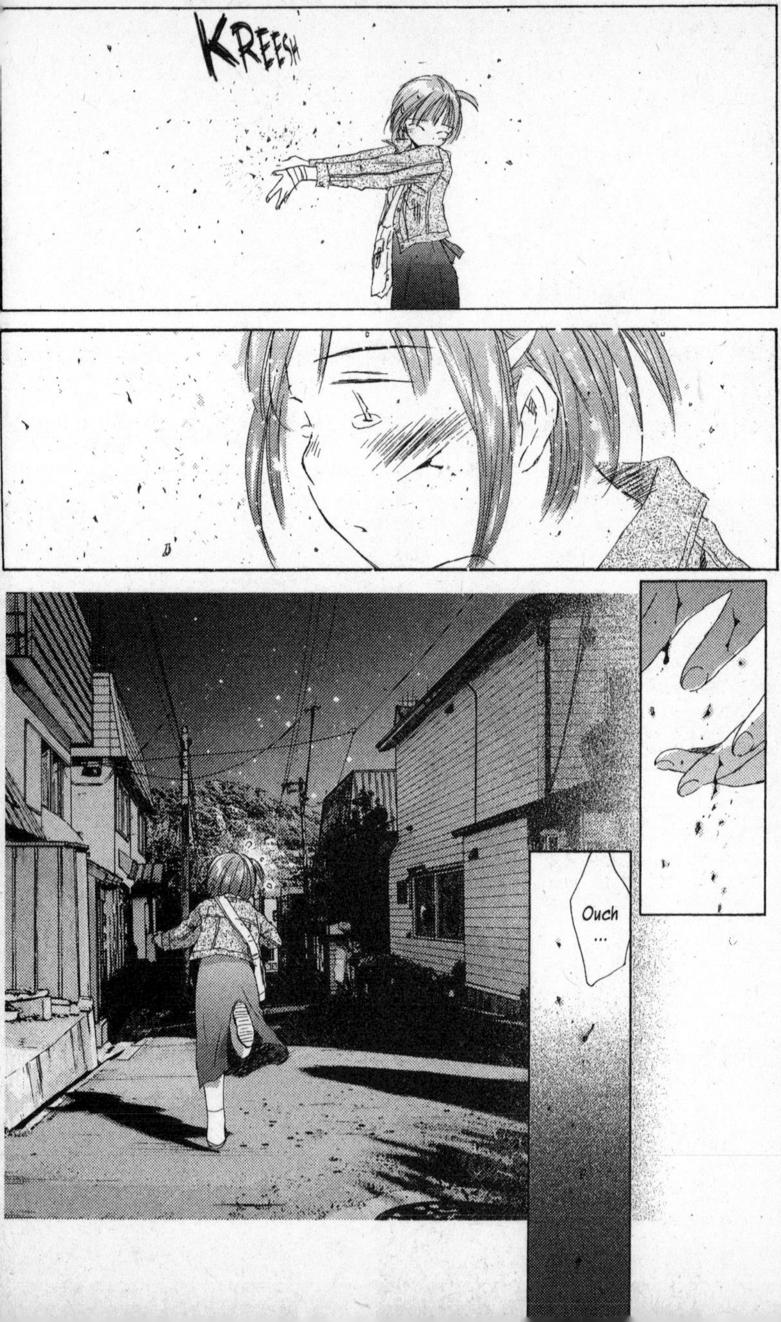
KREESH
Ouch ...

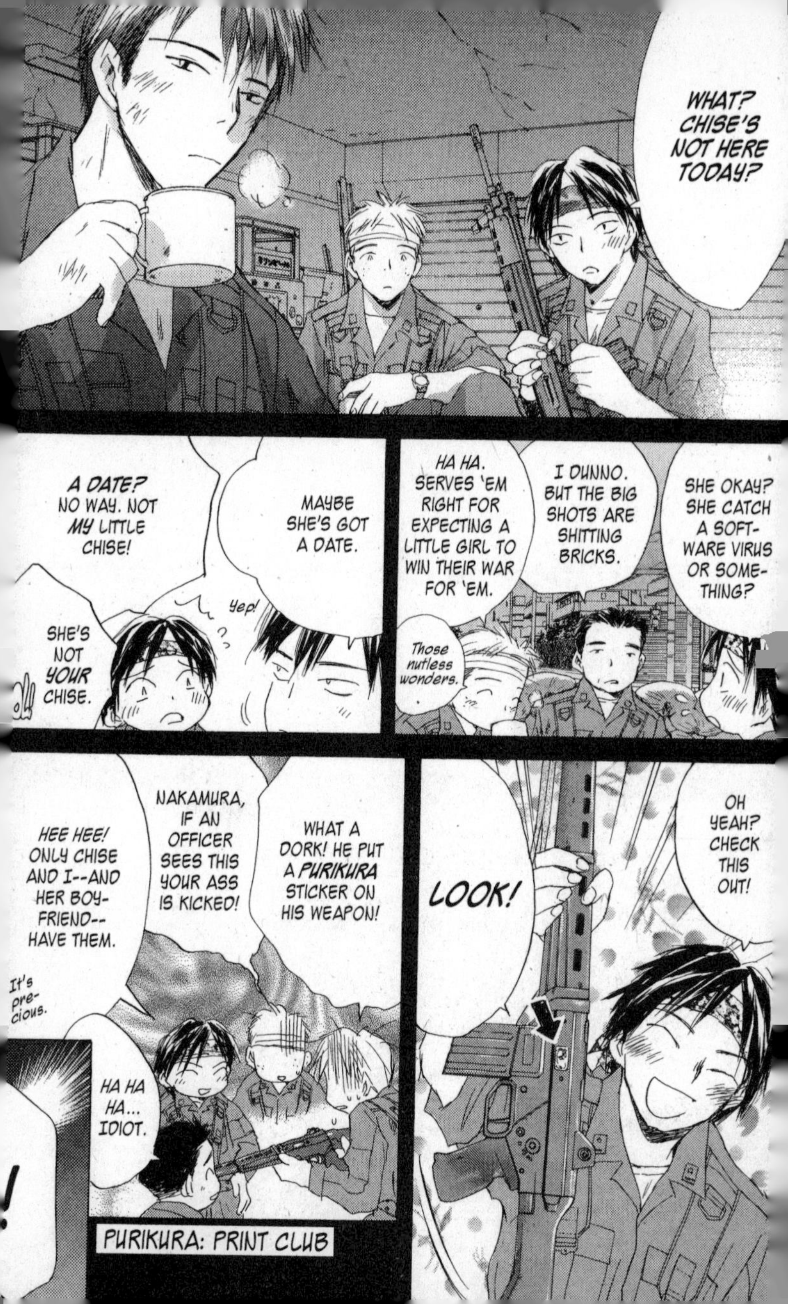

WHAT? CHISE'S NOT HERE TODAY?
SHE OKAY? SHE CATCH A SOFT-WARE VIRUS OR SOME-THING?
I DUNNO. BUT THE BIG SHOTS ARE SHITTING BRICKS.
HA HA. SERVES 'EM RIGHT FOR EXPECTING A LITTLE GIRL TO WIN THEIR WAR FOR 'EM.
Those nutless wonders.
MAYBE SHE'S GOT A DATE.
A DATE? NO WAY. NOT MY LITTLE CHISE!
Yep!
SHE'S NOT YOUR CHISE.
OH YEAH? CHECK THIS OUT!
LOOK!
WHAT A DORK! HE PUT A PURIKURA STICKER ON HIS WEAPON!
NAKAMURA, IF AN OFFICER SEES THIS YOUR ASS IS KICKED!
HEE HEE! ONLY CHISE AND I--AND HER BOY-FRIEND--HAVE THEM.
It's pre-cious.
HA HA HA... IDIOT.
PURIKURA: PRINT CLUB

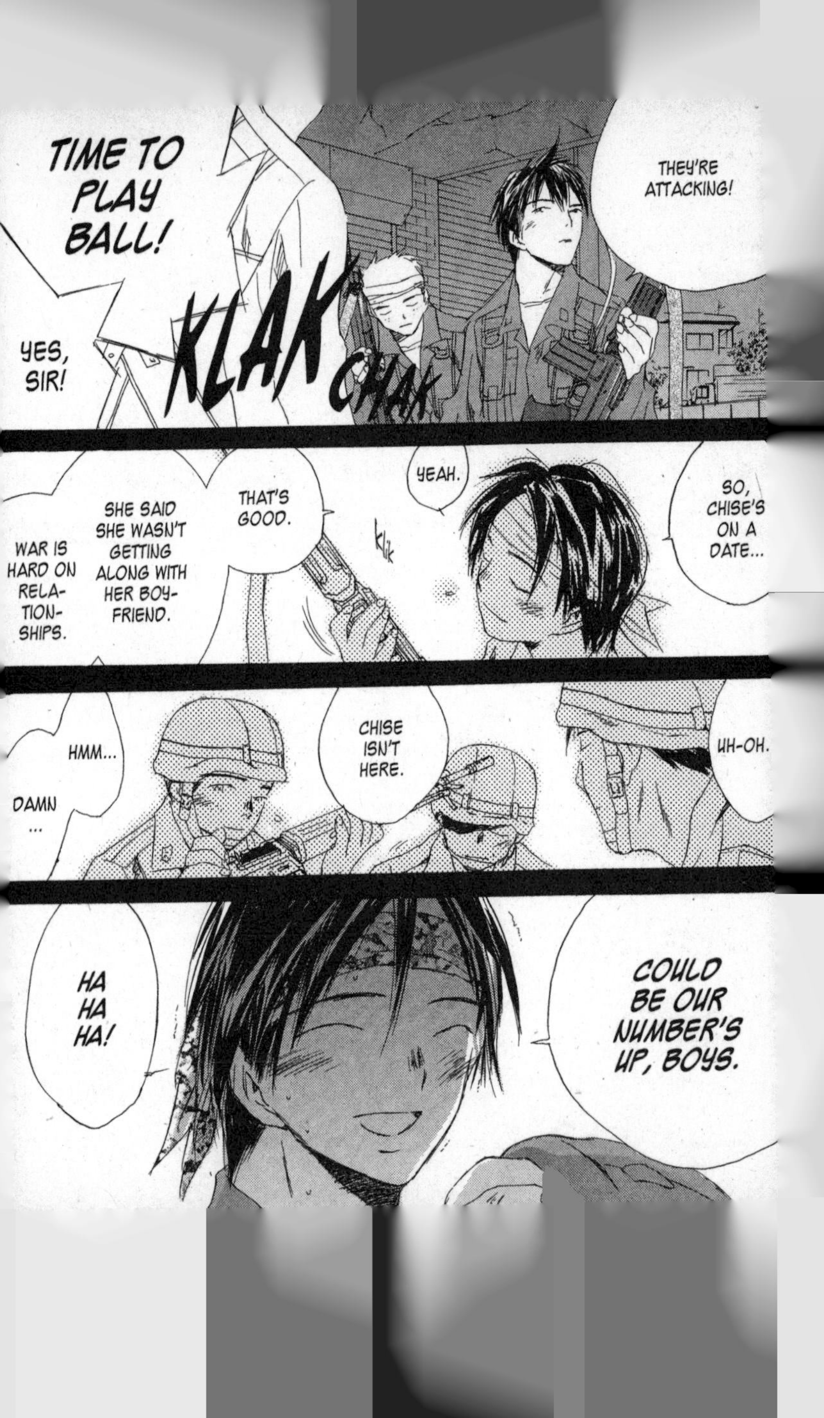
THEY'RE ATTACKING!
TIME TO PLAY BALL!
KLAK
CHAK
YES, SIR!
SO, CHISE'S ON A DATE...
YEAH.
klik
THAT'S GOOD.
SHE SAID SHE WASN'T GETTING ALONG WITH HER BOY-FRIEND.
WAR IS HARD ON RELA-TION-SHIPS.
UH-OH.
CHISE ISN'T HERE.
HMM...
DAMN ...
COULD BE OUR NUMBER'S UP, BOYS.
HA HA HA!

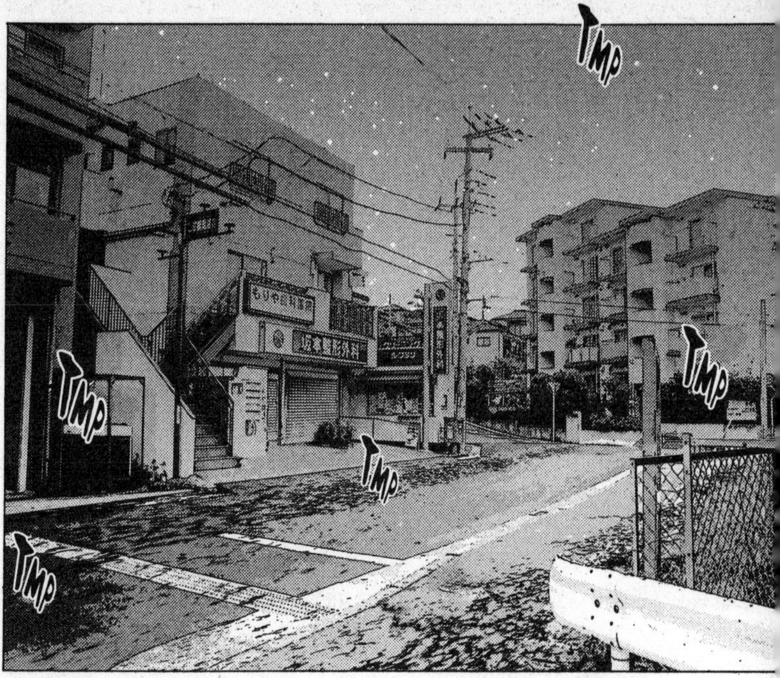
TMP
TMP
TMP
TMP
TMP

THE LAST LOVE SONG ON THIS LITTLE PLANET.

CHAPTER 5: *On This Planet. (1)*

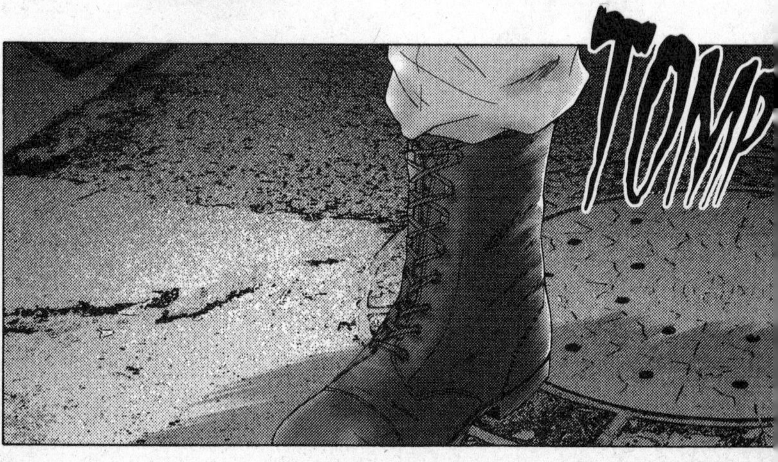
TOMP

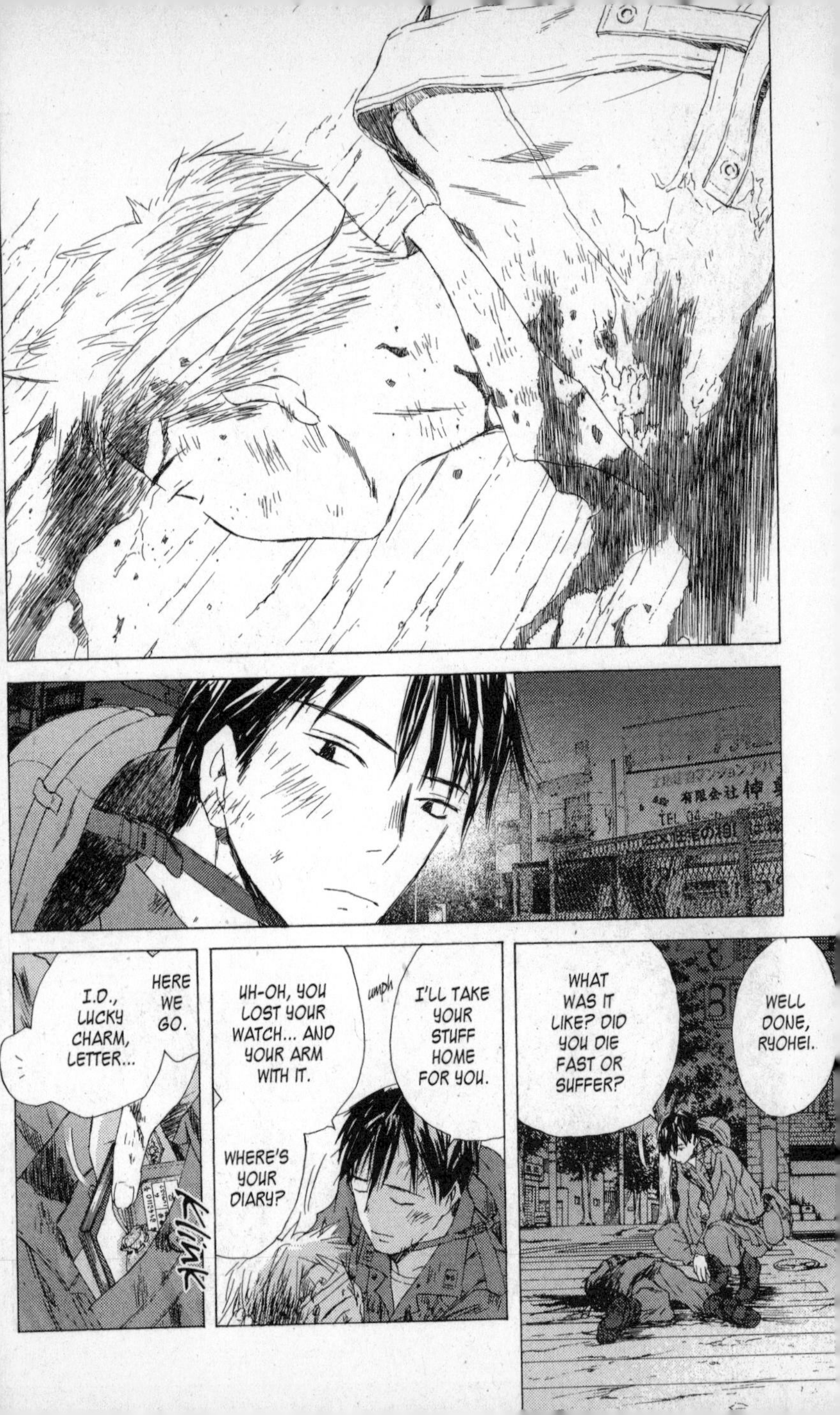
WELL DONE, RYOHEI.
WHAT WAS IT LIKE? DID YOU DIE FAST OR SUFFER?
I'LL TAKE YOUR STUFF HOME FOR YOU.
umph
UH-OH, YOU LOST YOUR WATCH... AND YOUR ARM WITH IT.
WHERE'S YOUR DIARY?
HERE WE GO.
I.D., LUCKY CHARM, LETTER...
Klink

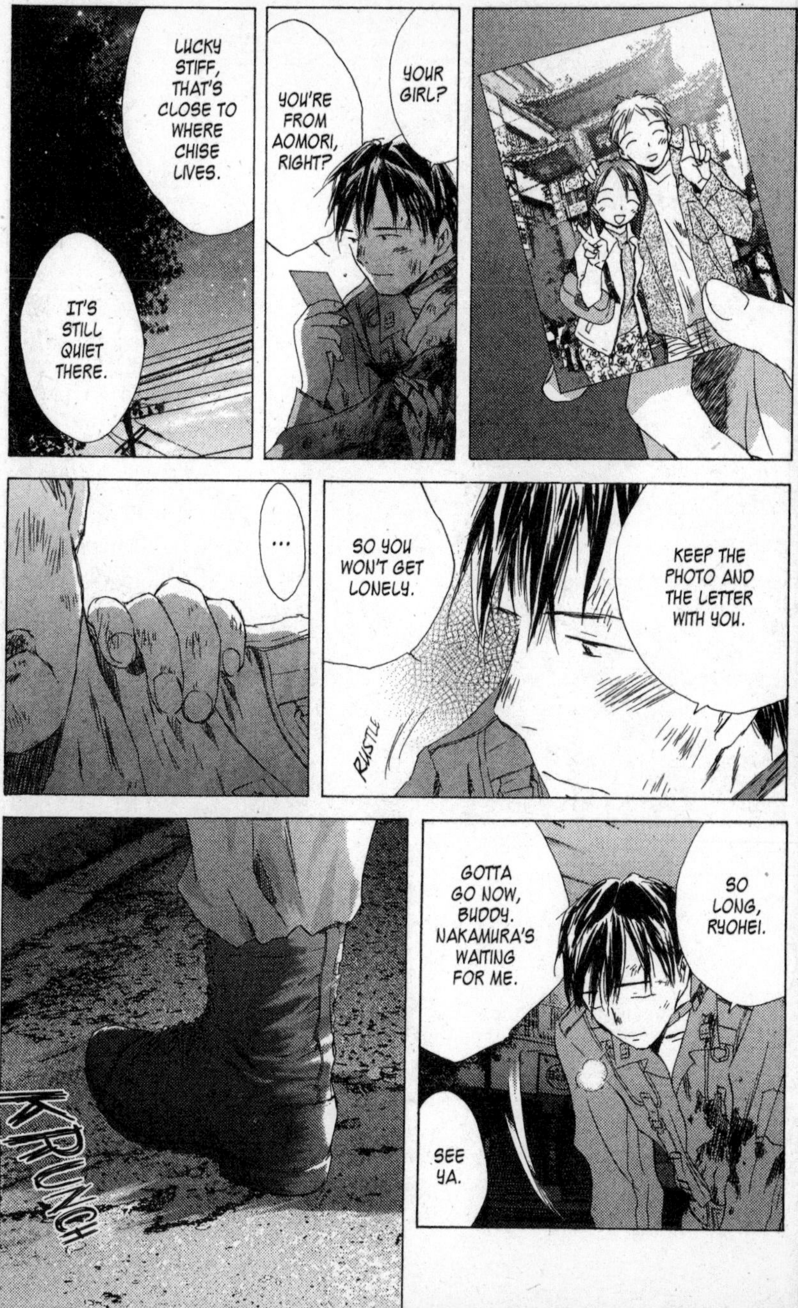
YOUR GIRL?
YOU'RE FROM AOMORI, RIGHT?
LUCKY STIFF, THAT'S CLOSE TO WHERE CHISE LIVES.
IT'S STILL QUIET THERE.
KEEP THE PHOTO AND THE LETTER WITH YOU.
SO YOU WON'T GET LONELY.
RUSTLE
...
SO LONG, RYOHEI.
GOTTA GO NOW, BUDDY. NAKAMURA'S WAITING FOR ME.
SEE YA.
KRUNCH

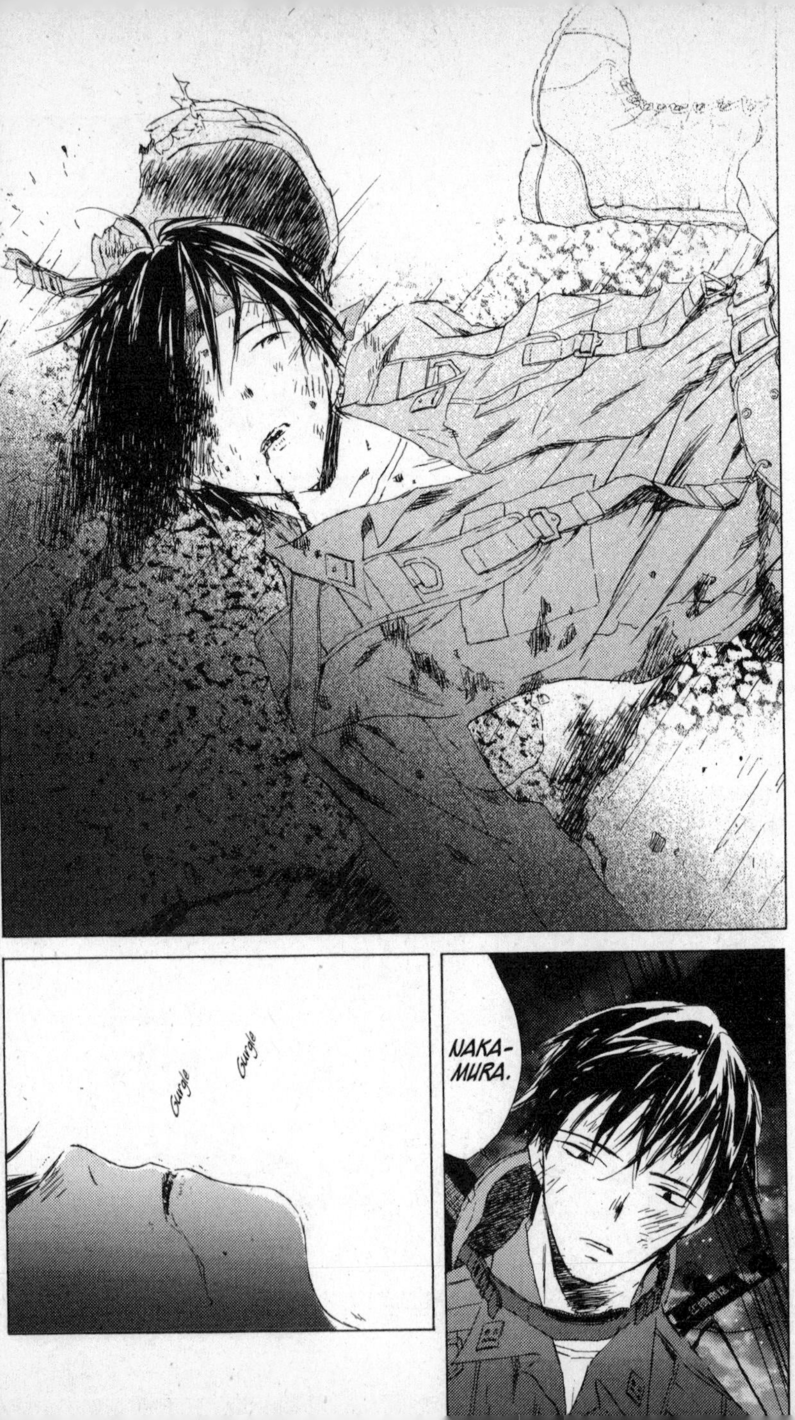
NAKA-
MURA.
Gurgle
Gurgle

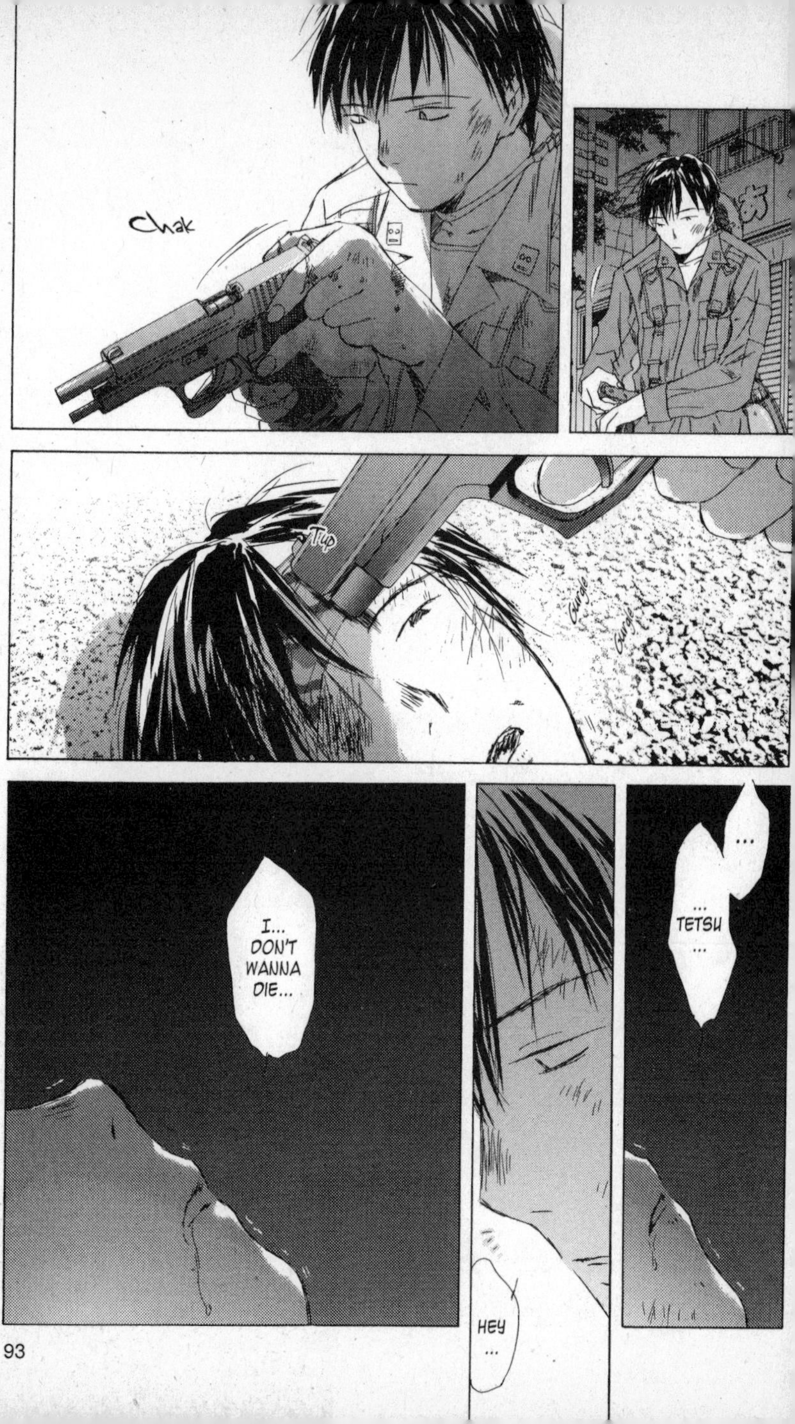
Chak
Tup
Gurgle
Gurgle
...
... TETSU ...
HEY ...
I... DON'T WANNA DIE...

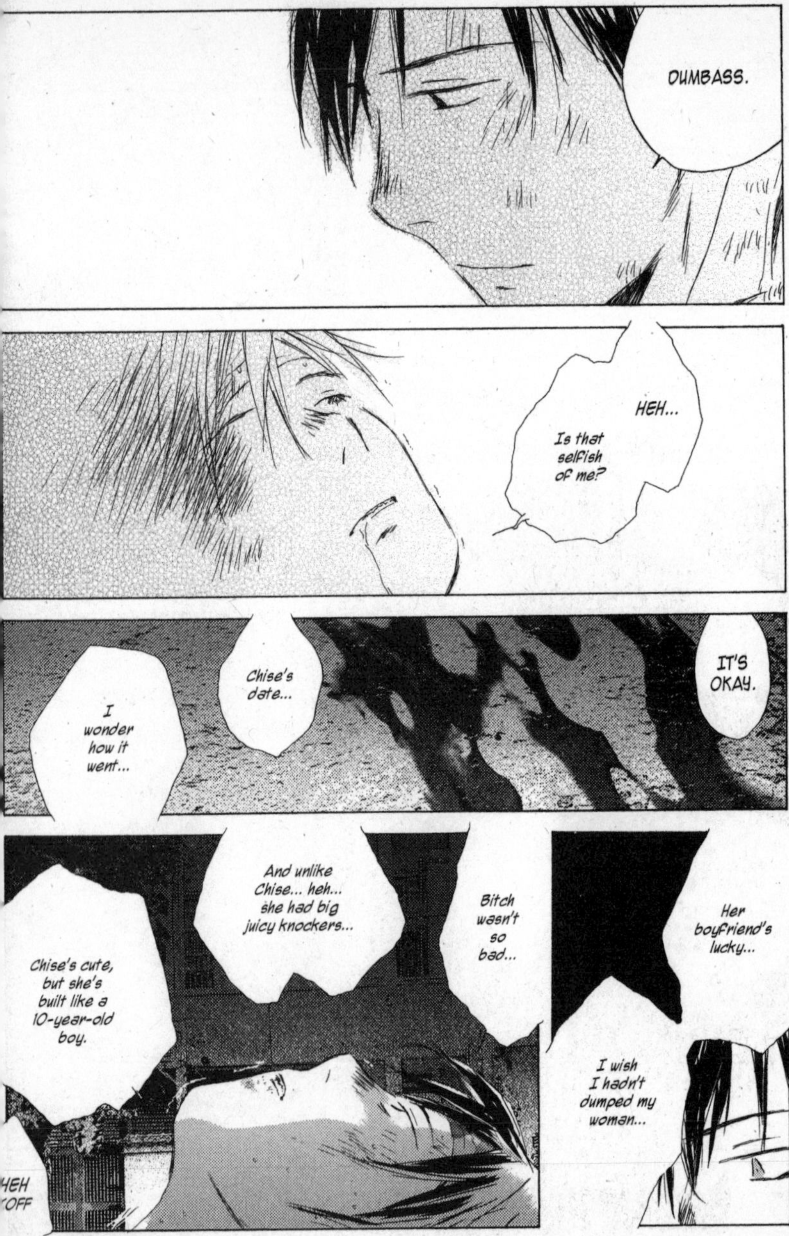
DUMBASS.
HEH...
Is that selfish of me?
IT'S OKAY.
Chise's date...
I wonder how it went...
Her boyfriend's lucky...
I wish I hadn't dumped my woman...
Bitch wasn't so bad...
And unlike Chise... heh... she had big juicy knockers...
Chise's cute, but she's built like a 10-year-old boy.
HEH

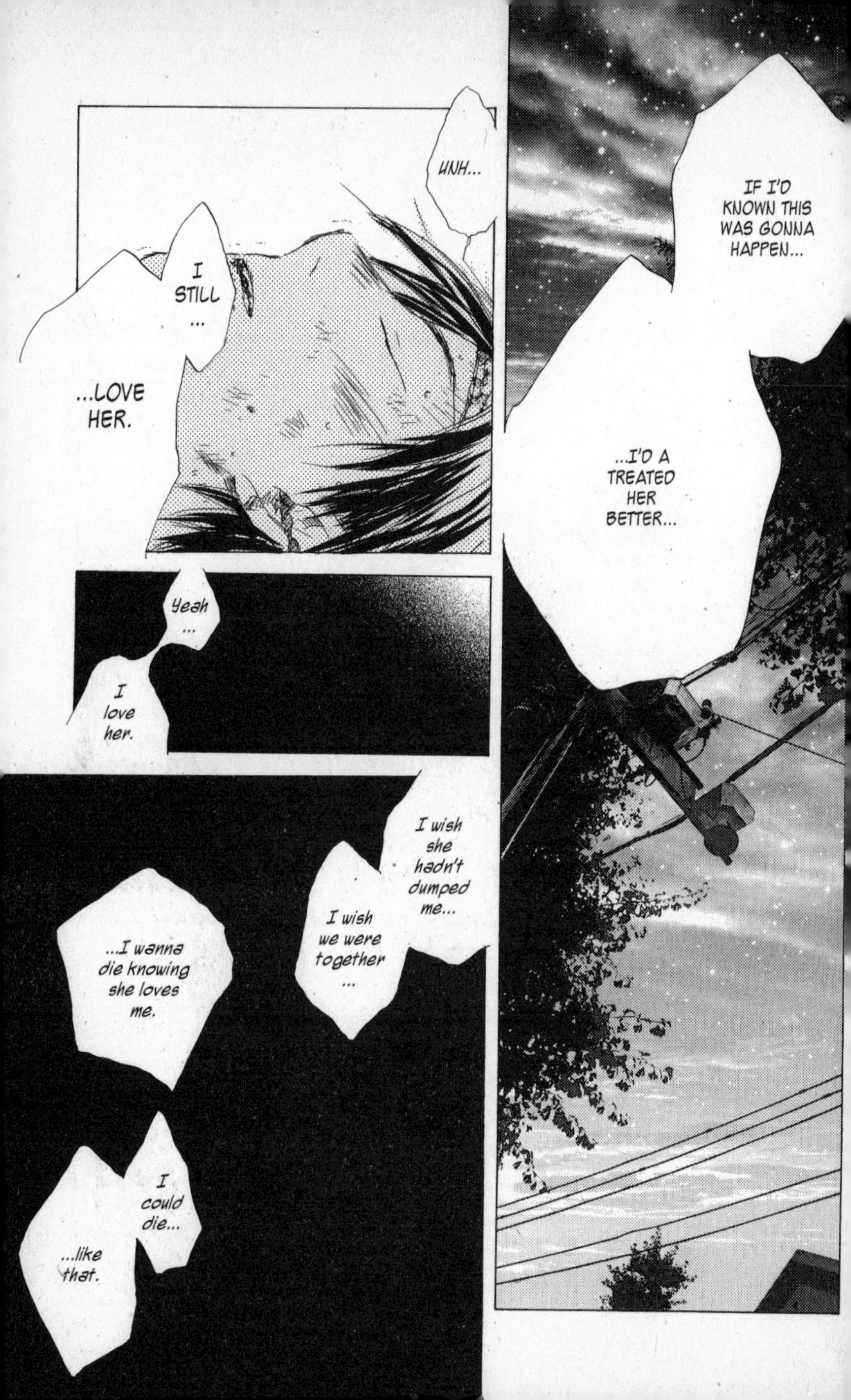
IF I'D KNOWN THIS WAS GONNA HAPPEN...
...I'D A TREATED HER BETTER...
UNH...
I STILL ...
...LOVE HER.
Yeah ...
I love her.
I wish she hadn't dumped me...
I wish we were together ...
...I wanna die knowing she loves me.
I could die...
...like that.

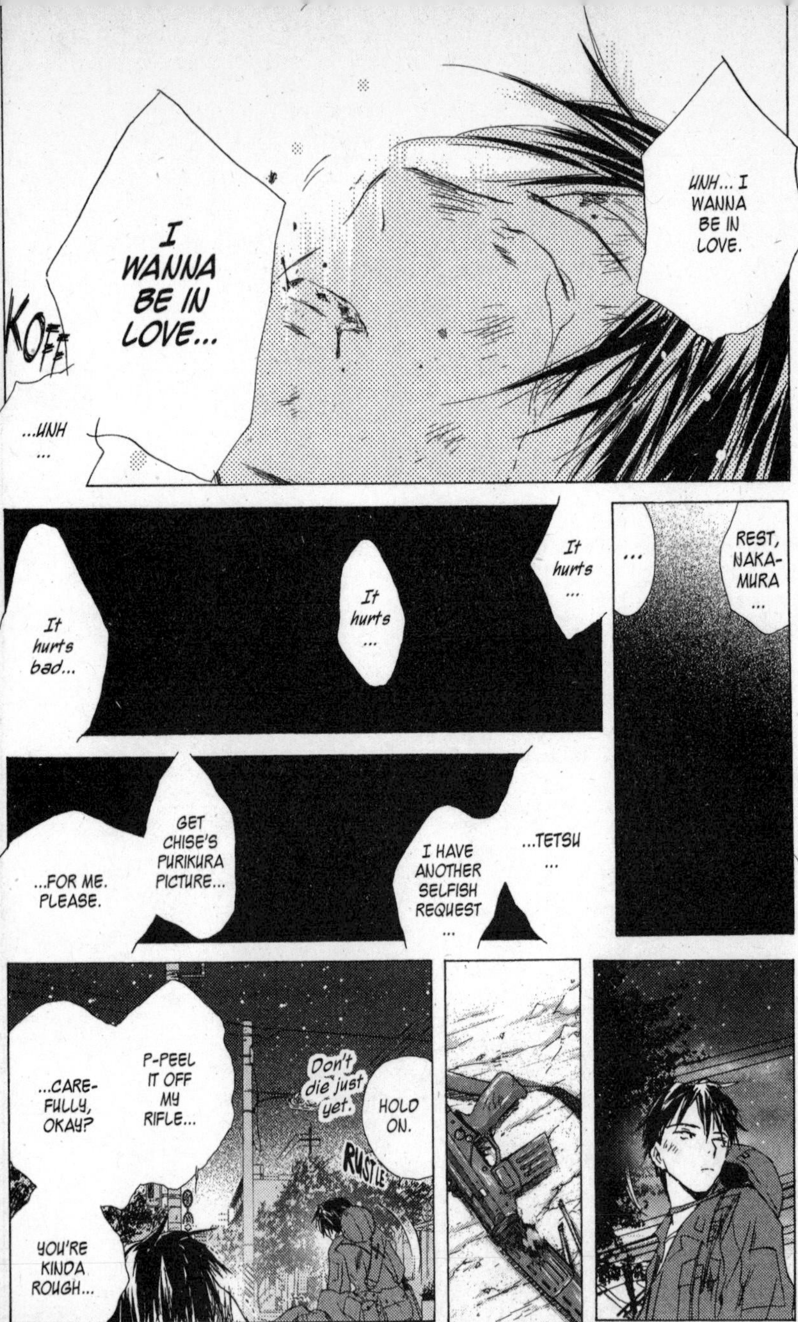
UNH... I WANNA BE IN LOVE.
I WANNA BE IN LOVE...
KOFF
...UNH ...
REST, NAKA-MURA ...
...
It hurts ...
It hurts ...
It hurts bad...
...TETSU ...
I HAVE ANOTHER SELFISH REQUEST ...
GET CHISE'S PURIKURA PICTURE...
...FOR ME. PLEASE.
HOLD ON.
Don't die just yet.
RUSTLE
P-PEEL IT OFF MY RIFLE...
...CARE-FULLY, OKAY?
YOU'RE KINDA ROUGH...

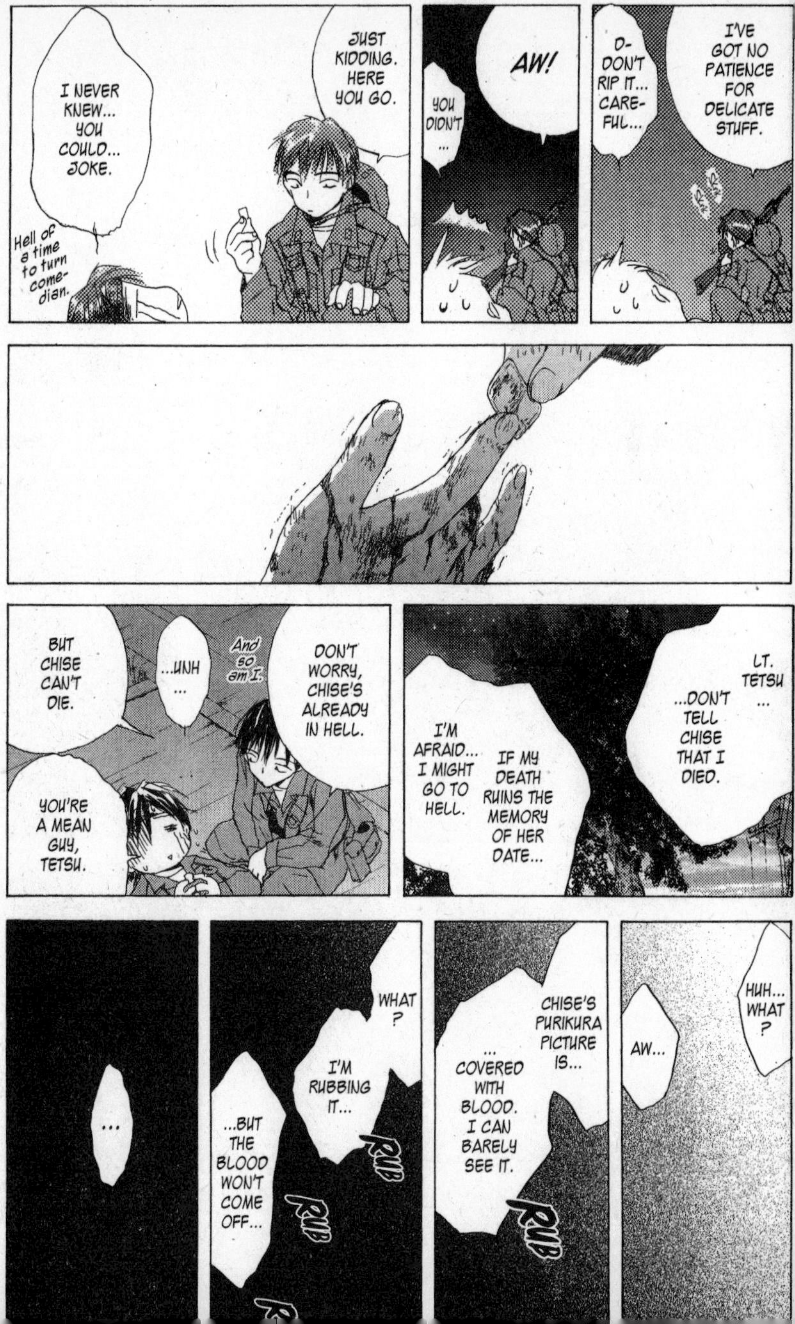
I'VE GOT NO PATIENCE FOR DELICATE STUFF.
Slak Slak
D-DON'T RIP IT... CAREFUL...
AW!
YOU DIDN'T...
JUST KIDDING. HERE YOU GO.
I NEVER KNEW... YOU COULD... JOKE.
Hell of a time to turn comedian.
LT. TETSU...
...DON'T TELL CHISE THAT I DIED.
IF MY DEATH RUINS THE MEMORY OF HER DATE...
I'M AFRAID... I MIGHT GO TO HELL.
DON'T WORRY, CHISE'S ALREADY IN HELL.
And so am I.
...UNH...
BUT CHISE CAN'T DIE.
YOU'RE A MEAN GUY, TETSU.
HUH... WHAT?
AW...
CHISE'S PURIKURA PICTURE IS...
...COVERED WITH BLOOD. I CAN BARELY SEE IT.
RUB
WHAT?
I'M RUBBING IT...
...BUT THE BLOOD WON'T COME OFF...
RUB
RUB
...

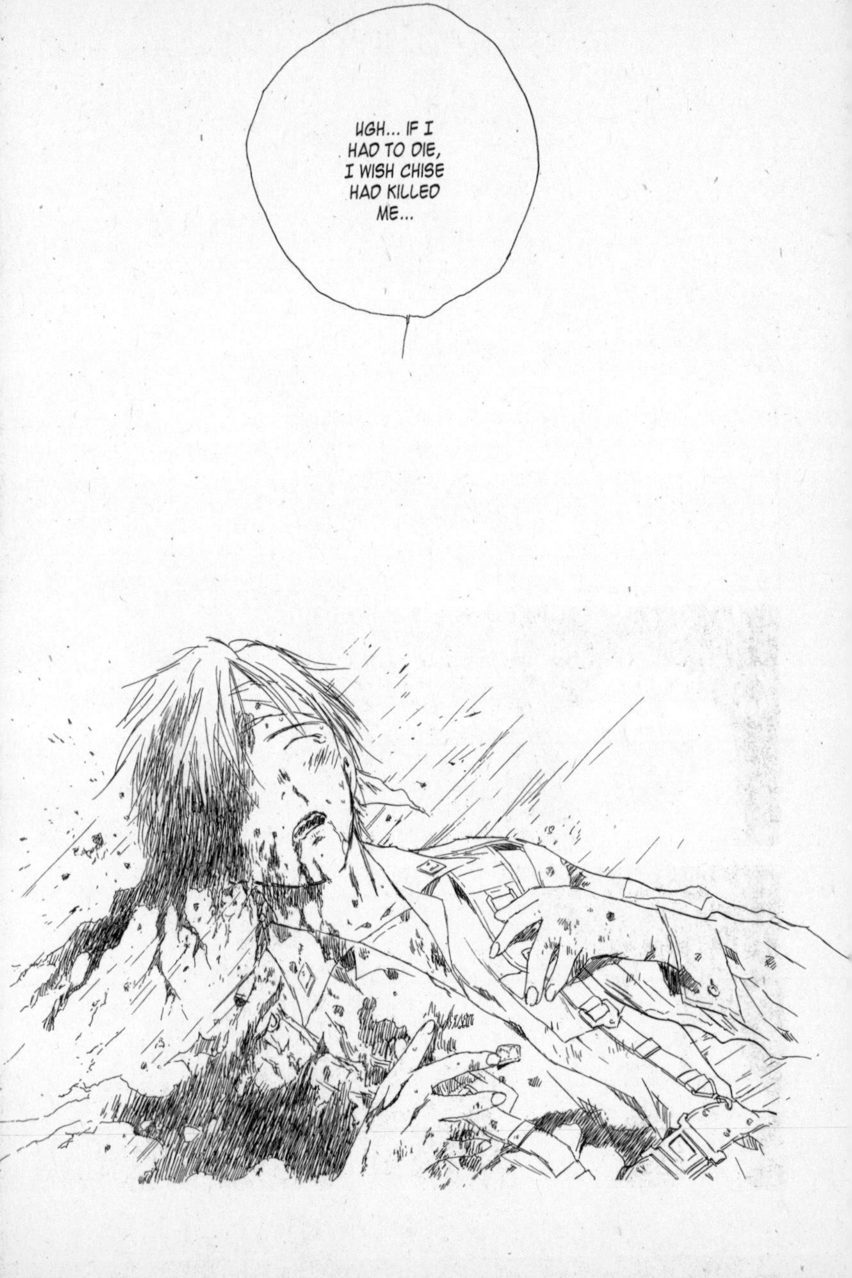
UGH... IF I HAD TO DIE, I WISH CHISE HAD KILLED ME...

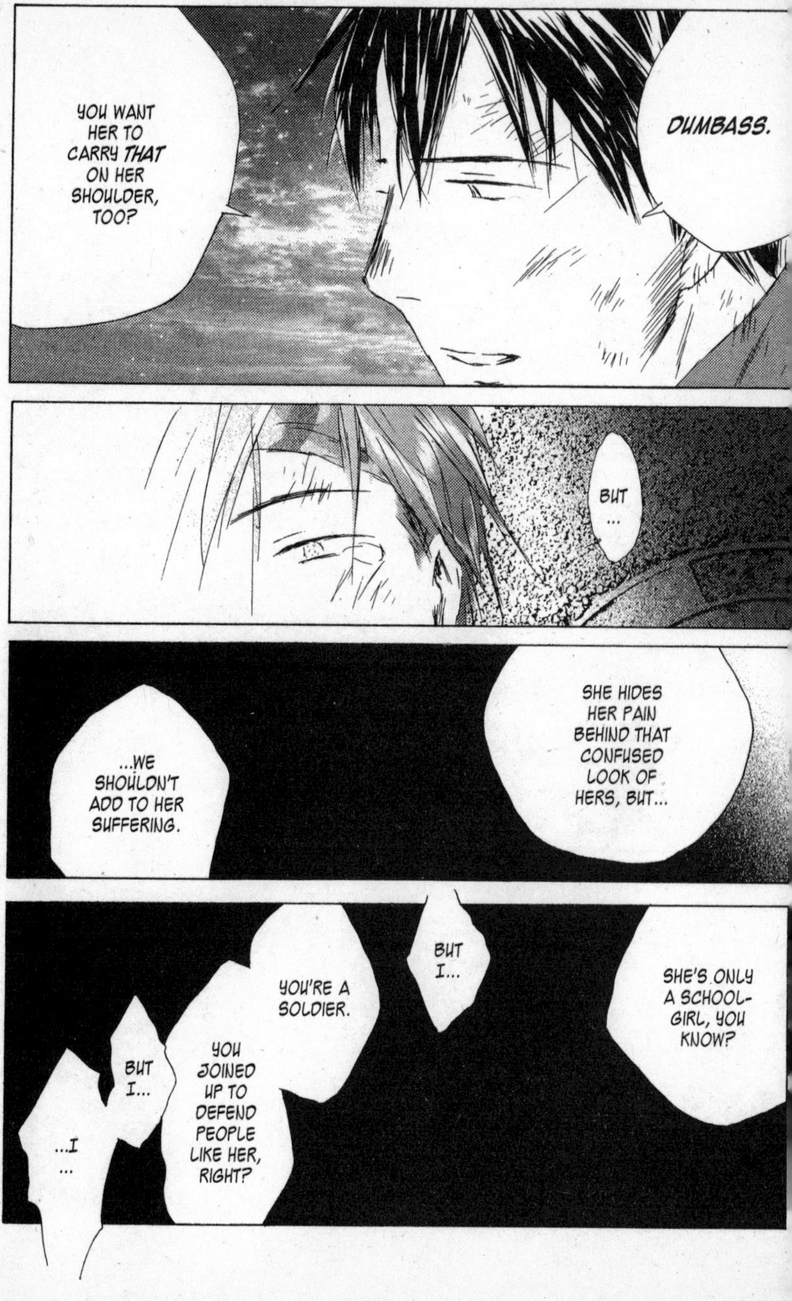
DUMBASS.
YOU WANT HER TO CARRY THAT ON HER SHOULDER, TOO?
BUT ...
SHE HIDES HER PAIN BEHIND THAT CONFUSED LOOK OF HERS, BUT...
...WE SHOULDN'T ADD TO HER SUFFERING.
SHE'S ONLY A SCHOOL-GIRL, YOU KNOW?
BUT I...
YOU'RE A SOLDIER.
YOU JOINED UP TO DEFEND PEOPLE LIKE HER, RIGHT?
BUT I...
...I ...

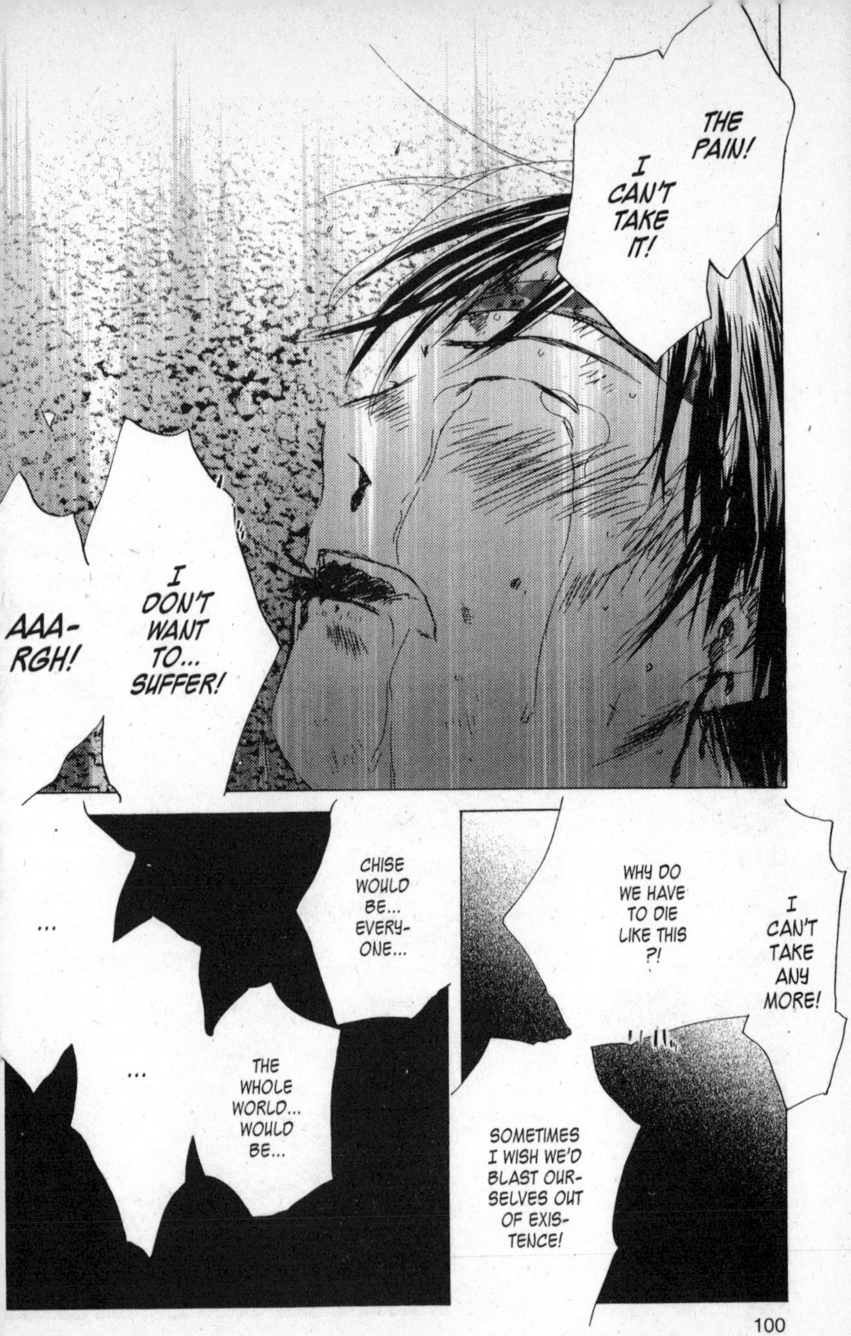

THE PAIN!
I CAN'T TAKE IT!
I DON'T WANT TO... SUFFER!
AAA-RGH!
I CAN'T TAKE ANY MORE!
WHY DO WE HAVE TO DIE LIKE THIS ?!
SOMETIMES I WISH WE'D BLAST OURSELVES OUT OF EXISTENCE!
CHISE WOULD BE... EVERYONE...
...
THE WHOLE WORLD... WOULD BE...
...

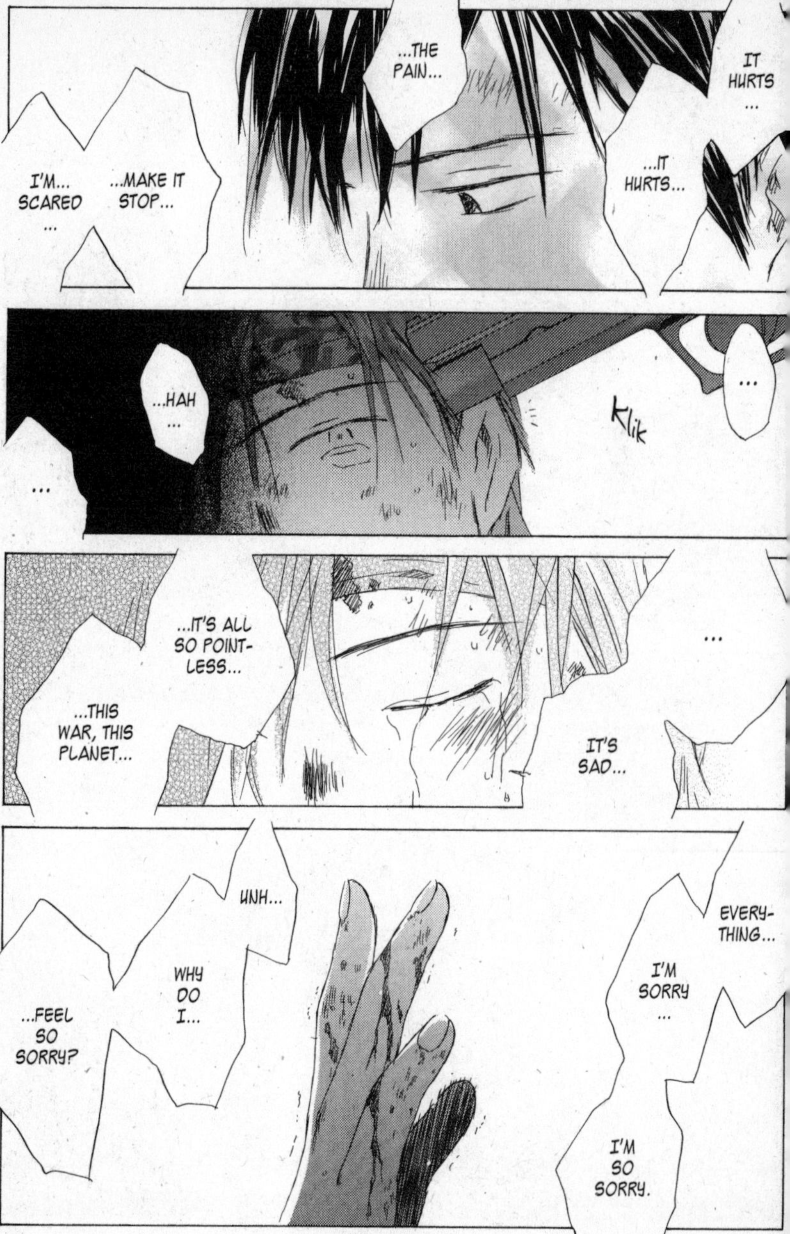
IT HURTS ...
...IT HURTS...
...THE PAIN...
...MAKE IT STOP...
I'M... SCARED ...
...
Klik
...HAH ...
...
...
IT'S SAD...
...IT'S ALL SO POINT-LESS...
...THIS WAR, THIS PLANET...
EVERY-THING...
I'M SORRY ...
I'M SO SORRY.
UNH...
WHY DO I...
...FEEL SO SORRY?

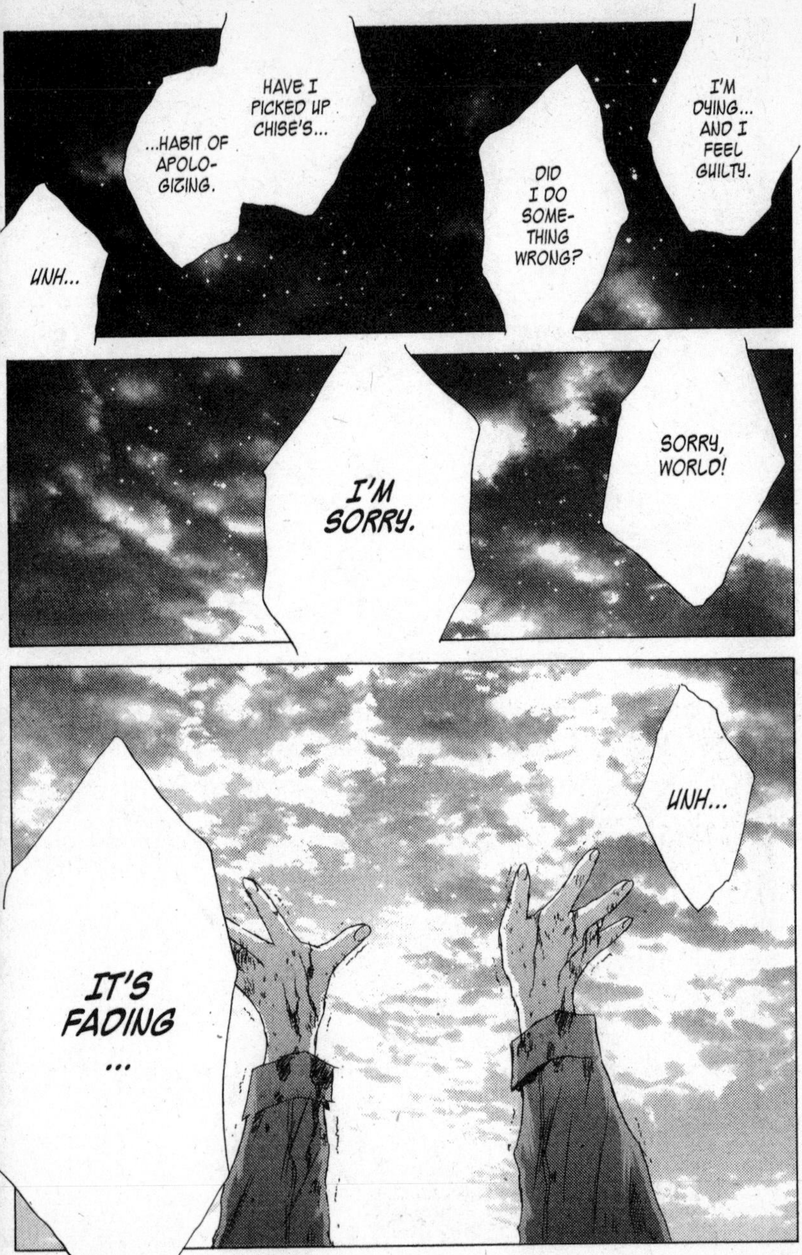
I'M DYING... AND I FEEL GUILTY.
DID I DO SOME-THING WRONG?
HAVE I PICKED UP CHISE'S...
...HABIT OF APOLO-GIZING.
UNH...
SORRY, WORLD!
I'M SORRY.
UNH...
IT'S FADING ...

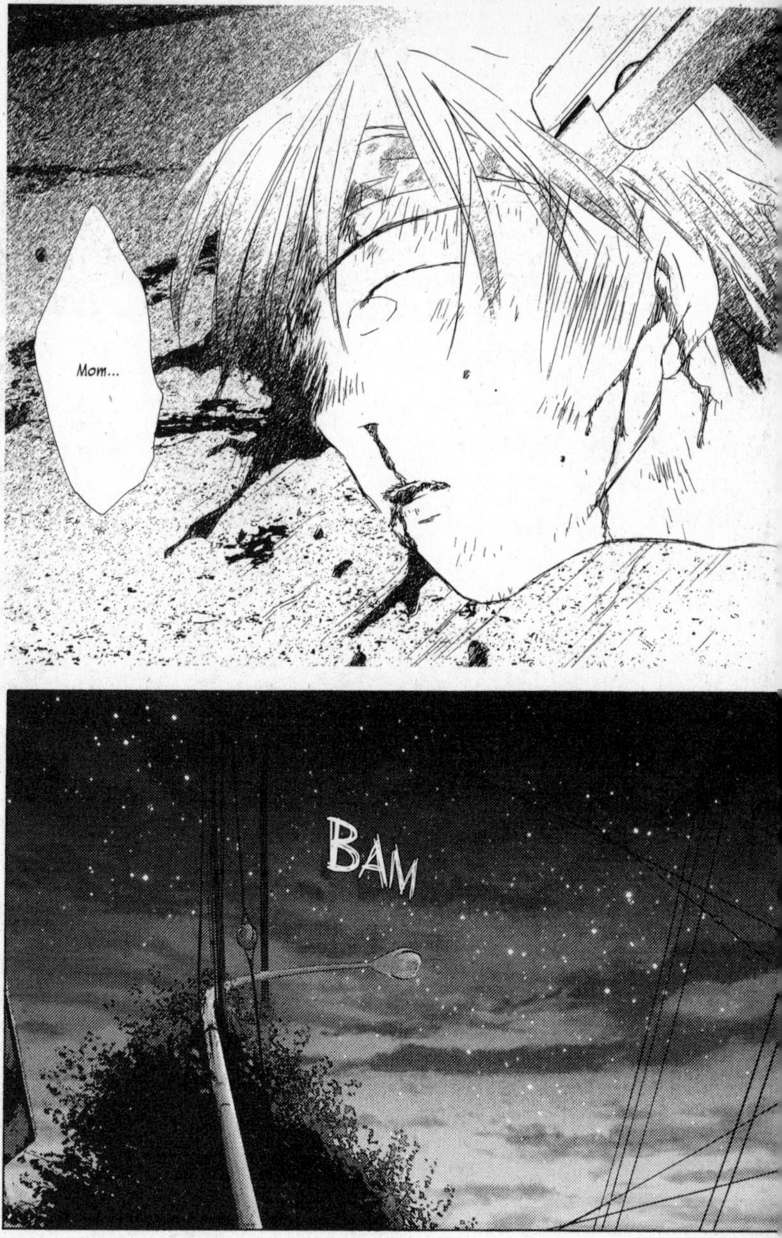
Mom...
BAM

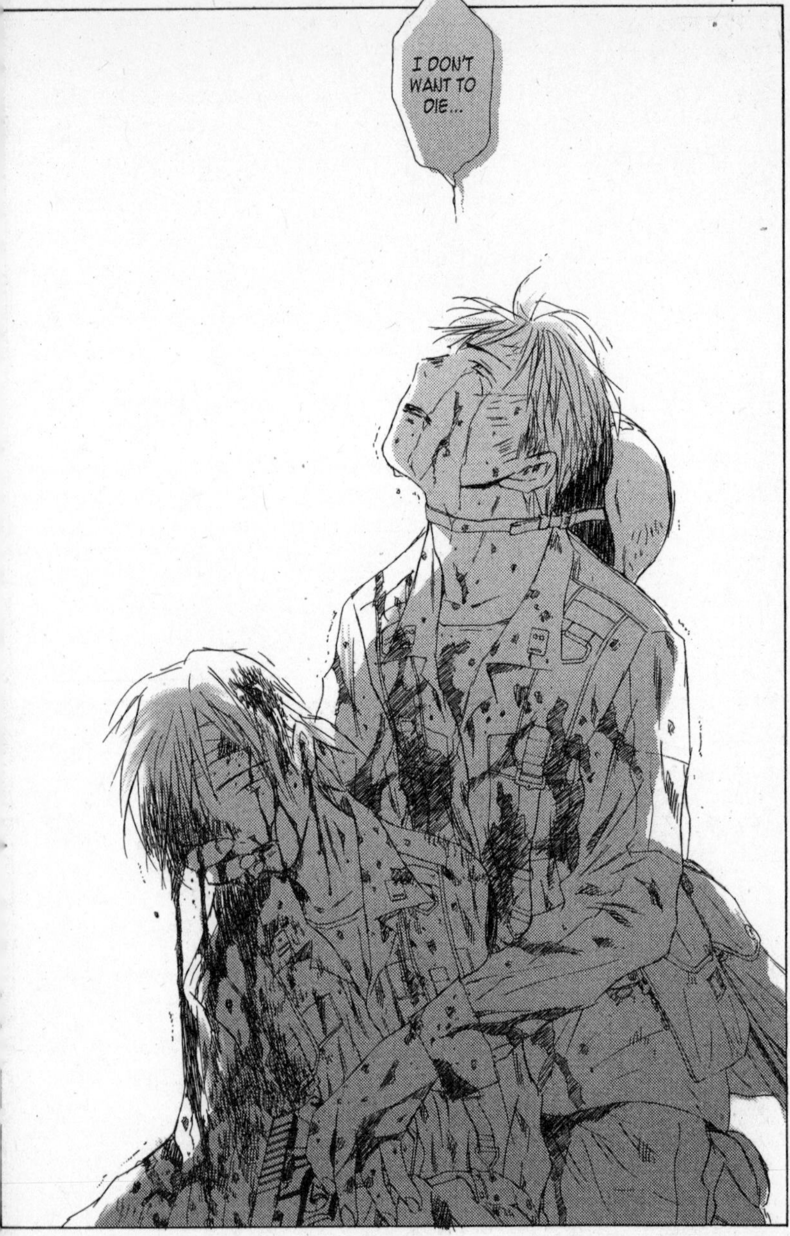
I DON'T WANT TO DIE...

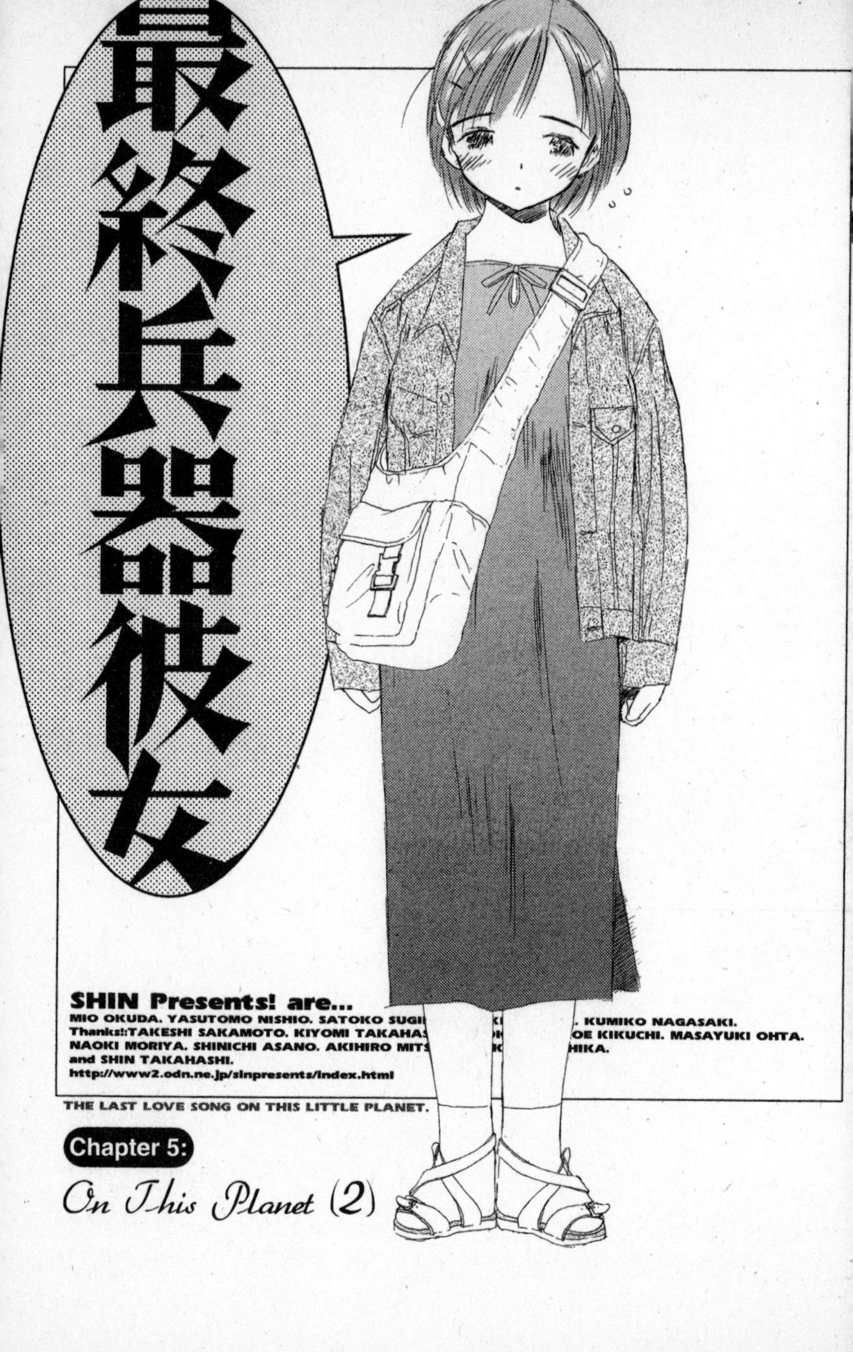
最終兵器彼女
SHIN Presents! are...
MIO OKUDA. YASUTOMO NISHIO. SATOKO SUGI . KUMIKO NAGASAKI.
Thanks!:TAKESHI SAKAMOTO. KIYOMI TAKAHAS OE KIKUCHI. MASAYUKI OHTA.
NAOKI MORIYA. SHINICHI ASANO. AKIHIRO MITS HIKA.
and SHIN TAKAHASHI.
http://www2.odn.ne.jp/sinpresents/index.html
THE LAST LOVE SONG ON THIS LITTLE PLANET.
Chapter 5:
On This Planet (2)

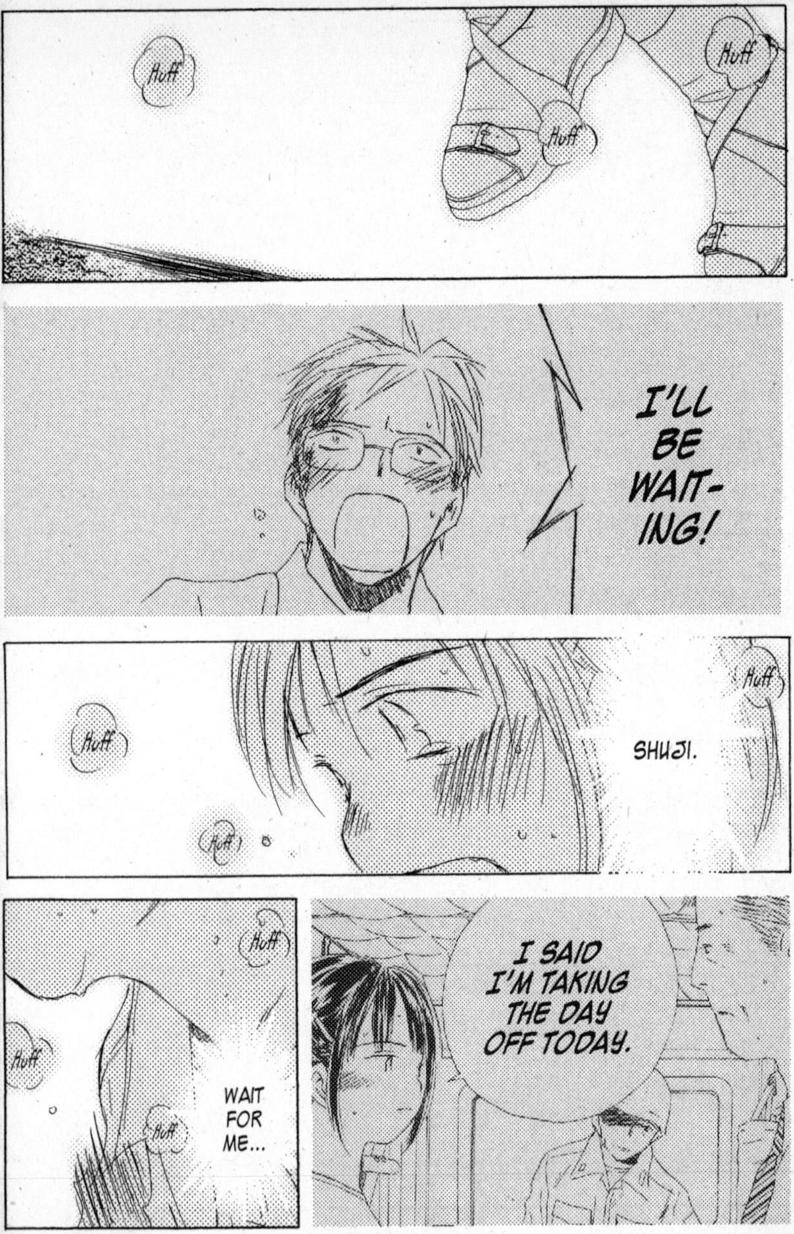
Huff
Huff
Huff
I'LL BE WAIT-ING!
Huff
SHUJI.
Huff
Huff
I SAID I'M TAKING THE DAY OFF TODAY.
Huff
Huff
WAIT FOR ME...
Huff

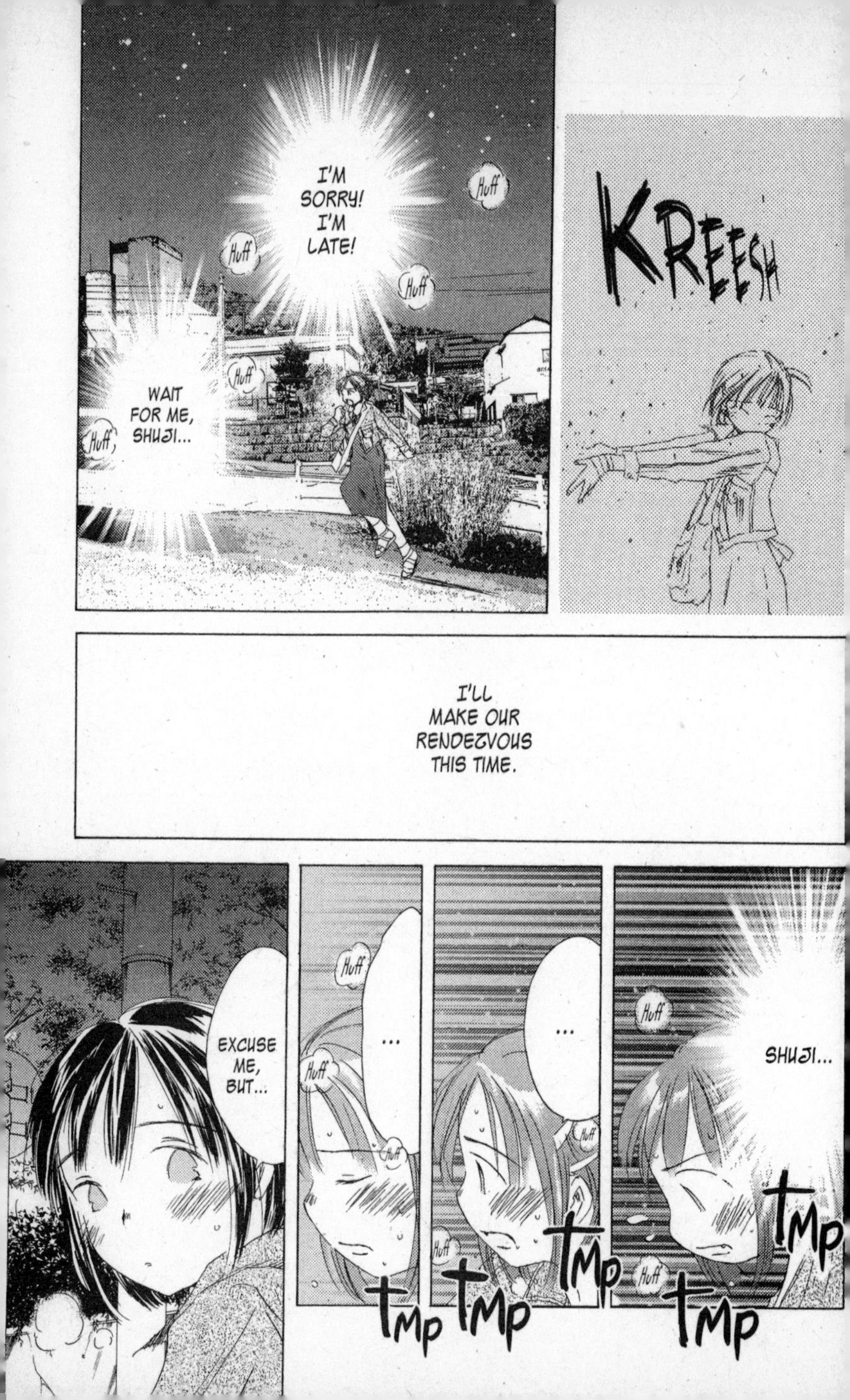
KREESH
Huff
I'M SORRY! I'M LATE!
Huff
Huff
Huff
WAIT FOR ME, SHUJI...
Huff
I'LL MAKE OUR RENDEZVOUS THIS TIME.
Huff
SHUJI...
Huff
tMp
tMp
Huff
...
Huff
Huff
tMp
tMp
Huff
...
Huff
Huff
tMp
EXCUSE ME, BUT...

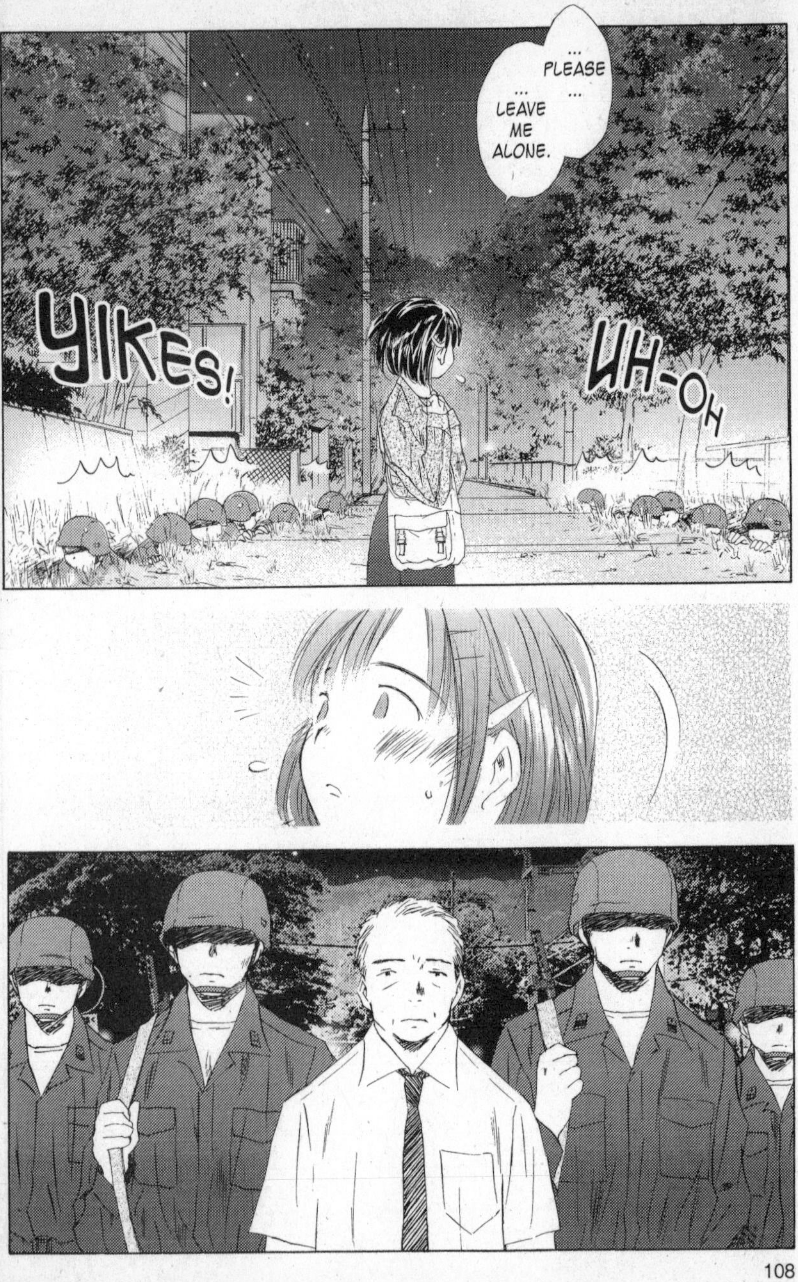
... PLEASE ... ... LEAVE ME ALONE.
UH-OH
YIKES!

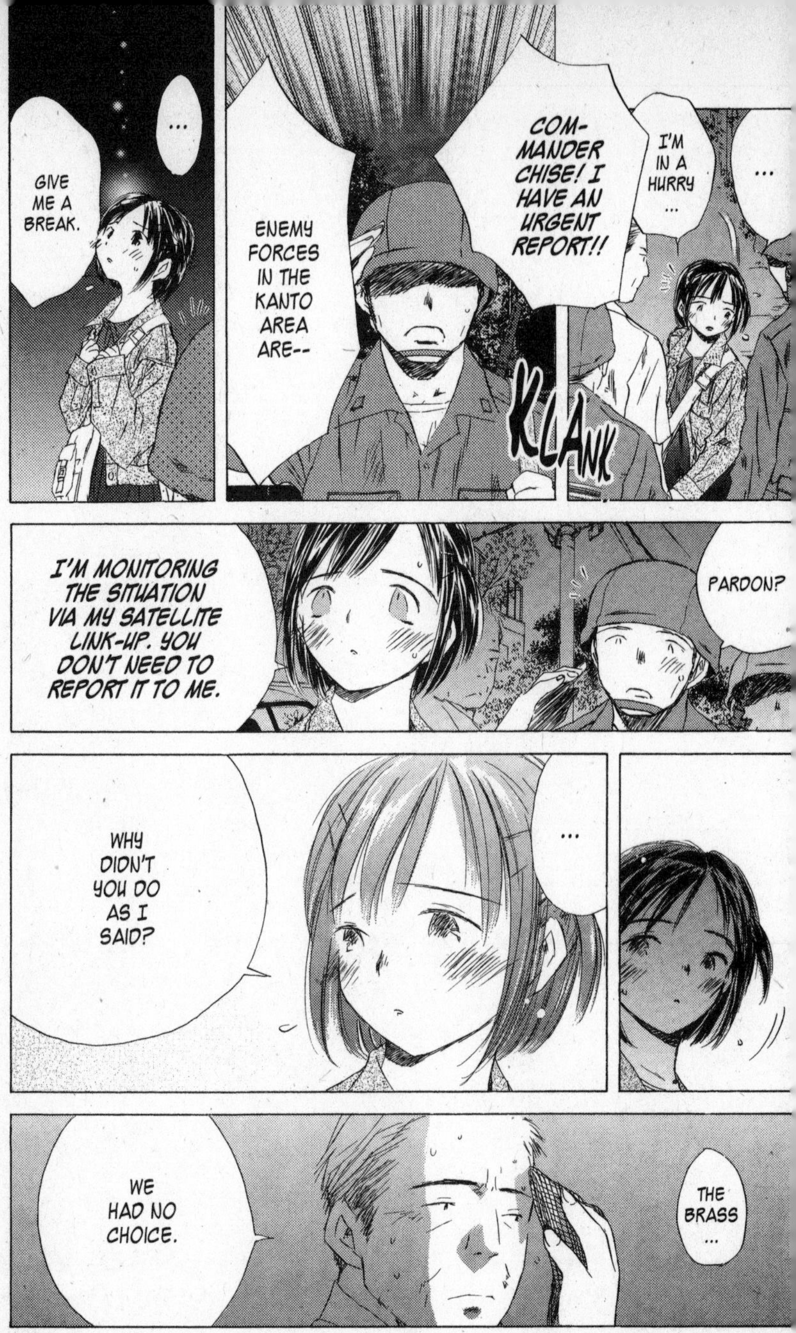
...
I'M IN A HURRY ...
COMMANDER CHISE! I HAVE AN URGENT REPORT!!
KLANK
ENEMY FORCES IN THE KANTO AREA ARE--
...
GIVE ME A BREAK.
PARDON?
I'M MONITORING THE SITUATION VIA MY SATELLITE LINK-UP. YOU DON'T NEED TO REPORT IT TO ME.
...
WHY DIDN'T YOU DO AS I SAID?
THE BRASS ...
WE HAD NO CHOICE.

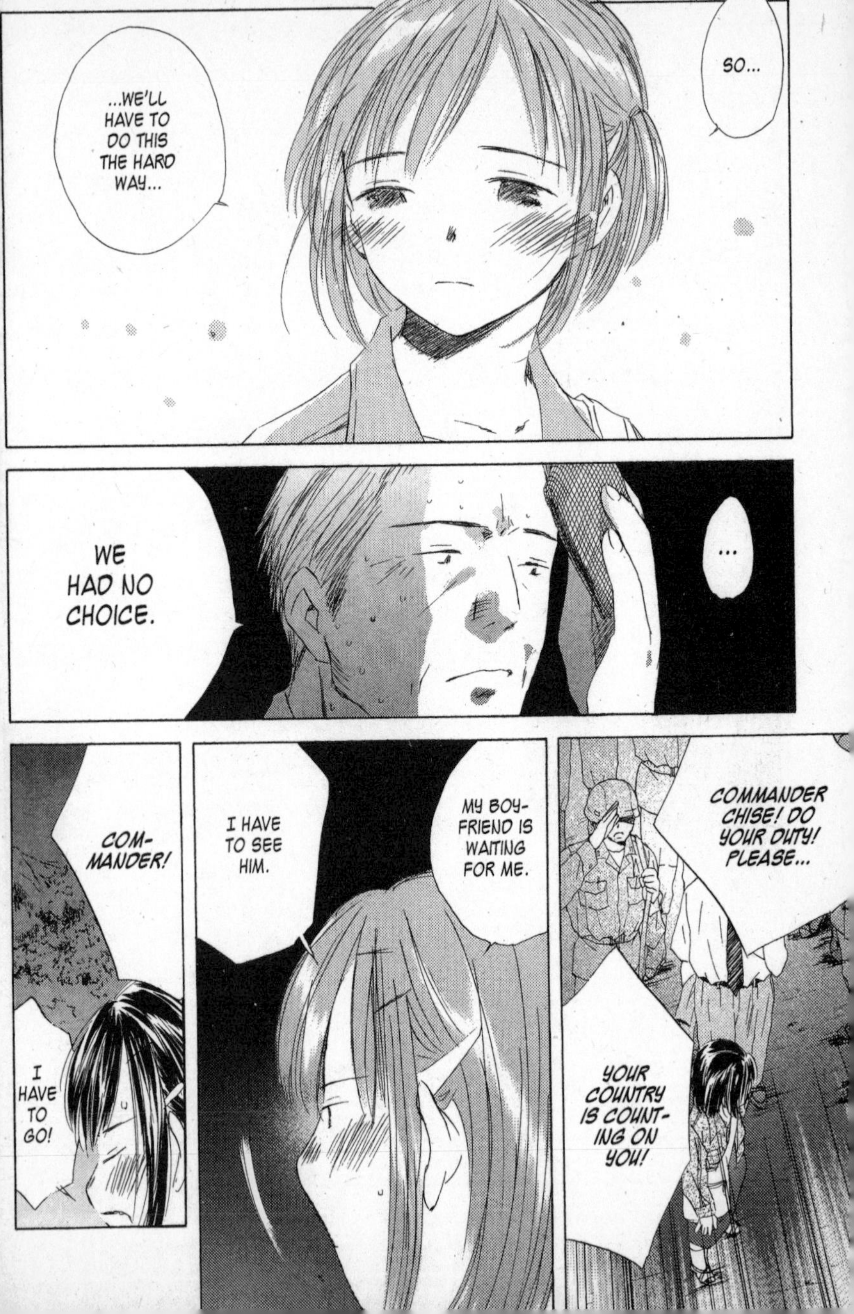
SO...
...WE'LL HAVE TO DO THIS THE HARD WAY...
...
WE HAD NO CHOICE.
COMMANDER CHISE! DO YOUR DUTY! PLEASE...
YOUR COUNTRY IS COUNTING ON YOU!
MY BOY-FRIEND IS WAITING FOR ME.
I HAVE TO SEE HIM.
COM-MANDER!
I HAVE TO GO!

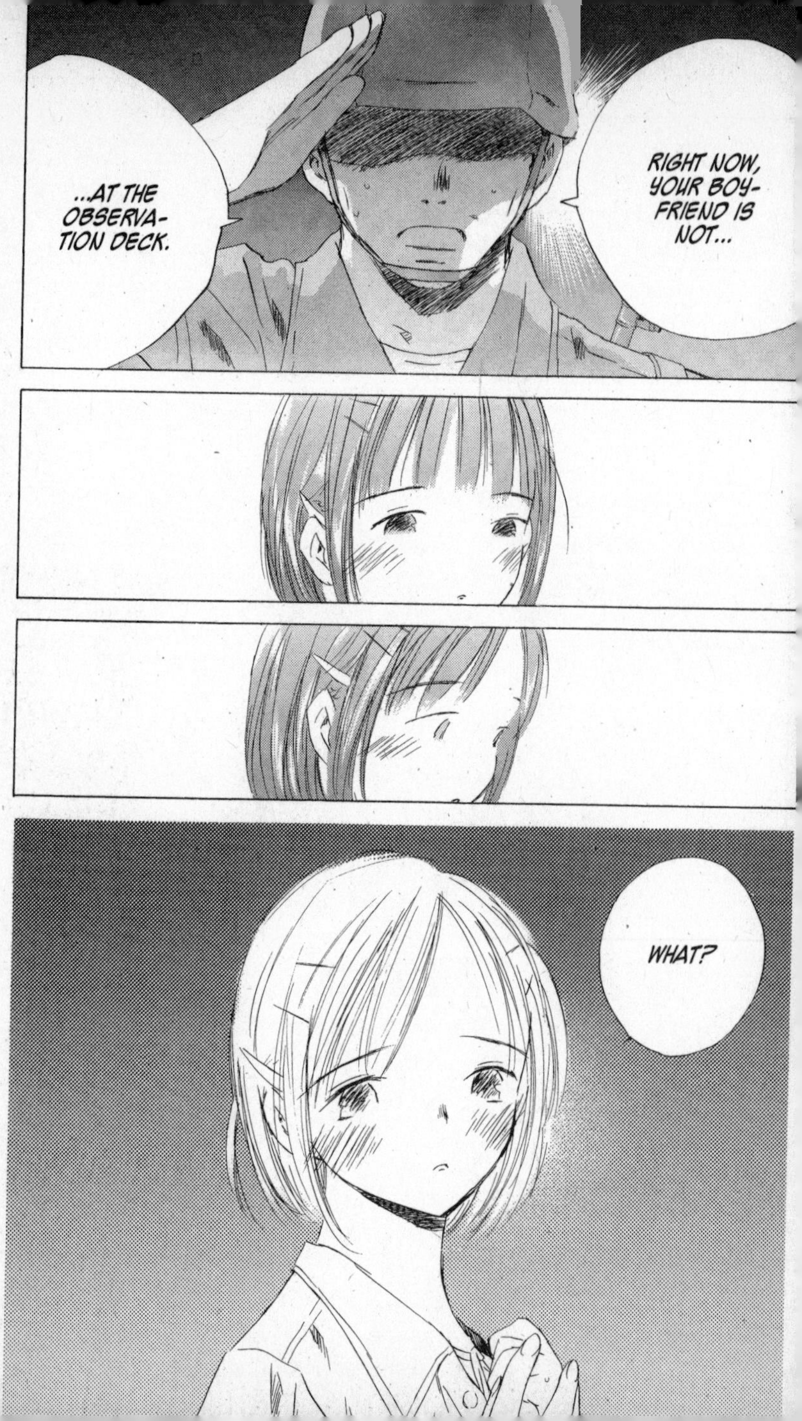
RIGHT NOW, YOUR BOY-FRIEND IS NOT...
...AT THE OBSERVATION DECK.
WHAT?

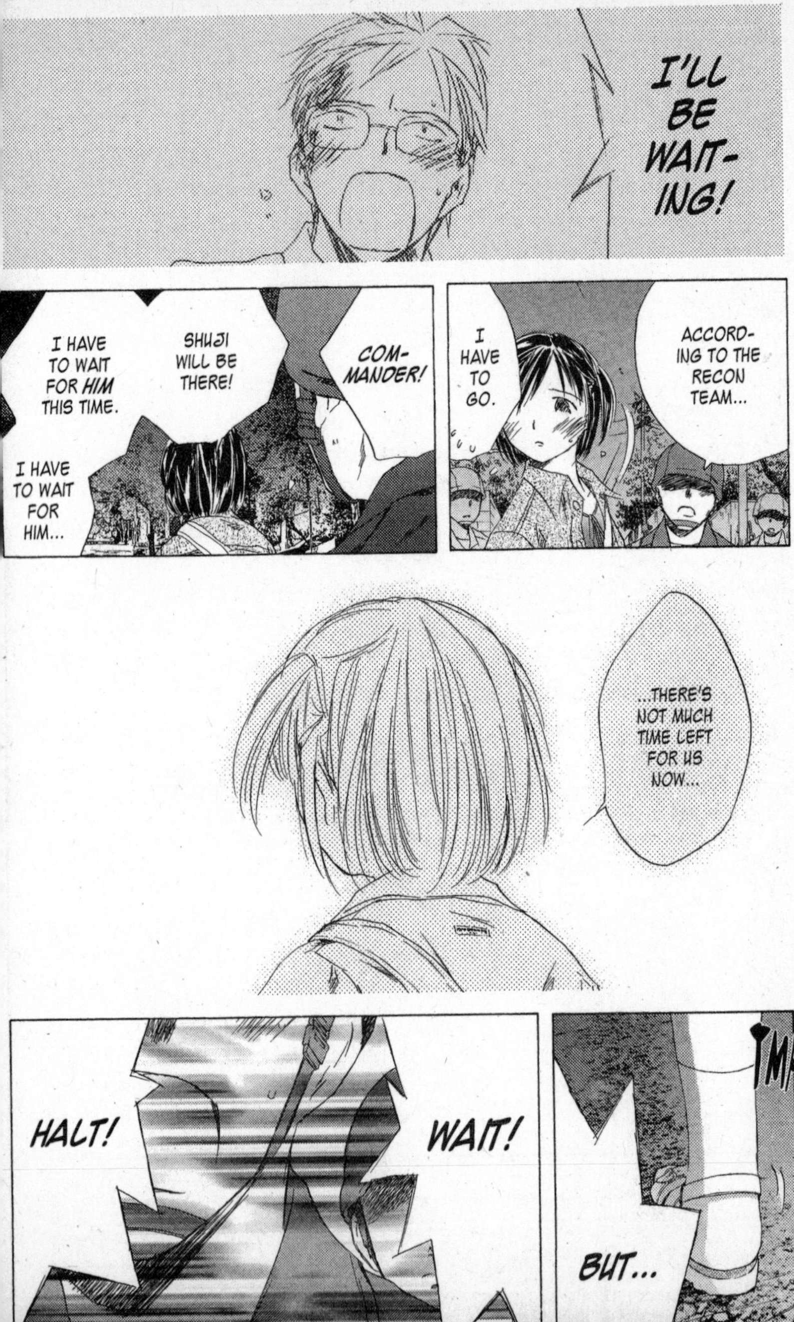
I'LL BE WAIT-ING!
ACCORD-ING TO THE RECON TEAM...
I HAVE TO GO.
COM-MANDER!
SHUJI WILL BE THERE!
I HAVE TO WAIT FOR HIM THIS TIME.
I HAVE TO WAIT FOR HIM...
...THERE'S NOT MUCH TIME LEFT FOR US NOW...
TMP
BUT...
WAIT!
HALT!

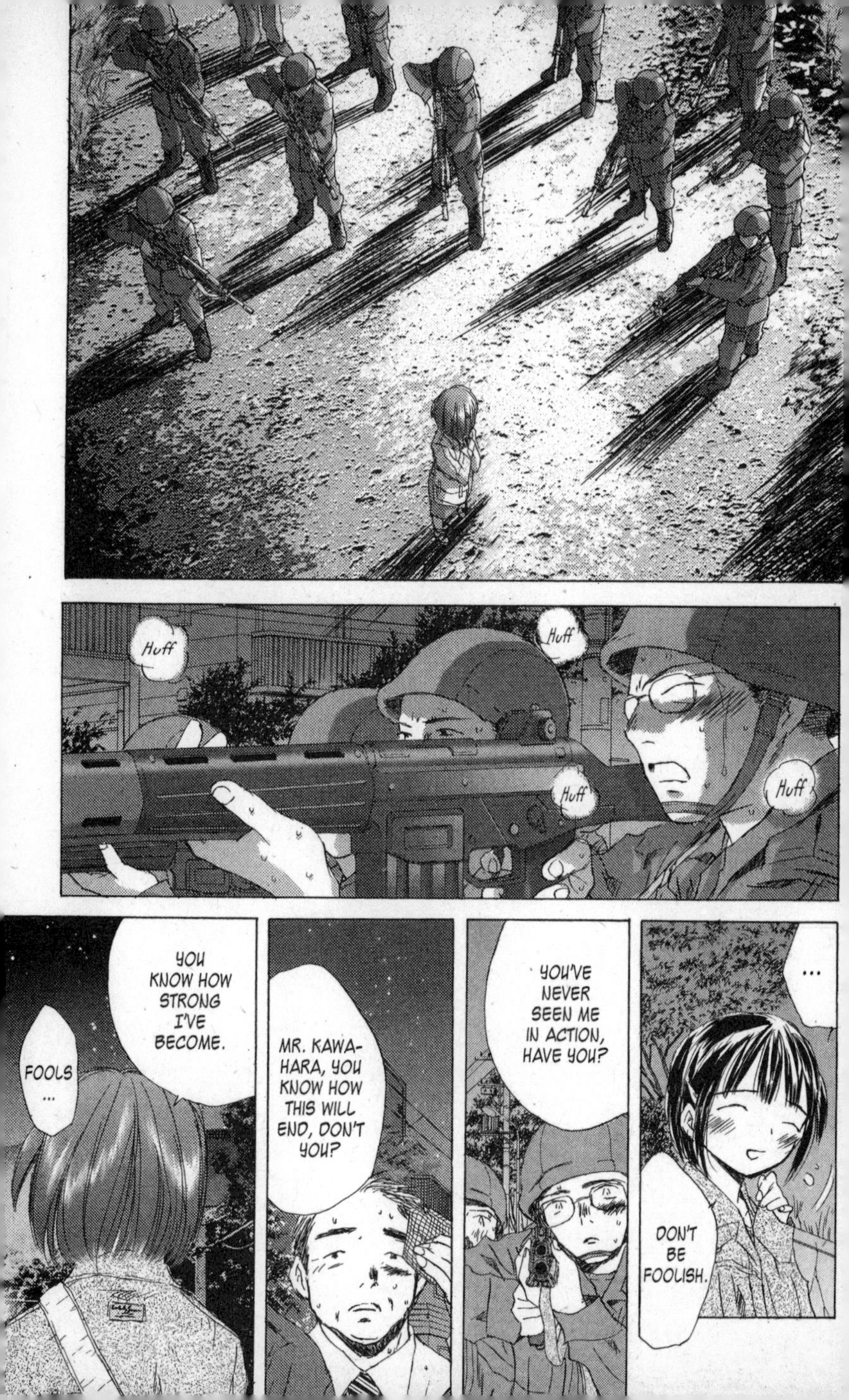
Huff
Huff
Huff
Huff
...
DON'T BE FOOLISH.
YOU'VE NEVER SEEN ME IN ACTION, HAVE YOU?
MR. KAWAHARA, YOU KNOW HOW THIS WILL END, DON'T YOU?
YOU KNOW HOW STRONG I'VE BECOME.
FOOLS ...

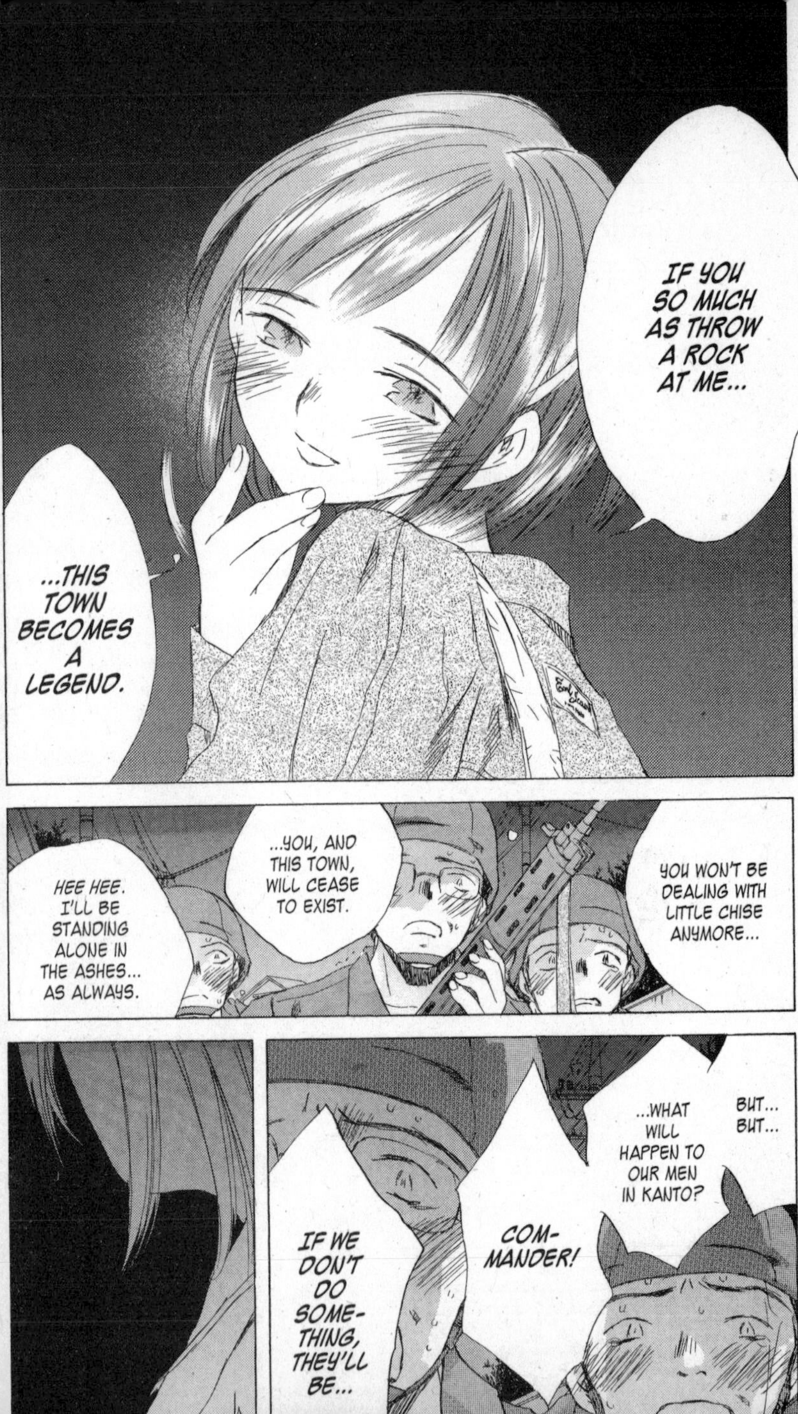
IF YOU SO MUCH AS THROW A ROCK AT ME...
...THIS TOWN BECOMES A LEGEND.
YOU WON'T BE DEALING WITH LITTLE CHISE ANYMORE...
...YOU, AND THIS TOWN, WILL CEASE TO EXIST.
HEE HEE. I'LL BE STANDING ALONE IN THE ASHES... AS ALWAYS.
BUT... BUT...
...WHAT WILL HAPPEN TO OUR MEN IN KANTO?
COM-MANDER!
IF WE DON'T DO SOME-THING, THEY'LL BE...

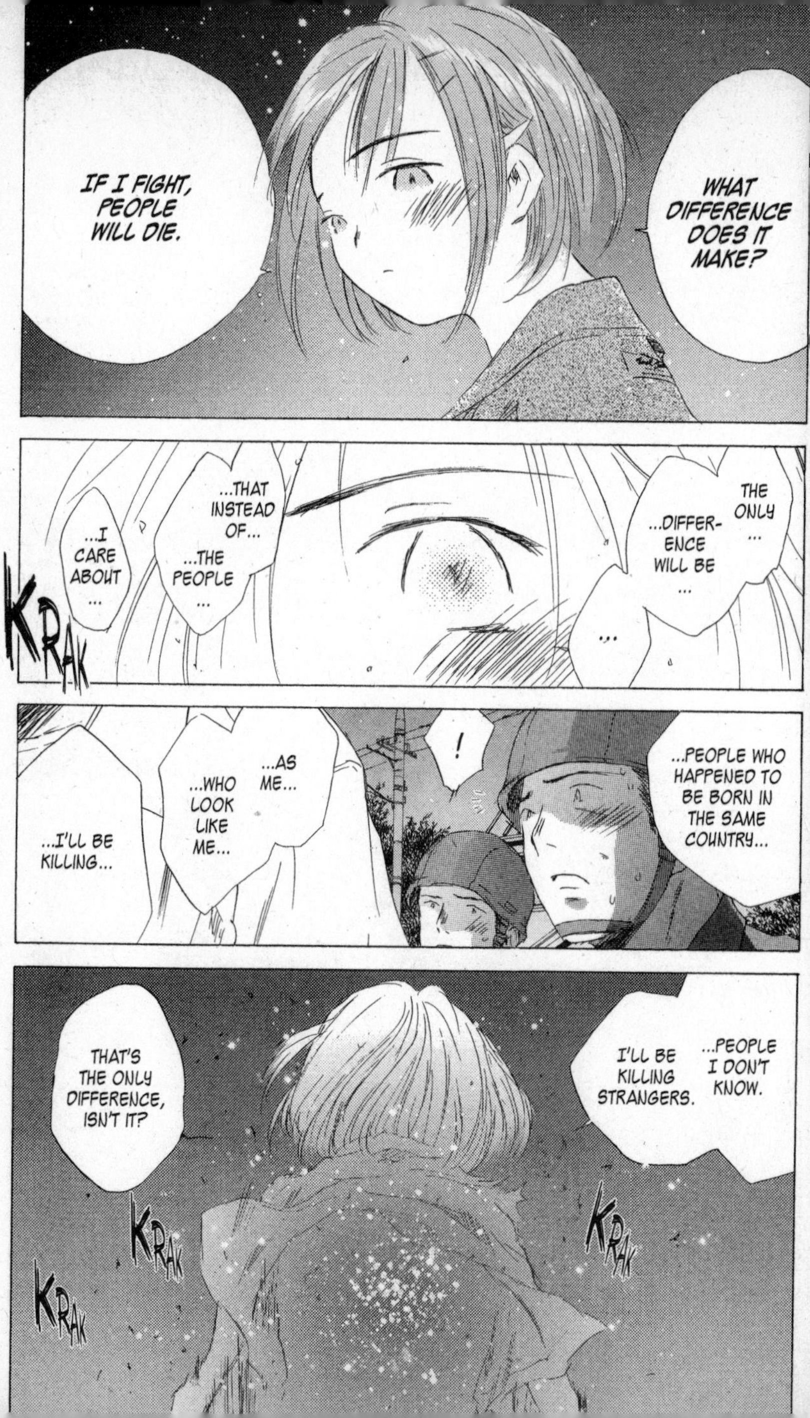
WHAT DIFFERENCE DOES IT MAKE?
IF I FIGHT, PEOPLE WILL DIE.
THE ONLY...
...DIFFERENCE WILL BE...
...
...THAT INSTEAD OF...
...THE PEOPLE...
...I CARE ABOUT...
KRAK
...PEOPLE WHO HAPPENED TO BE BORN IN THE SAME COUNTRY...
!
...AS ME...
...WHO LOOK LIKE ME...
...I'LL BE KILLING...
...PEOPLE I DON'T KNOW.
I'LL BE KILLING STRANGERS.
THAT'S THE ONLY DIFFERENCE, ISN'T IT?
KRAK
KRAK
KRAK

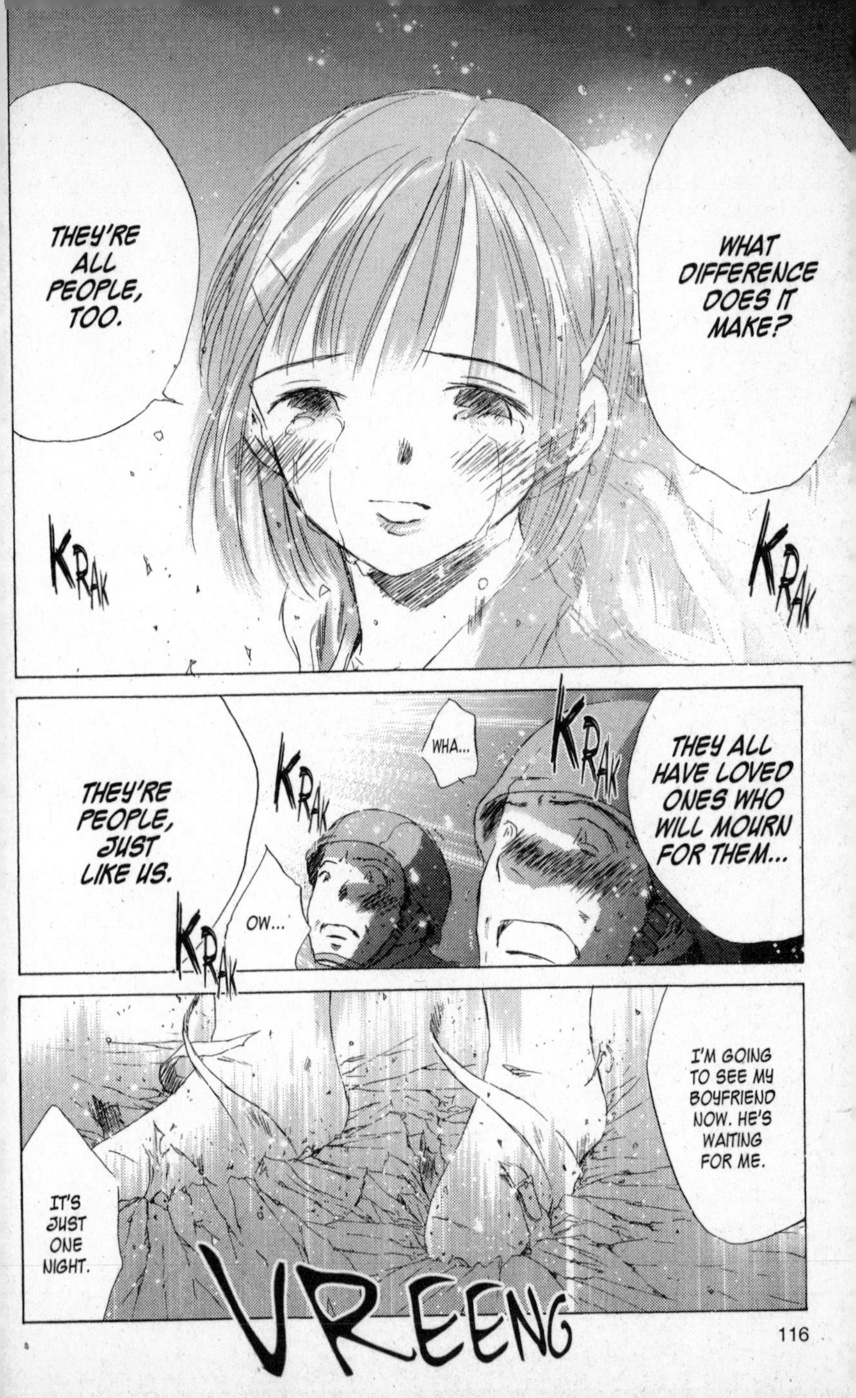
WHAT DIFFERENCE DOES IT MAKE?
KRAK
THEY'RE ALL PEOPLE, TOO.
KRAK
KRAK
THEY ALL HAVE LOVED ONES WHO WILL MOURN FOR THEM...
WHA...
KRAK
THEY'RE PEOPLE, JUST LIKE US.
OW...
KRAK
I'M GOING TO SEE MY BOYFRIEND NOW. HE'S WAITING FOR ME.
IT'S JUST ONE NIGHT.
VREENG

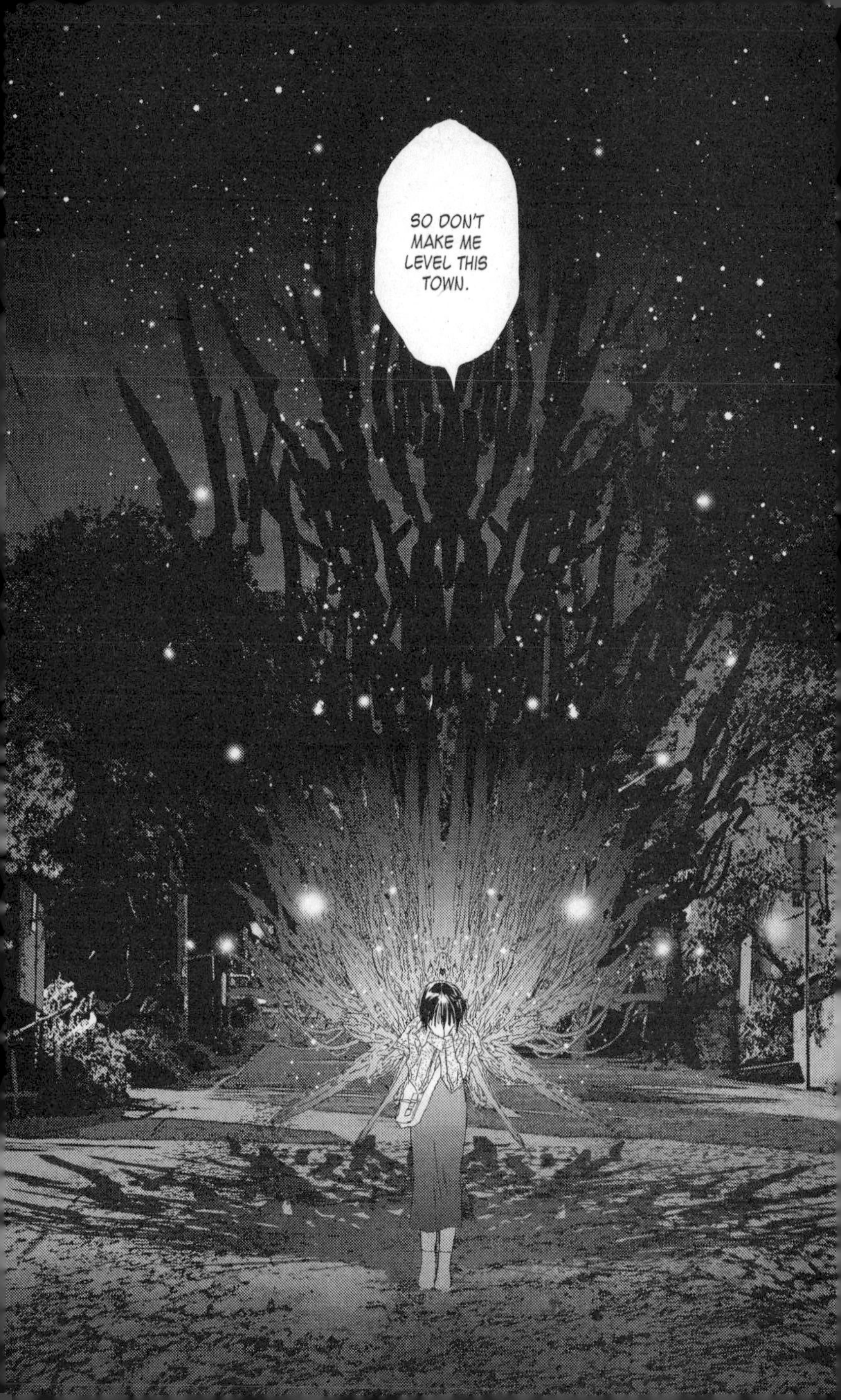
SO DON'T MAKE ME LEVEL THIS TOWN.

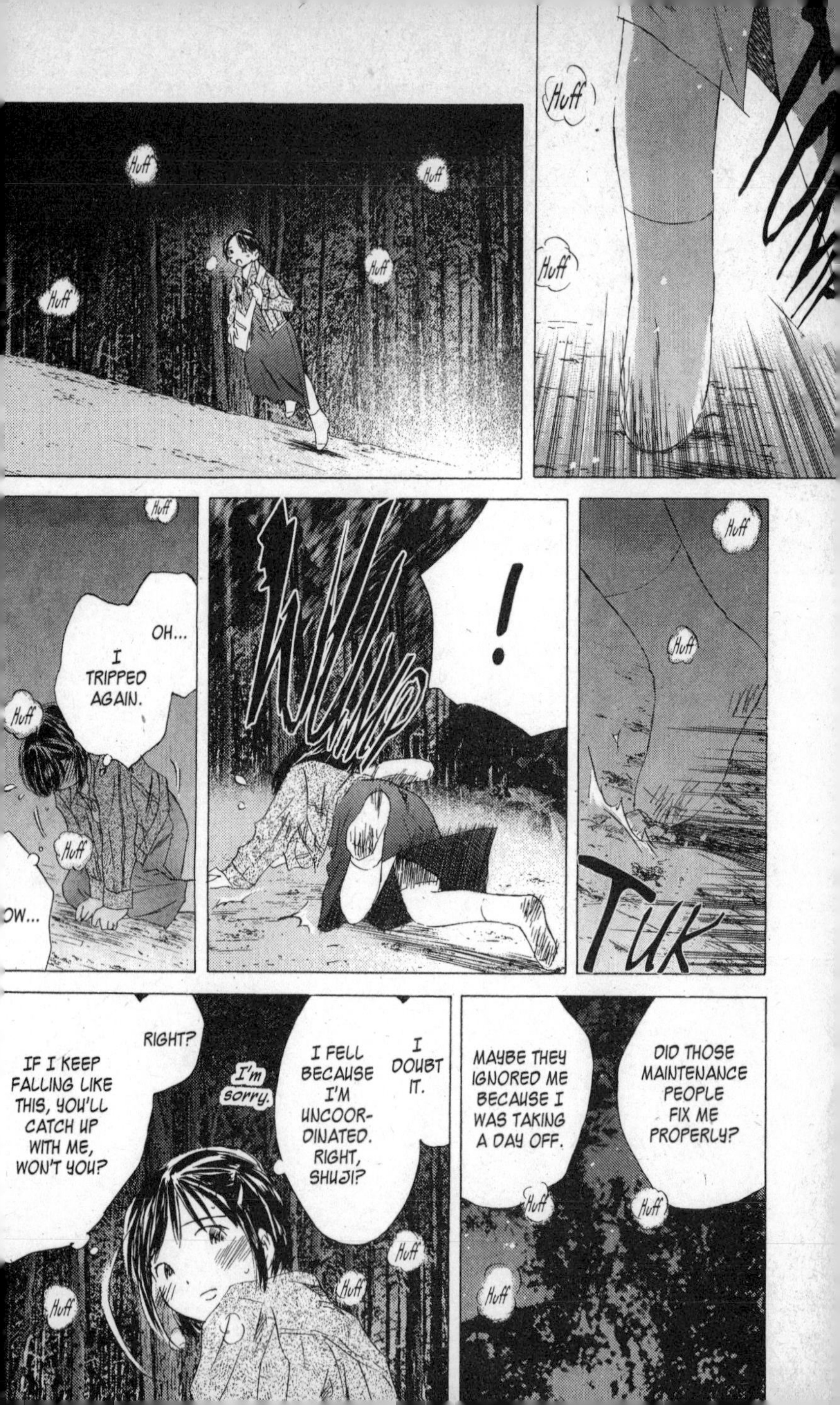
Huff
Huff
Huff
Huff
Huff
Huff
Huff
Huff
TUK
!
Huff
OH... I TRIPPED AGAIN.
Huff
Huff
OW...
DID THOSE MAINTENANCE PEOPLE FIX ME PROPERLY?
MAYBE THEY IGNORED ME BECAUSE I WAS TAKING A DAY OFF.
Huff
Huff
Huff
I DOUBT IT.
I FELL BECAUSE I'M UNCOORDINATED. RIGHT, SHUJI?
I'm sorry.
RIGHT?
IF I KEEP FALLING LIKE THIS, YOU'LL CATCH UP WITH ME, WON'T YOU?
Huff
Huff
Huff

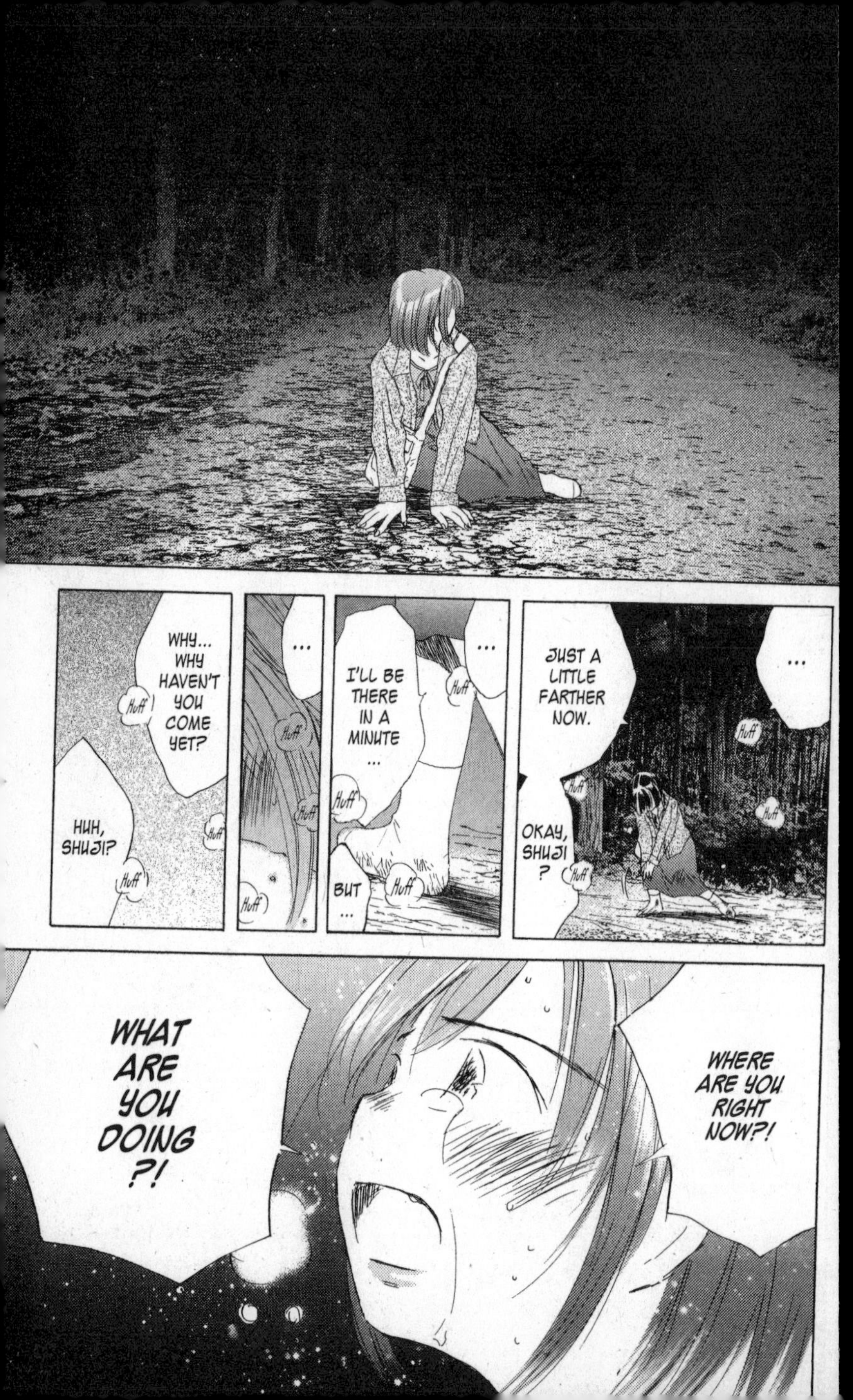
...
Huff
JUST A LITTLE FARTHER NOW.
Huff
OKAY, SHUJI?
Huff
...
Huff
I'LL BE THERE IN A MINUTE ...
Huff
BUT ...
Huff
...
Huff
Huff
Huff
WHY... WHY HAVEN'T YOU COME YET?
Huff
Huff
HUH, SHUJI?
Huff
WHERE ARE YOU RIGHT NOW?!
WHAT ARE YOU DOING ?!

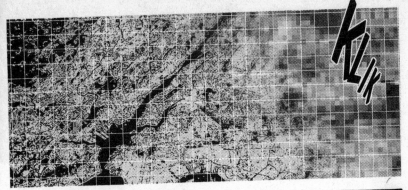

KLIK

WHAT?

WHAT?

OW...

ACCESS-ING...

SHUJI'S ...

...SURVEIL-LANCE RECORD?!

...HIS DATA?

KLIK

WHAT?

INFOR-MATION?

NO...

I DON'T WANT TO DO THAT!

KLIK

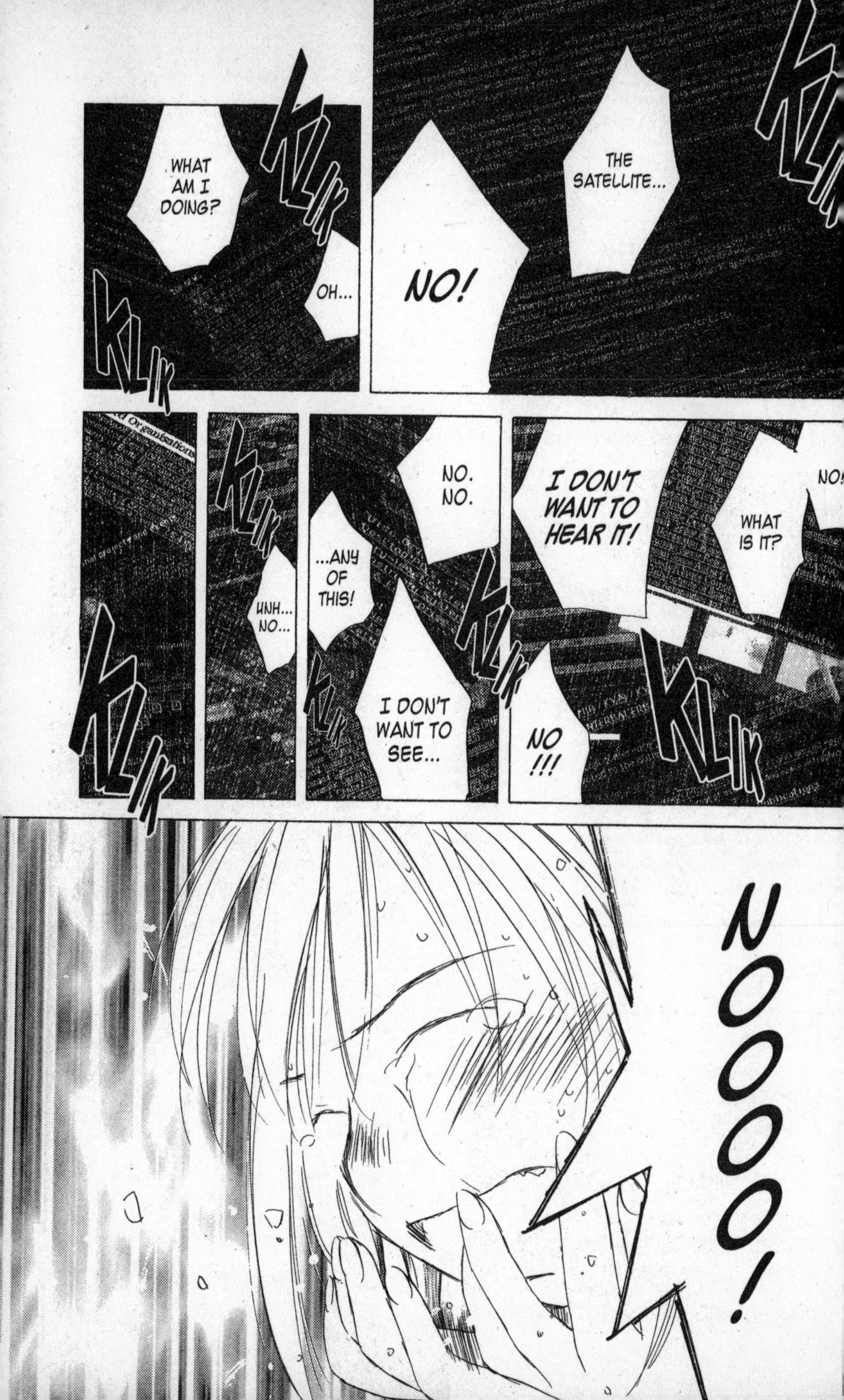
KLIK
THE SATELLITE...
NO!
KLIK
WHAT AM I DOING?
OH...
KLIK
NO!
WHAT IS IT?
I DON'T WANT TO HEAR IT!
KLIK
NO !!!
NO. NO.
...ANY OF THIS!
KLIK
I DON'T WANT TO SEE...
KLIK
KLIK
UNH... NO...
KLIK
NOOOO!

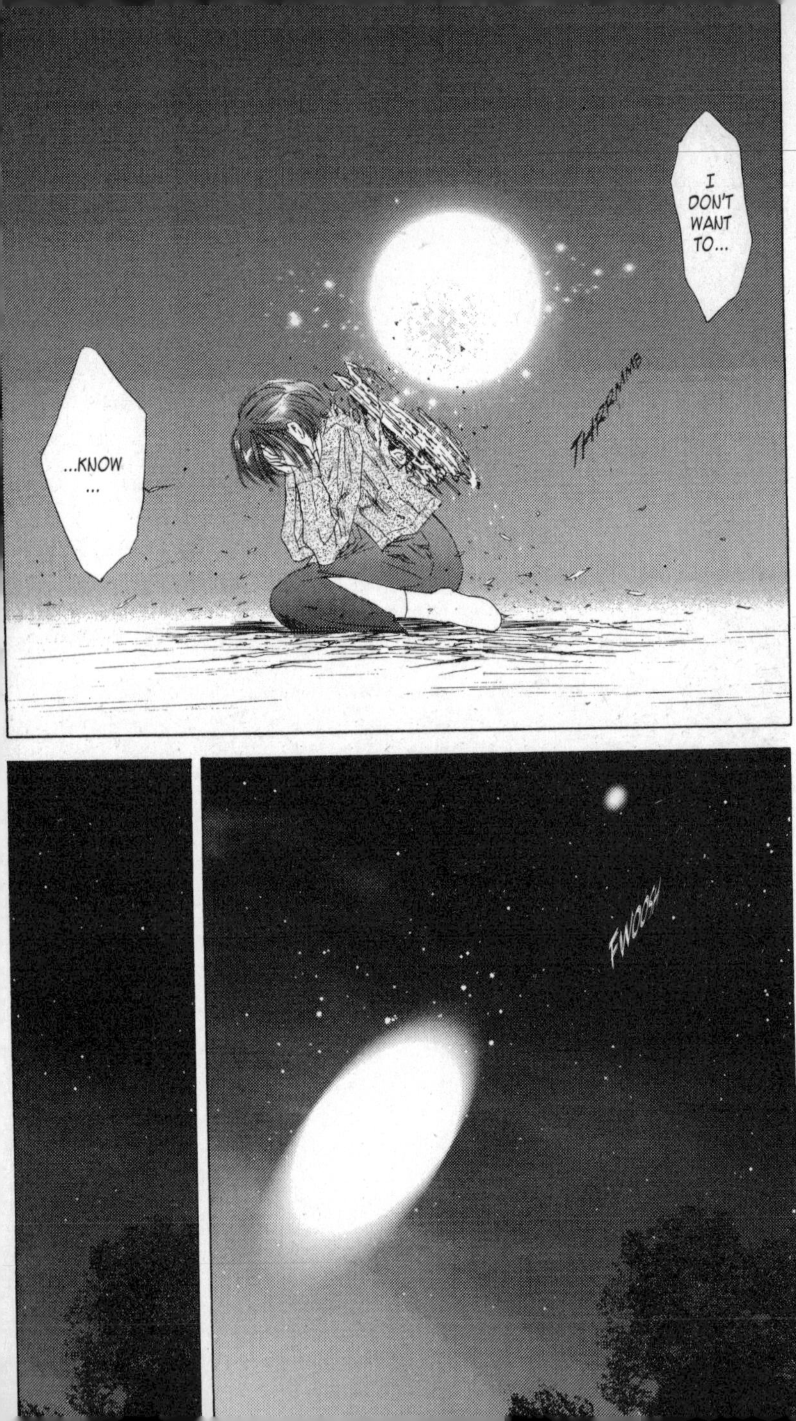
I DON'T WANT TO...
...KNOW ...
FWOOSH

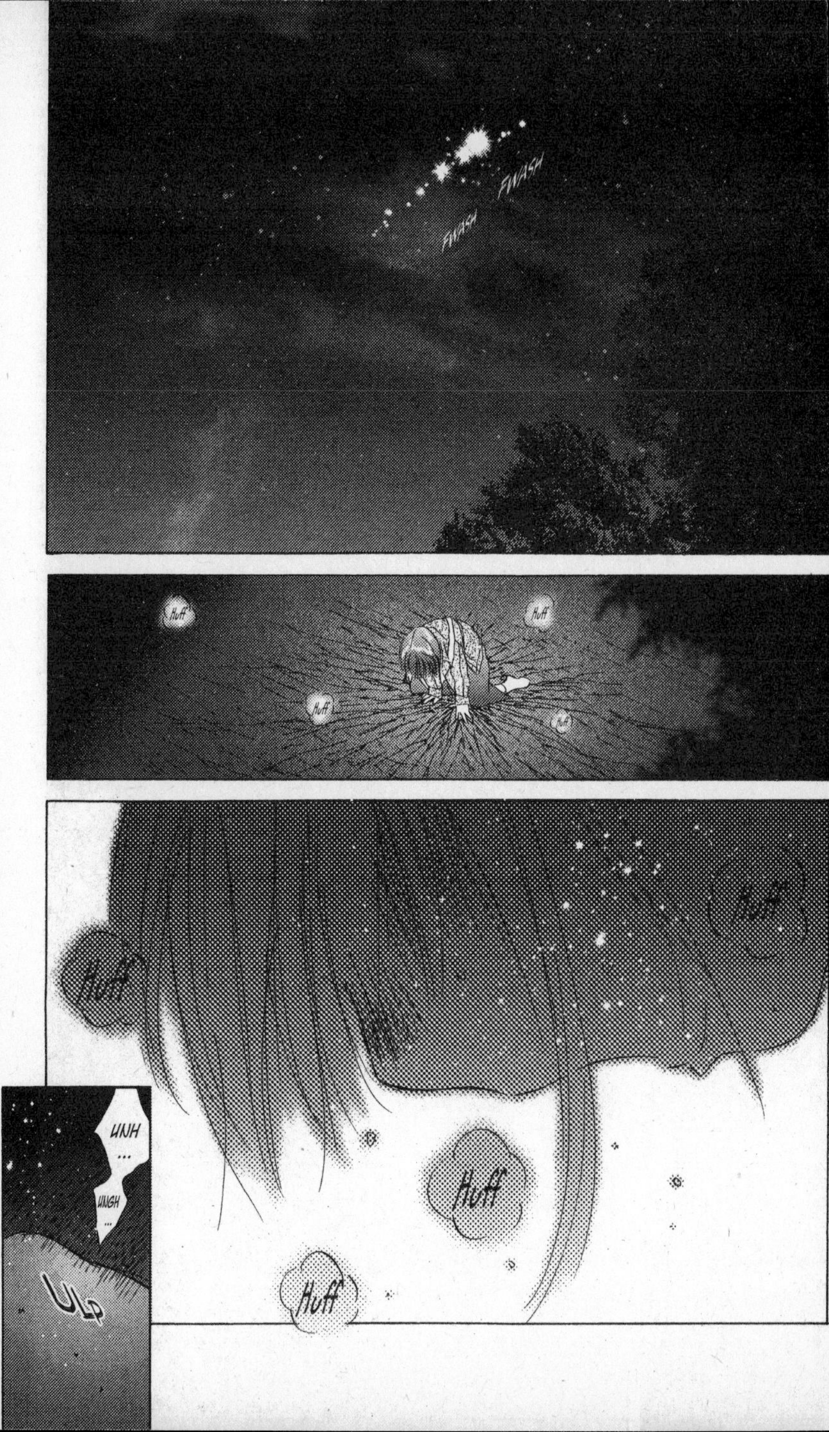
FWASH
FWASH
Huff
Huff
Huff
Huff
Huff
Huff
Huff
Huff
UNH ...
UNGH ...
Ulp

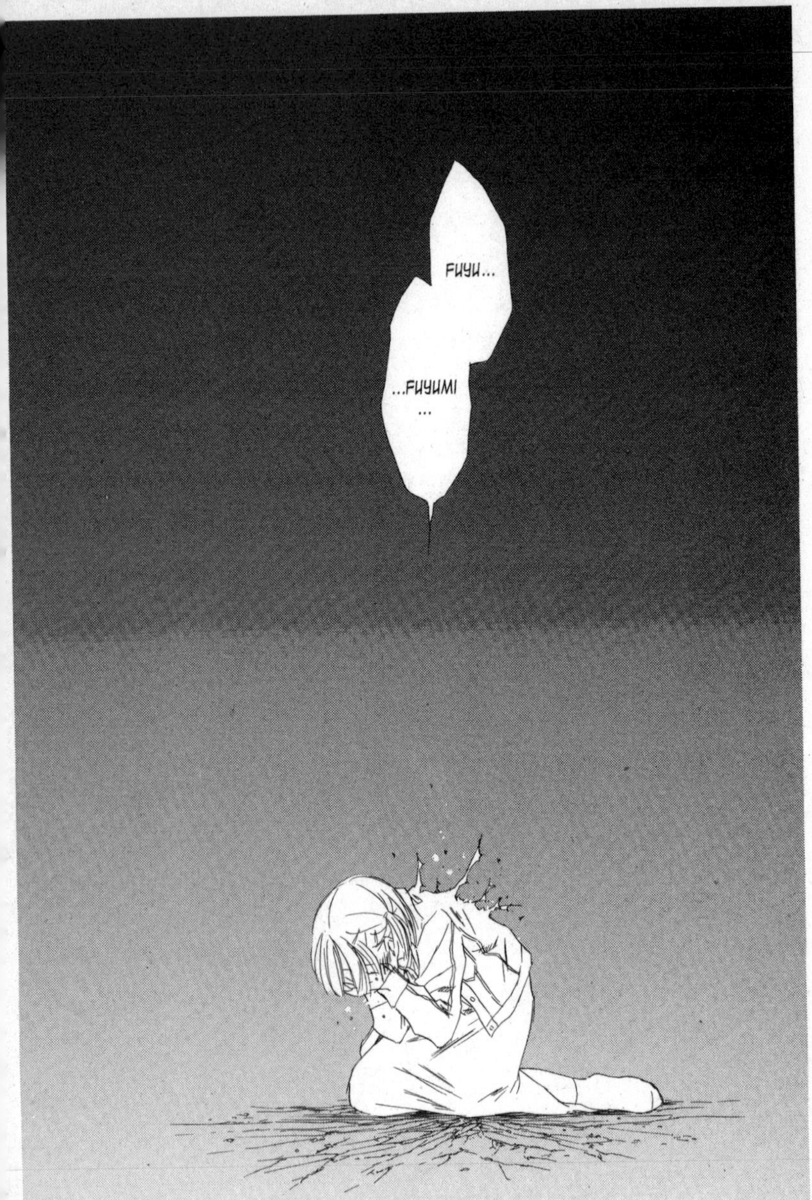
FUYU...
...FUYUMI
...

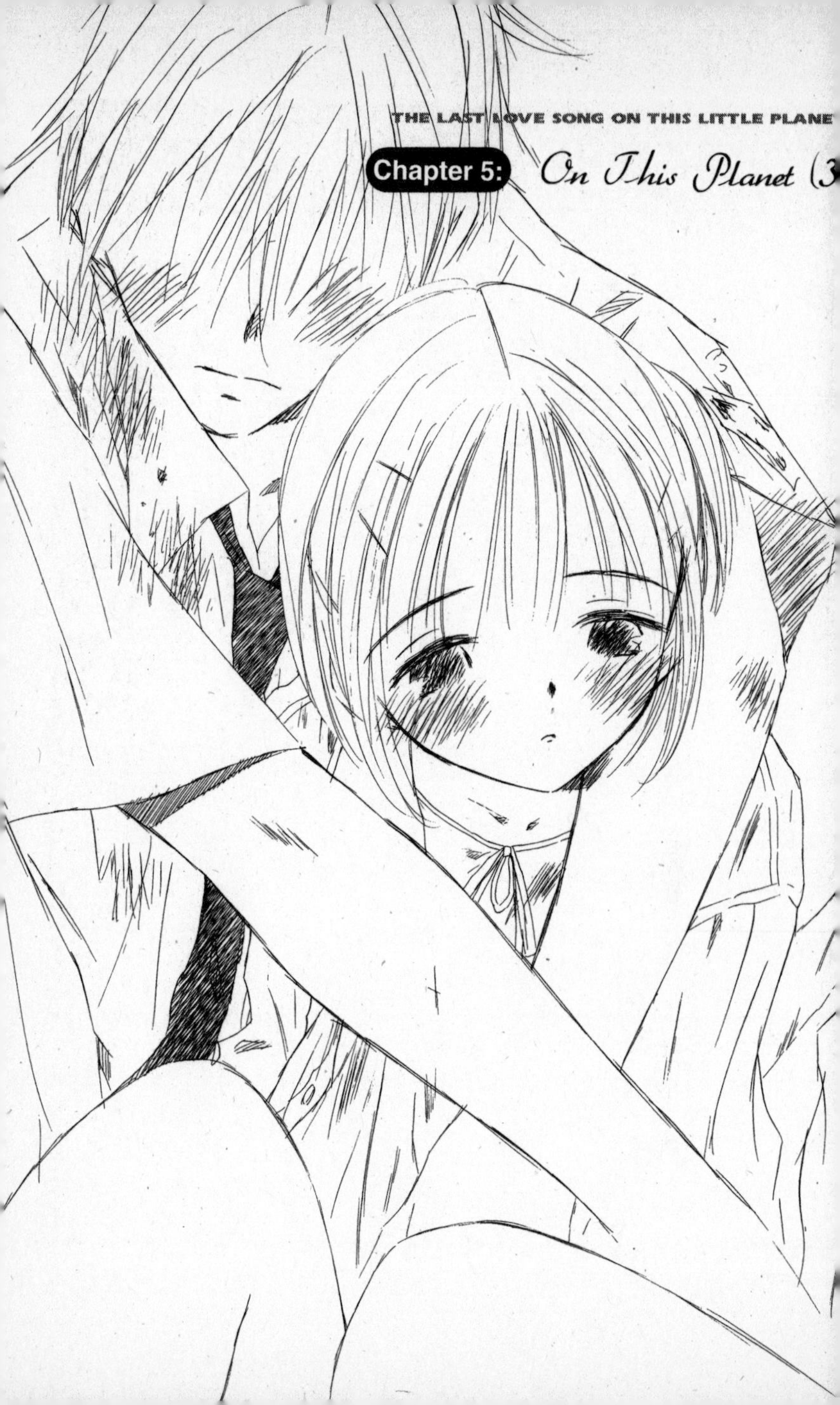
THE LAST LOVE SONG ON THIS LITTLE PLANE
Chapter 5: On This Planet (3

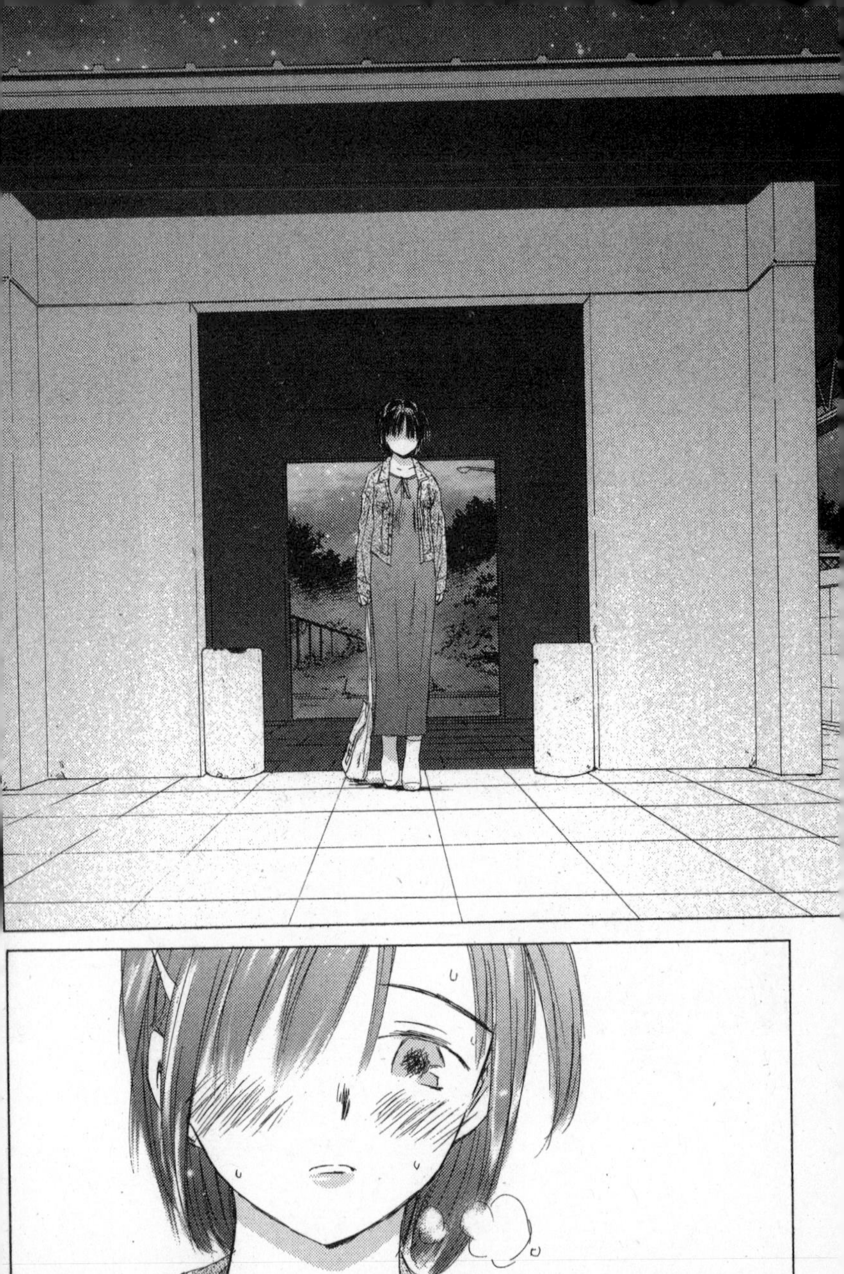

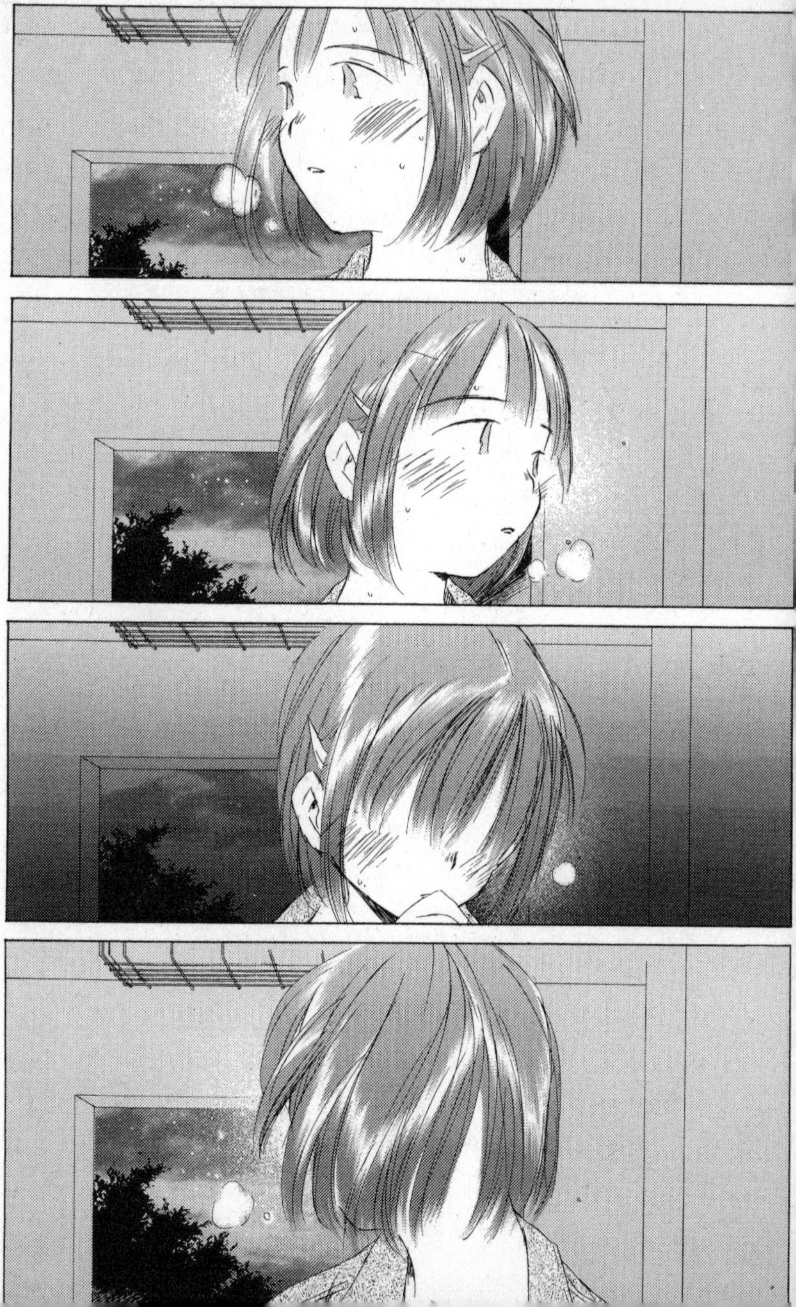

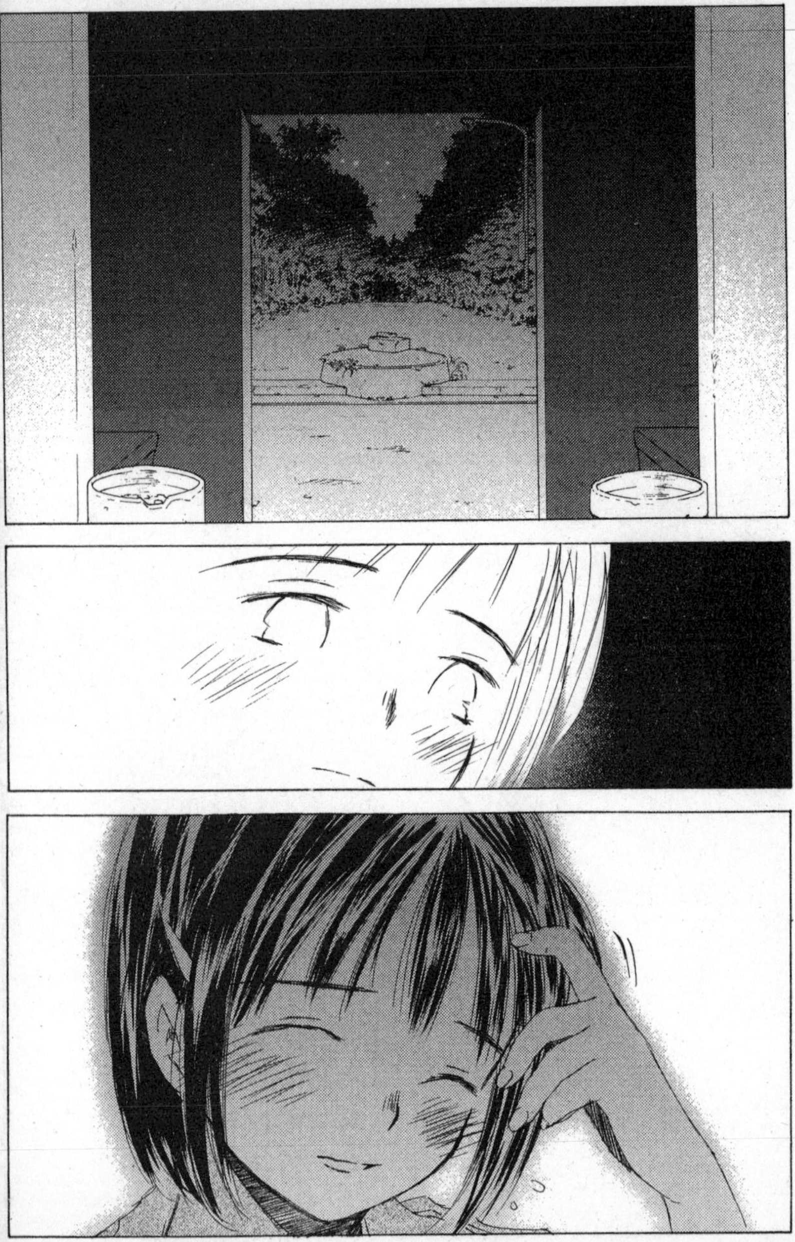

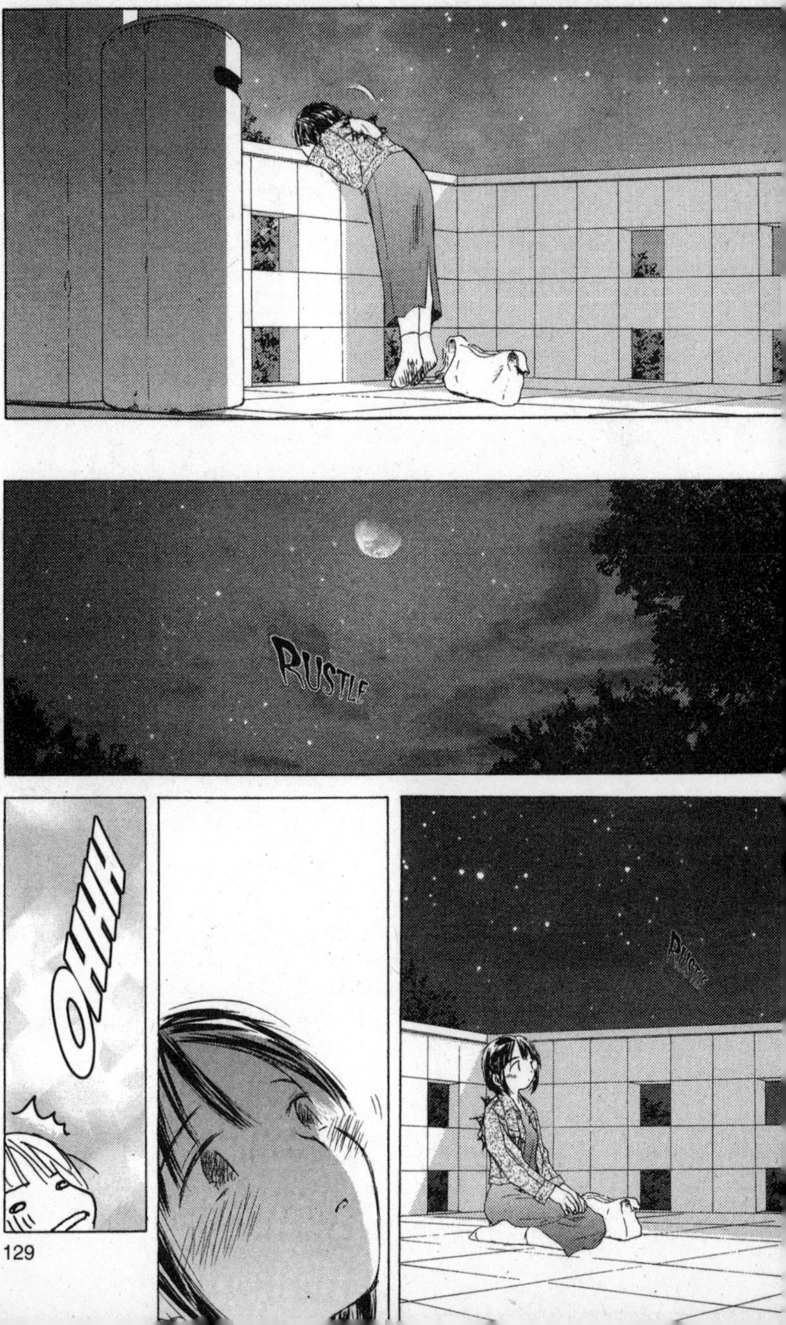
RUSTLE
RUSTLE
OHHH

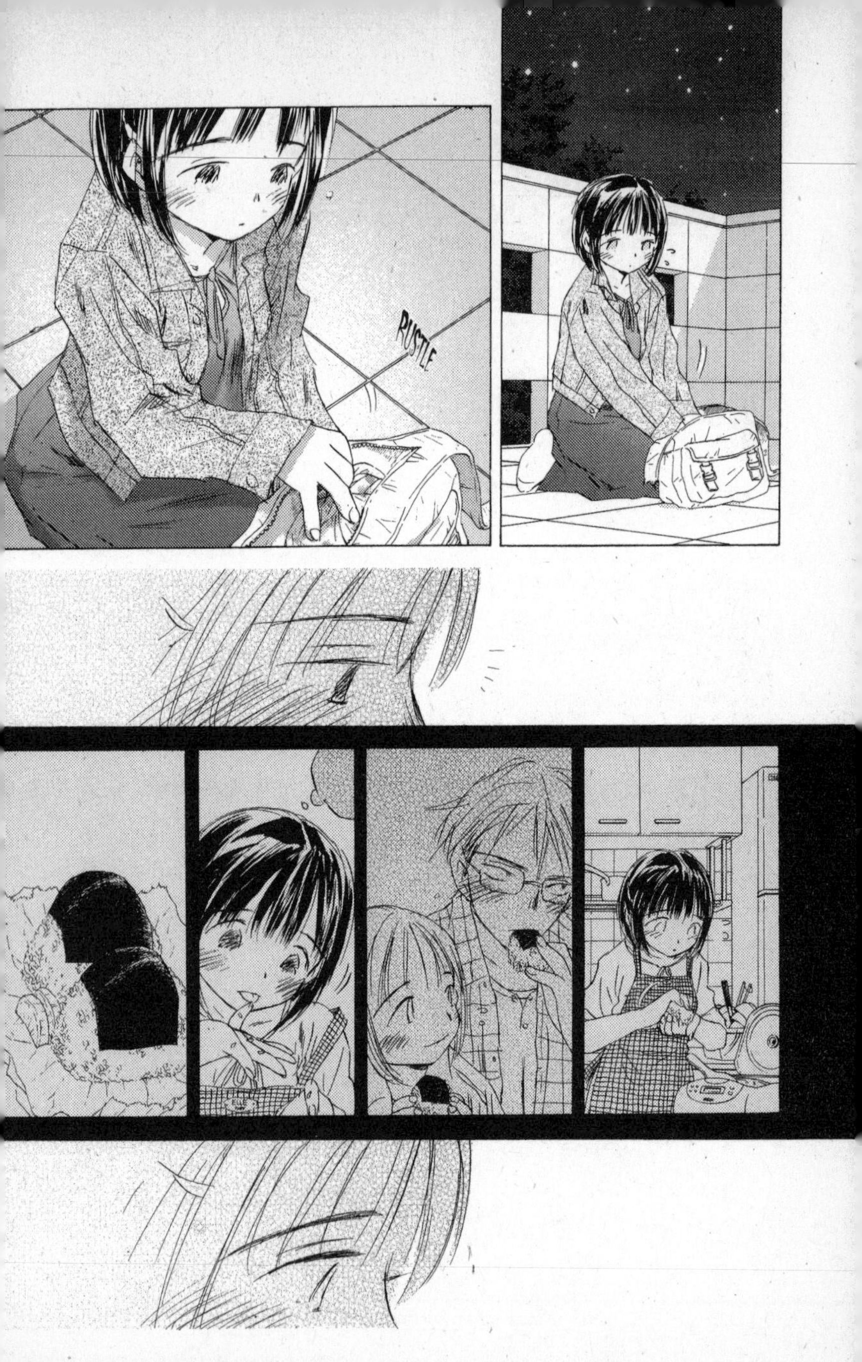
RUSTLE

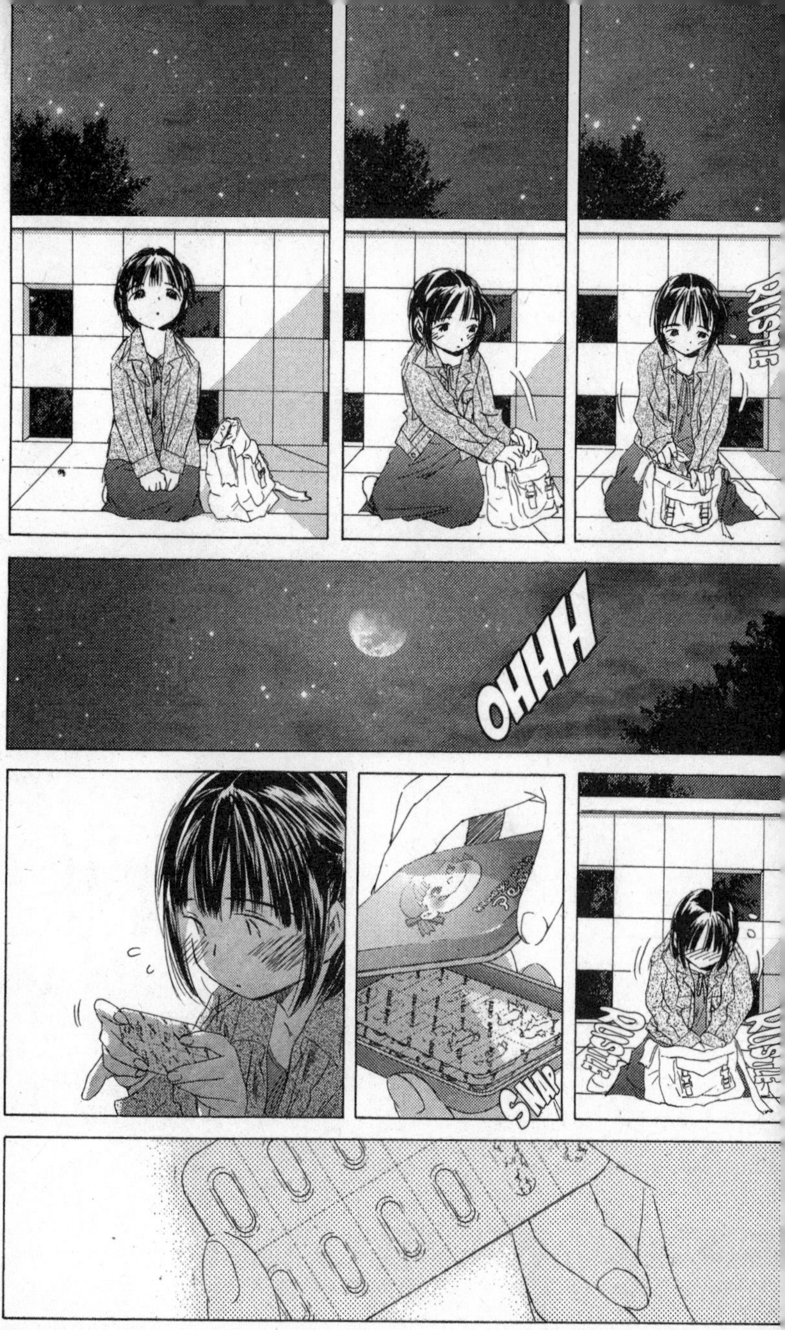
RUSTLE
OHHH
RUSTLE
RUSTLE
SNAP

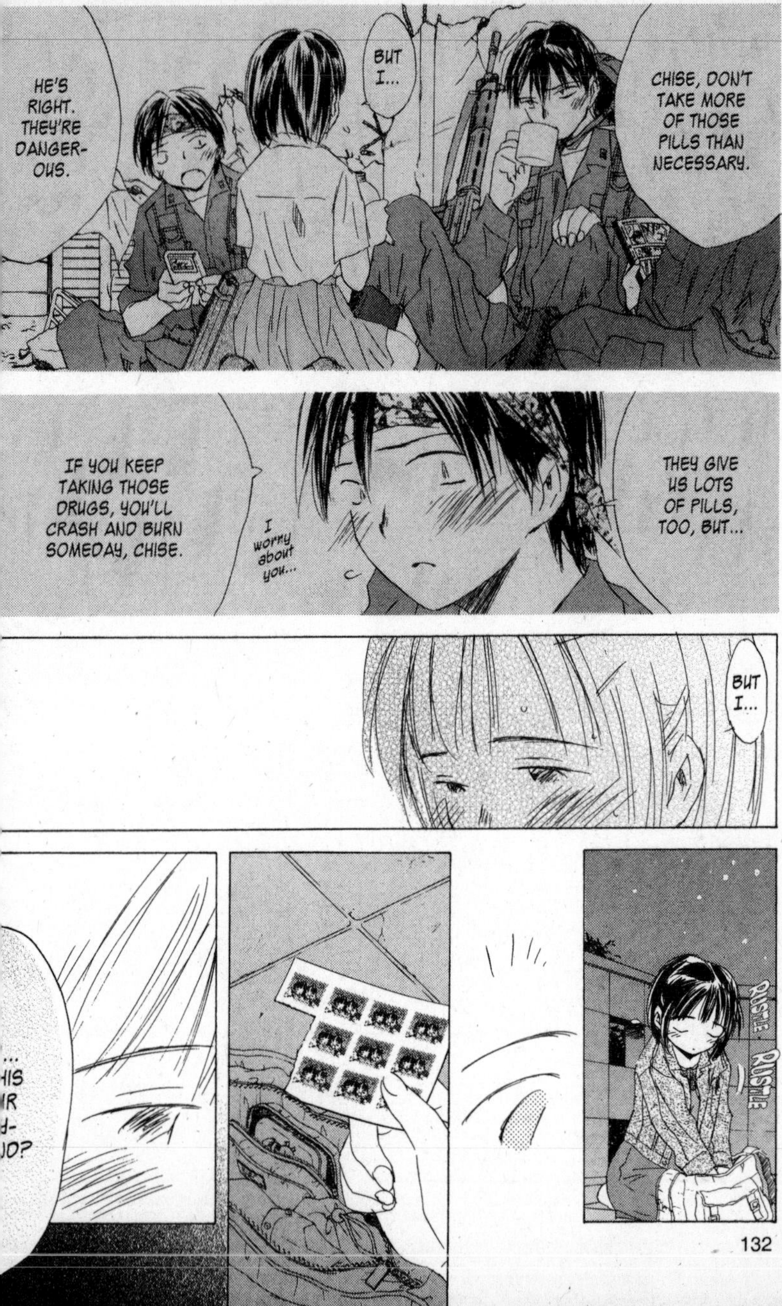
CHISE, DON'T TAKE MORE OF THOSE PILLS THAN NECESSARY.
BUT I...
HE'S RIGHT. THEY'RE DANGER-OUS.
THEY GIVE US LOTS OF PILLS, TOO, BUT...
I worry about you...
IF YOU KEEP TAKING THOSE DRUGS, YOU'LL CRASH AND BURN SOMEDAY, CHISE.
BUT I...
RUSTLE
RUSTLE

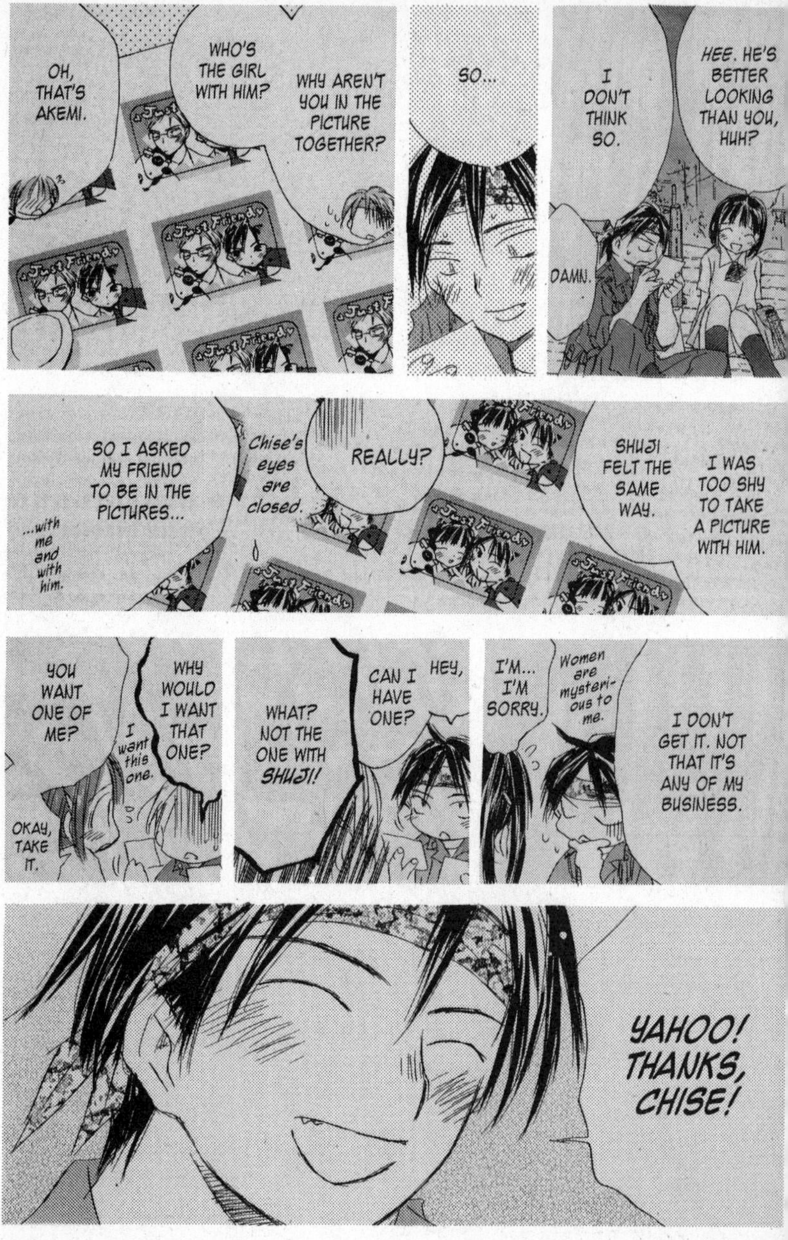
HEE. HE'S BETTER LOOKING THAN YOU, HUH?
I DON'T THINK SO.
DAMN.
SO...
WHY AREN'T YOU IN THE PICTURE TOGETHER?
WHO'S THE GIRL WITH HIM?
OH, THAT'S AKEMI.
I WAS TOO SHY TO TAKE A PICTURE WITH HIM.
SHUJI FELT THE SAME WAY.
REALLY?
Chise's eyes are closed.
SO I ASKED MY FRIEND TO BE IN THE PICTURES...
...with me and with him.
I DON'T GET IT. NOT THAT IT'S ANY OF MY BUSINESS.
Women are mysterious to me.
I'M... I'M SORRY.
HEY,
CAN I HAVE ONE?
WHAT? NOT THE ONE WITH SHUJI!
WHY WOULD I WANT THAT ONE?
YOU WANT ONE OF ME?
I want this one.
OKAY, TAKE IT.
YAHOO! THANKS, CHISE!

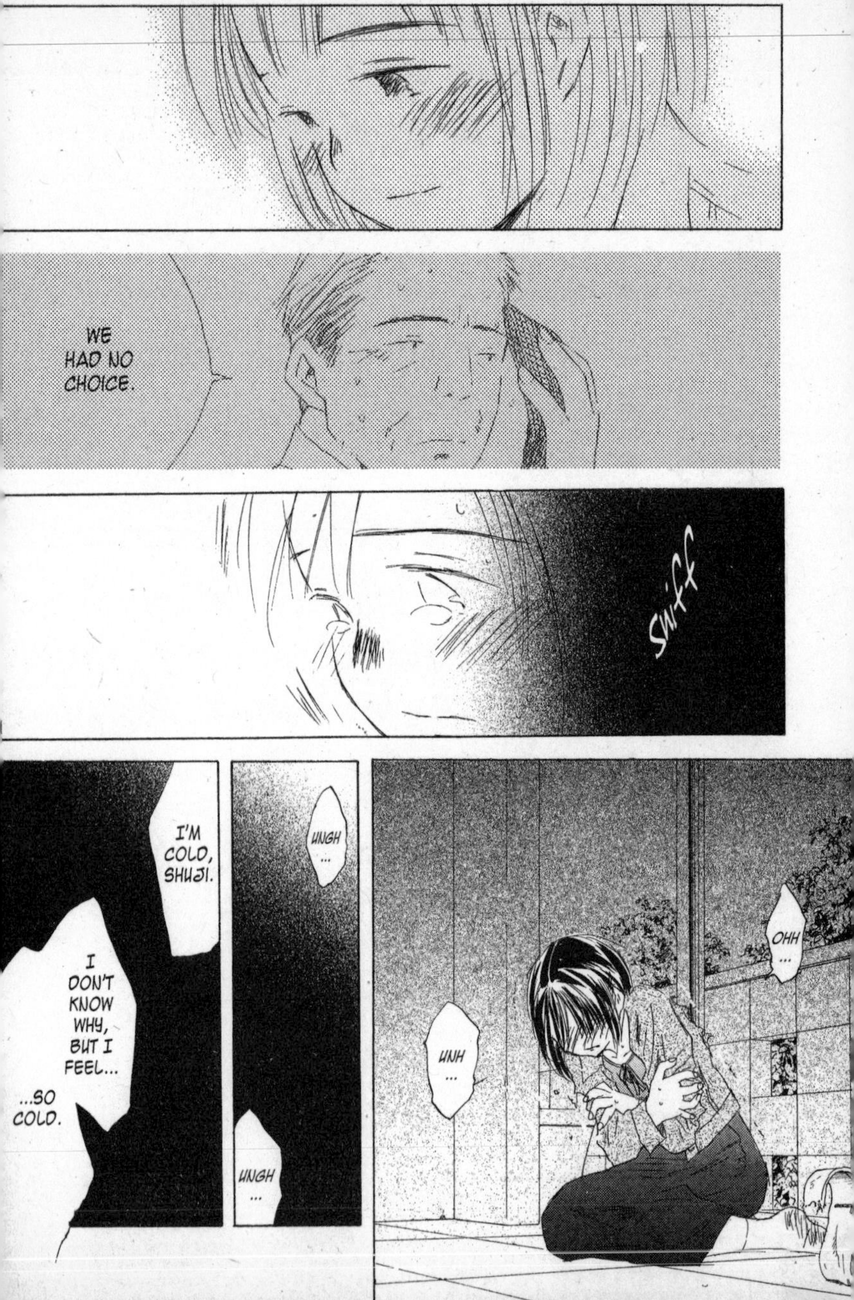

WE HAD NO CHOICE.
Sniff
OHH ...
UNH ...
UNGH ...
UNGH ...
I'M COLD, SHUJI.
I DON'T KNOW WHY, BUT I FEEL...
...SO COLD.

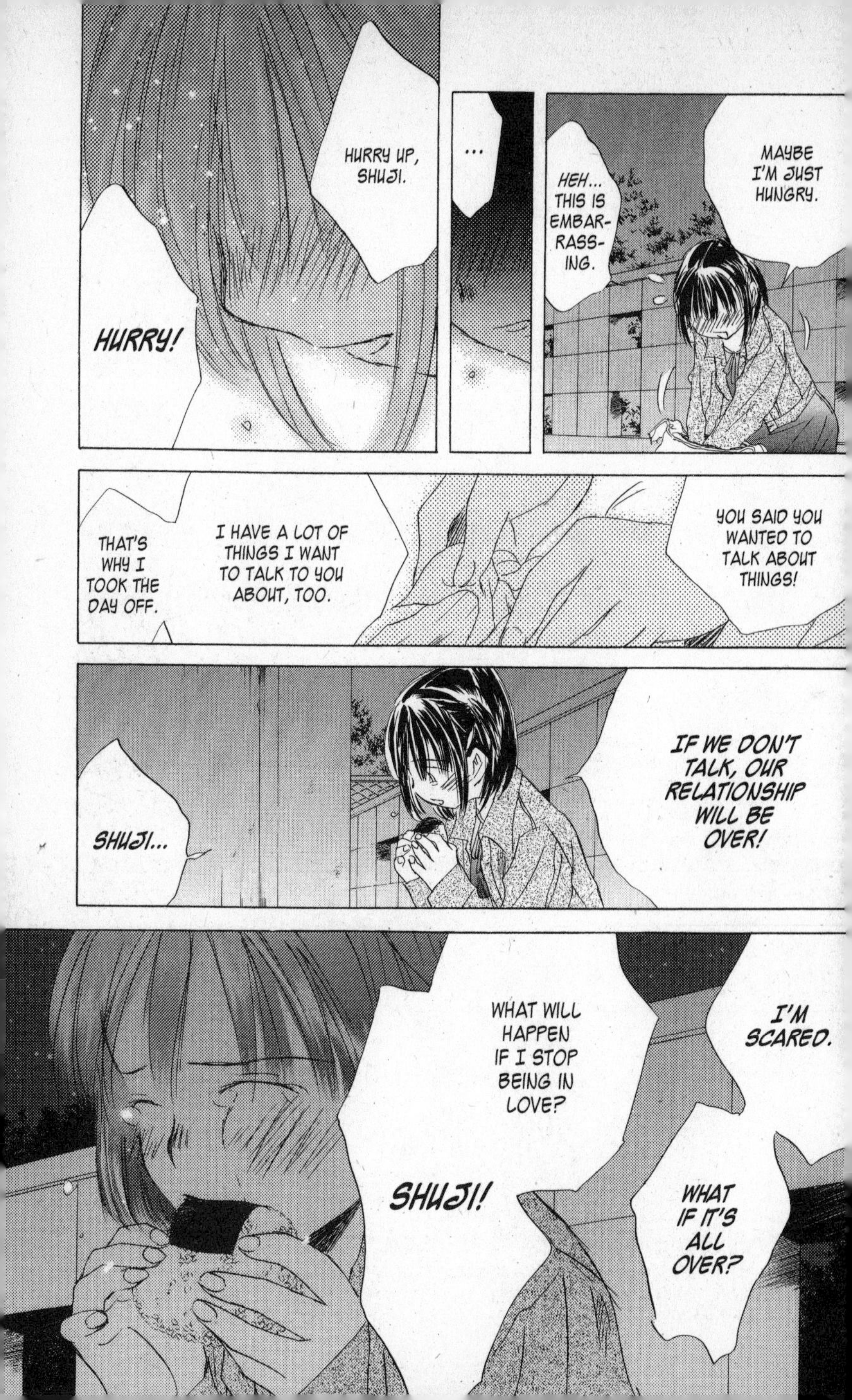
MAYBE I'M JUST HUNGRY.
HEH... THIS IS EMBARRASSING.
...
HURRY UP, SHUJI.
HURRY!
YOU SAID YOU WANTED TO TALK ABOUT THINGS!
I HAVE A LOT OF THINGS I WANT TO TALK TO YOU ABOUT, TOO.
THAT'S WHY I TOOK THE DAY OFF.
IF WE DON'T TALK, OUR RELATIONSHIP WILL BE OVER!
SHUJI...
I'M SCARED.
WHAT WILL HAPPEN IF I STOP BEING IN LOVE?
WHAT IF IT'S ALL OVER?
SHUJI!

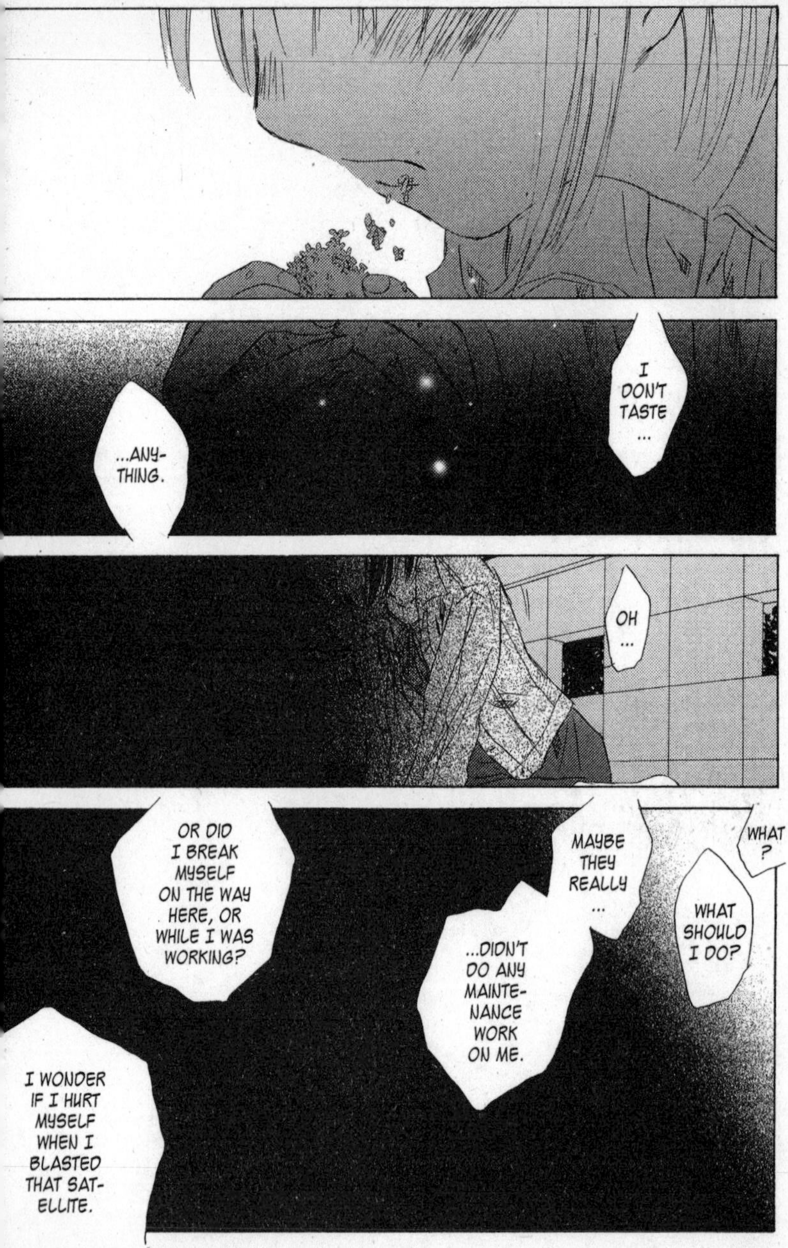
I DON'T TASTE ...
...ANYTHING.
OH ...
WHAT ?
WHAT SHOULD I DO?
MAYBE THEY REALLY ...
...DIDN'T DO ANY MAINTENANCE WORK ON ME.
OR DID I BREAK MYSELF ON THE WAY HERE, OR WHILE I WAS WORKING?
I WONDER IF I HURT MYSELF WHEN I BLASTED THAT SATELLITE.

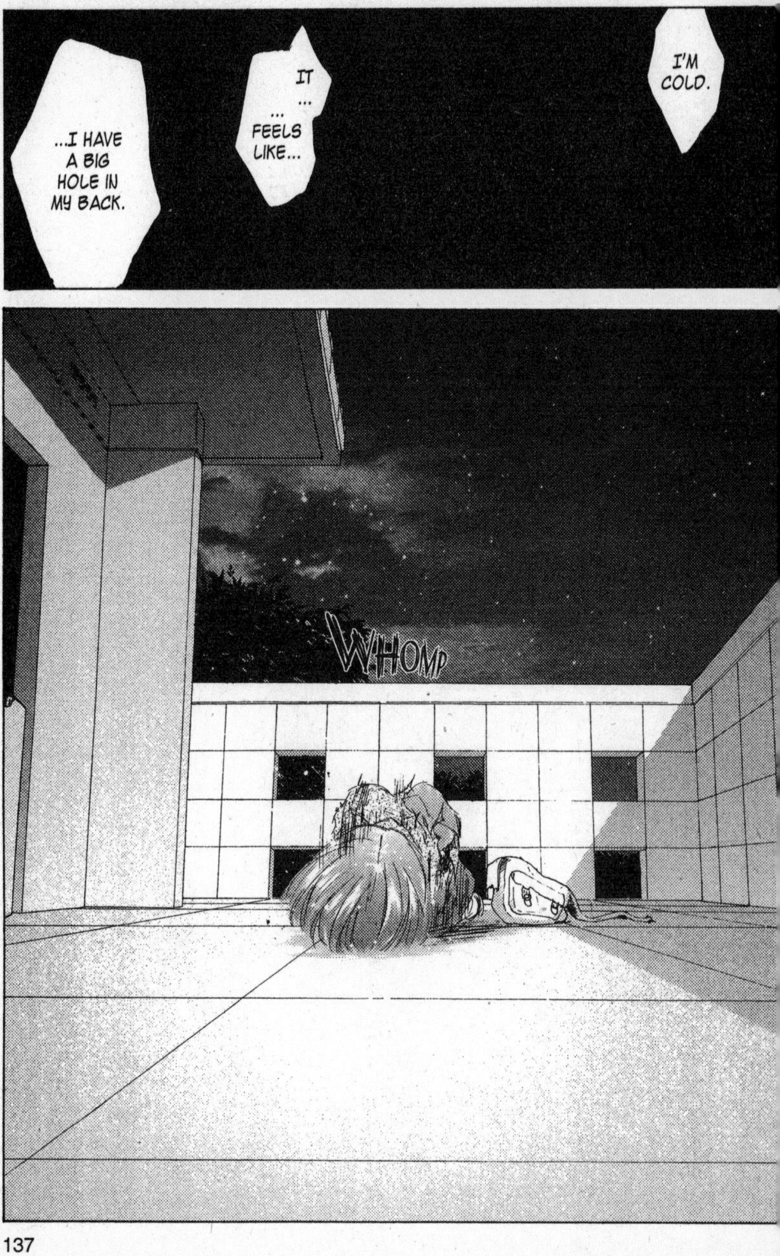
I'M COLD.
IT ... ... FEELS LIKE...
...I HAVE A BIG HOLE IN MY BACK.
WHOMP

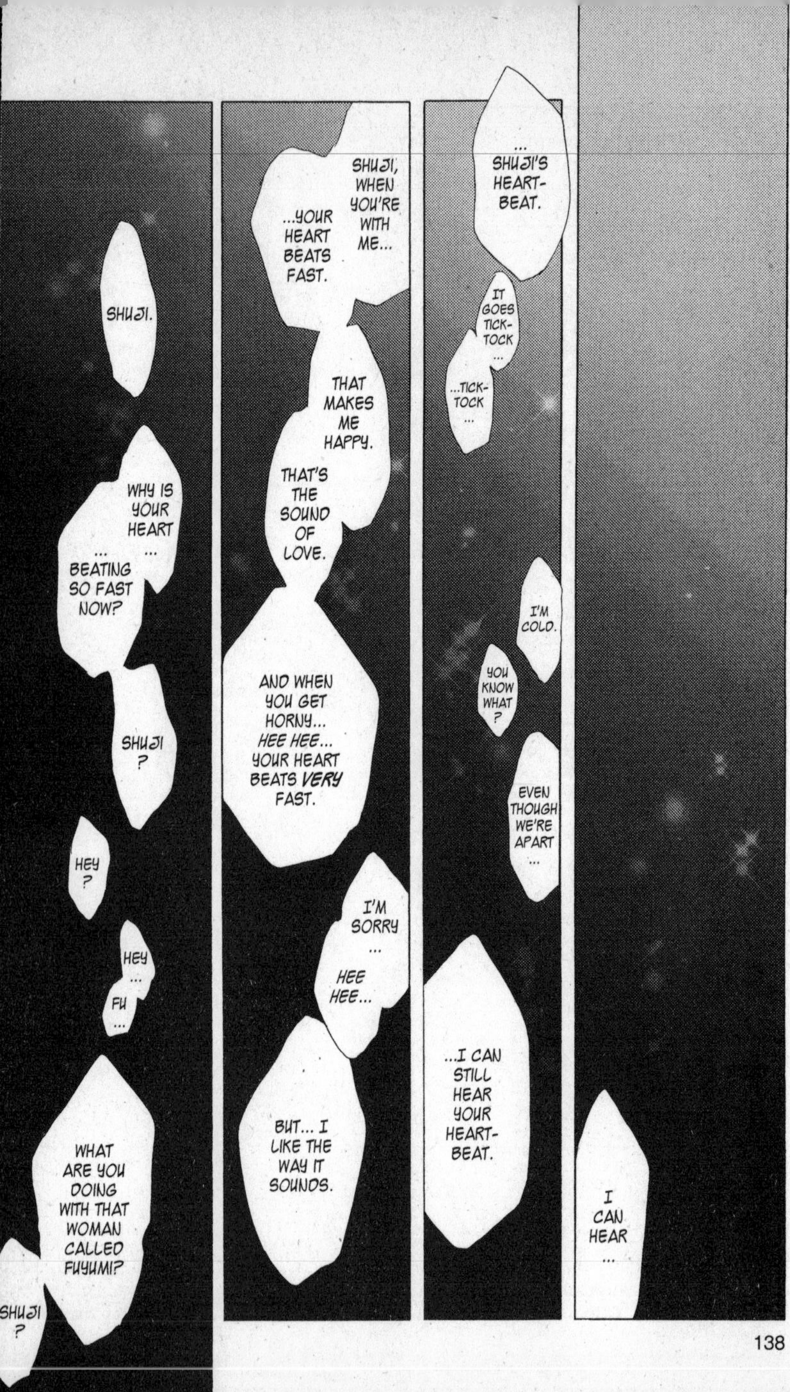
I CAN HEAR ...
... SHUJI'S HEART-BEAT.
IT GOES TICK-TOCK ...
...TICK-TOCK ...
I'M COLD.
YOU KNOW WHAT ?
EVEN THOUGH WE'RE APART ...
...I CAN STILL HEAR YOUR HEART-BEAT.
SHUJI, WHEN YOU'RE WITH ME...
...YOUR HEART BEATS FAST.
THAT MAKES ME HAPPY.
THAT'S THE SOUND OF LOVE.
AND WHEN YOU GET HORNY... *HEE HEE...* YOUR HEART BEATS ***VERY*** FAST.
I'M SORRY ...
HEE HEE...
BUT... I LIKE THE WAY IT SOUNDS.
SHUJI.
WHY IS YOUR HEART ...
... BEATING SO FAST NOW?
SHUJI ?
HEY ?
HEY ...
FU ...
WHAT ARE YOU DOING WITH THAT WOMAN CALLED FUYUMI?
SHUJI ?

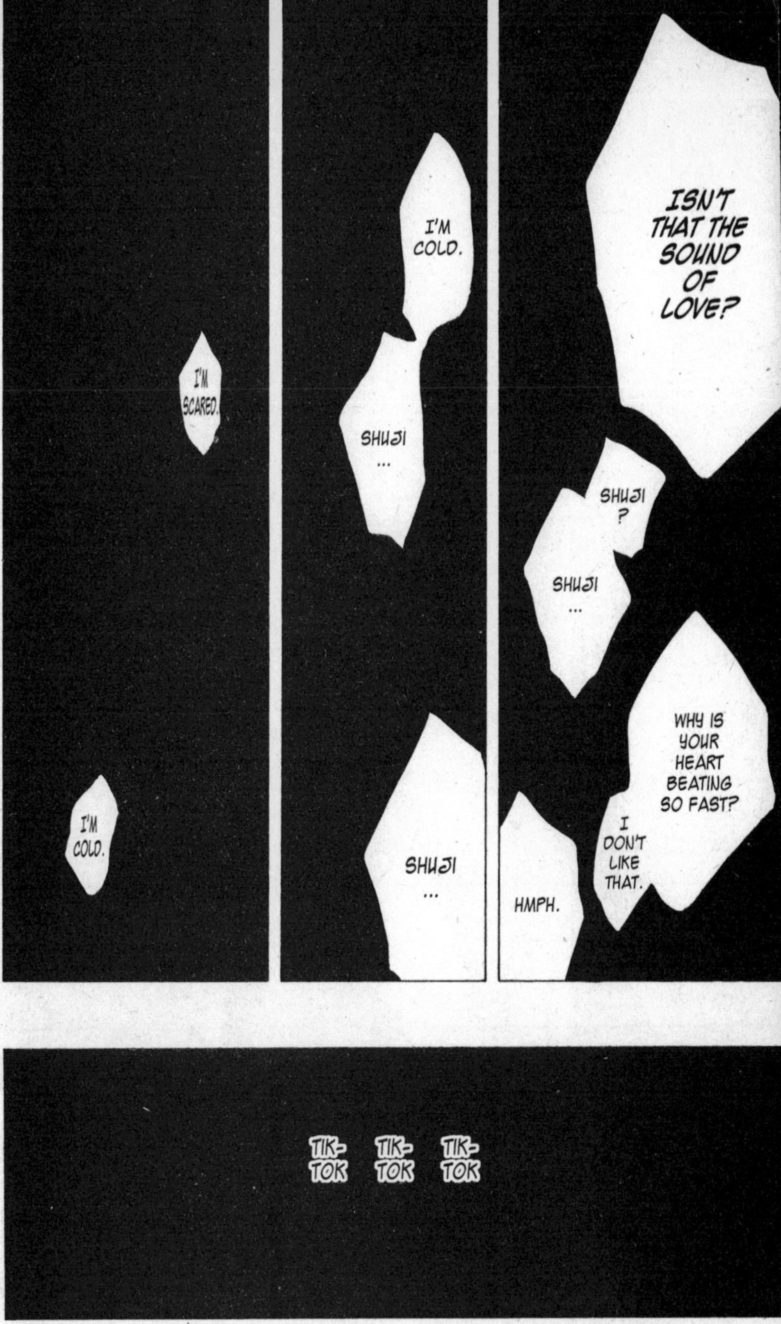
ISN'T THAT THE SOUND OF LOVE?
SHUJI?
SHUJI...
WHY IS YOUR HEART BEATING SO FAST?
I DON'T LIKE THAT.
HMPH.
I'M COLD.
SHUJI...
SHUJI...
I'M SCARED.
I'M COLD.
TIK-TOK TIK-TOK TIK-TOK

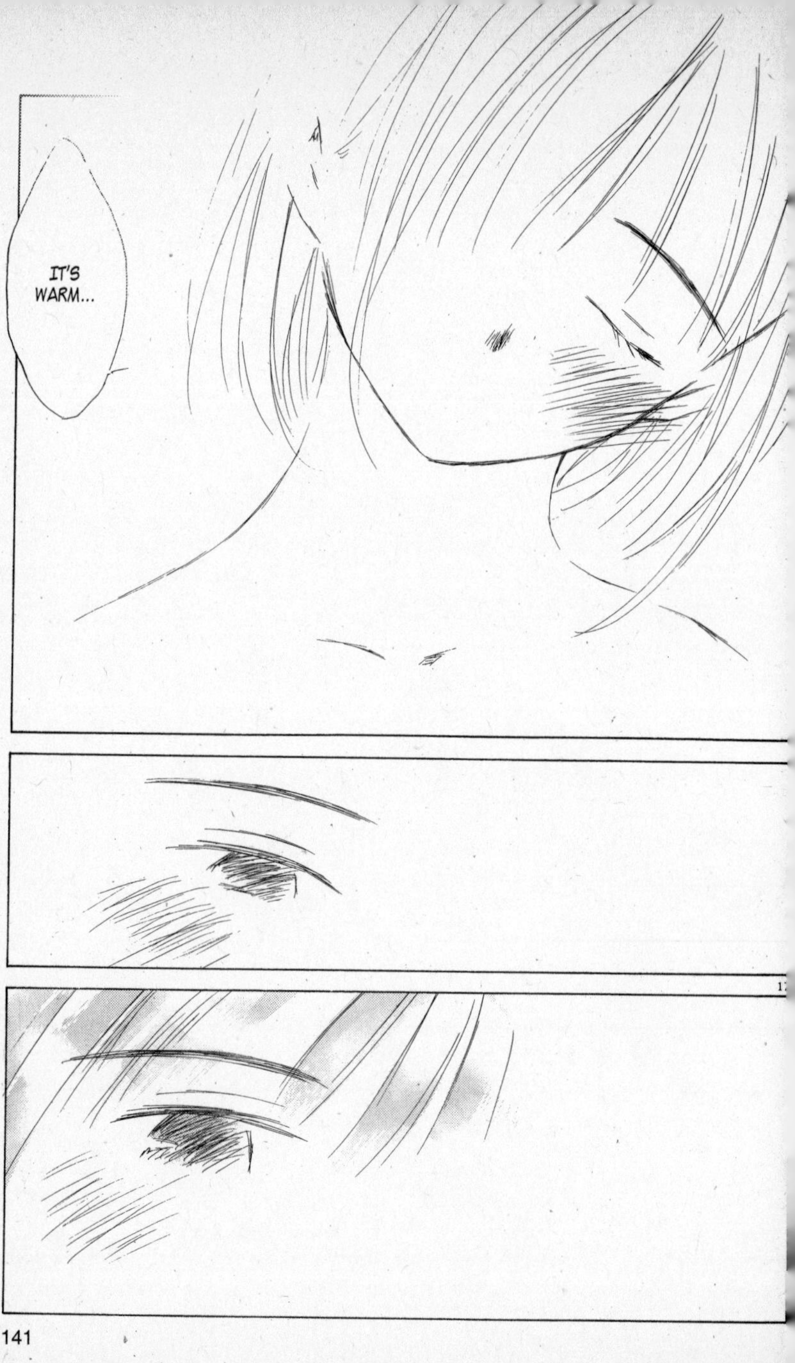
IT'S WARM...

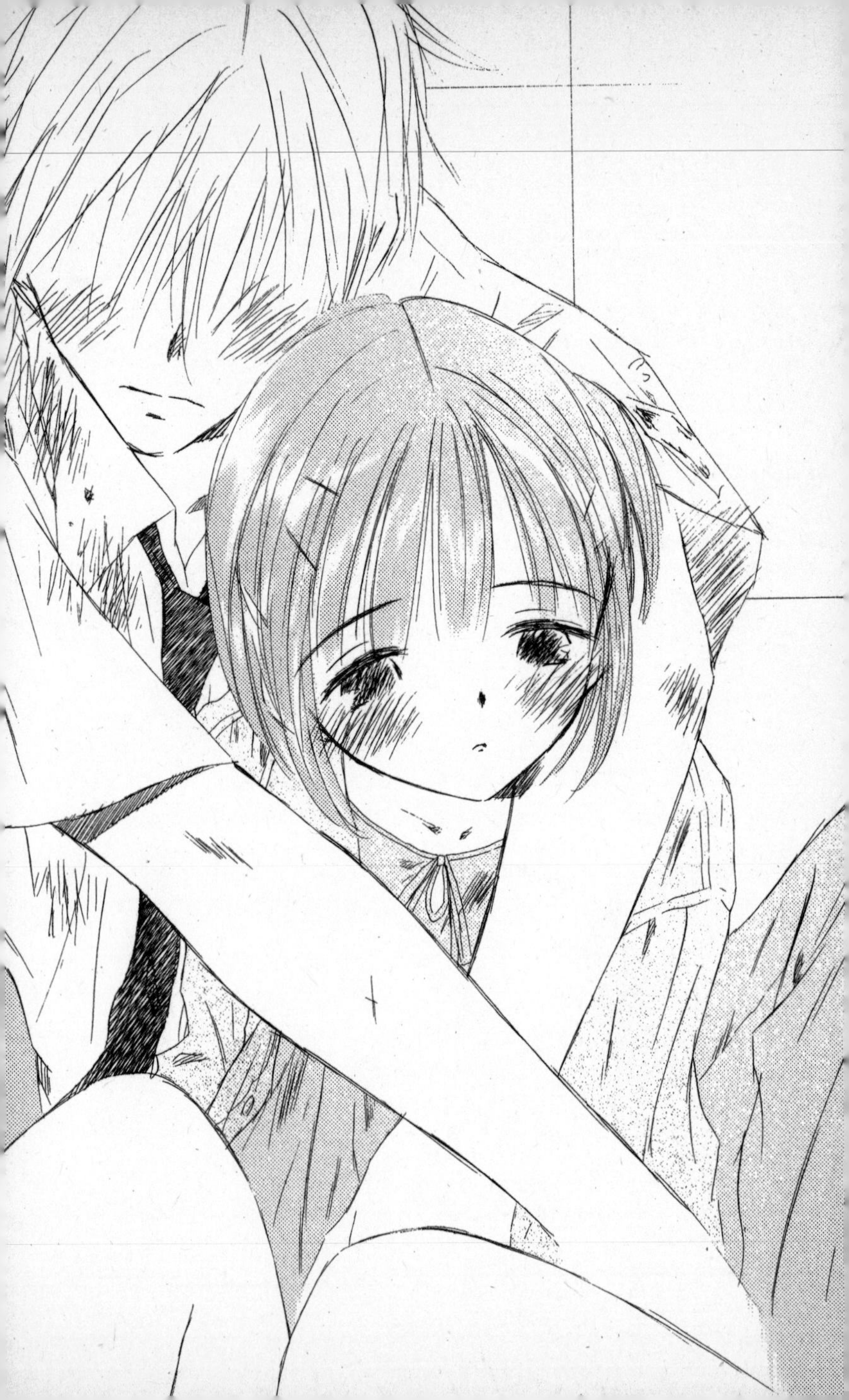

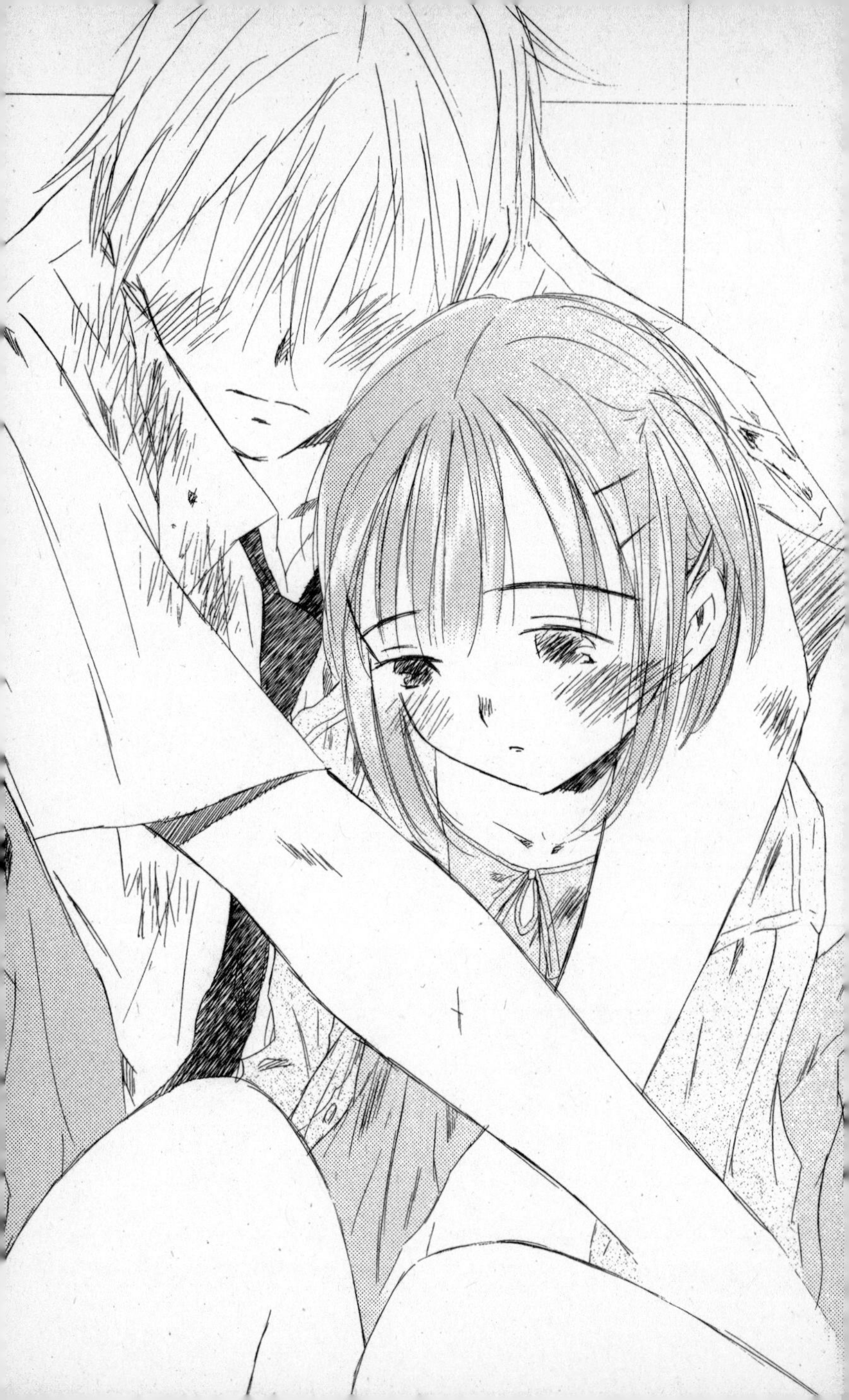

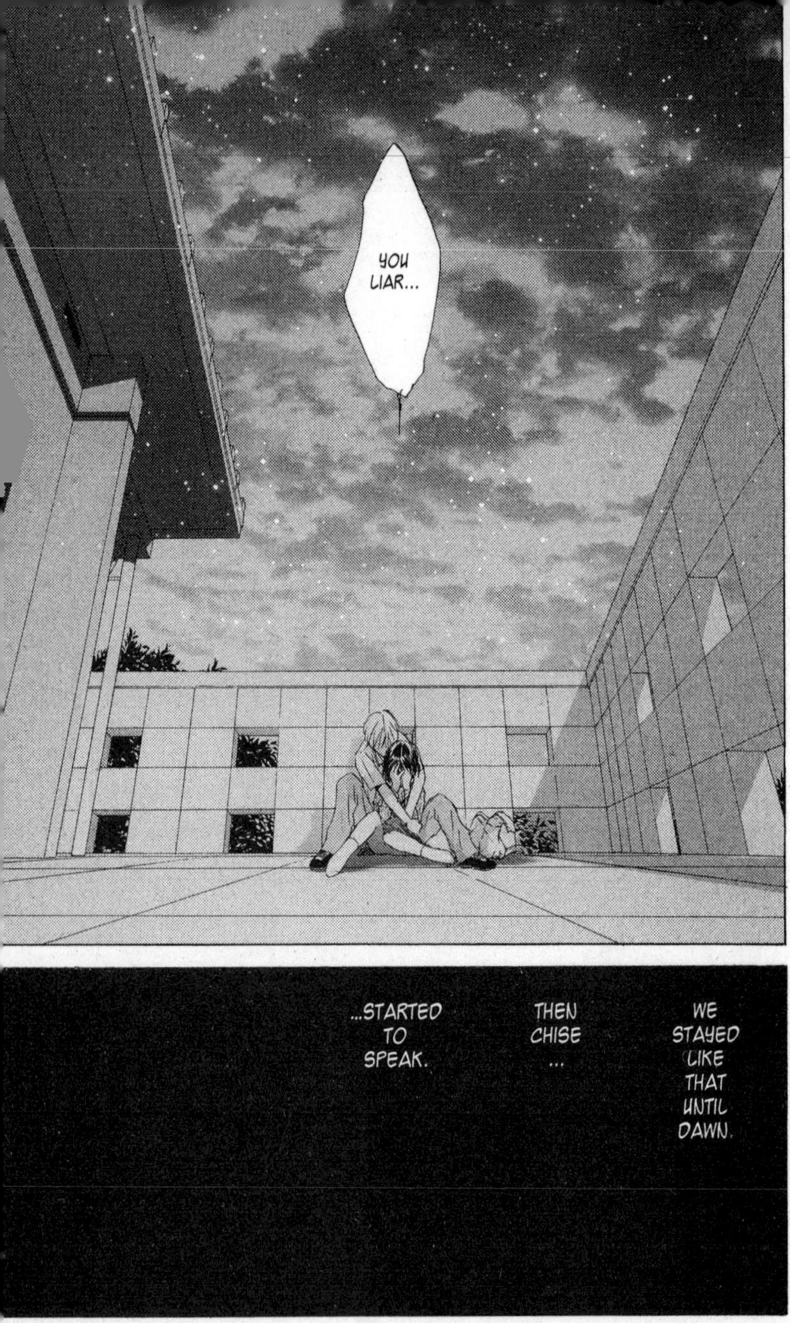
YOU LIAR...
WE STAYED LIKE THAT UNTIL DAWN.
THEN CHISE ...
...STARTED TO SPEAK.

THE LAST LOVE SONG ON THIS LITTLE PLANET.

Chapter 5: On This Planet (4)

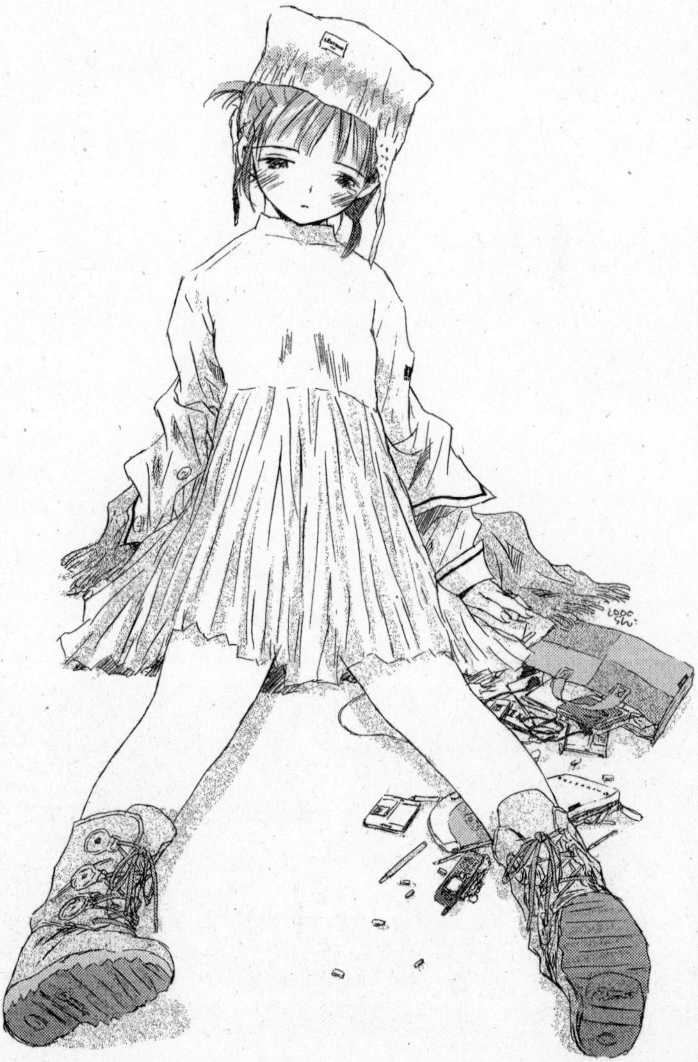

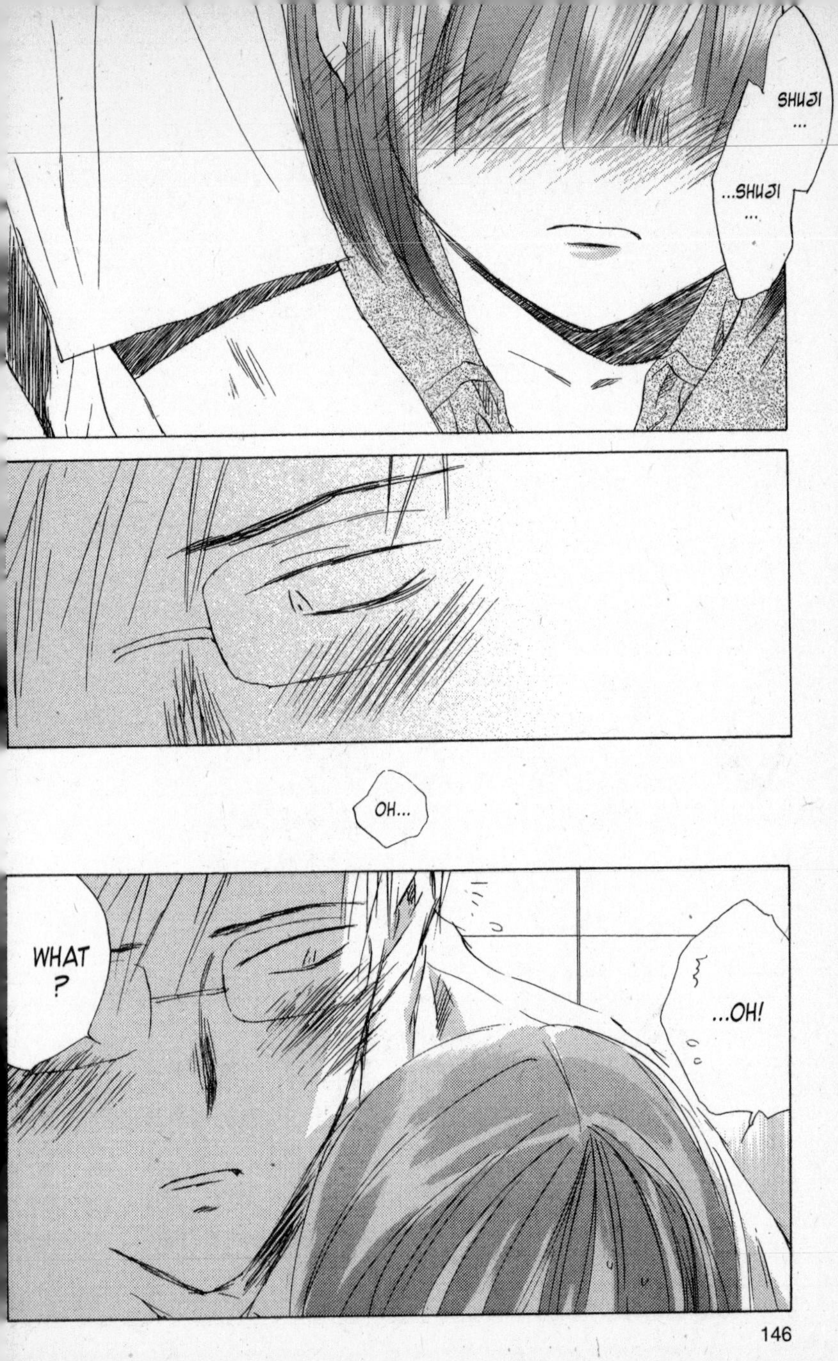
SHUJI ...
...SHUJI ...
OH...
...OH!
WHAT ?

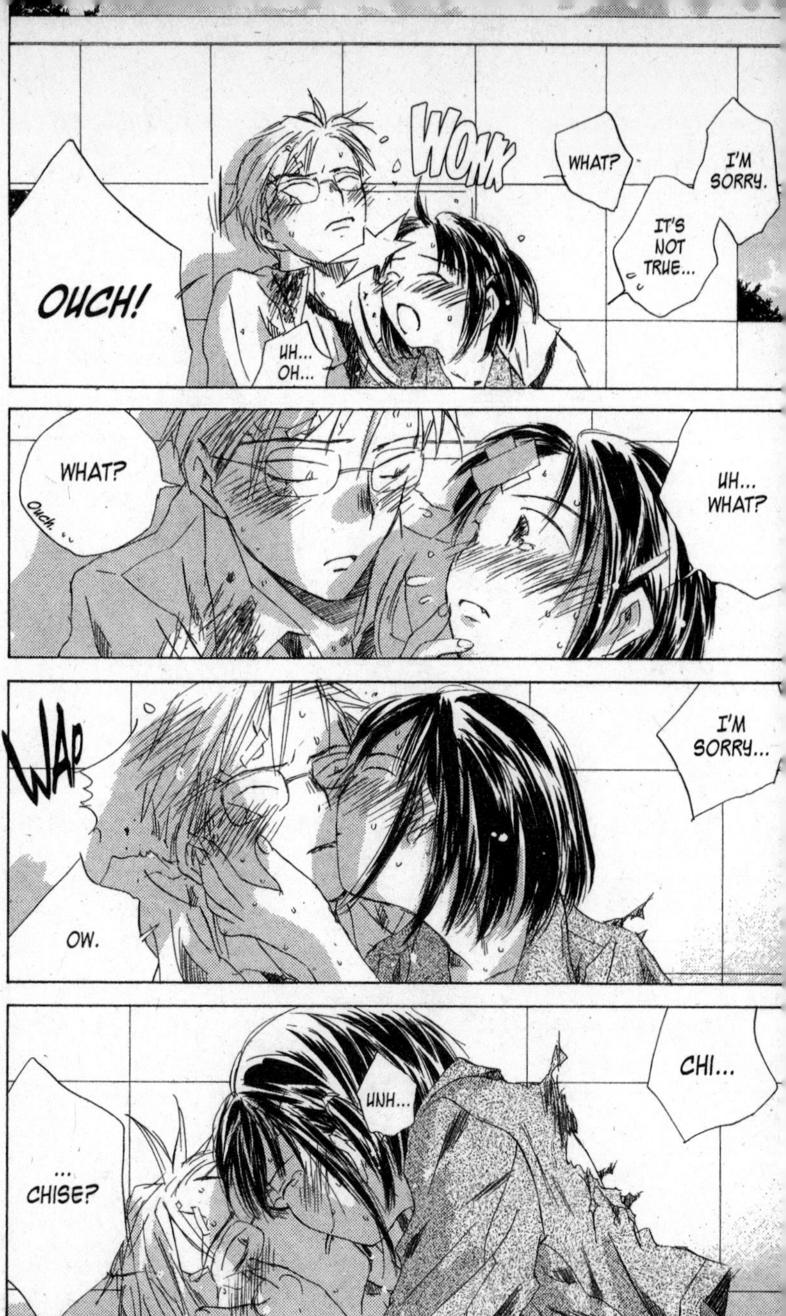
I'M SORRY.
IT'S NOT TRUE...
WHAT?
WONK
OUCH!
UH... OH...
UH... WHAT?
WHAT?
Ouch.
I'M SORRY...
WAP
OW.
CHI...
UNH...
... CHISE?

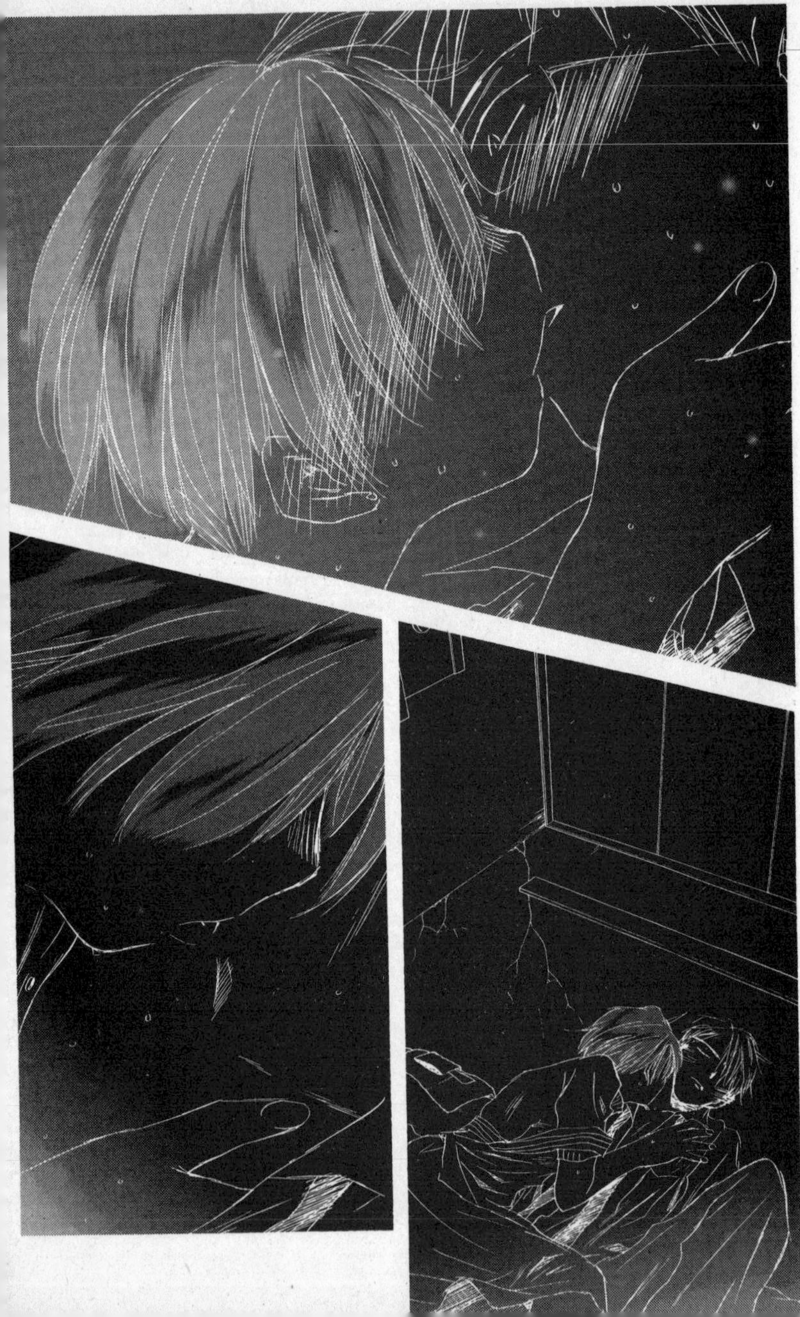

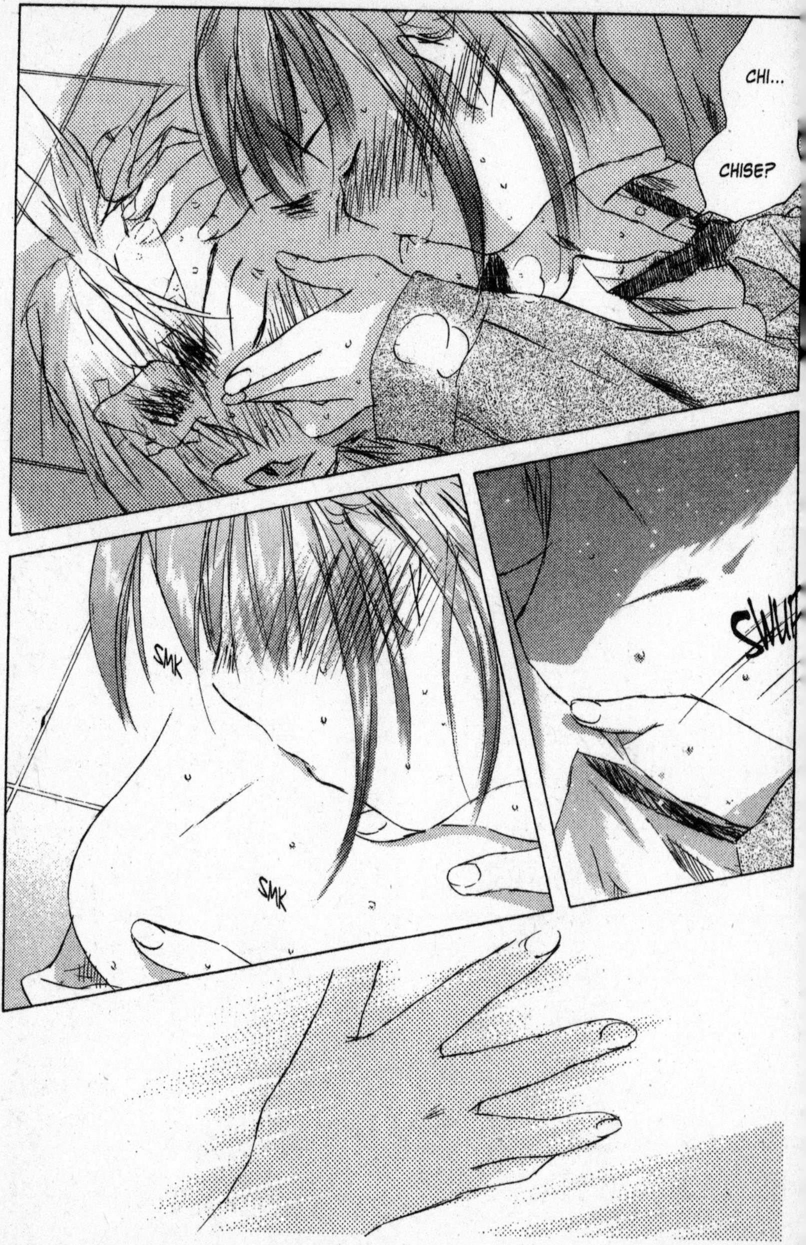
CHI...
CHISE?
SWU
SMK
SMK

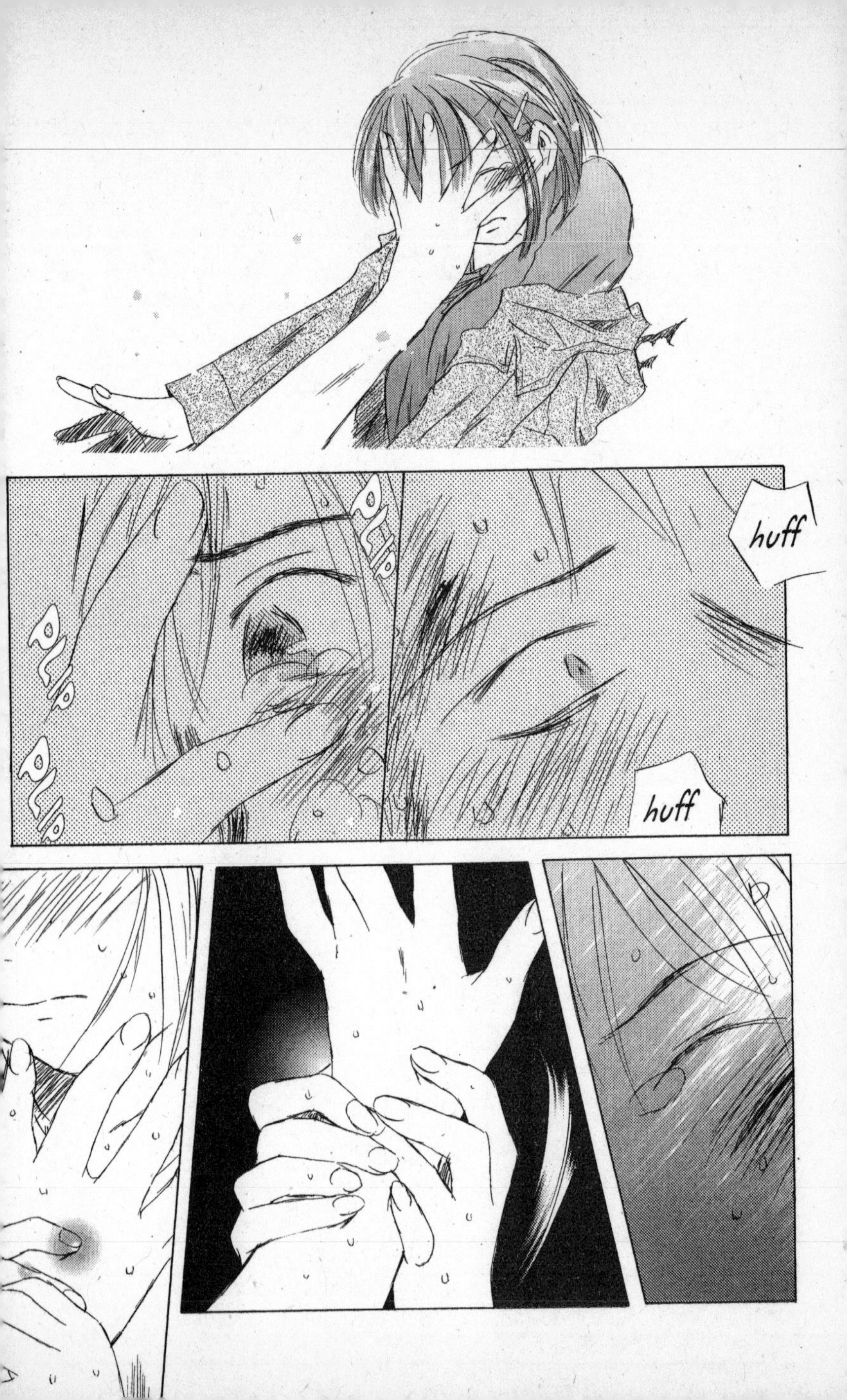
huff
huff
PLIP
PLIP
PLIP
PLIP

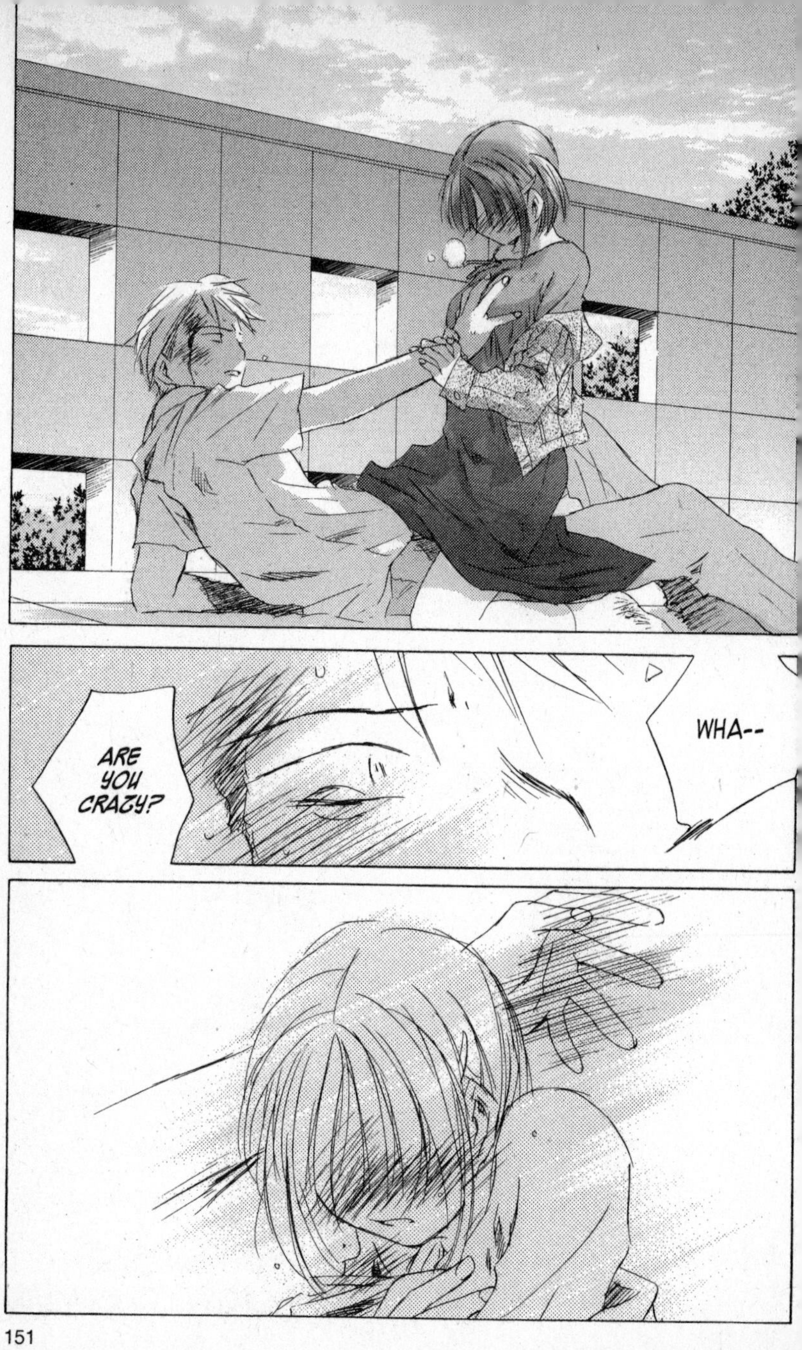
WHA--
ARE YOU CRAZY?

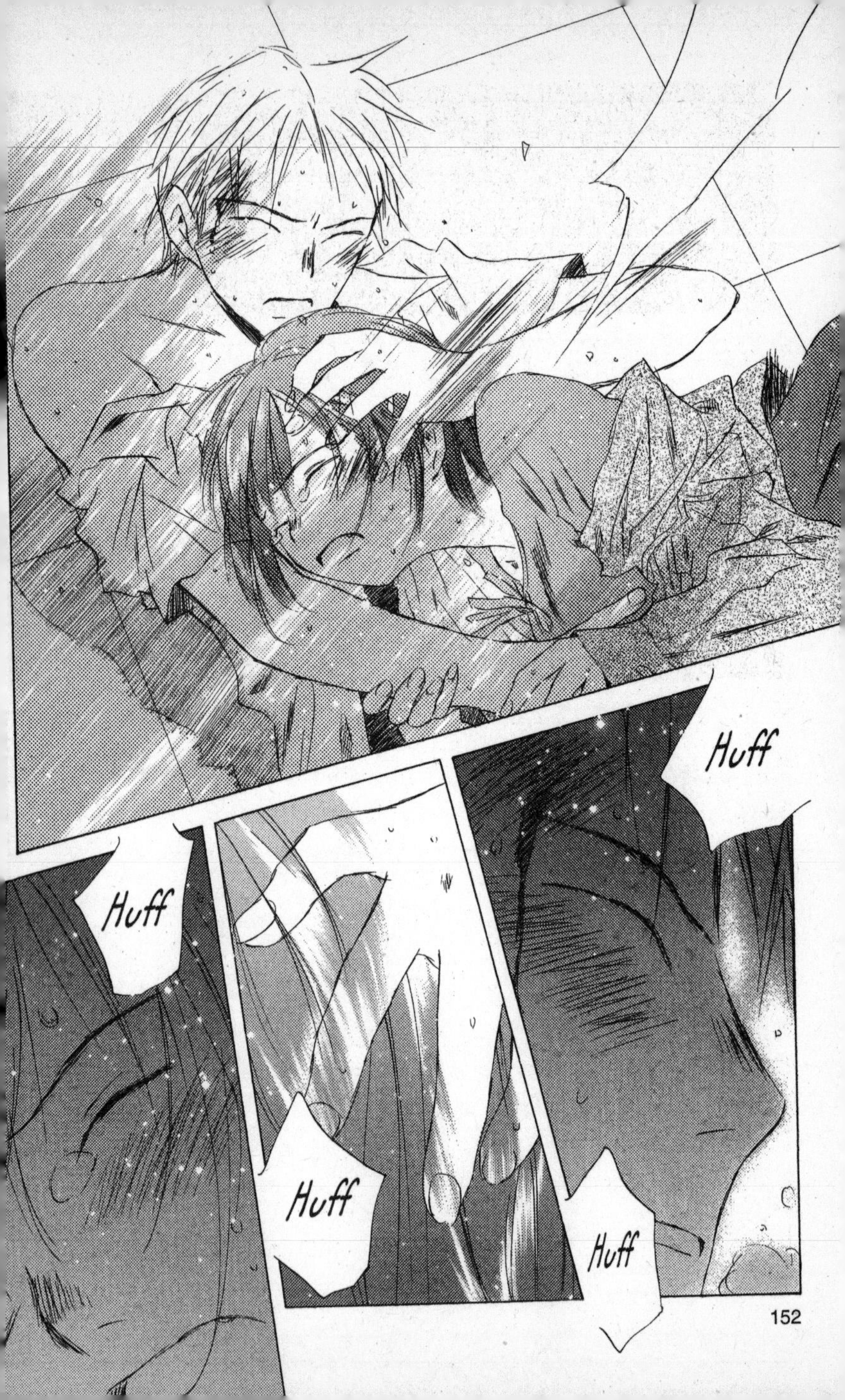
Huff
Huff
Huff
Huff

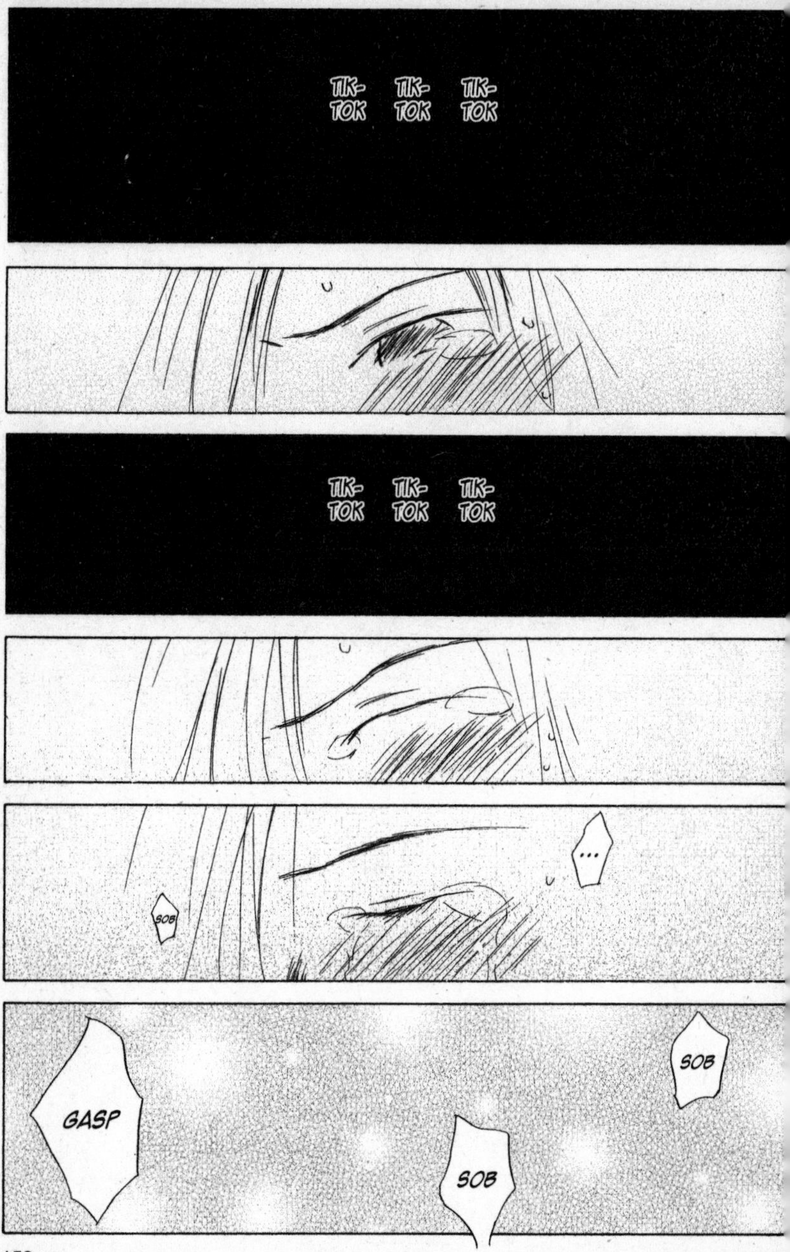

TIK-TOK TIK-TOK TIK-TOK
TIK-TOK TIK-TOK TIK-TOK
...
SOB
SOB
SOB
GASP

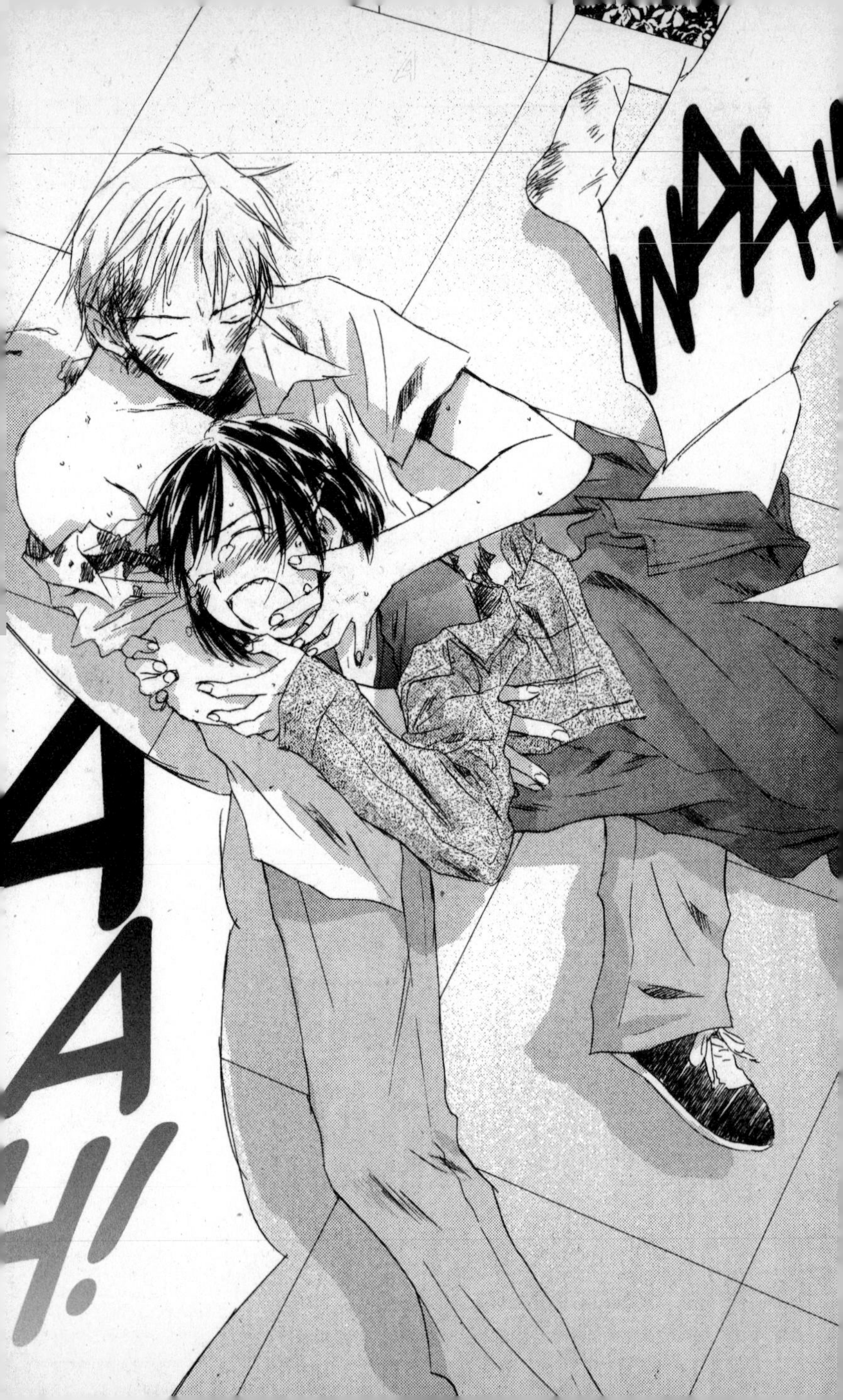
WAAH
AAH!

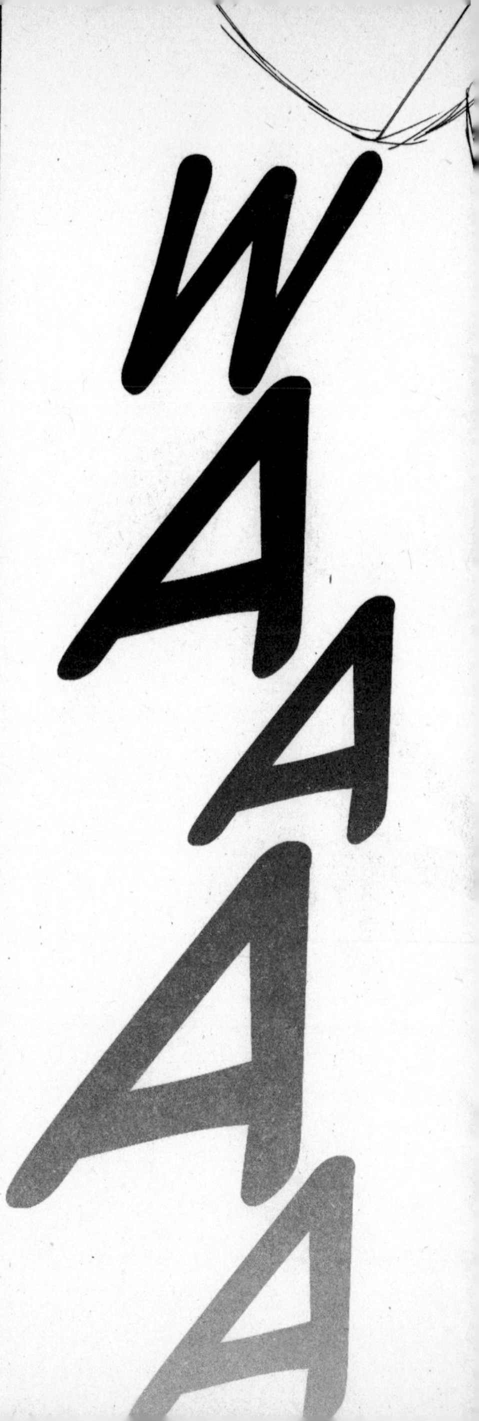
WAAAA

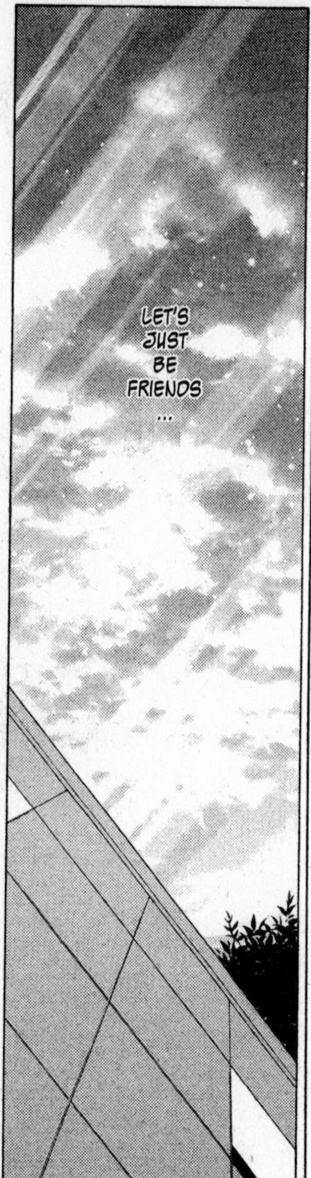
LET'S JUST BE FRIENDS ...

SHUJI, LET'S JUST BE FRIENDS...

...LIKE WE WERE BEFORE.

LET'S GO BACK TO BEFORE WE WERE BOY-FRIEND AND GIRL-FRIEND.

IF WE HADN'T STARTED GOING OUT, WE WOULDN'T HURT LIKE THIS.

I WOULDN'T HAVE HAD TO FEEL THIS PAIN!

I DON'T WANT TO LEARN TO DIS-TRUST PEOPLE.

I DON'T WANT TO [LE]ARN WHAT [A]N AWFUL PERSON [I] CAN BE [W]HEN I'M [I]N LOVE.

I DON'T WANT TO LEARN WHAT PAIN IS.

LET'S GO BACK TO THE WAY WE WERE BEFORE WE STARTED DATING.

THEN ...

...I CAN ADORE YOU FROM AFAR.

LET'S JUST BE FRIENDS.

IT'LL BE AWKWARD WHEN WE SEE EACH OTHER AT SCHOOL, BUT WE'LL GET USED TO IT.

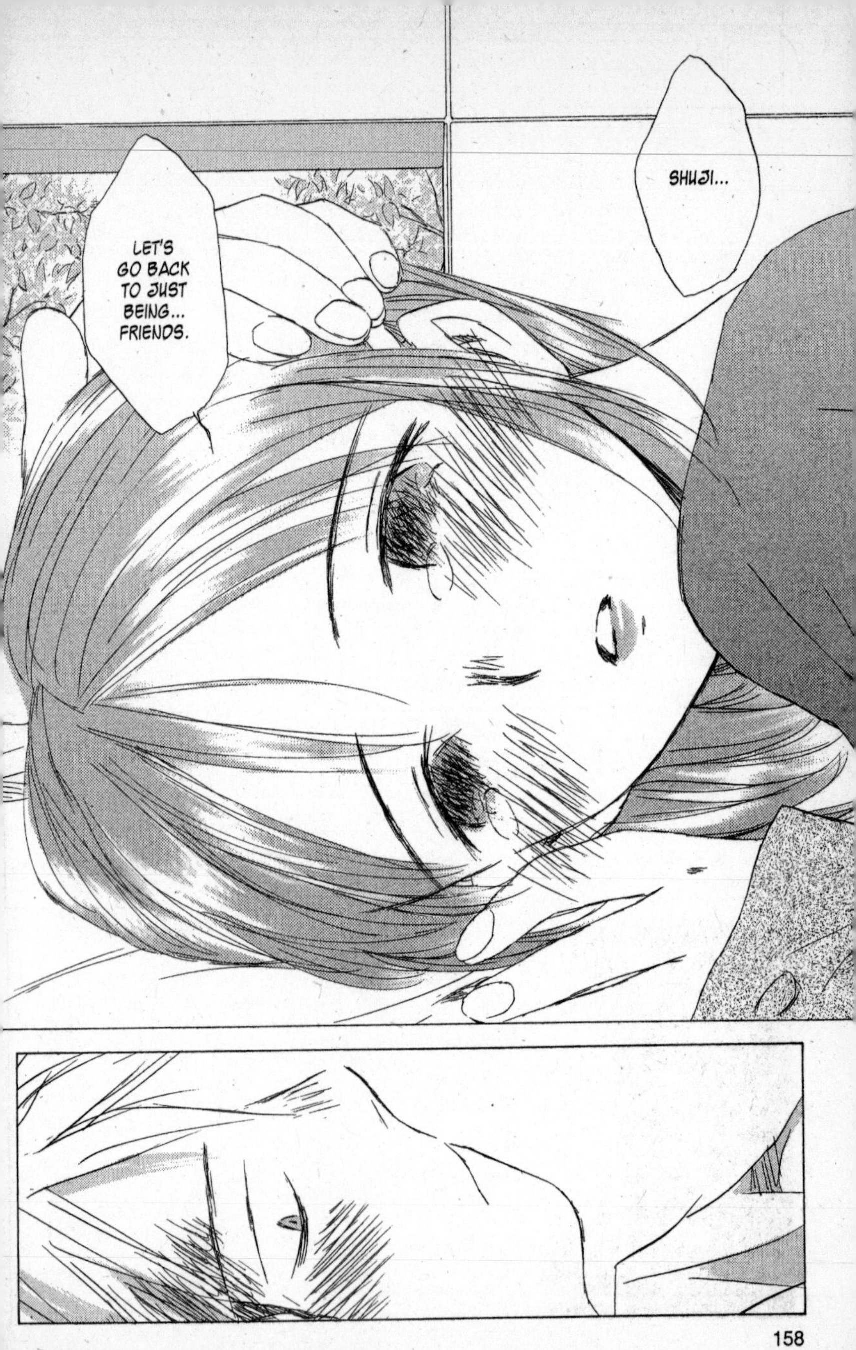
SHUJI...
LET'S GO BACK TO JUST BEING... FRIENDS.

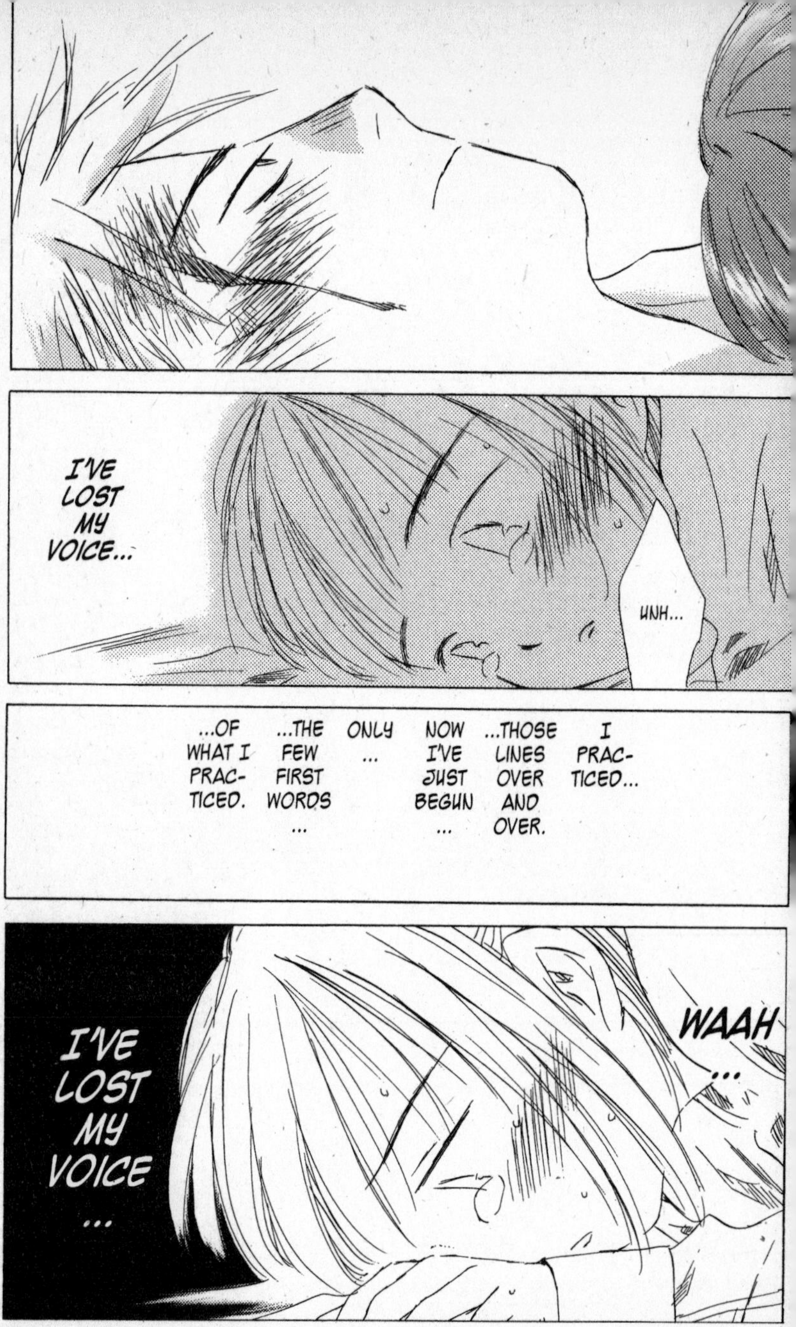
UNH...
I'VE LOST MY VOICE...
I PRACTICED...
...THOSE LINES OVER AND OVER.
NOW I'VE JUST BEGUN...
ONLY...
...THE FEW FIRST WORDS...
...OF WHAT I PRACTICED.
WAAH...
I'VE LOST MY VOICE...

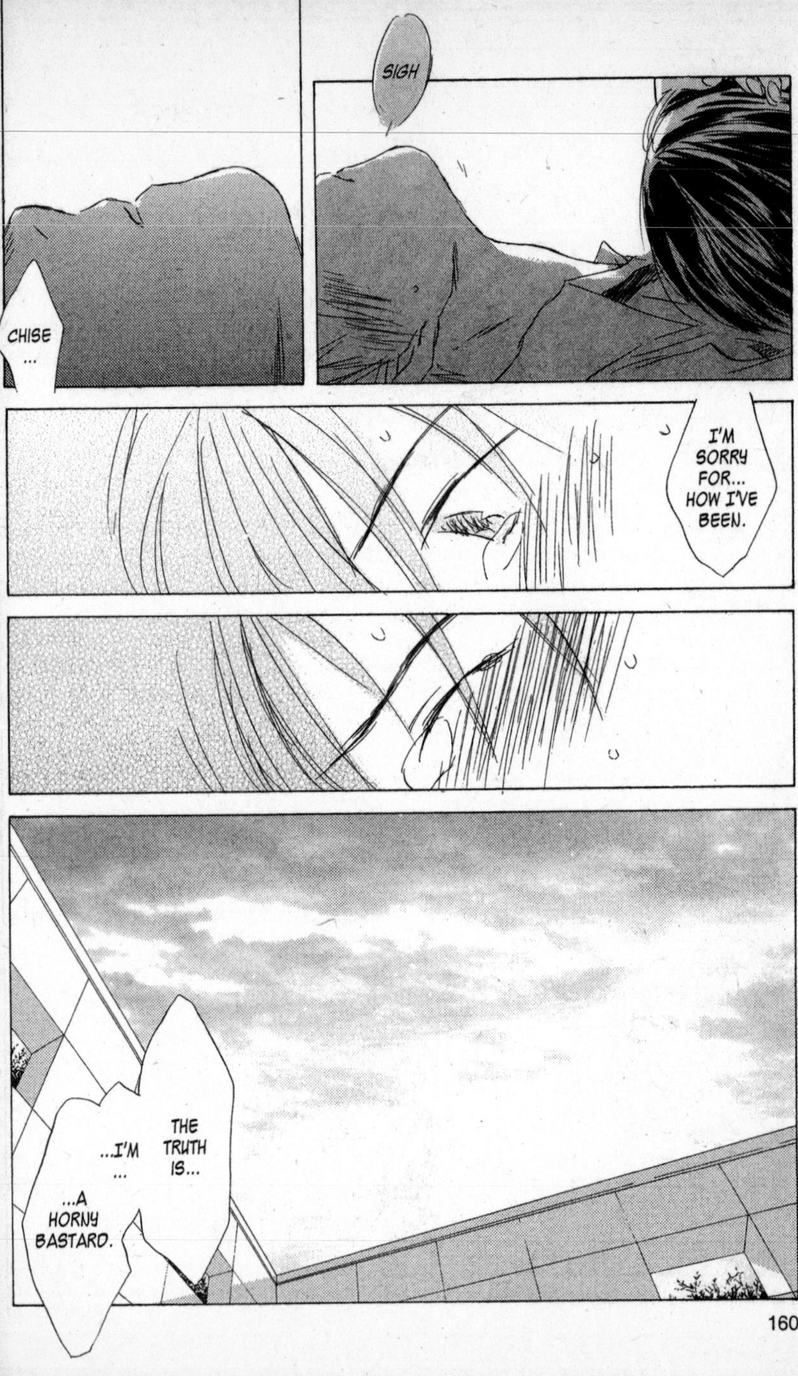
SIGH
CHISE ...
I'M SORRY FOR... HOW I'VE BEEN.
THE TRUTH IS...
...I'M ...
...A HORNY BASTARD.

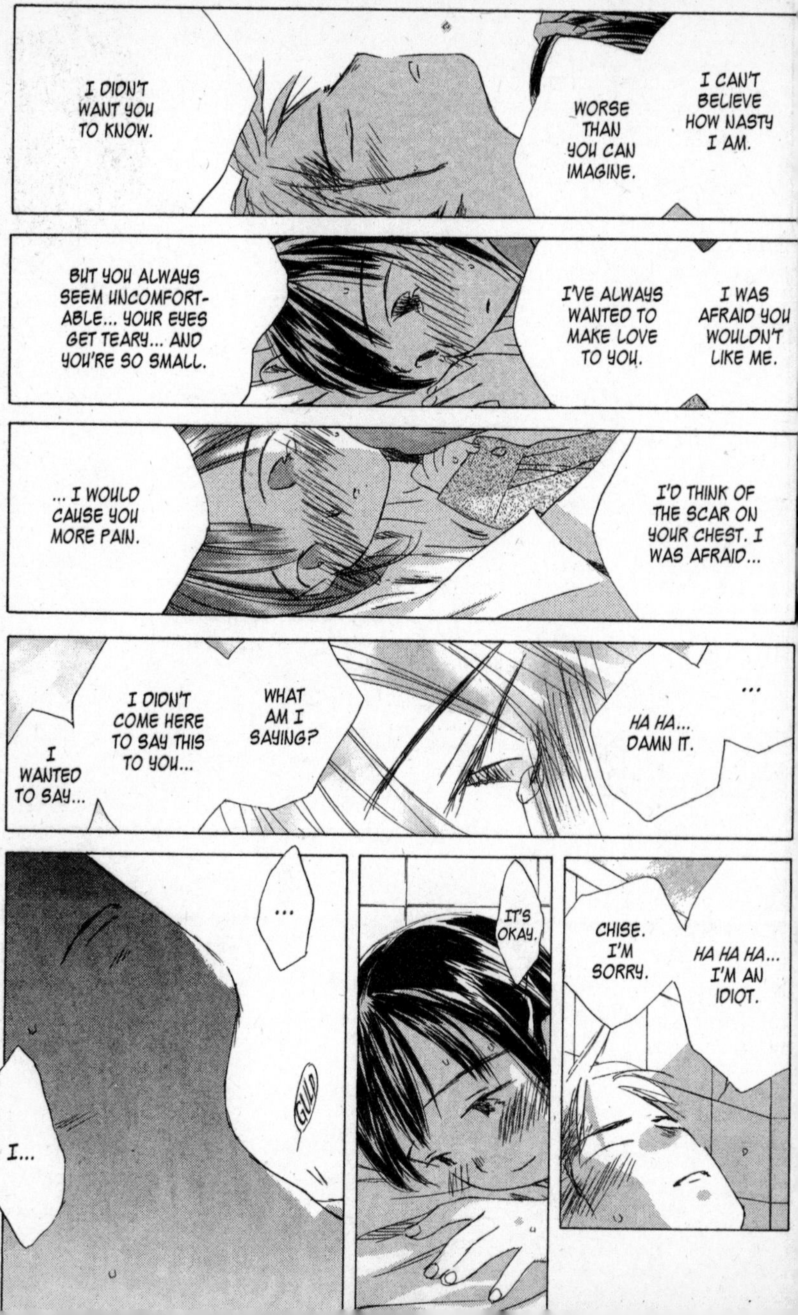
I CAN'T BELIEVE HOW NASTY I AM.
WORSE THAN YOU CAN IMAGINE.
I DIDN'T WANT YOU TO KNOW.
I WAS AFRAID YOU WOULDN'T LIKE ME.
I'VE ALWAYS WANTED TO MAKE LOVE TO YOU.
BUT YOU ALWAYS SEEM UNCOMFORT-ABLE... YOUR EYES GET TEARY... AND YOU'RE SO SMALL.
I'D THINK OF THE SCAR ON YOUR CHEST. I WAS AFRAID...
... I WOULD CAUSE YOU MORE PAIN.
...
HA HA... DAMN IT.
WHAT AM I SAYING?
I DIDN'T COME HERE TO SAY THIS TO YOU...
I WANTED TO SAY...
HA HA HA... I'M AN IDIOT.
CHISE. I'M SORRY.
IT'S OKAY.
...
GULP
I...

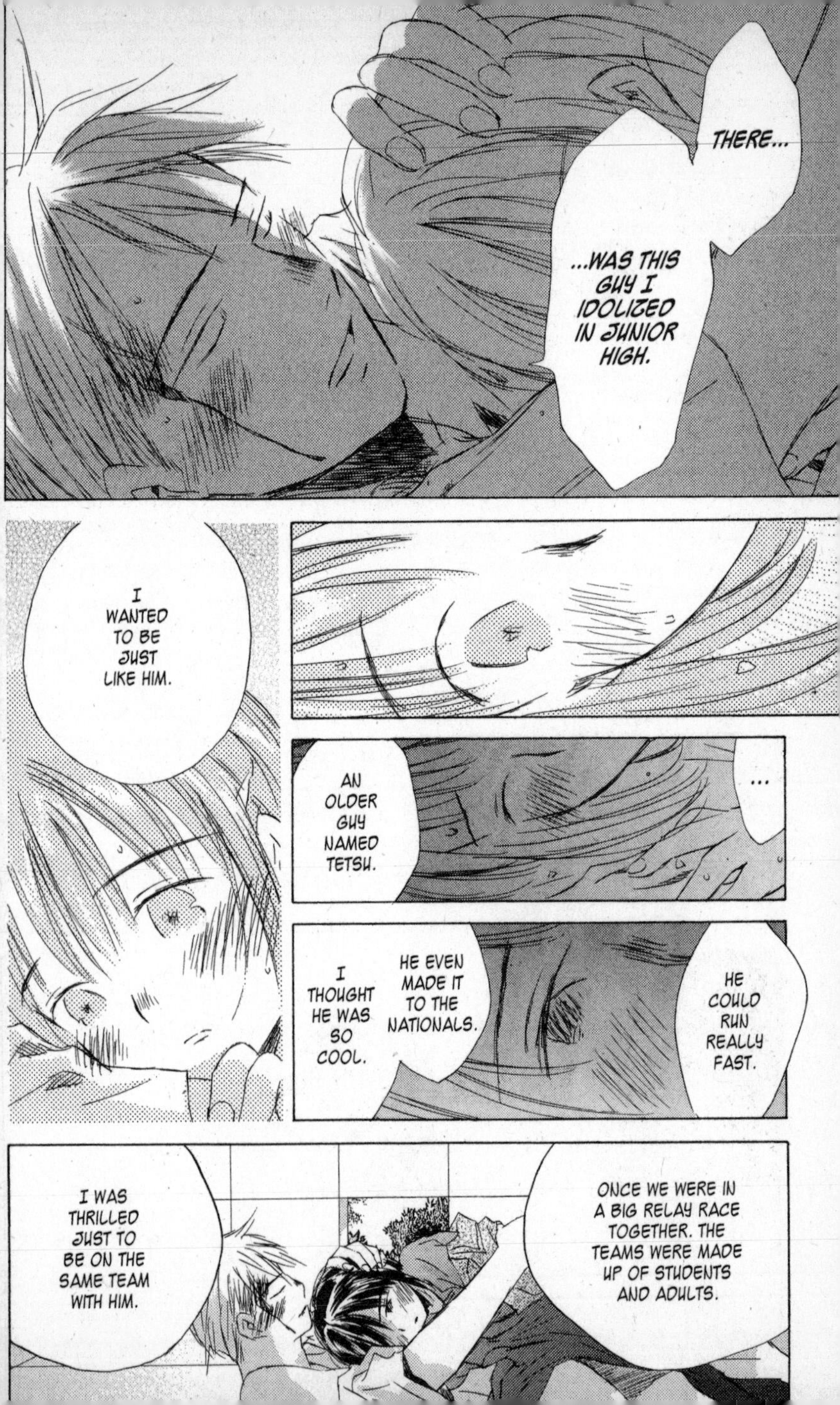
THERE...
...WAS THIS GUY I IDOLIZED IN JUNIOR HIGH.
...
AN OLDER GUY NAMED TETSU.
HE COULD RUN REALLY FAST.
HE EVEN MADE IT TO THE NATIONALS.
I THOUGHT HE WAS SO COOL.
I WANTED TO BE JUST LIKE HIM.
ONCE WE WERE IN A BIG RELAY RACE TOGETHER. THE TEAMS WERE MADE UP OF STUDENTS AND ADULTS.
I WAS THRILLED JUST TO BE ON THE SAME TEAM WITH HIM.

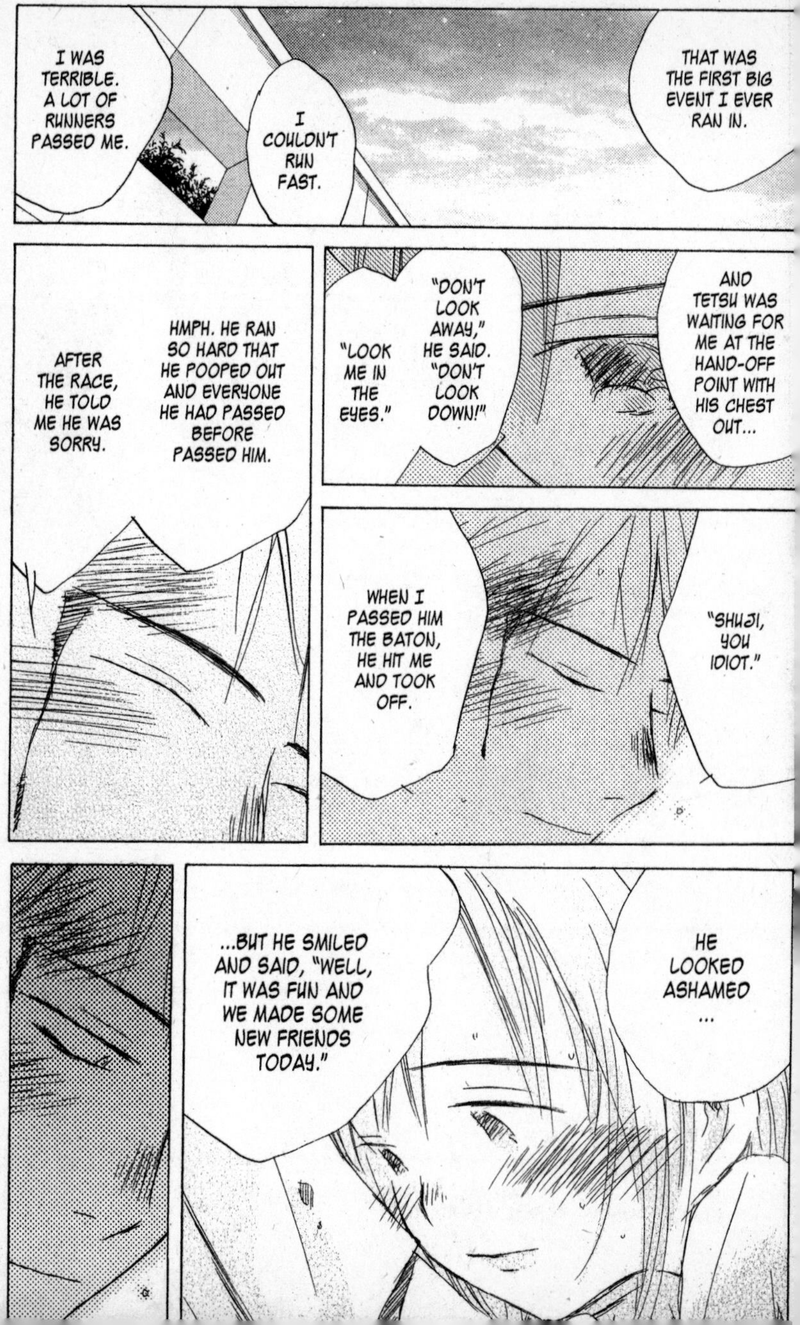
THAT WAS THE FIRST BIG EVENT I EVER RAN IN.
I COULDN'T RUN FAST.
I WAS TERRIBLE. A LOT OF RUNNERS PASSED ME.
AND TETSU WAS WAITING FOR ME AT THE HAND-OFF POINT WITH HIS CHEST OUT...
"DON'T LOOK AWAY," HE SAID. "DON'T LOOK DOWN!"
"LOOK ME IN THE EYES."
"SHUJI, YOU IDIOT."
WHEN I PASSED HIM THE BATON, HE HIT ME AND TOOK OFF.
HMPH. HE RAN SO HARD THAT HE POOPED OUT AND EVERYONE HE HAD PASSED BEFORE PASSED HIM.
AFTER THE RACE, HE TOLD ME HE WAS SORRY.
HE LOOKED ASHAMED ...
...BUT HE SMILED AND SAID, "WELL, IT WAS FUN AND WE MADE SOME NEW FRIENDS TODAY."

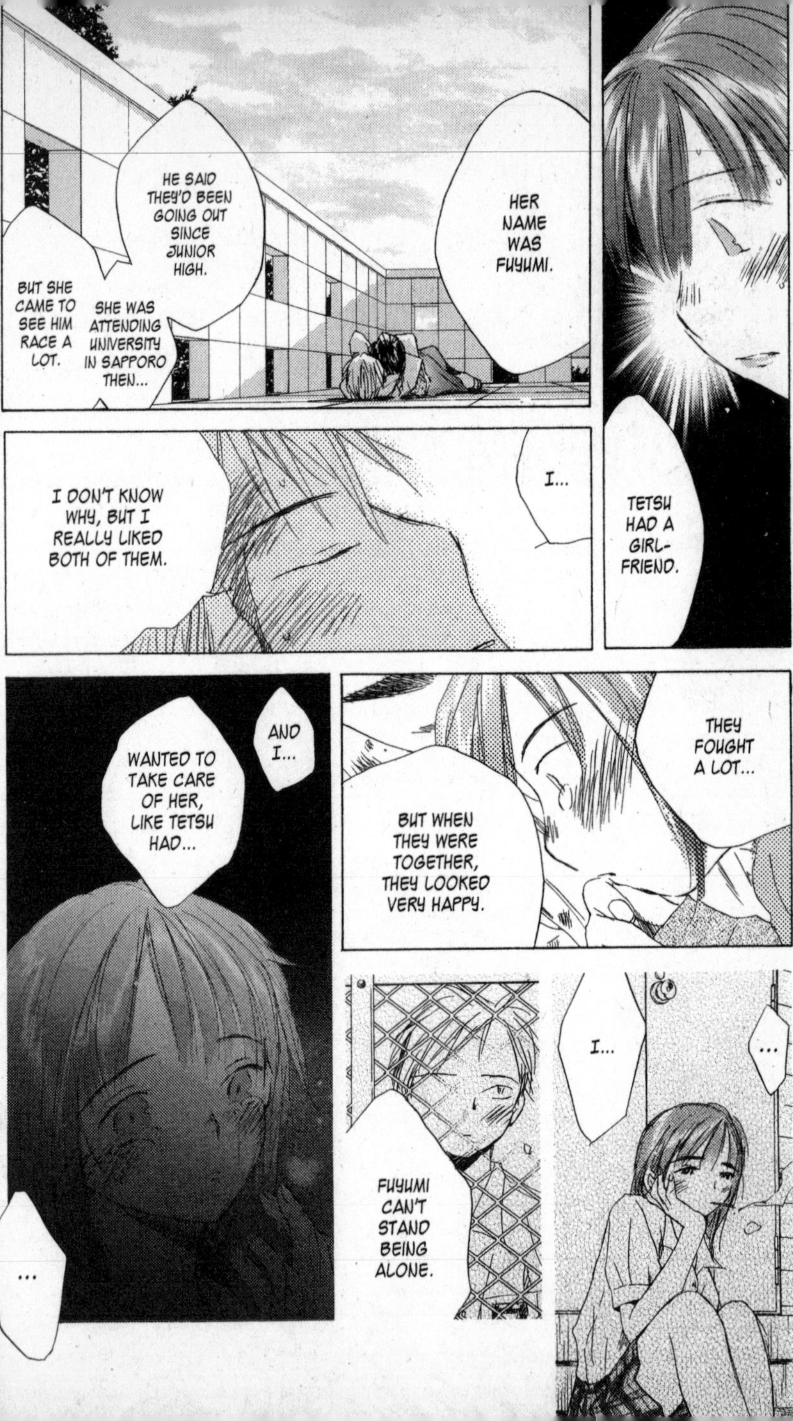
TETSU HAD A GIRL-FRIEND.
HER NAME WAS FUYUMI.
HE SAID THEY'D BEEN GOING OUT SINCE JUNIOR HIGH.
SHE WAS ATTENDING UNIVERSITY IN SAPPORO THEN...
BUT SHE CAME TO SEE HIM RACE A LOT.
I...
I DON'T KNOW WHY, BUT I REALLY LIKED BOTH OF THEM.
THEY FOUGHT A LOT...
BUT WHEN THEY WERE TOGETHER, THEY LOOKED VERY HAPPY.
...
I...
FUYUMI CAN'T STAND BEING ALONE.
AND I...
WANTED TO TAKE CARE OF HER, LIKE TETSU HAD...
...

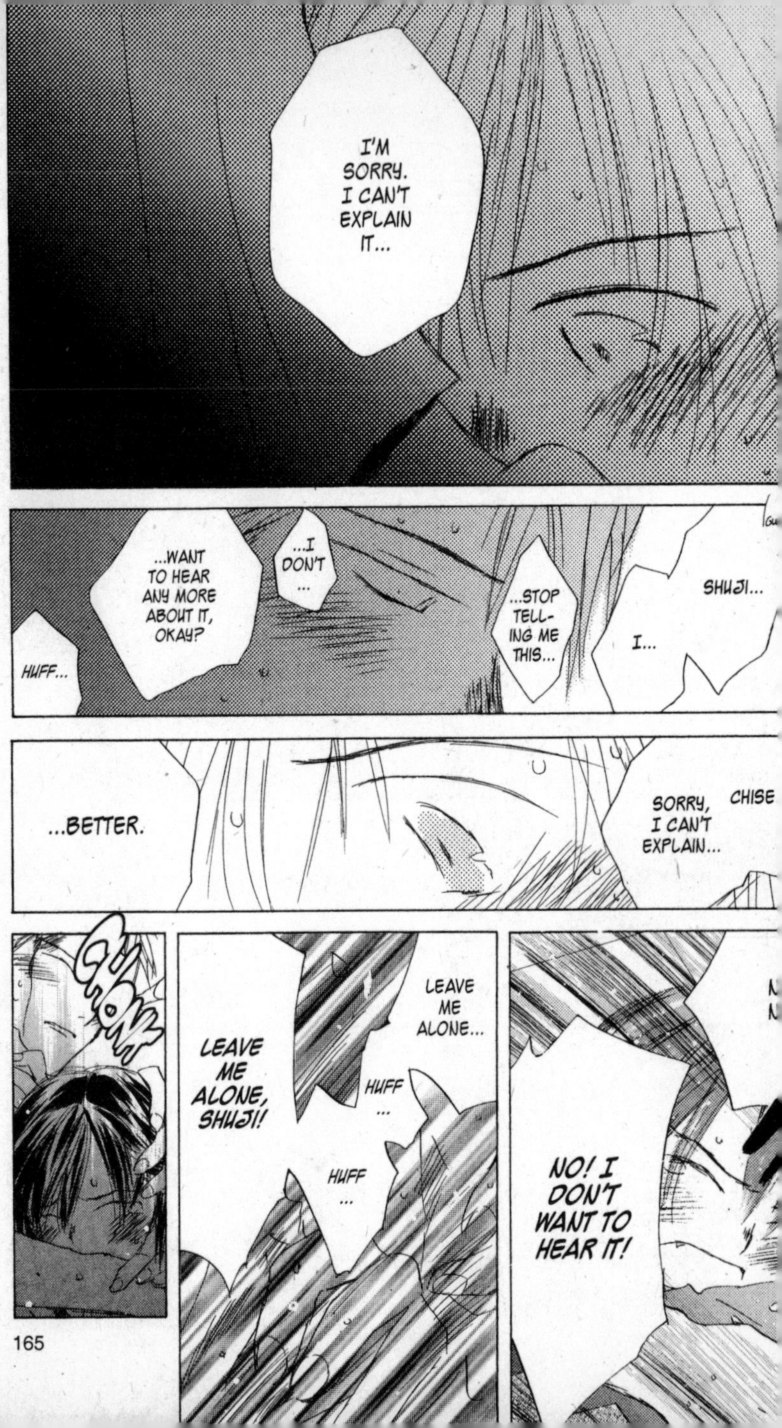
I'M SORRY. I CAN'T EXPLAIN IT...
SHUJI...
I...
...STOP TELL-ING ME THIS...
...I DON'T ...
...WANT TO HEAR ANY MORE ABOUT IT, OKAY?
HUFF...
CHISE
SORRY, I CAN'T EXPLAIN...
...BETTER.
NO! I DON'T WANT TO HEAR IT!
LEAVE ME ALONE...
HUFF ...
HUFF ...
LEAVE ME ALONE, SHUJI!
CHOMP

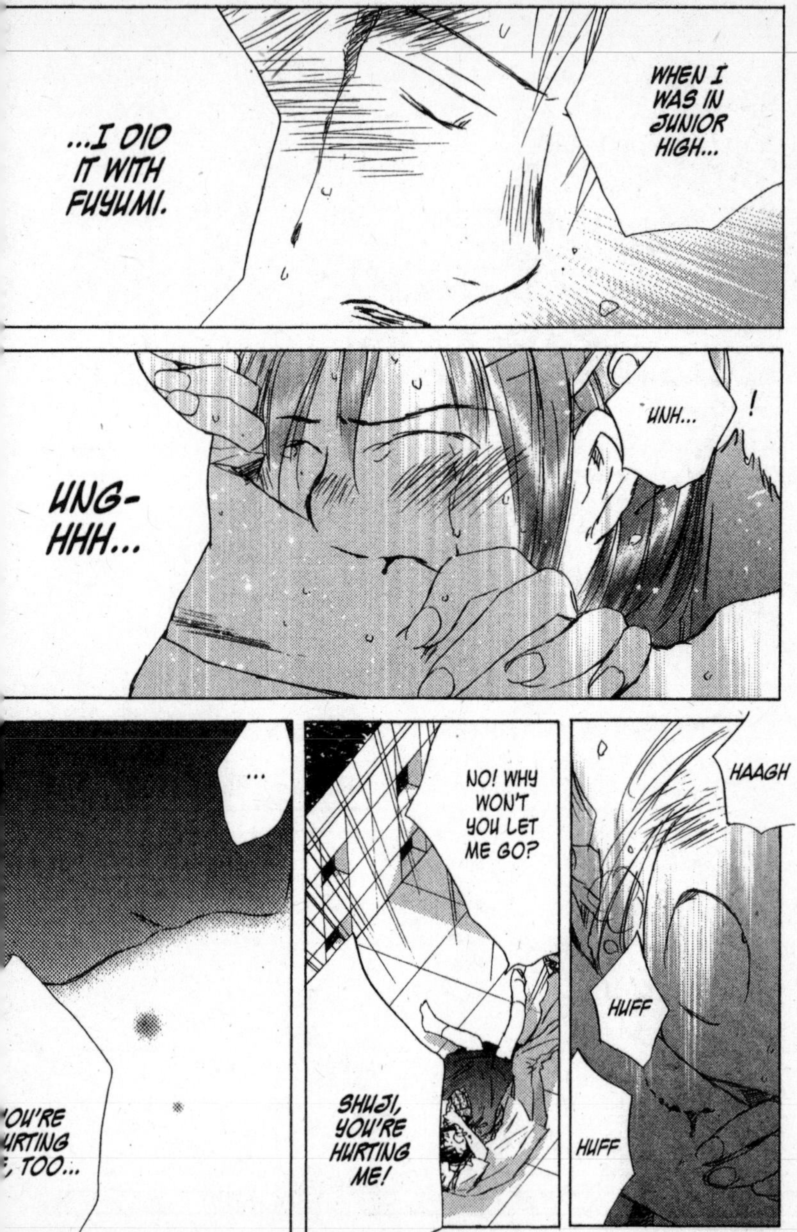
WHEN I WAS IN JUNIOR HIGH...
...I DID IT WITH FUYUMI.
UNH...
!
UNG-HHH...
HAAGH
HUFF
HUFF
NO! WHY WON'T YOU LET ME GO?
SHUJI, YOU'RE HURTING ME!
...
OU'RE URTING , TOO...

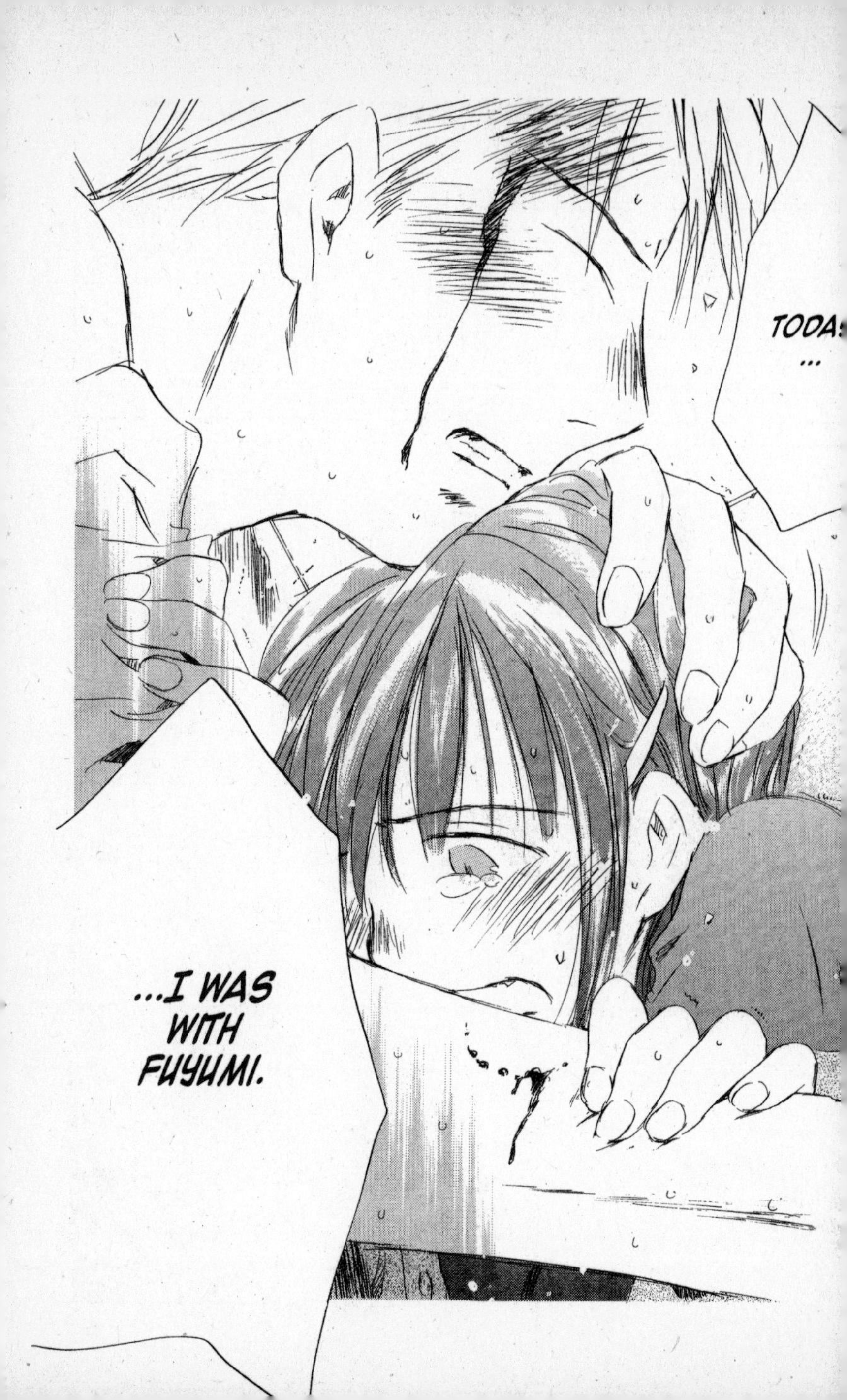
TODA!
...
...I WAS WITH FUYUMI.

I
WAS
SCARED.

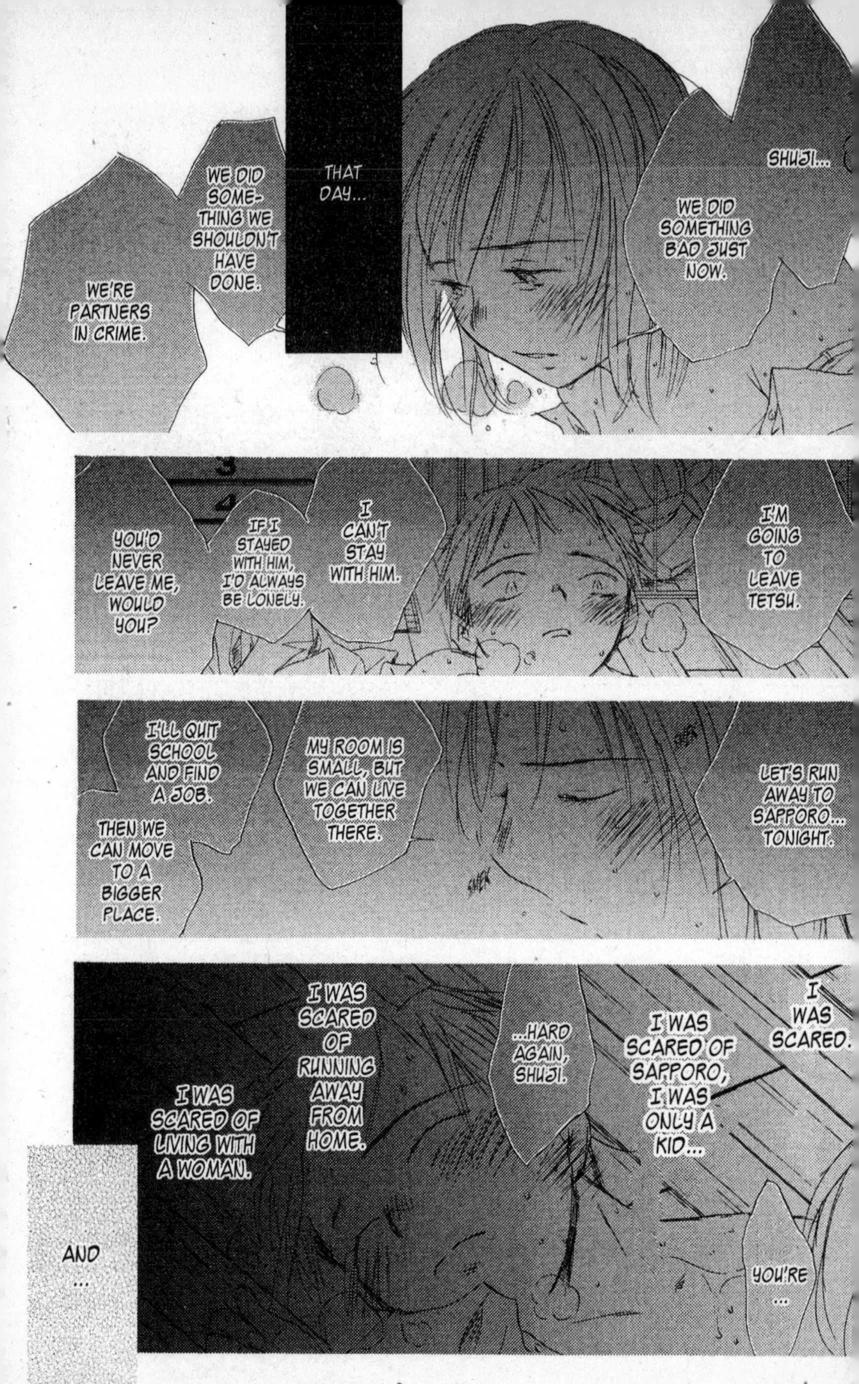
SHUJI...
WE DID SOMETHING BAD JUST NOW.
THAT DAY...
WE DID SOME-THING WE SHOULDN'T HAVE DONE.
WE'RE PARTNERS IN CRIME.
I'M GOING TO LEAVE TETSU.
I CAN'T STAY WITH HIM.
IF I STAYED WITH HIM, I'D ALWAYS BE LONELY.
YOU'D NEVER LEAVE ME, WOULD YOU?
LET'S RUN AWAY TO SAPPORO... TONIGHT.
MY ROOM IS SMALL, BUT WE CAN LIVE TOGETHER THERE.
I'LL QUIT SCHOOL AND FIND A JOB.
THEN WE CAN MOVE TO A BIGGER PLACE.
I WAS SCARED.
I WAS SCARED OF SAPPORO, I WAS ONLY A KID...
YOU'RE ...
...HARD AGAIN, SHUJI.
I WAS SCARED OF RUNNING AWAY FROM HOME.
I WAS SCARED OF LIVING WITH A WOMAN.
AND ...

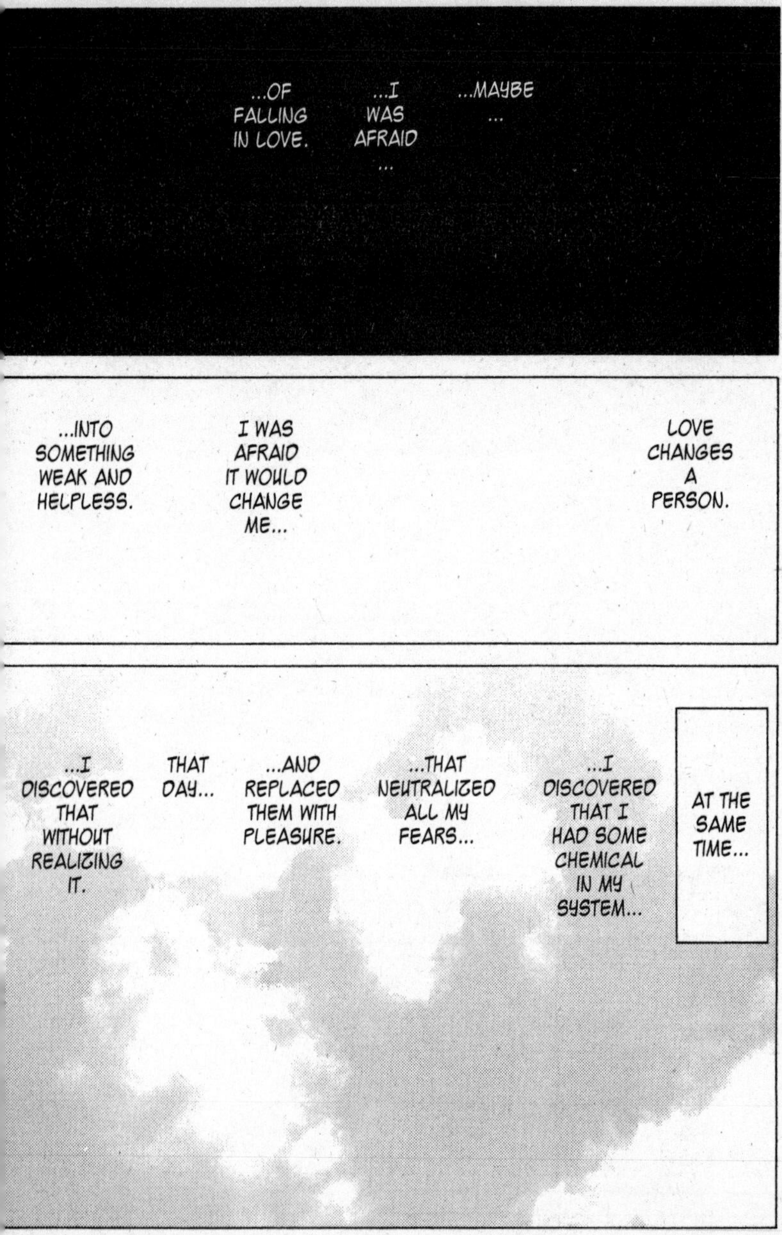

...MAYBE ...
...I WAS AFRAID ...
...OF FALLING IN LOVE.
LOVE CHANGES A PERSON.
I WAS AFRAID IT WOULD CHANGE ME...
...INTO SOMETHING WEAK AND HELPLESS.
AT THE SAME TIME...
...I DISCOVERED THAT I HAD SOME CHEMICAL IN MY SYSTEM...
...THAT NEUTRALIZED ALL MY FEARS...
...AND REPLACED THEM WITH PLEASURE.
THAT DAY...
...I DISCOVERED THAT WITHOUT REALIZING IT.

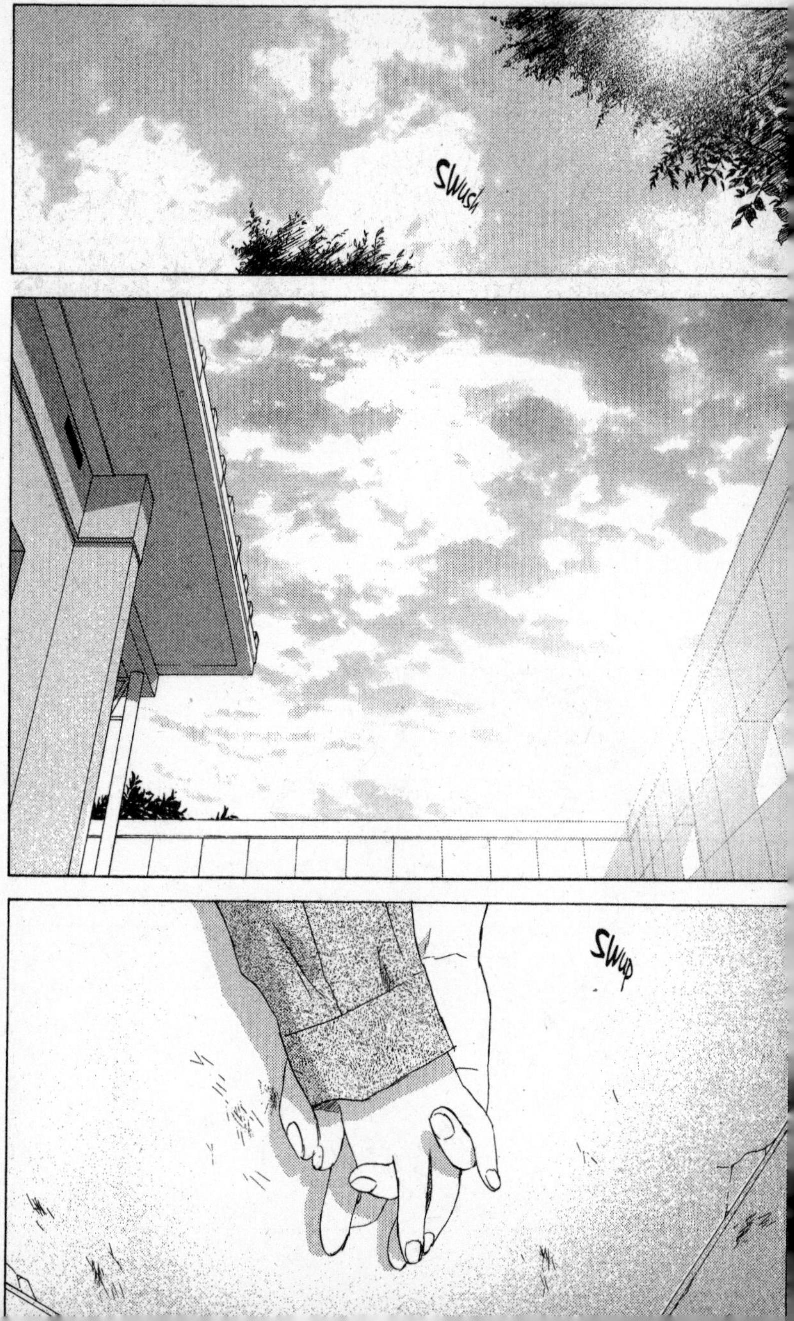
Swush
Swup

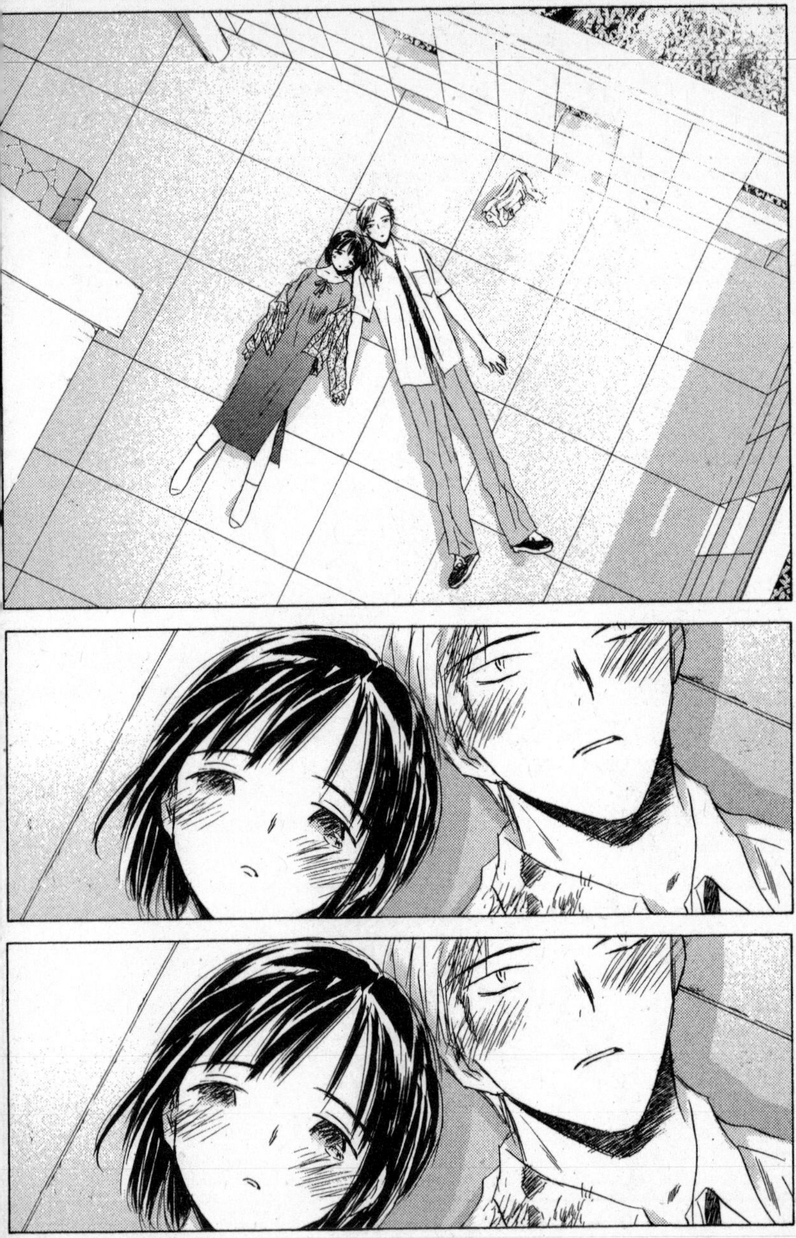

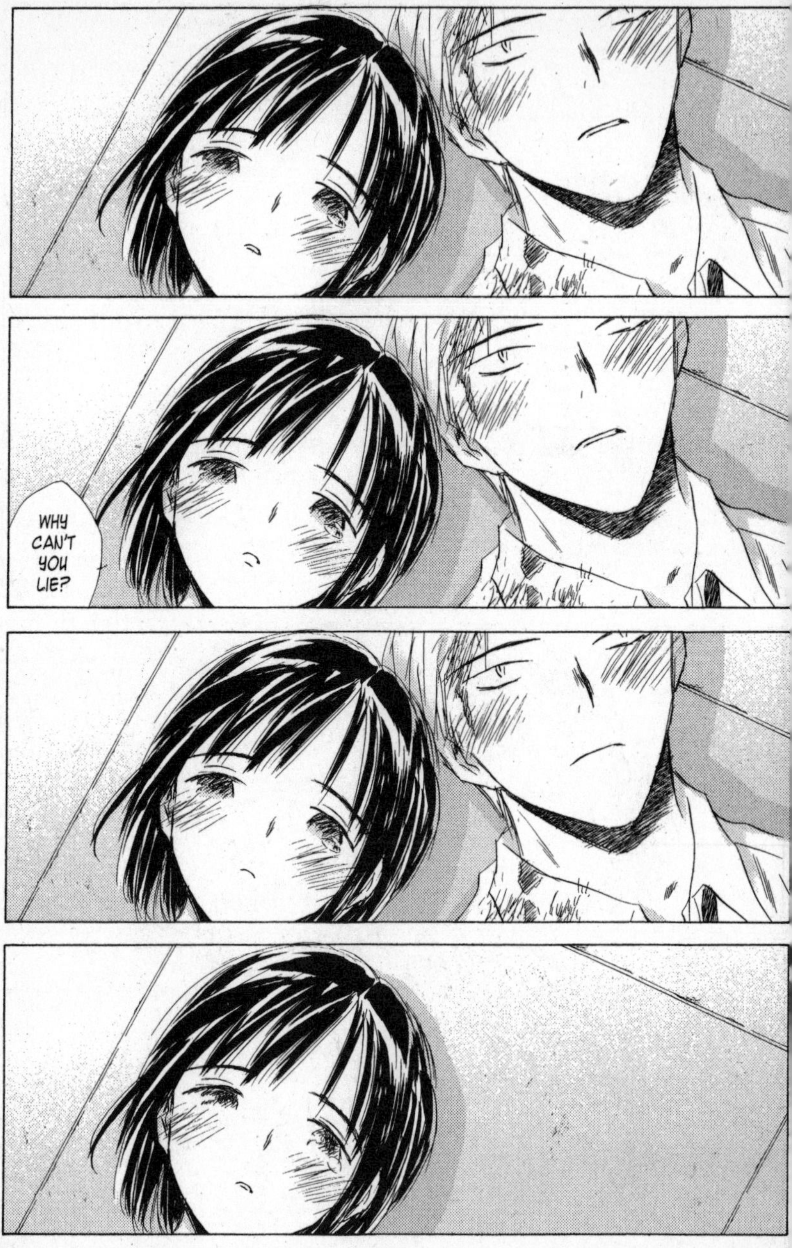
WHY CAN'T YOU LIE?

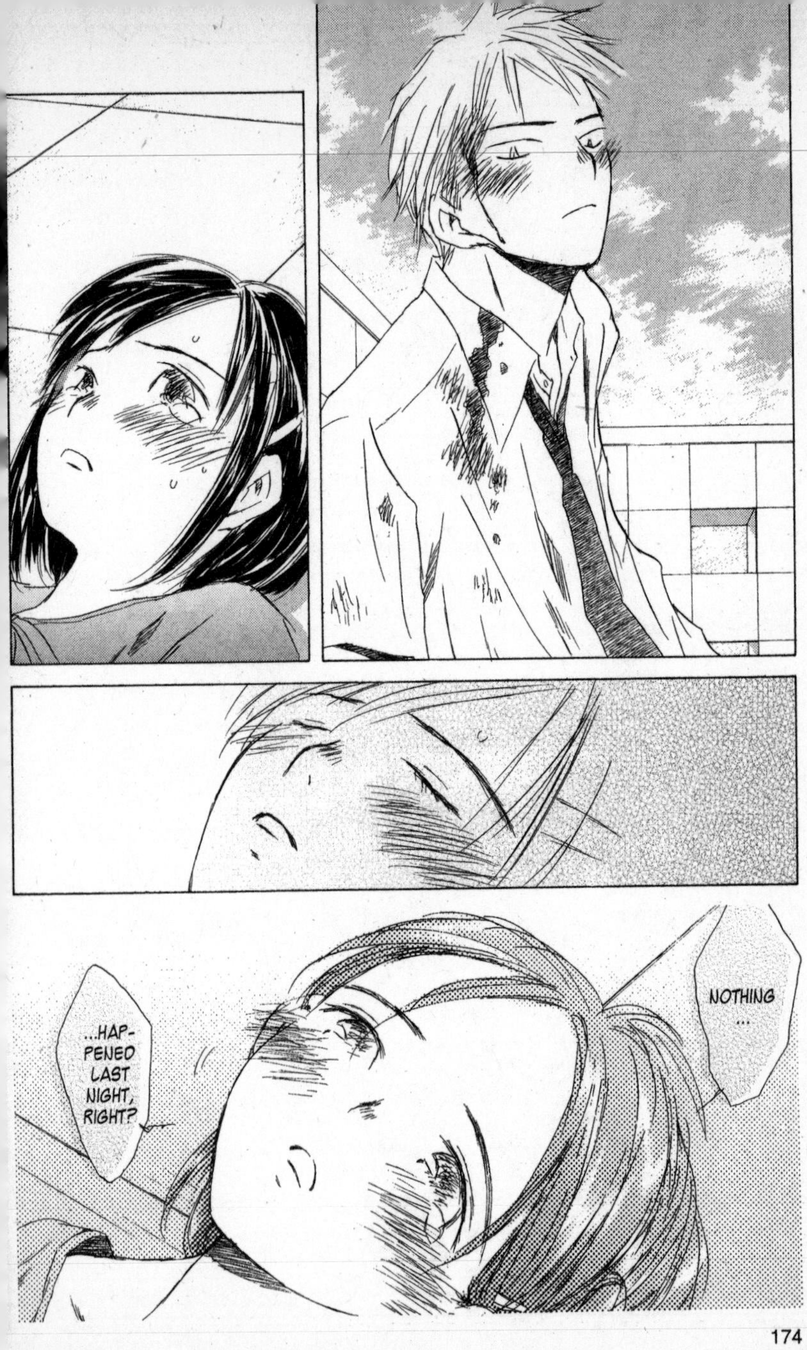
NOTHING ...
...HAP-PENED LAST NIGHT, RIGHT?

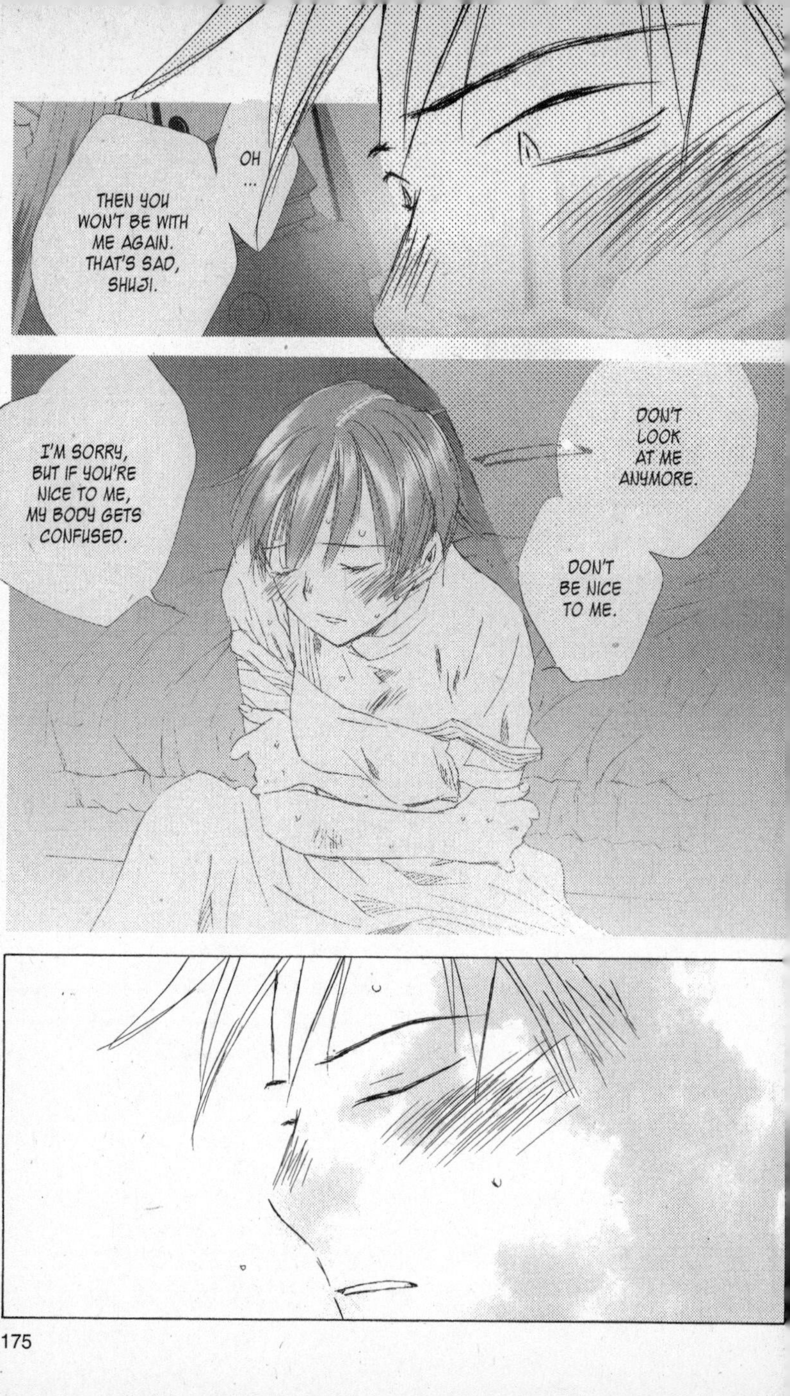
OH ...
THEN YOU WON'T BE WITH ME AGAIN. THAT'S SAD, SHUJI.
DON'T LOOK AT ME ANYMORE.
DON'T BE NICE TO ME.
I'M SORRY, BUT IF YOU'RE NICE TO ME, MY BODY GETS CONFUSED.

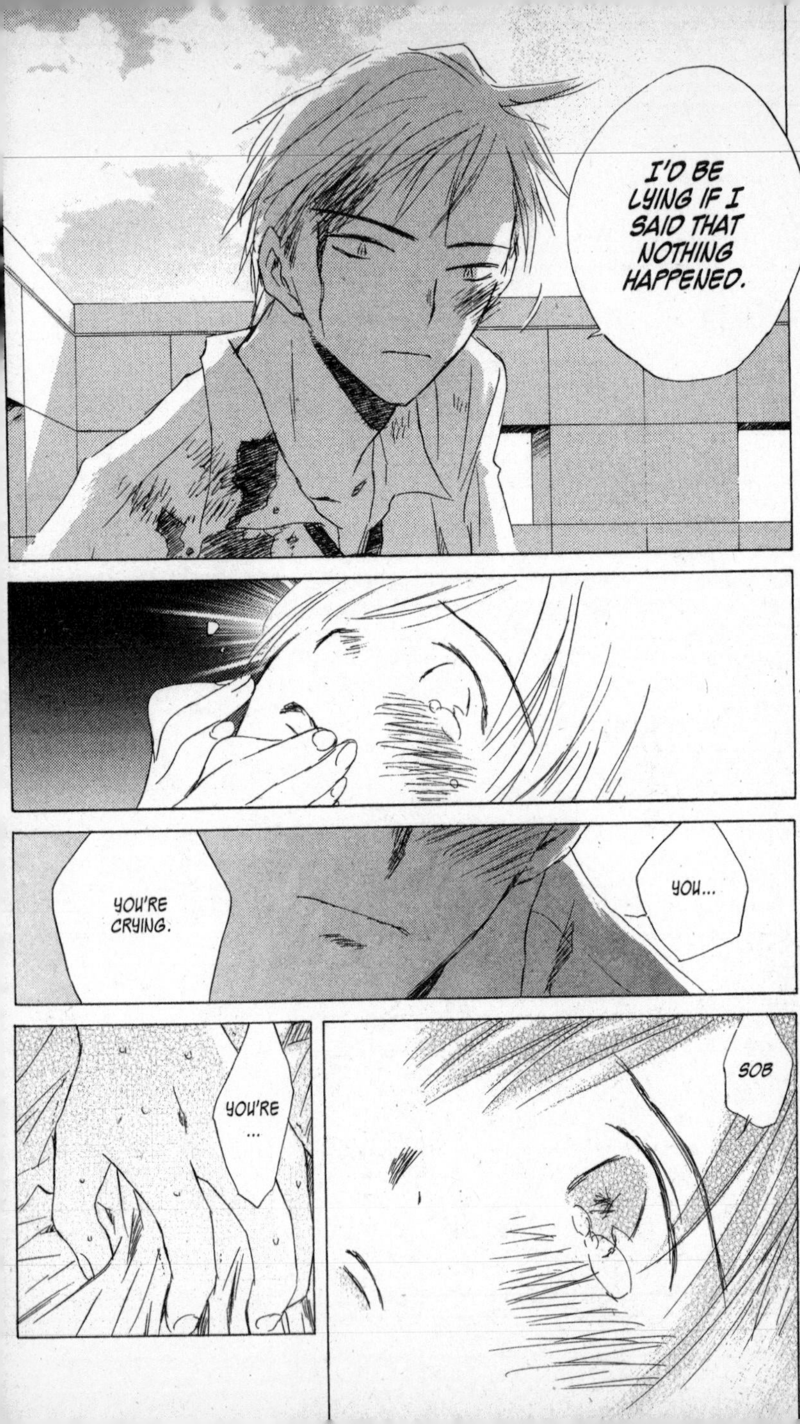
I'D BE LYING IF I SAID THAT NOTHING HAPPENED.
YOU...
YOU'RE CRYING.
SOB
YOU'RE
...

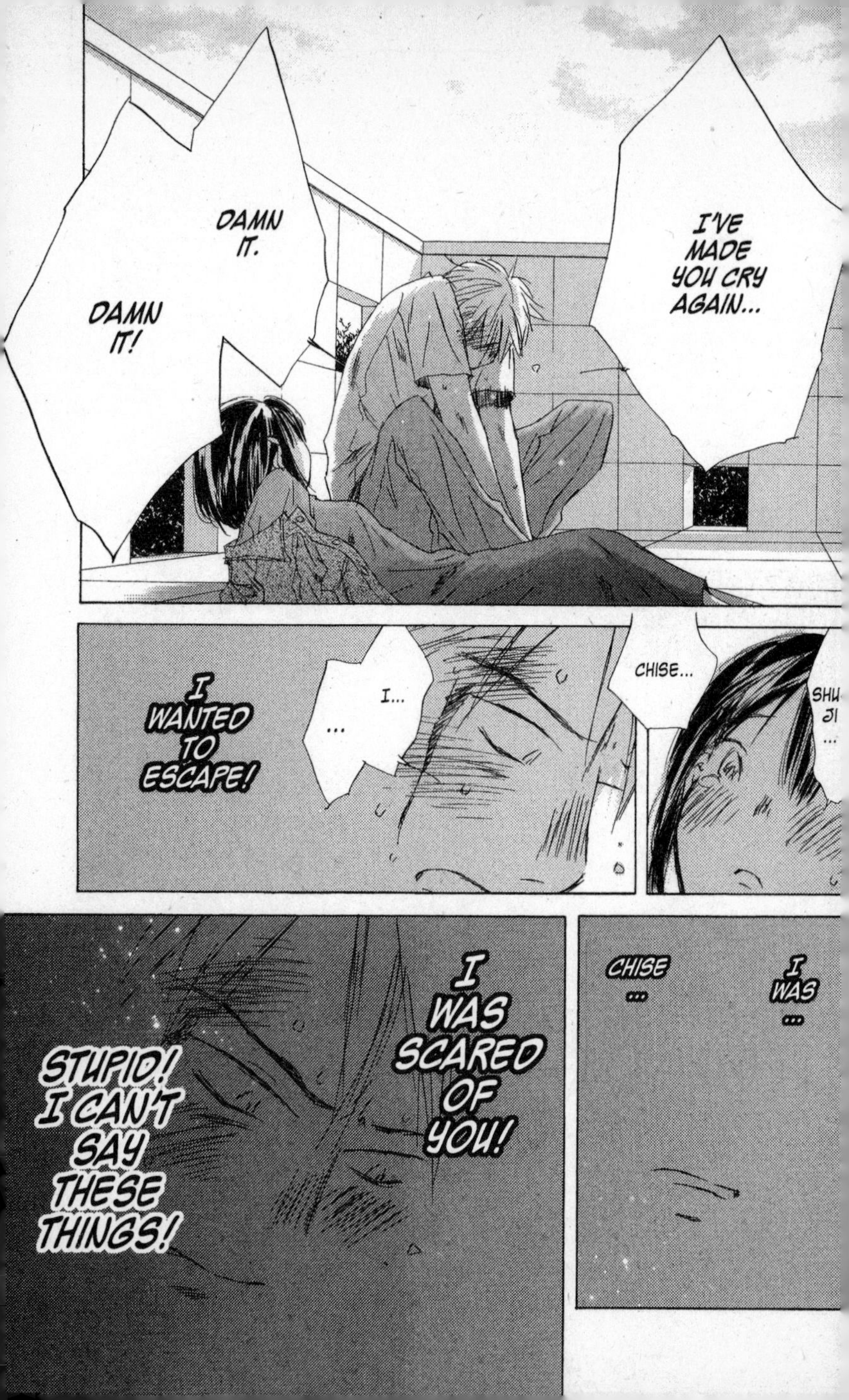
I'VE MADE YOU CRY AGAIN...
DAMN IT.
DAMN IT!
CHISE...
SHUJI...
I... ...
I WANTED TO ESCAPE!
I WAS...
CHISE...
I WAS SCARED OF YOU!
STUPID! I CAN'T SAY THESE THINGS!

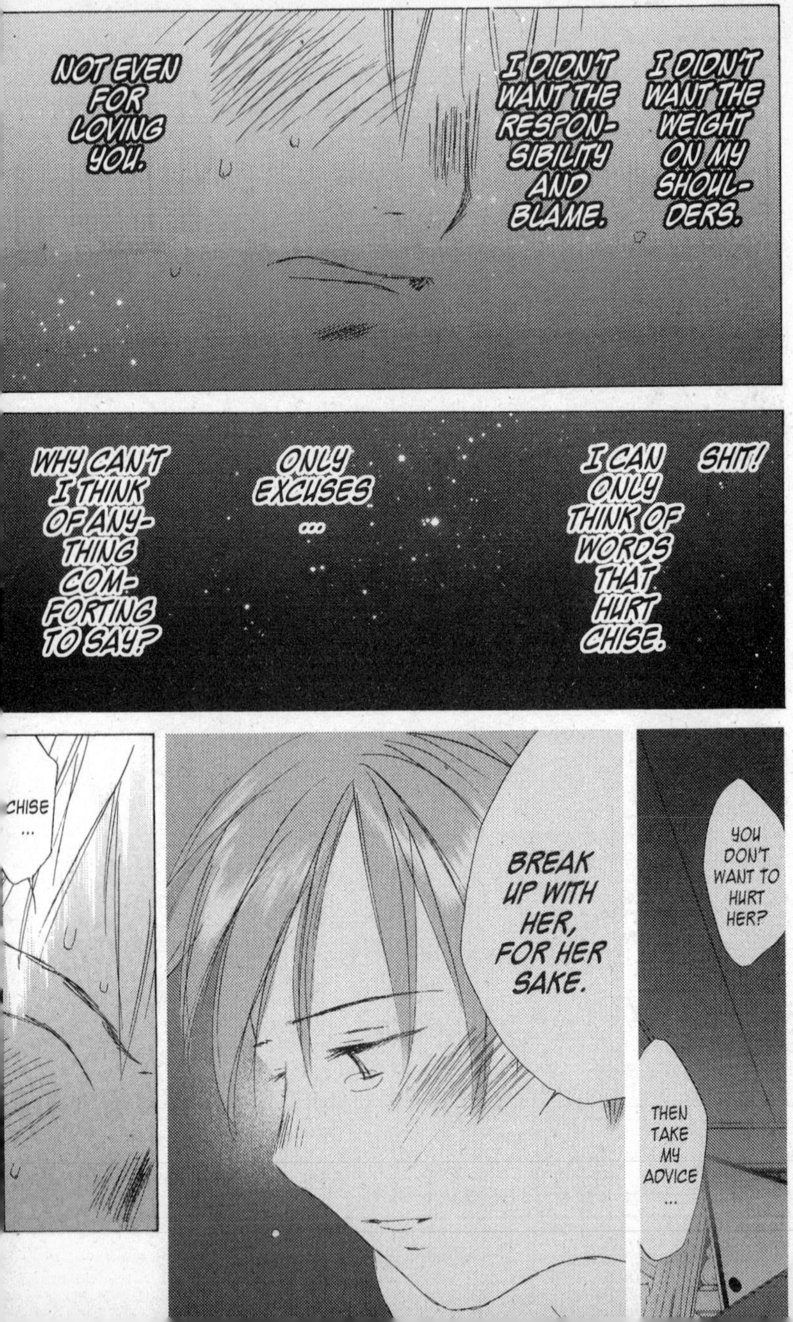
I DIDN'T WANT THE WEIGHT ON MY SHOULDERS.
I DIDN'T WANT THE RESPONSIBILITY AND BLAME.
NOT EVEN FOR LOVING YOU.
SHIT!
I CAN ONLY THINK OF WORDS THAT HURT CHISE.
ONLY EXCUSES...
WHY CAN'T I THINK OF ANYTHING COMFORTING TO SAY?
YOU DON'T WANT TO HURT HER?
THEN TAKE MY ADVICE...
BREAK UP WITH HER, FOR HER SAKE.
CHISE...

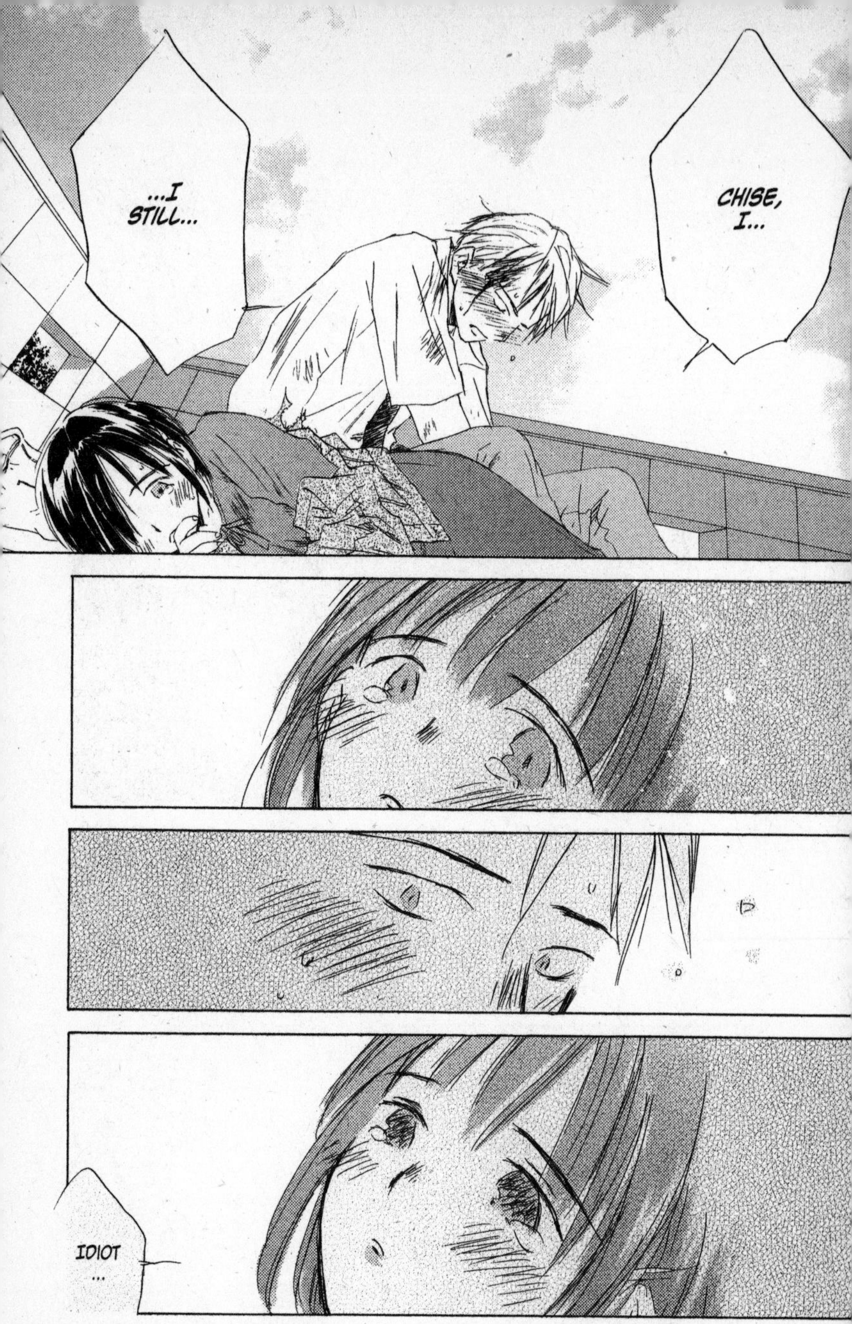
CHISE, I...
...I STILL...
IDIOT ...

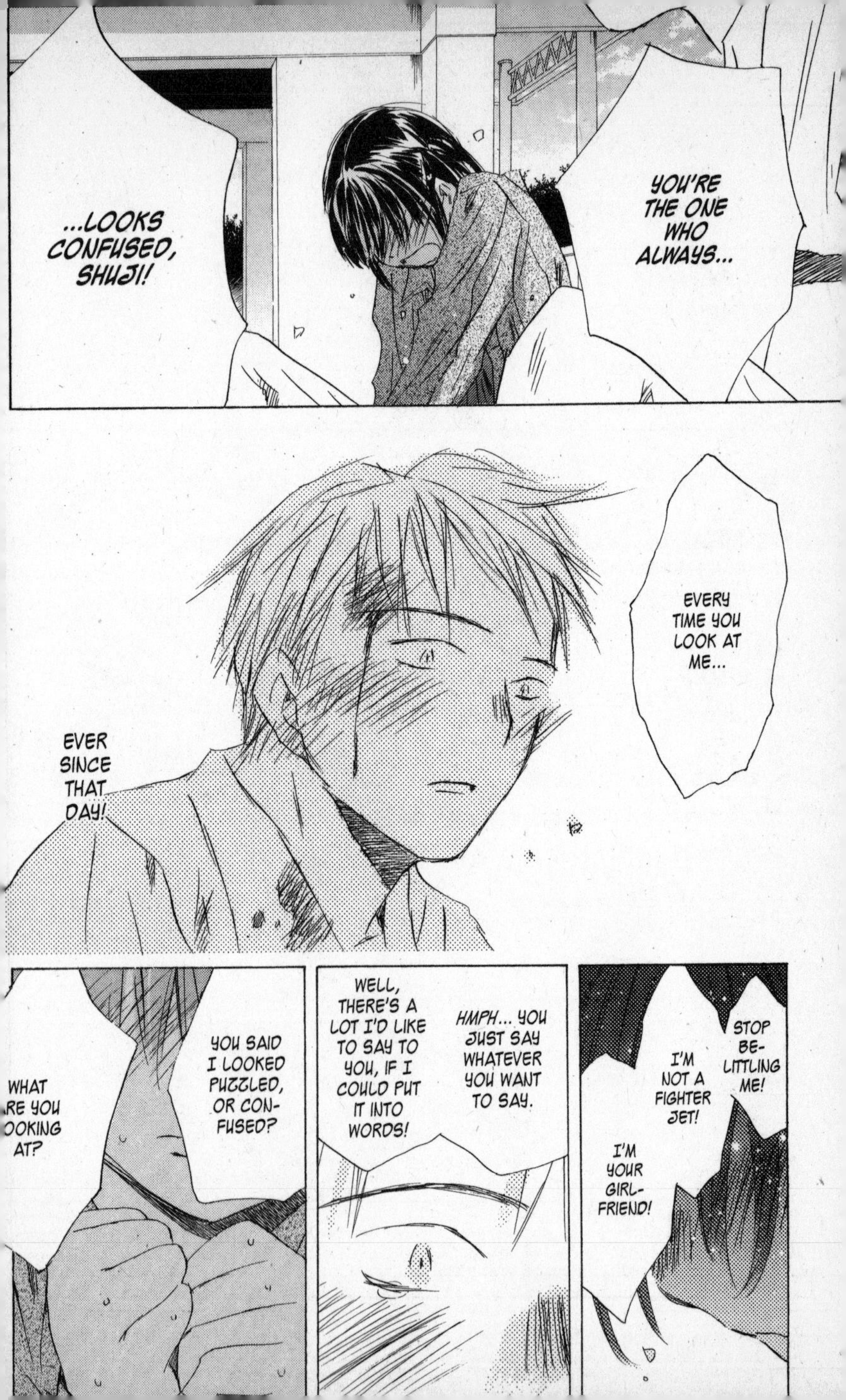
YOU'RE THE ONE WHO ALWAYS...
...LOOKS CONFUSED, SHUJI!
EVERY TIME YOU LOOK AT ME...
EVER SINCE THAT DAY!
STOP BE-LITTLING ME!
I'M NOT A FIGHTER JET!
I'M YOUR GIRL-FRIEND!
HMPH... YOU JUST SAY WHATEVER YOU WANT TO SAY.
WELL, THERE'S A LOT I'D LIKE TO SAY TO YOU, IF I COULD PUT IT INTO WORDS!
YOU SAID I LOOKED PUZZLED, OR CON-FUSED?
WHAT RE YOU OOKING AT?

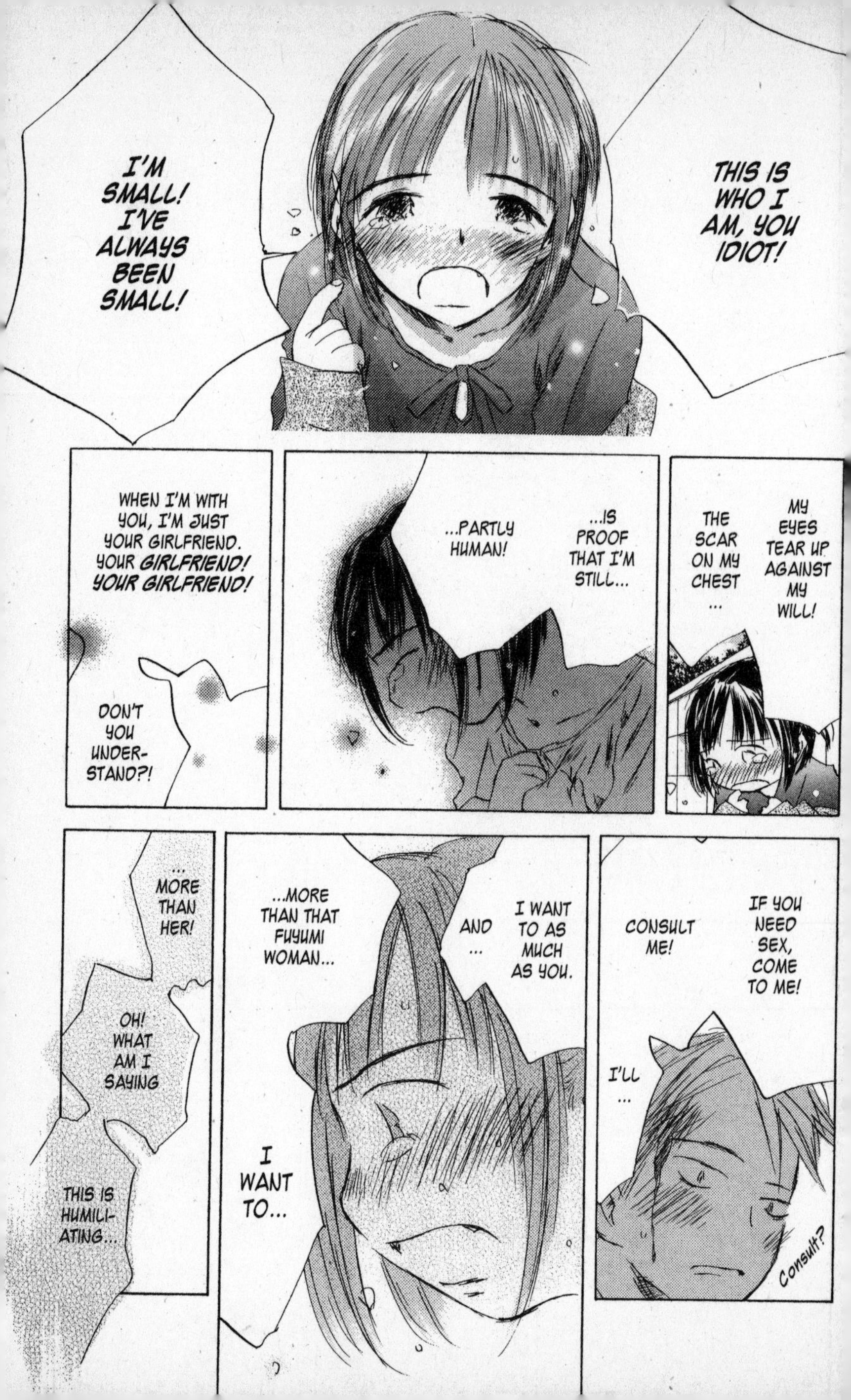
THIS IS WHO I AM, YOU IDIOT!
I'M SMALL! I'VE ALWAYS BEEN SMALL!
MY EYES TEAR UP AGAINST MY WILL!
THE SCAR ON MY CHEST...
...IS PROOF THAT I'M STILL...
...PARTLY HUMAN!
WHEN I'M WITH YOU, I'M JUST YOUR GIRLFRIEND. YOUR GIRLFRIEND! YOUR GIRLFRIEND!
DON'T YOU UNDER-STAND?!
IF YOU NEED SEX, COME TO ME!
CONSULT ME!
I'LL...
Consult?
I WANT TO AS MUCH AS YOU.
AND...
...MORE THAN THAT FUYUMI WOMAN...
I WANT TO...
...MORE THAN HER!
OH! WHAT AM I SAYING
THIS IS HUMILI-ATING...

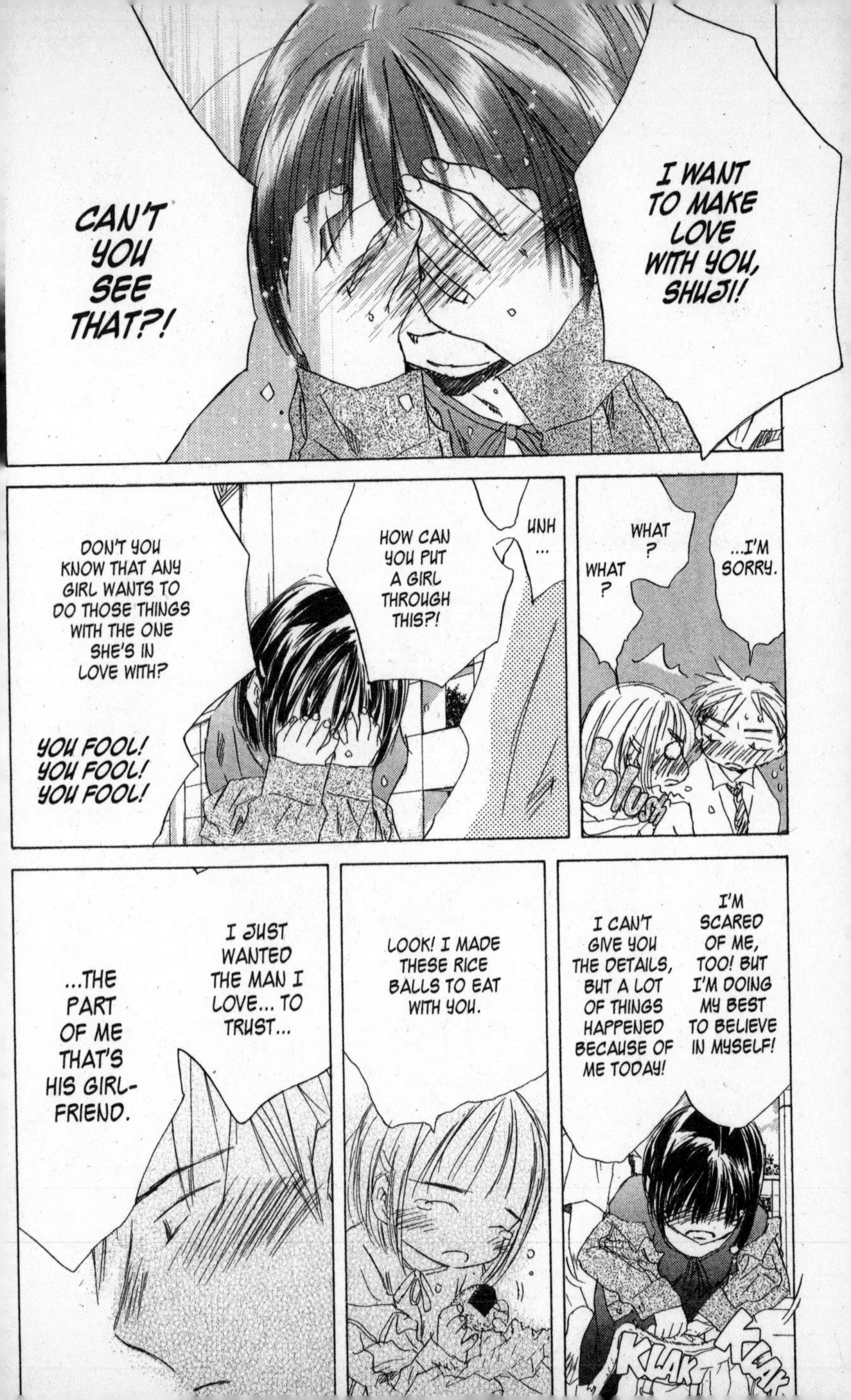
I WANT TO MAKE LOVE WITH YOU, SHUJI!
CAN'T YOU SEE THAT?!
...I'M SORRY.
WHAT?
WHAT?
blush
UNH ...
HOW CAN YOU PUT A GIRL THROUGH THIS?!
DON'T YOU KNOW THAT ANY GIRL WANTS TO DO THOSE THINGS WITH THE ONE SHE'S IN LOVE WITH?
YOU FOOL! YOU FOOL! YOU FOOL!
I'M SCARED OF ME, TOO! BUT I'M DOING MY BEST TO BELIEVE IN MYSELF!
I CAN'T GIVE YOU THE DETAILS, BUT A LOT OF THINGS HAPPENED BECAUSE OF ME TODAY!
KLAK
KLAK
LOOK! I MADE THESE RICE BALLS TO EAT WITH YOU.
I JUST WANTED THE MAN I LOVE... TO TRUST...
...THE PART OF ME THAT'S HIS GIRL-FRIEND.

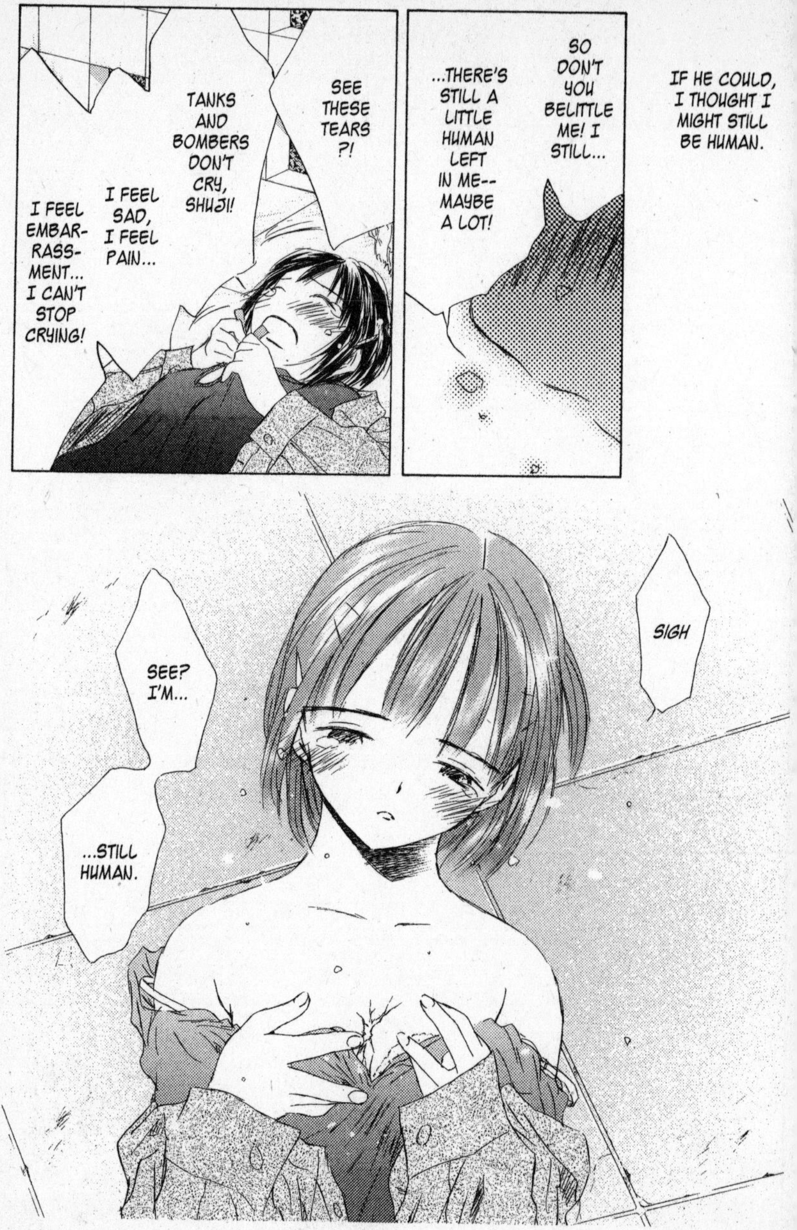
IF HE COULD, I THOUGHT I MIGHT STILL BE HUMAN.
SO DON'T YOU BELITTLE ME! I STILL...
...THERE'S STILL A LITTLE HUMAN LEFT IN ME-- MAYBE A LOT!
SEE THESE TEARS ?!
TANKS AND BOMBERS DON'T CRY, SHUJI!
I FEEL SAD, I FEEL PAIN...
I FEEL EMBAR-RASS-MENT... I CAN'T STOP CRYING!
SIGH
SEE? I'M...
...STILL HUMAN.

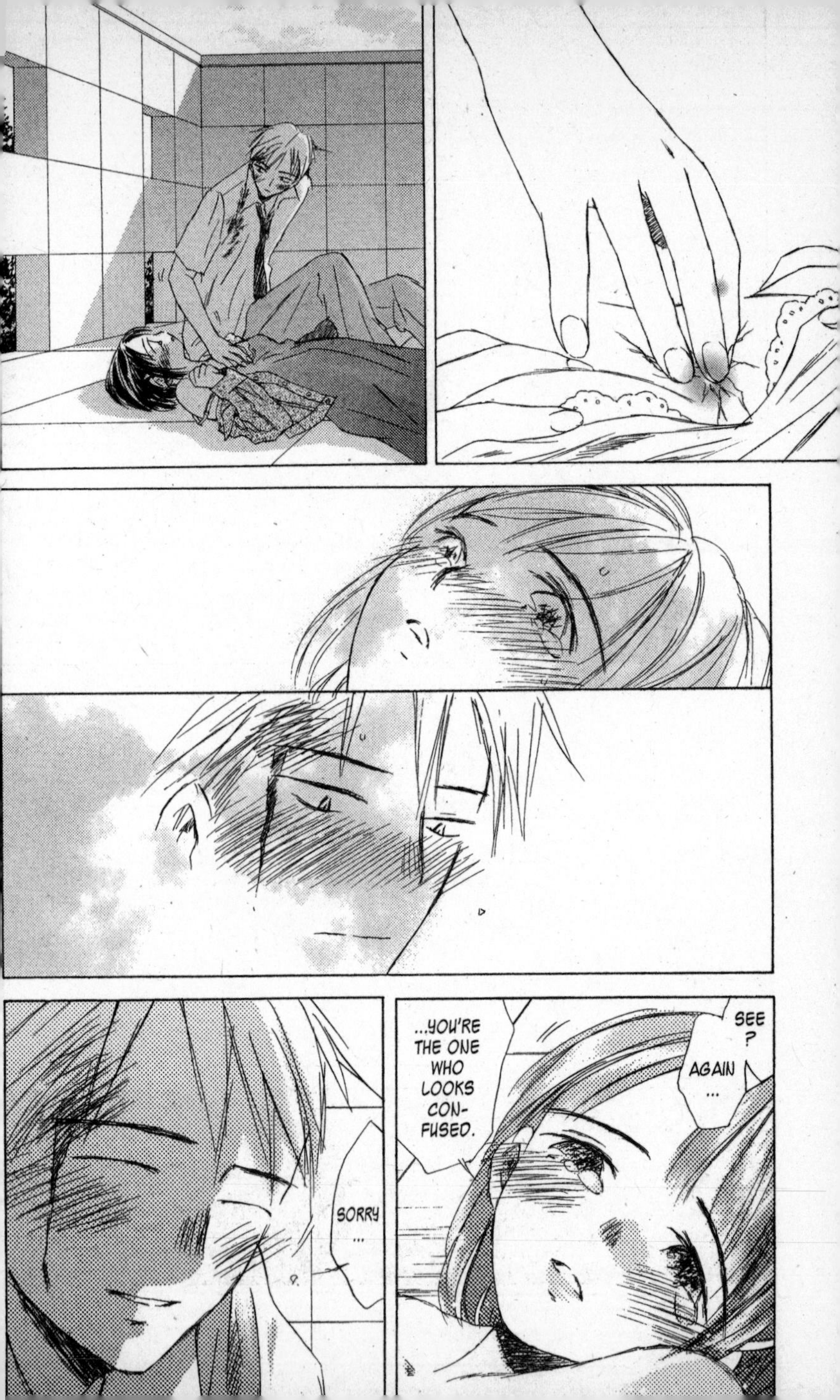
SEE?
AGAIN...
...YOU'RE THE ONE WHO LOOKS CON-FUSED.
SORRY...

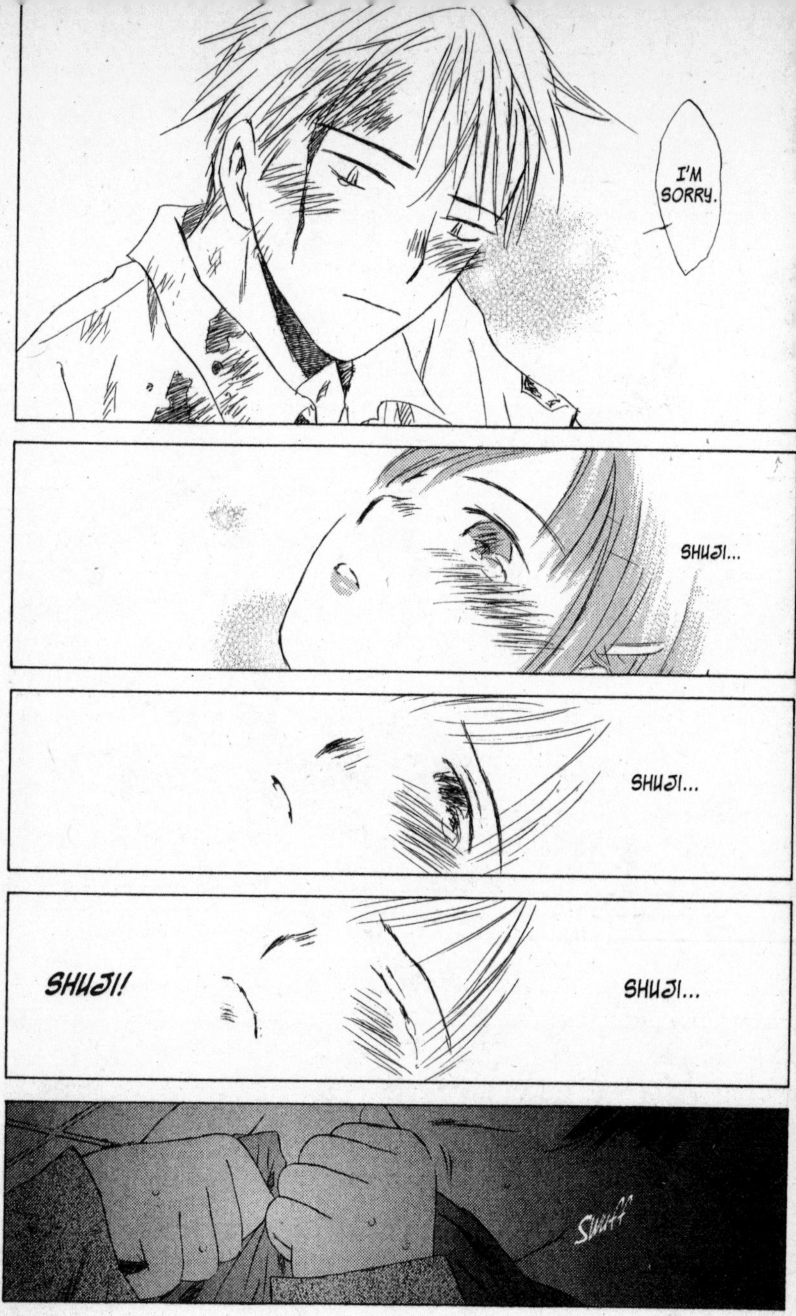
I'M SORRY.
SHUJI...
SHUJI...
SHUJI...
SHUJI!
Swuff

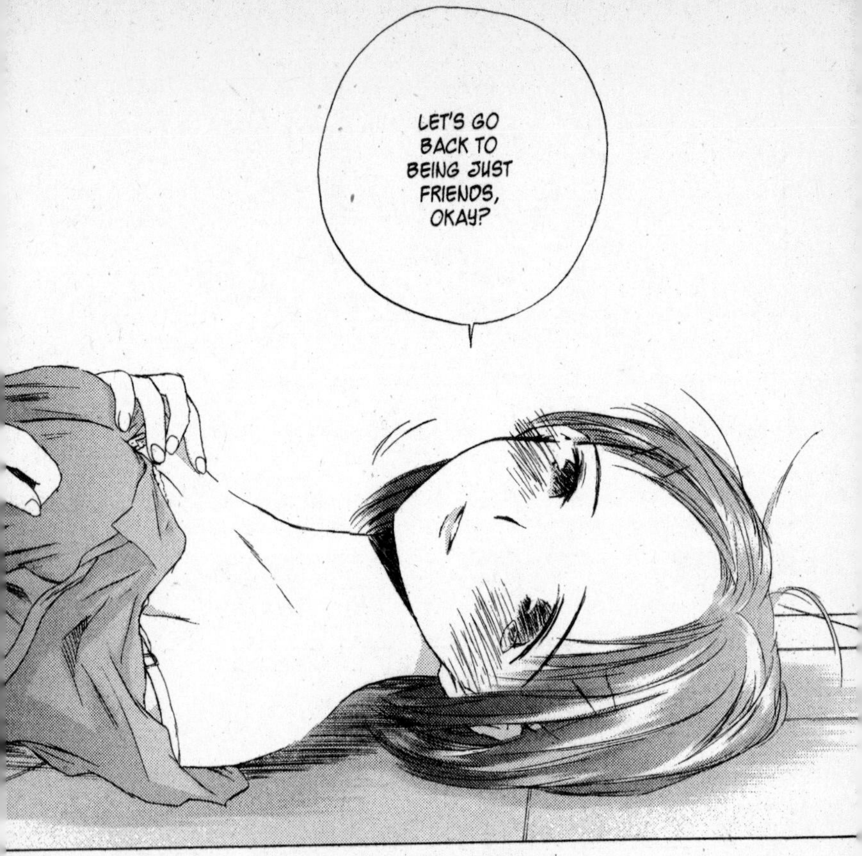
LET'S GO BACK TO BEING JUST FRIENDS, OKAY?
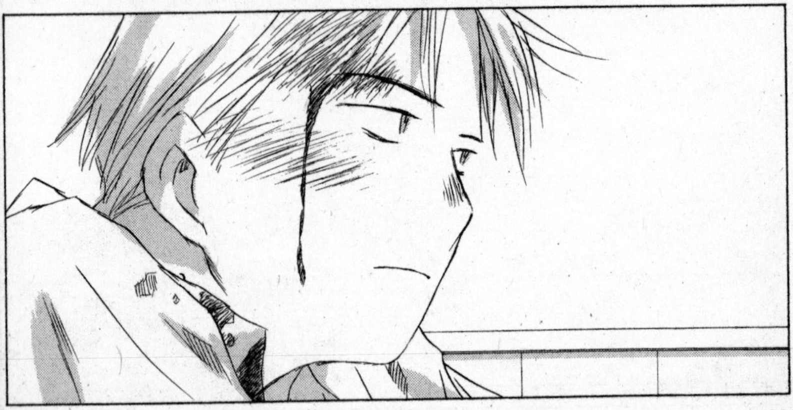

ON THAT DAY...

...WE WERE LATE FOR SCHOOL...

...TWO HOURS LATE. THE TEACHER YELLED AT US.

ON THAT DAY...

...WE BROKE UP.

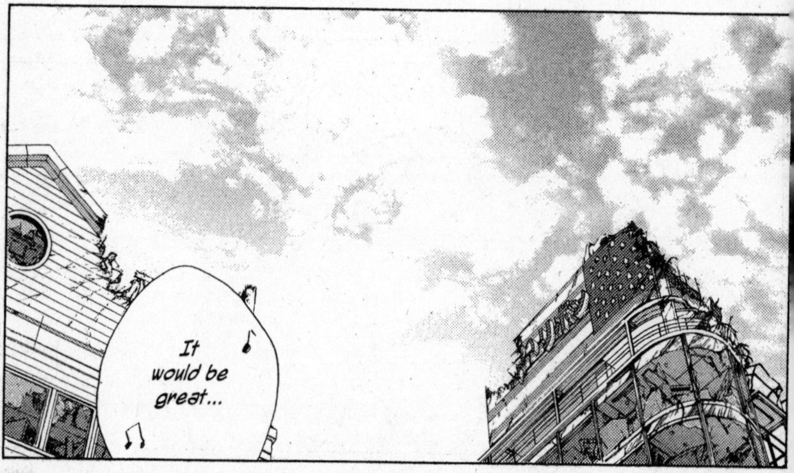
It would be great...

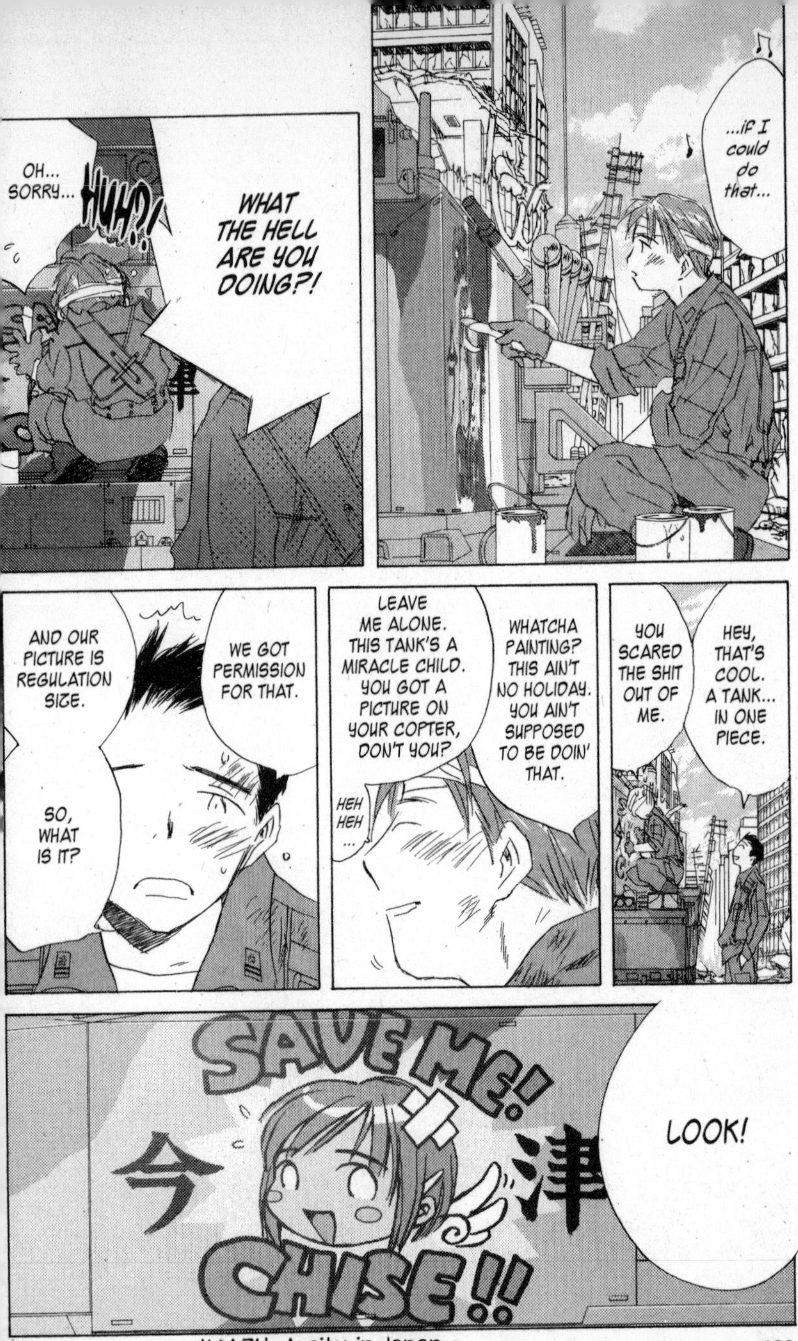
...if I could do that...
WHAT THE HELL ARE YOU DOING?!
HUH?!
OH... SORRY...
HEY, THAT'S COOL. A TANK... IN ONE PIECE.
YOU SCARED THE SHIT OUT OF ME.
WHATCHA PAINTING? THIS AIN'T NO HOLIDAY. YOU AIN'T SUPPOSED TO BE DOIN' THAT.
LEAVE ME ALONE. THIS TANK'S A MIRACLE CHILD. YOU GOT A PICTURE ON YOUR COPTER, DON'T YOU?
HEH HEH ...
WE GOT PERMISSION FOR THAT.
AND OUR PICTURE IS REGULATION SIZE.
SO, WHAT IS IT?
LOOK!
SAVE ME!
今
津
CHISE!!

IMAZU: A city in Japan

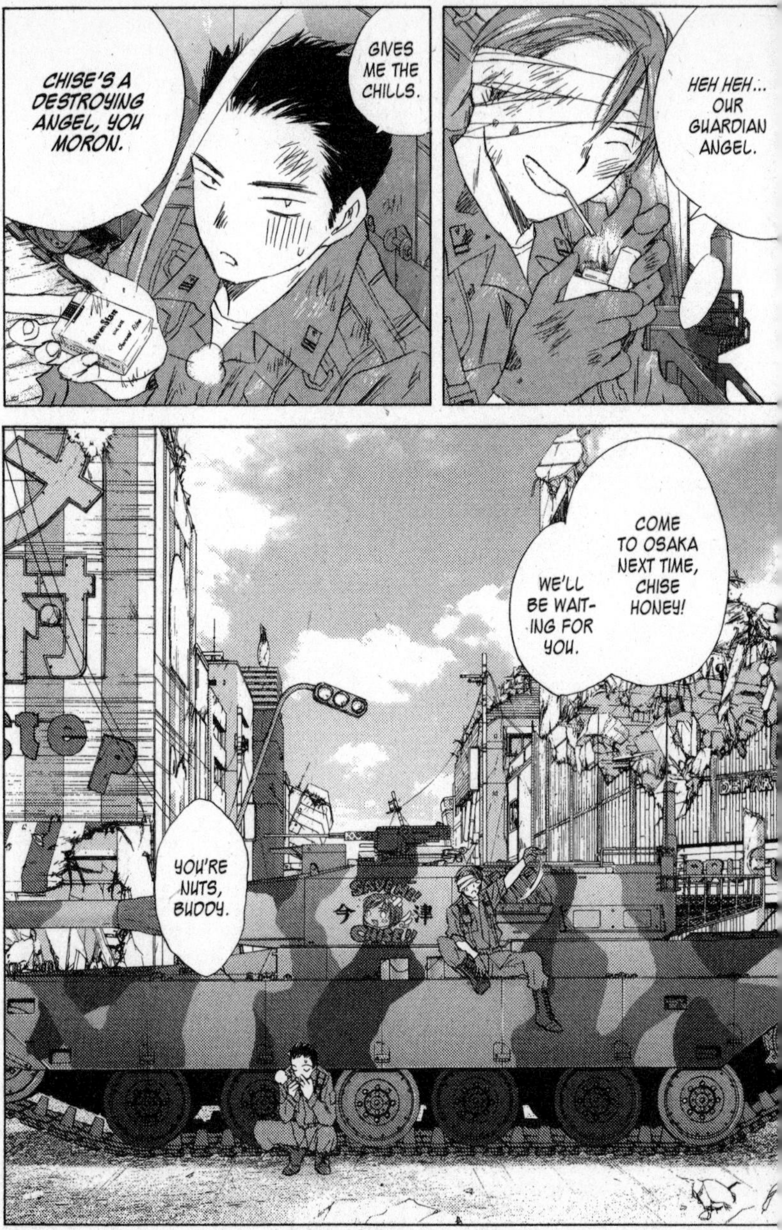
HEH HEH... OUR GUARDIAN ANGEL.
GIVES ME THE CHILLS.
CHISE'S A DESTROYING ANGEL, YOU MORON.
COME TO OSAKA NEXT TIME, CHISE HONEY!
WE'LL BE WAIT-ING FOR YOU.
YOU'RE NUTS, BUDDY.

END OF SAIKANO CHAPTER 5

Saikano Volume 3

STAFF

Graphics:
Mio Okuda
Yasutomo Nishio
Takeshi Sakamoto
Rie Okada
Naoe Kikuchi
Fumiko Tomochika
Kumiko Nagasaki
Shin Takahashi

Editing:
Tokie Komuro (Shogakukan)
Yasuki Hori (Shogakukan)
Icho-sha

Bookbinding:
Yoshiyuki Seki (Volare, Inc.)
Yukio Hoshino (Volare, Inc.)

Finishing:
Mio Okuda
Yasutomo Nishio
Takeshi Sakamoto
Rie Okada
Naoe Kikuchi
Akihiro Mitsui
Shin'ichi Asano
Fumiko Tomochika
Kumiko Nagasaki
Tomoko Ishii
Asami Maeda

CG:
Satoko Sugimoto
Naoki Moriya
Masayuki Ohta
Akemi Hara
Tomoko Ishii
Shin Takahashi

Mechanical Design:
Shin Takahashi

Cleanup:
Kiyomi Takahashi

Director:
Shin Takahashi

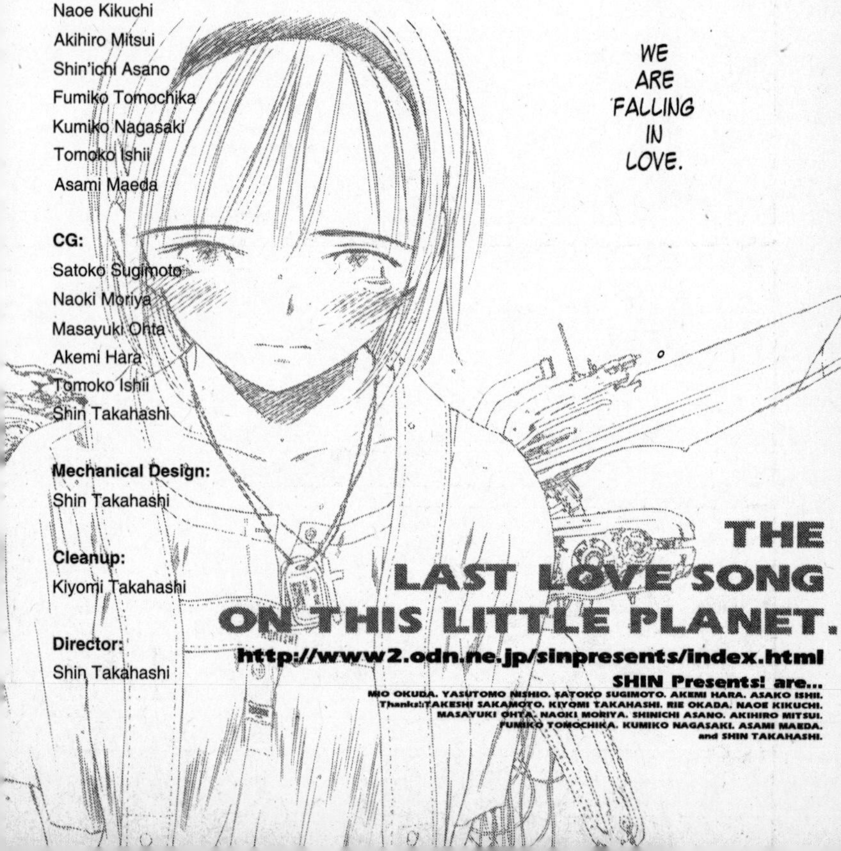
WE ARE FALLING IN LOVE.
THE LAST LOVE SONG ON THIS LITTLE PLANET.
http://www2.odn.ne.jp/sinpresents/index.html
SHIN Presents! are...
MIO OKUDA. YASUTOMO NISHIO. SATOKO SUGIMOTO. AKEMI HARA. ASAKO ISHII.
Thanks!:TAKESHI SAKAMOTO. KIYOMI TAKAHASHI. RIE OKADA. NAOE KIKUCHI.
MASAYUKI OHTA. NAOKI MORIYA. SHINICHI ASANO. AKIHIRO MITSUI.
FUMIKO TOMOCHIKA. KUMIKO NAGASAKI. ASAMI MAEDA.
and SHIN TAKAHASHI.

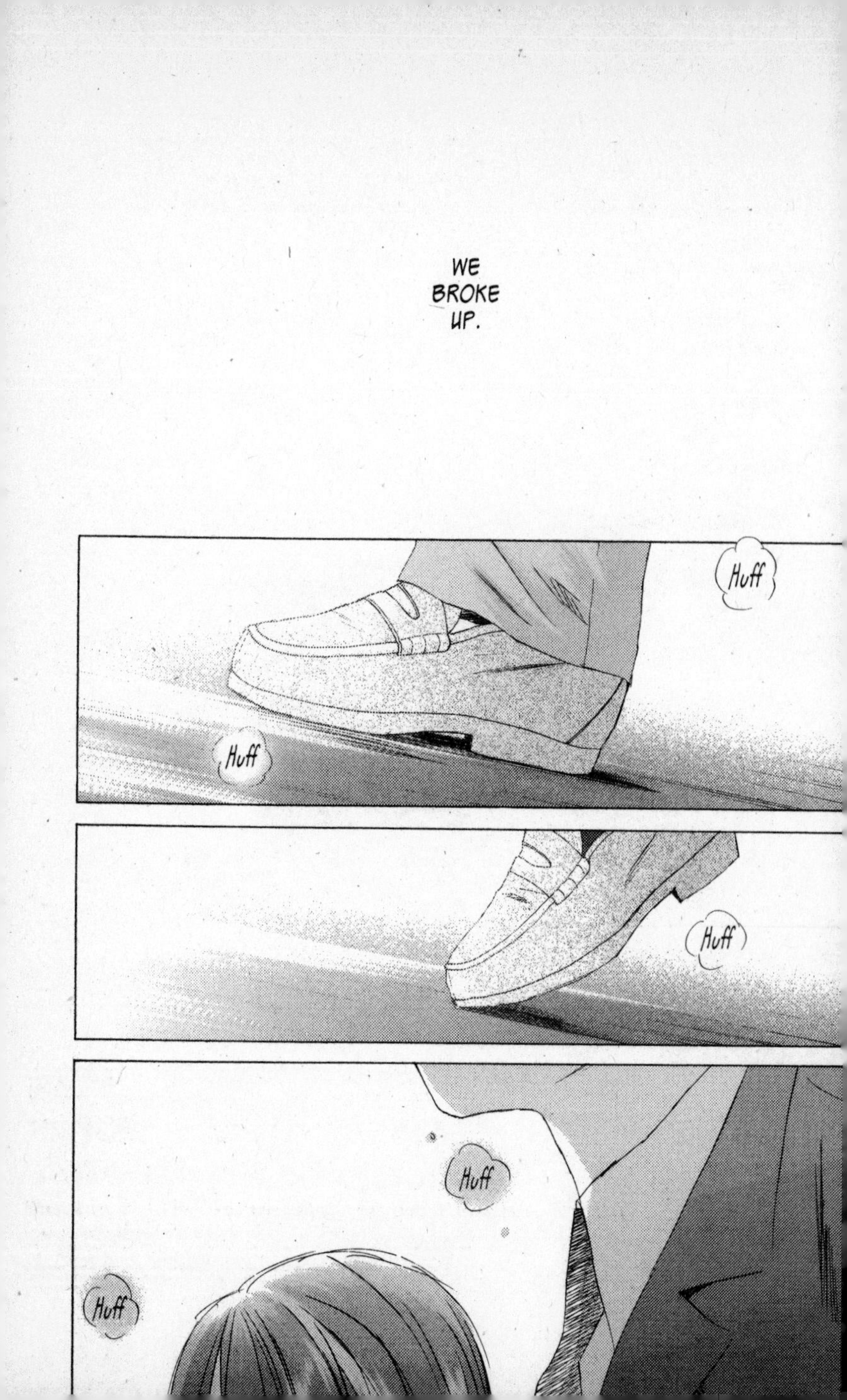
WE BROKE UP.
Huff
Huff
Huff
Huff
Huff

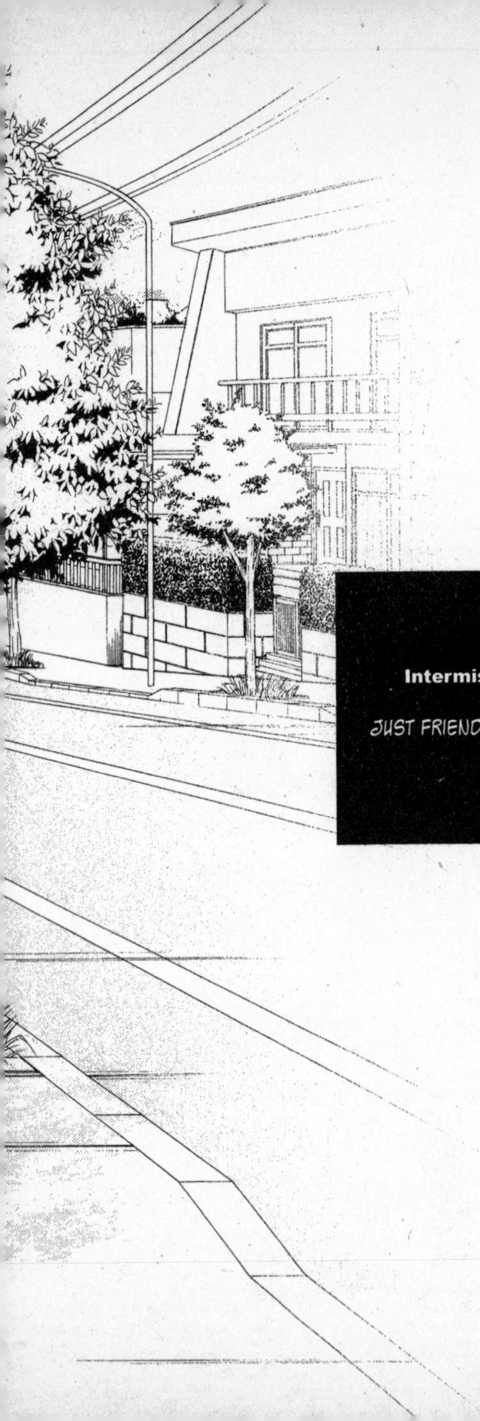

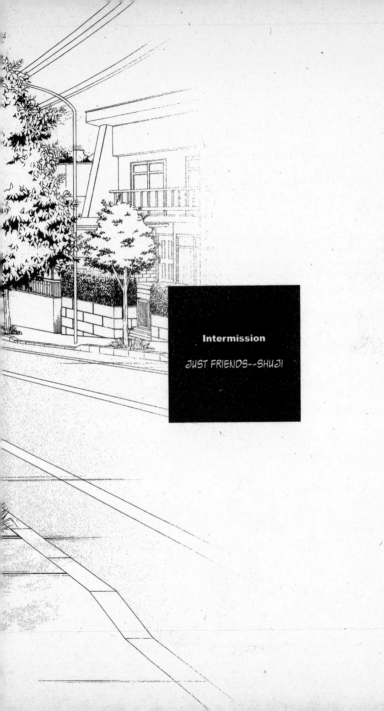

Intermission

JUST FRIENDS--SHUJI

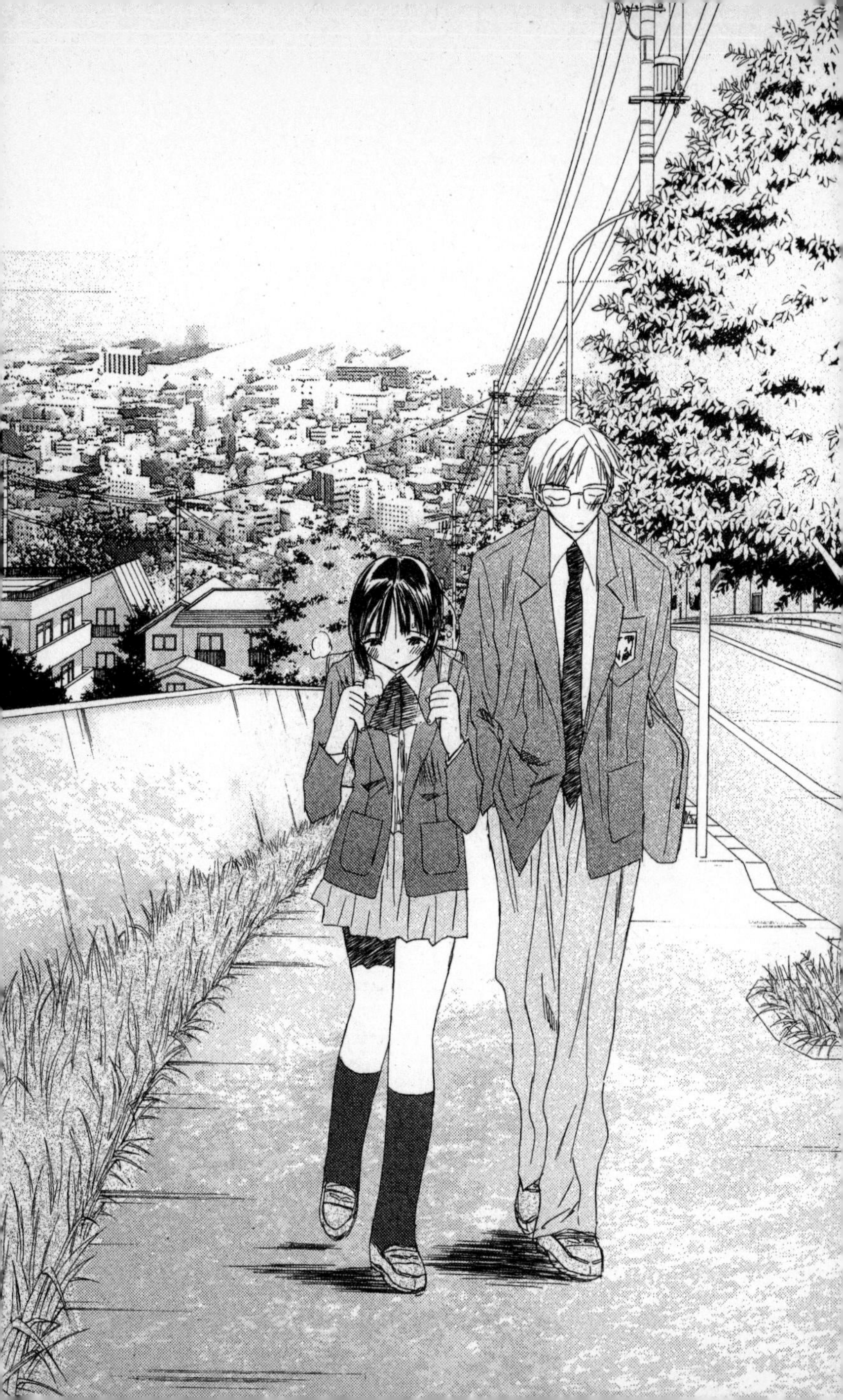

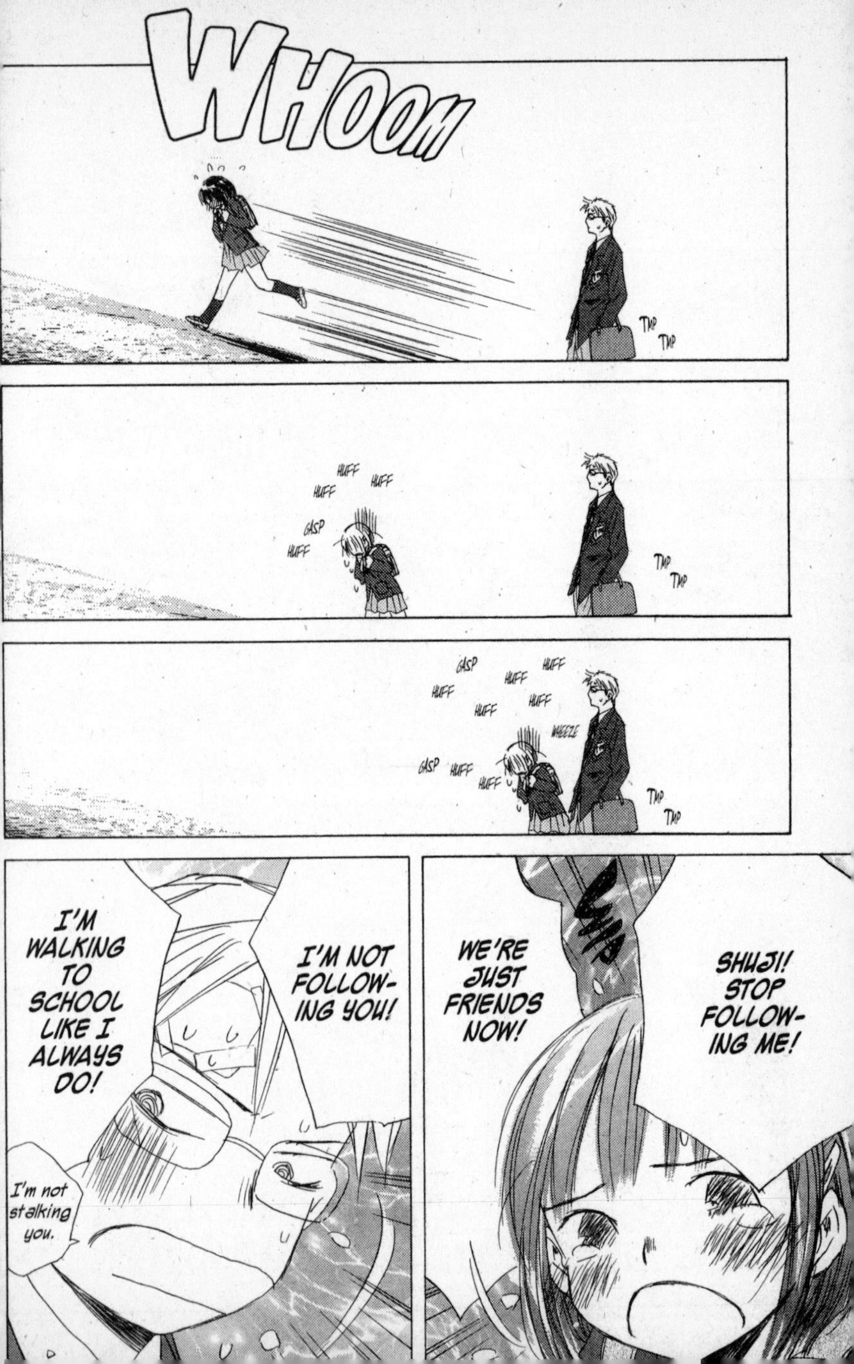
WHOOM
TMP
TMP
HUFF
HUFF
HUFF
GASP
HUFF
TMP
TMP
HUFF
GASP
HUFF
HUFF
HUFF
HUFF
WHEEZE
HUFF
HUFF
GASP
TMP
TMP
SHUJI! STOP FOLLOW-ING ME!
WE'RE JUST FRIENDS NOW!
I'M NOT FOLLOW-ING YOU!
I'M WALKING TO SCHOOL LIKE I ALWAYS DO!
I'm not stalking you.

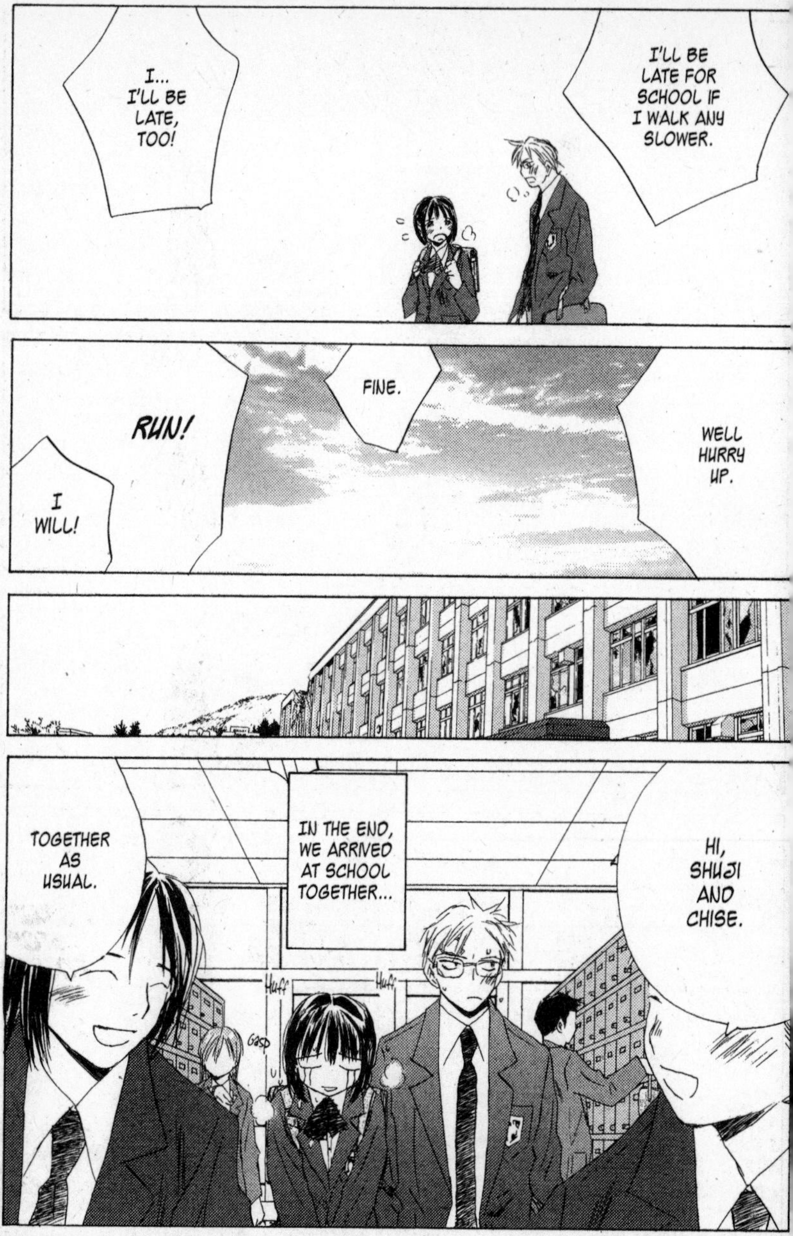
I'LL BE LATE FOR SCHOOL IF I WALK ANY SLOWER.
I... I'LL BE LATE, TOO!
WELL HURRY UP.
FINE.
RUN!
I WILL!
HI, SHUJI AND CHISE.
IN THE END, WE ARRIVED AT SCHOOL TOGETHER...
Huff
Huff
Gasp
TOGETHER AS USUAL.

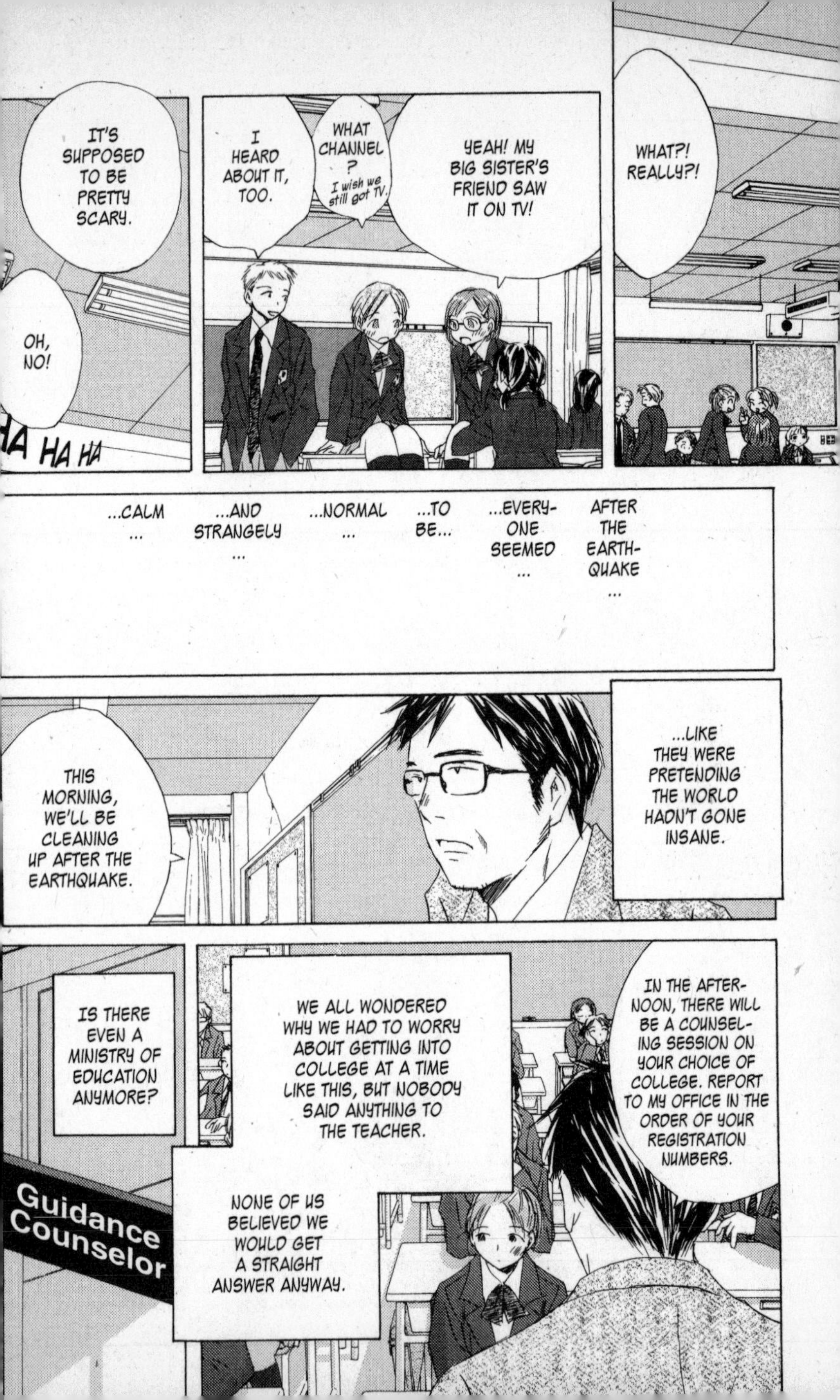
WHAT?! REALLY?!
YEAH! MY BIG SISTER'S FRIEND SAW IT ON TV!
WHAT CHANNEL ?
I wish we still got TV.
I HEARD ABOUT IT, TOO.
IT'S SUPPOSED TO BE PRETTY SCARY.
OH, NO!
HA HA HA
AFTER THE EARTH-QUAKE ...
...EVERY-ONE SEEMED ...
...TO BE...
...NORMAL ...
...AND STRANGELY ...
...CALM ...
...LIKE THEY WERE PRETENDING THE WORLD HADN'T GONE INSANE.
THIS MORNING, WE'LL BE CLEANING UP AFTER THE EARTHQUAKE.
IN THE AFTER-NOON, THERE WILL BE A COUNSEL-ING SESSION ON YOUR CHOICE OF COLLEGE. REPORT TO MY OFFICE IN THE ORDER OF YOUR REGISTRATION NUMBERS.
WE ALL WONDERED WHY WE HAD TO WORRY ABOUT GETTING INTO COLLEGE AT A TIME LIKE THIS, BUT NOBODY SAID ANYTHING TO THE TEACHER.
NONE OF US BELIEVED WE WOULD GET A STRAIGHT ANSWER ANYWAY.
IS THERE EVEN A MINISTRY OF EDUCATION ANYMORE?
Guidance Counselor

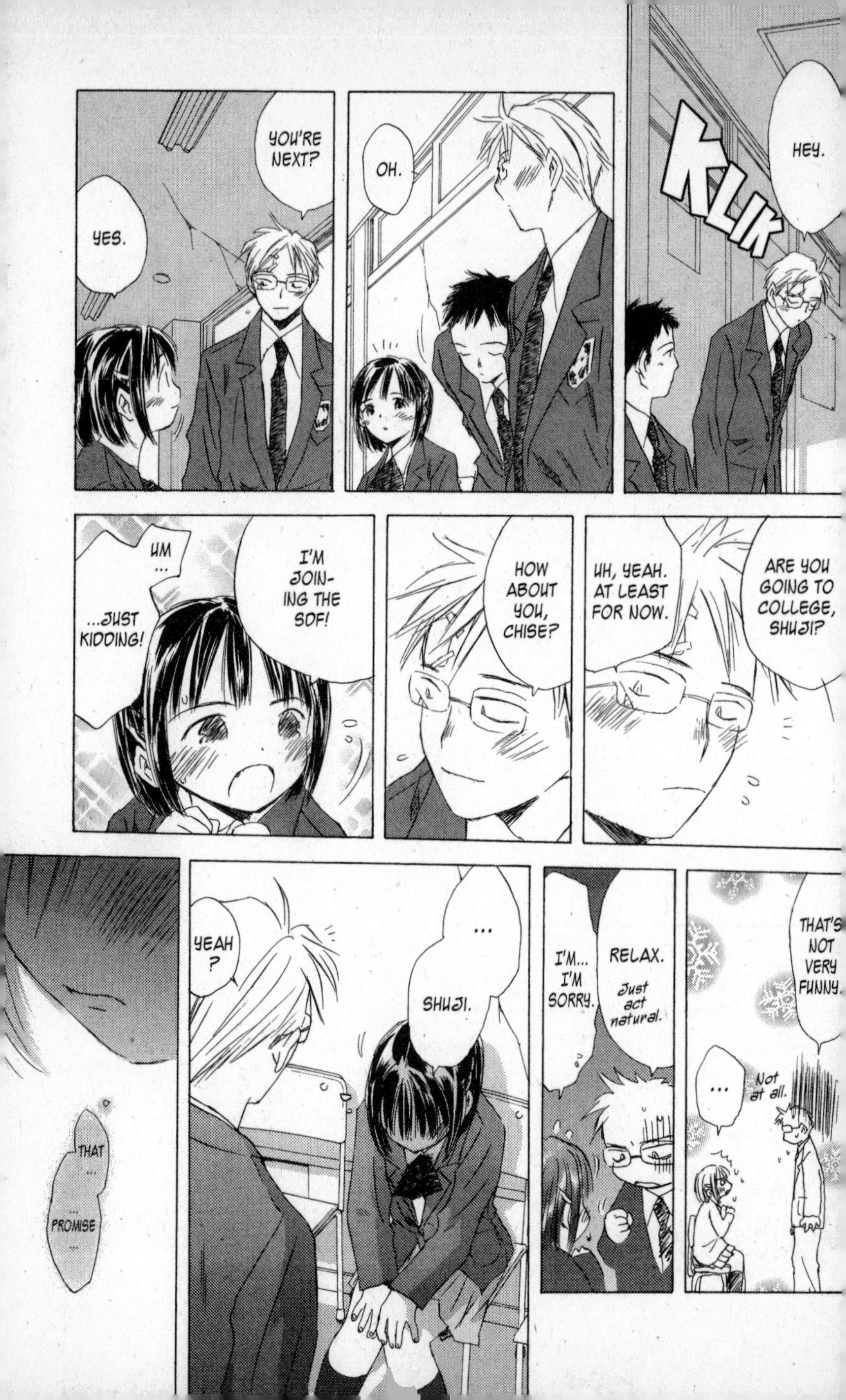
HEY.
KLIK
OH.
YOU'RE NEXT?
YES.
ARE YOU GOING TO COLLEGE, SHUJI?
UH, YEAH. AT LEAST FOR NOW.
HOW ABOUT YOU, CHISE?
I'M JOINING THE SDF!
UM ...
...JUST KIDDING!
THAT'S NOT VERY FUNNY.
Not at all.
...
RELAX.
Just act natural.
I'M... I'M SORRY.
...
SHUJI.
YEAH ?
THAT ... ... PROMISE ...

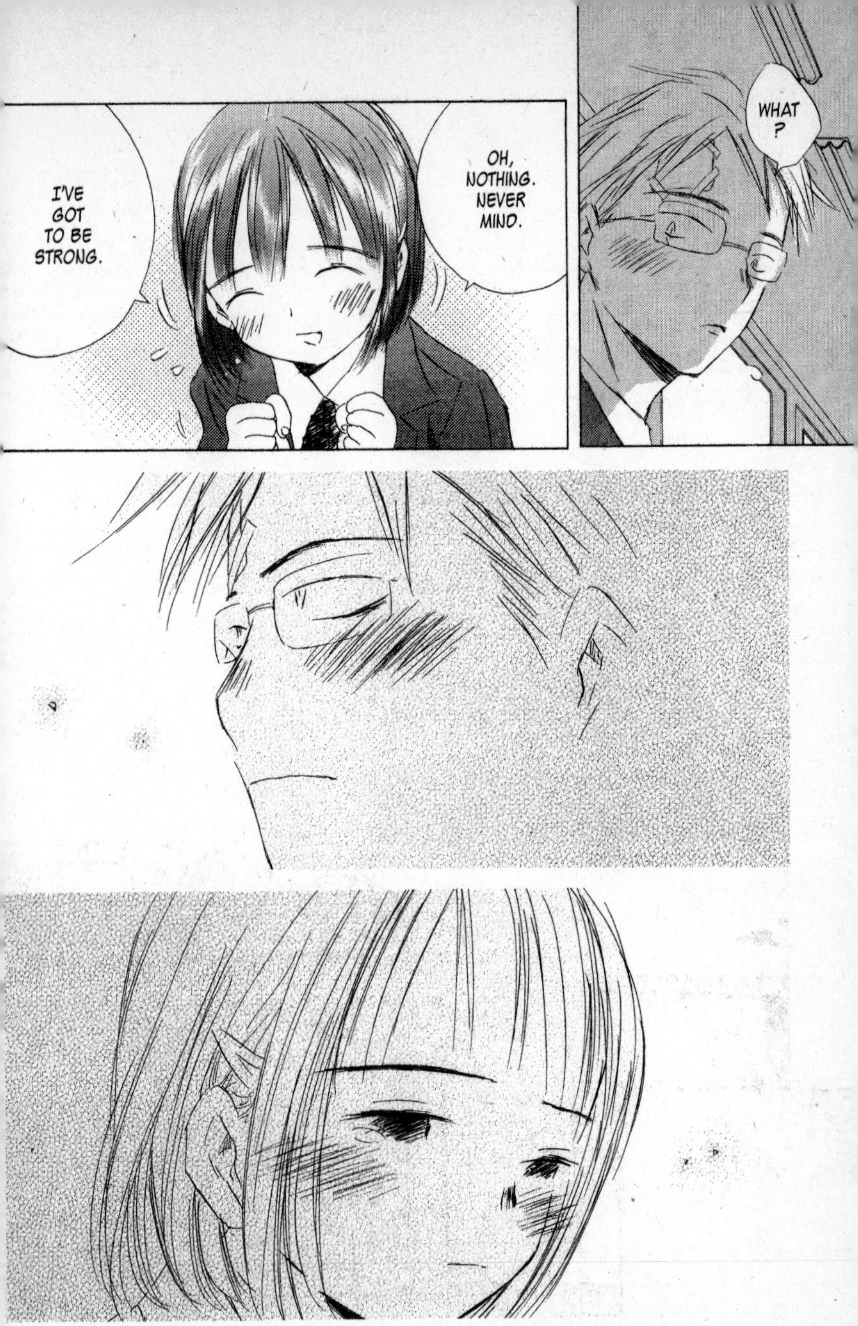
WHAT?
OH, NOTHING. NEVER MIND.
I'VE GOT TO BE STRONG.

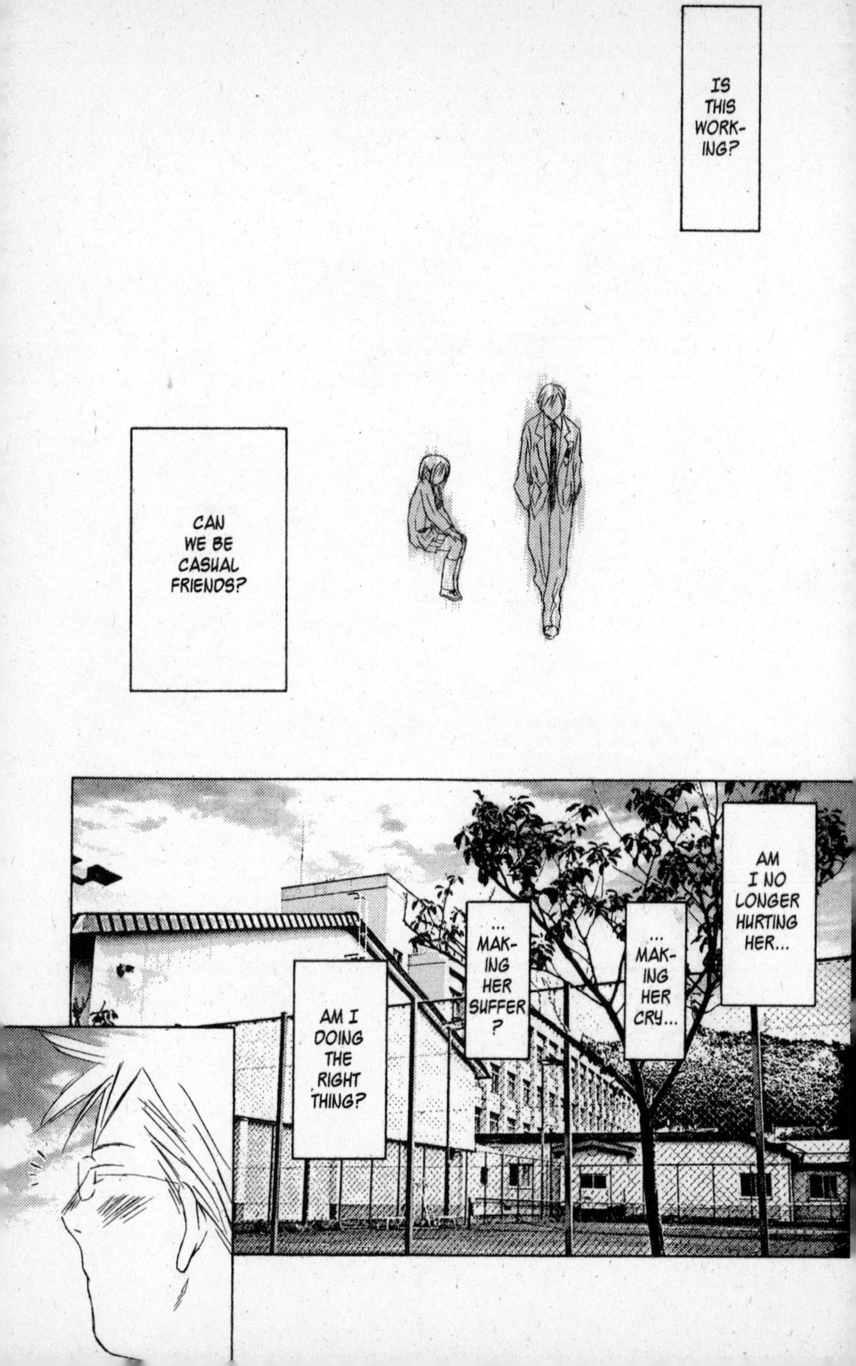
IS THIS WORKING?
CAN WE BE CASUAL FRIENDS?
AM I NO LONGER HURTING HER...
...MAKING HER CRY...
...MAKING HER SUFFER?
AM I DOING THE RIGHT THING?

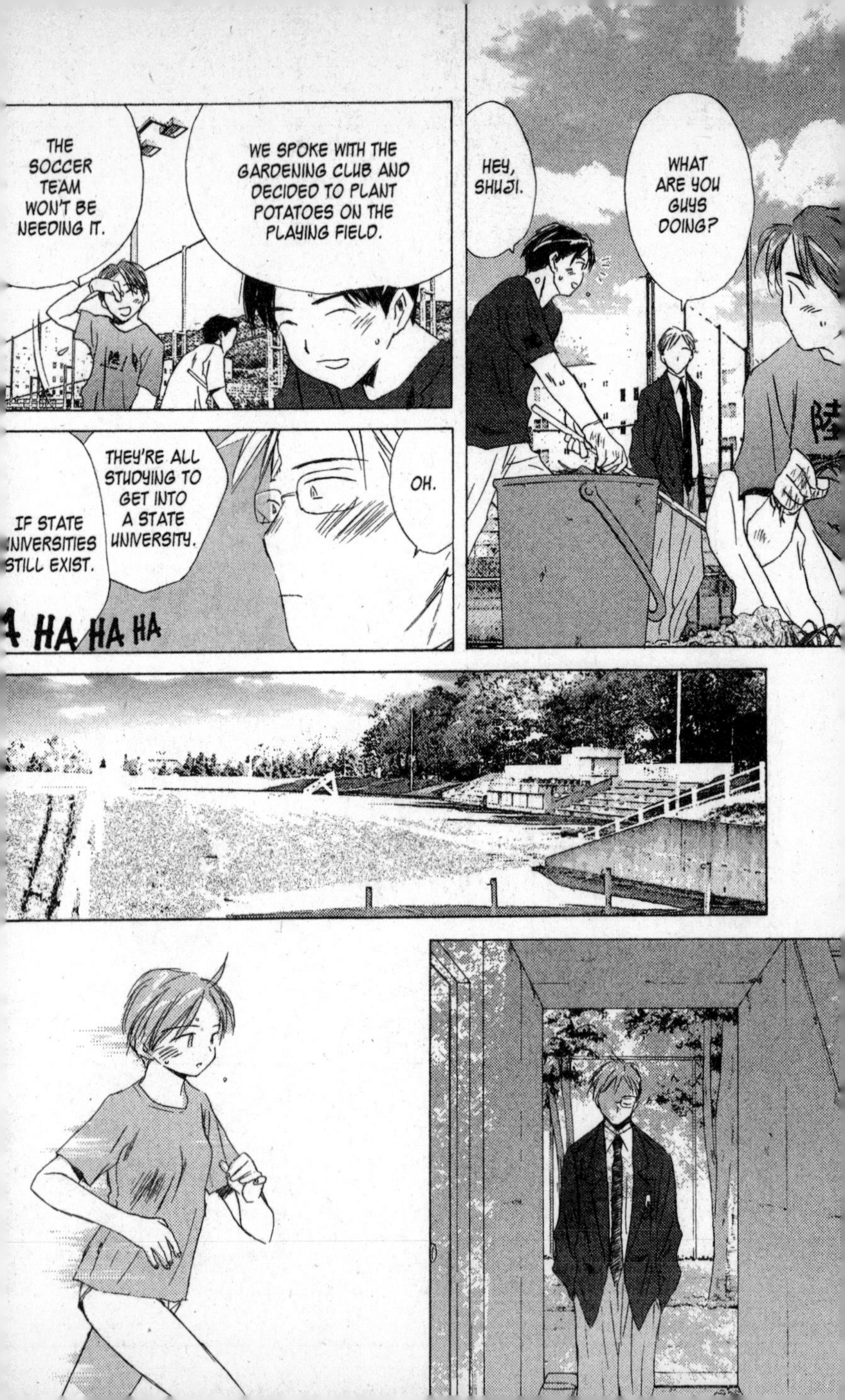

HEY, SHUJI.
WHAT ARE YOU GUYS DOING?
WE SPOKE WITH THE GARDENING CLUB AND DECIDED TO PLANT POTATOES ON THE PLAYING FIELD.
THE SOCCER TEAM WON'T BE NEEDING IT.
OH.
THEY'RE ALL STUDYING TO GET INTO A STATE UNIVERSITY.
IF STATE UNIVERSITIES STILL EXIST.
HA HA HA

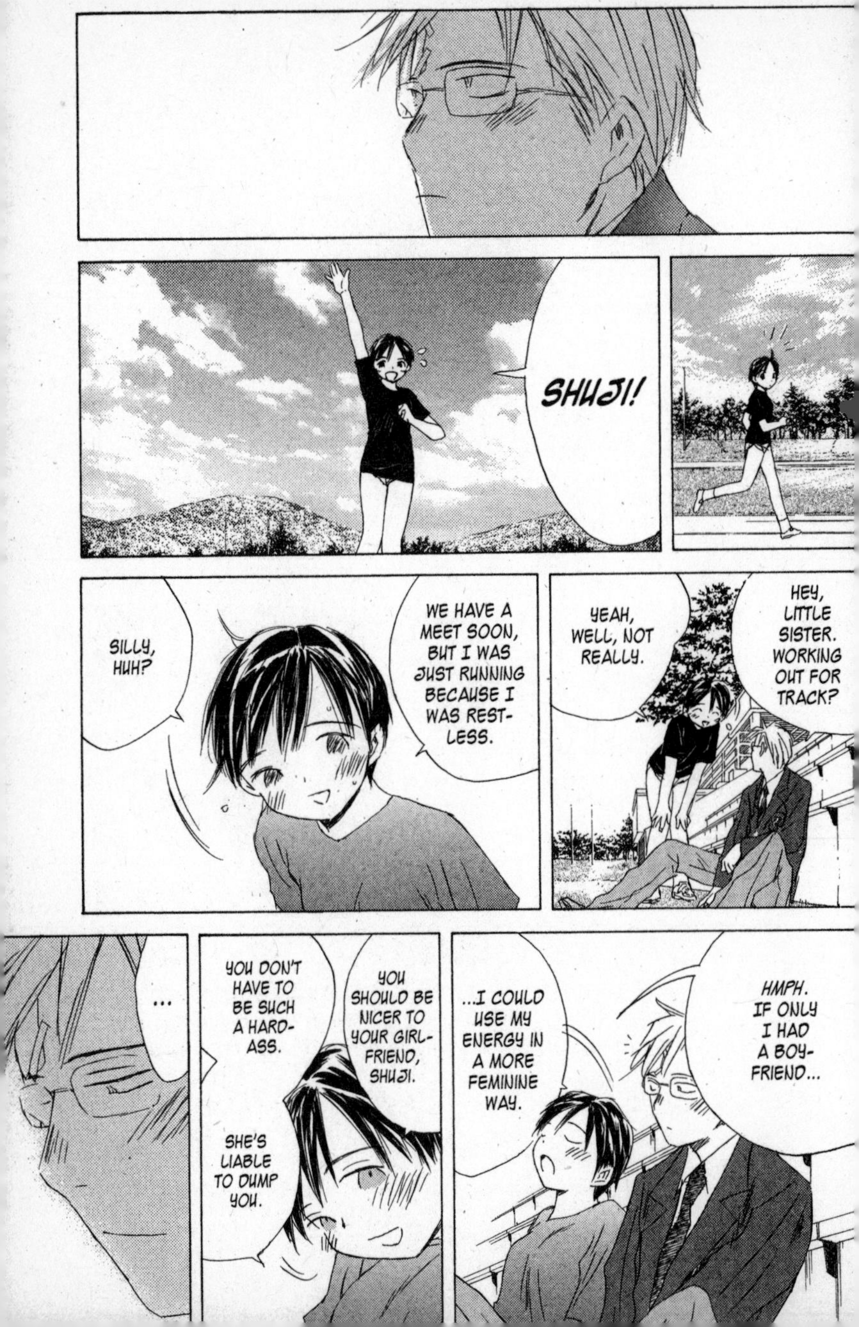
SHUJI!
HEY, LITTLE SISTER. WORKING OUT FOR TRACK?
YEAH, WELL, NOT REALLY.
WE HAVE A MEET SOON, BUT I WAS JUST RUNNING BECAUSE I WAS REST-LESS.
SILLY, HUH?
HMPH. IF ONLY I HAD A BOY-FRIEND...
...I COULD USE MY ENERGY IN A MORE FEMININE WAY.
YOU SHOULD BE NICER TO YOUR GIRL-FRIEND, SHUJI.
YOU DON'T HAVE TO BE SUCH A HARD-ASS.
SHE'S LIABLE TO DUMP YOU.
...

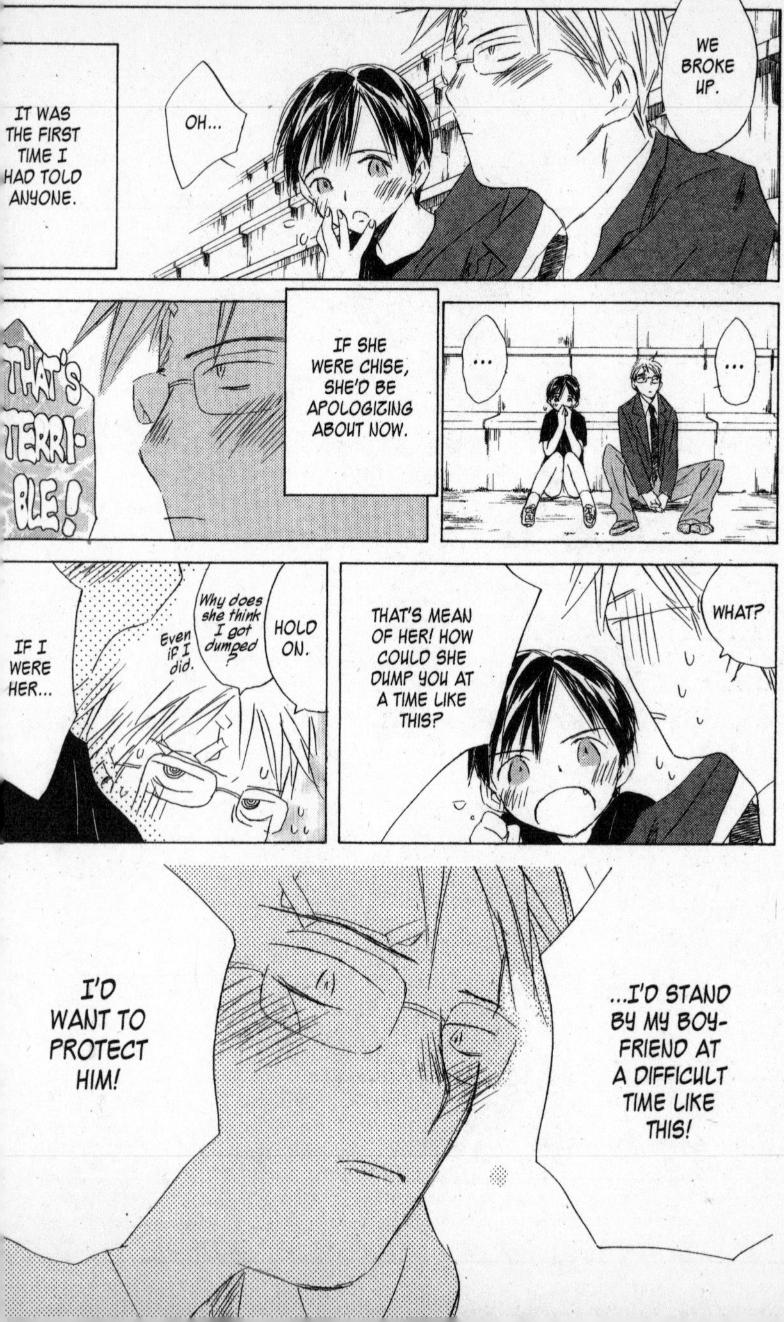
WE BROKE UP.
OH...
IT WAS THE FIRST TIME I HAD TOLD ANYONE.
...
...
IF SHE WERE CHISE, SHE'D BE APOLOGIZING ABOUT NOW.
THAT'S TERRI-BLE!
WHAT?
THAT'S MEAN OF HER! HOW COULD SHE DUMP YOU AT A TIME LIKE THIS?
HOLD ON.
Why does she think I got dumped?
Even if I did.
IF I WERE HER...
...I'D STAND BY MY BOY-FRIEND AT A DIFFICULT TIME LIKE THIS!
I'D WANT TO PROTECT HIM!

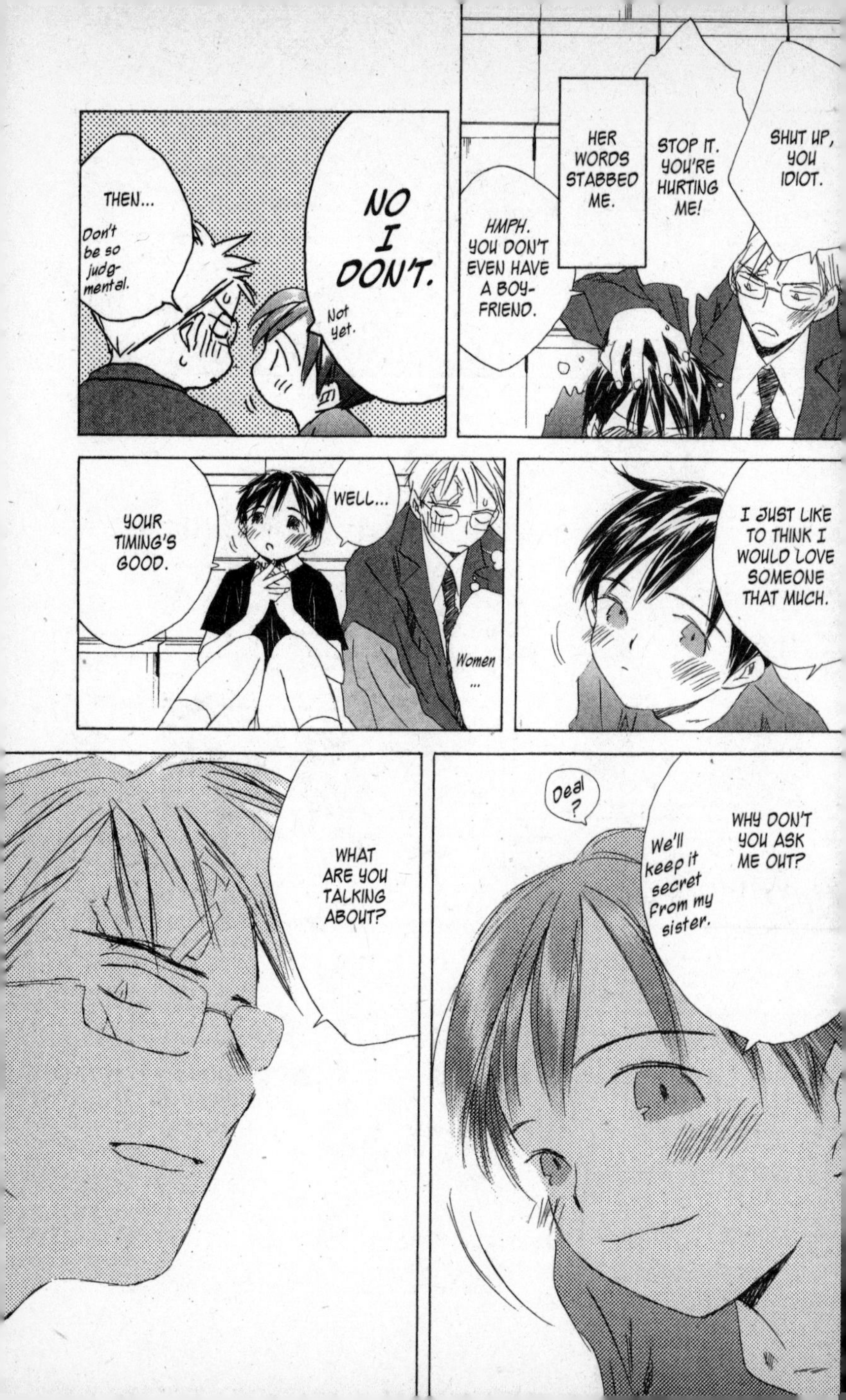
SHUT UP, YOU IDIOT.
STOP IT. YOU'RE HURTING ME!
HER WORDS STABBED ME.
HMPH. YOU DON'T EVEN HAVE A BOY-FRIEND.
NO I DON'T.
Not yet.
THEN...
Don't be so judg-mental.
I JUST LIKE TO THINK I WOULD LOVE SOMEONE THAT MUCH.
WELL...
YOUR TIMING'S GOOD.
Women ...
WHY DON'T YOU ASK ME OUT?
We'll keep it secret from my sister.
Deal?
WHAT ARE YOU TALKING ABOUT?

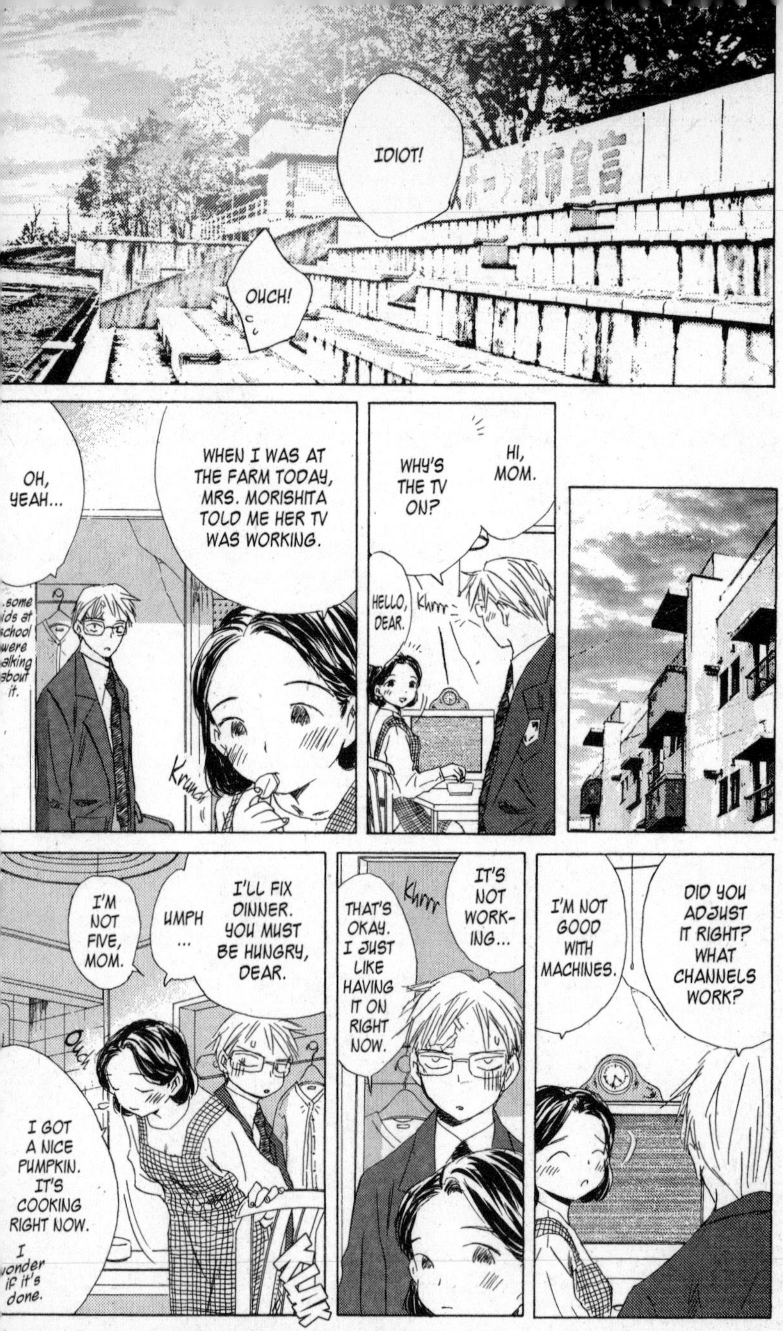
IDIOT!
OUCH!
HI, MOM.
WHY'S THE TV ON?
HELLO, DEAR.
Khrrr
WHEN I WAS AT THE FARM TODAY, MRS. MORISHITA TOLD ME HER TV WAS WORKING.
OH, YEAH...
...some kids at school were talking about it.
Krunch
DID YOU ADJUST IT RIGHT? WHAT CHANNELS WORK?
I'M NOT GOOD WITH MACHINES.
IT'S NOT WORKING...
Khrrr
THAT'S OKAY. I JUST LIKE HAVING IT ON RIGHT NOW.
I'LL FIX DINNER. YOU MUST BE HUNGRY, DEAR.
UMPH...
I'M NOT FIVE, MOM.
Ouch
I GOT A NICE PUMPKIN. IT'S COOKING RIGHT NOW.
I wonder if it's done.
YANK

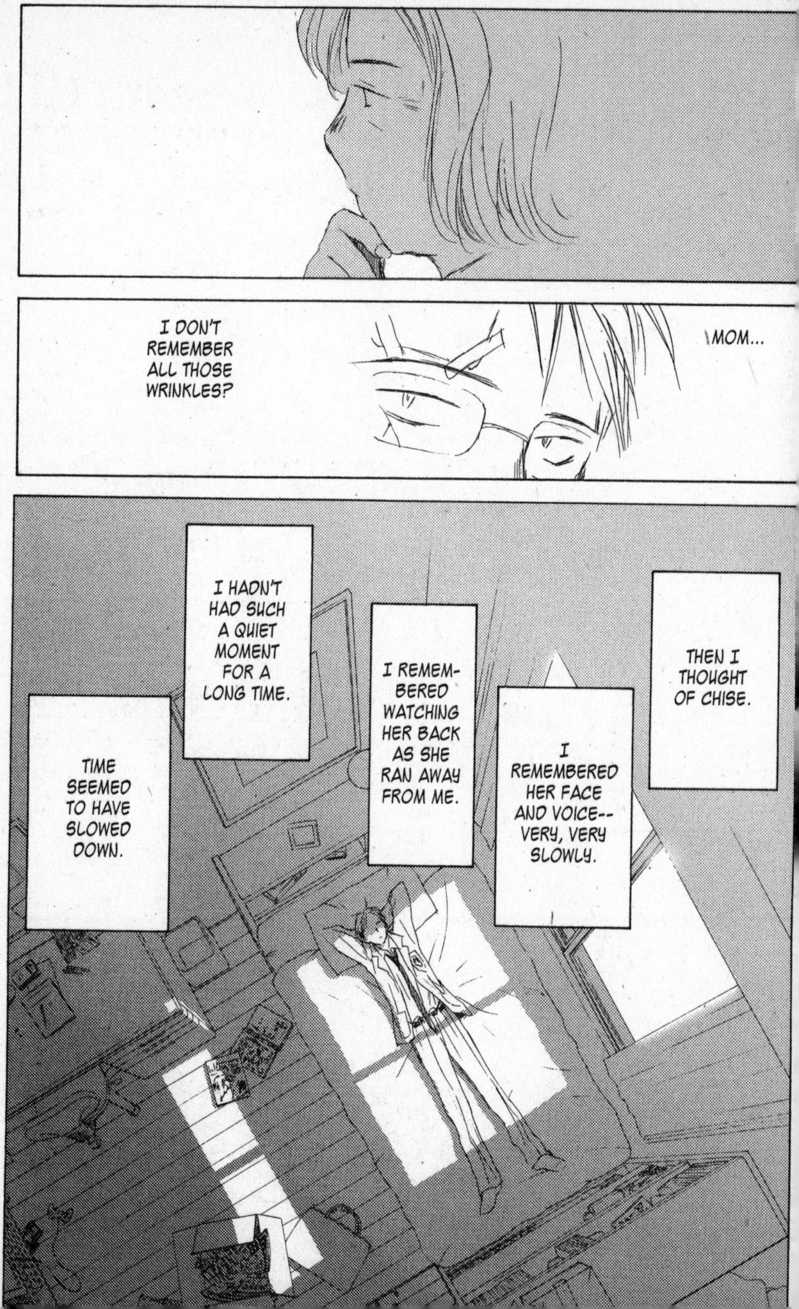
MOM...
I DON'T REMEMBER ALL THOSE WRINKLES?
THEN I THOUGHT OF CHISE.
I REMEMBERED HER FACE AND VOICE--VERY, VERY SLOWLY.
I REMEMBERED WATCHING HER BACK AS SHE RAN AWAY FROM ME.
I HADN'T HAD SUCH A QUIET MOMENT FOR A LONG TIME.
TIME SEEMED TO HAVE SLOWED DOWN.

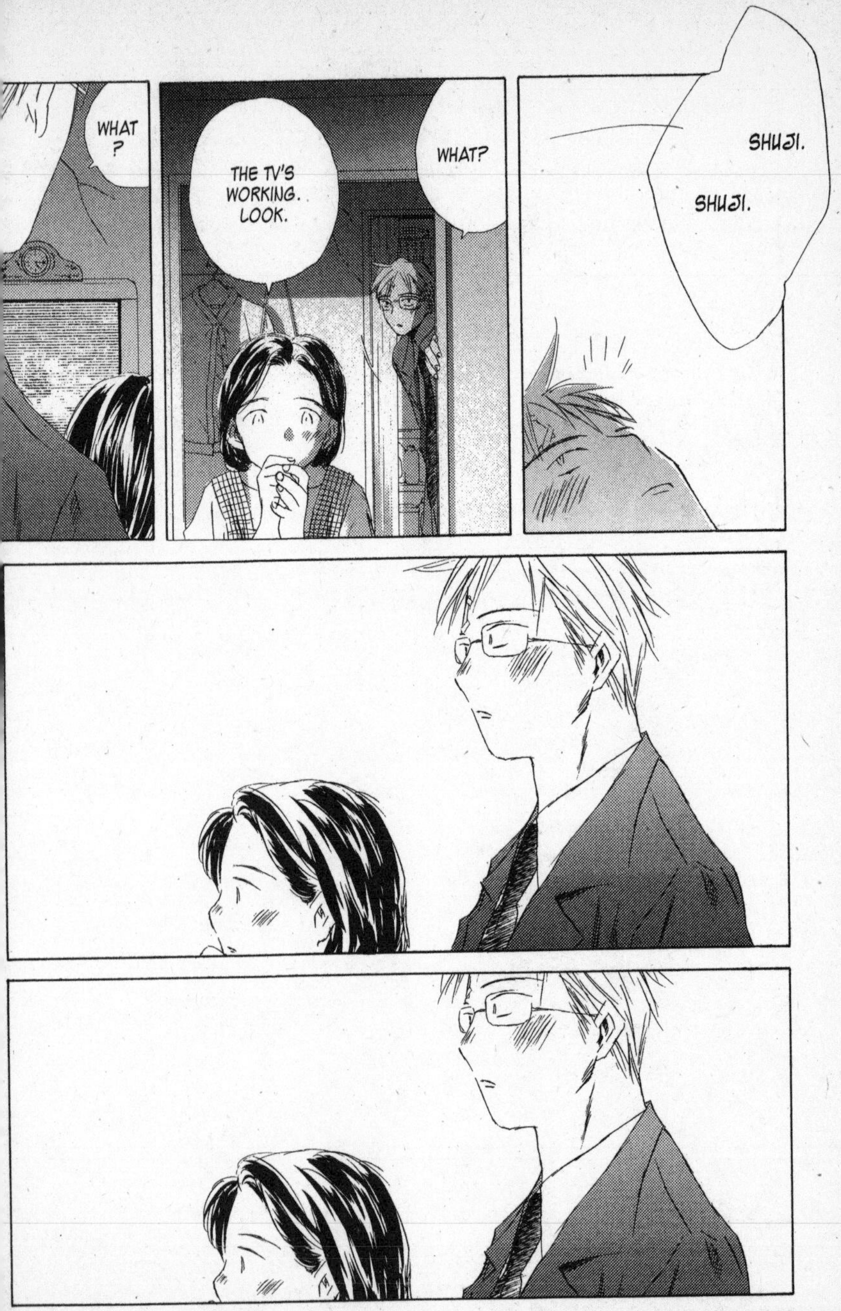
SHUJI.
SHUJI.
WHAT?
THE TV'S WORKING. LOOK.
WHAT ?

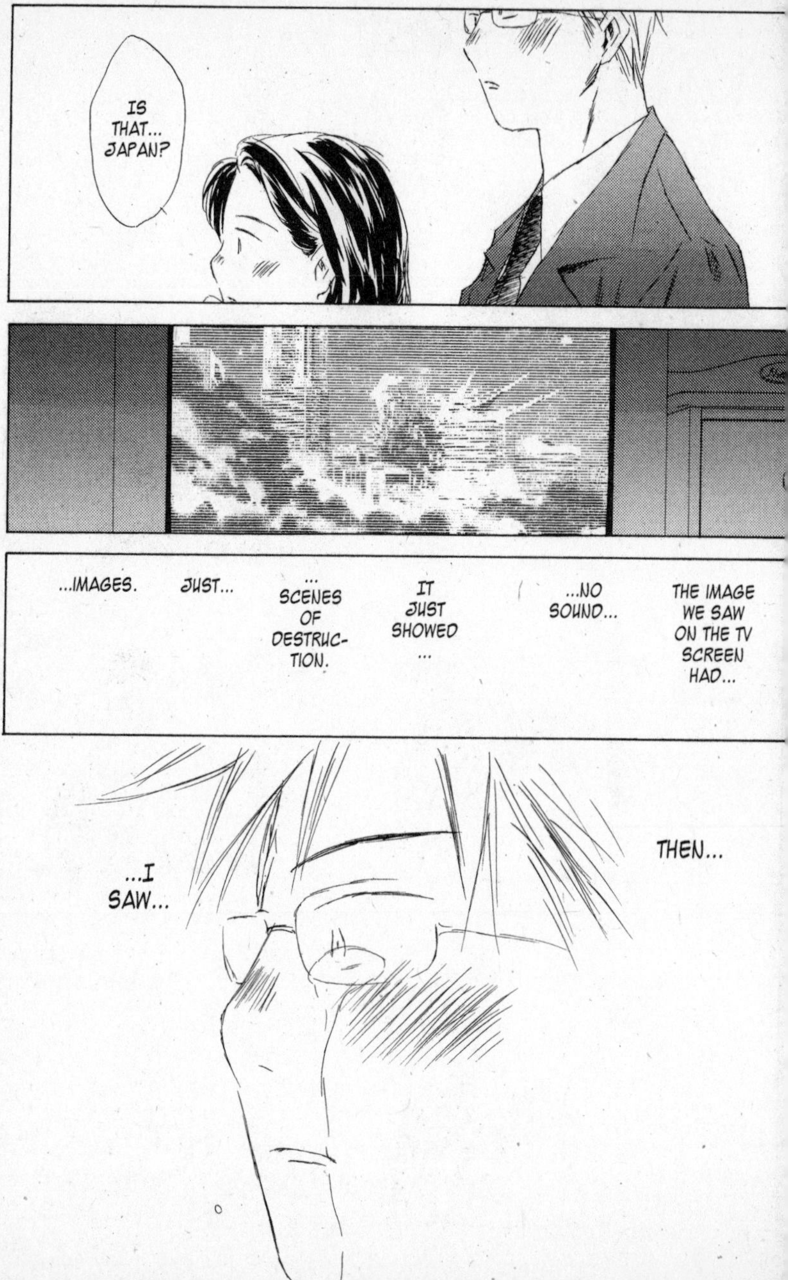
IS THAT... JAPAN?
THE IMAGE WE SAW ON THE TV SCREEN HAD...
...NO SOUND...
IT JUST SHOWED ...
... SCENES OF DESTRUC- TION.
JUST...
...IMAGES.
THEN...
...I SAW...

...HER.

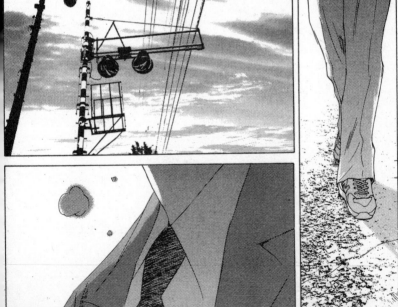

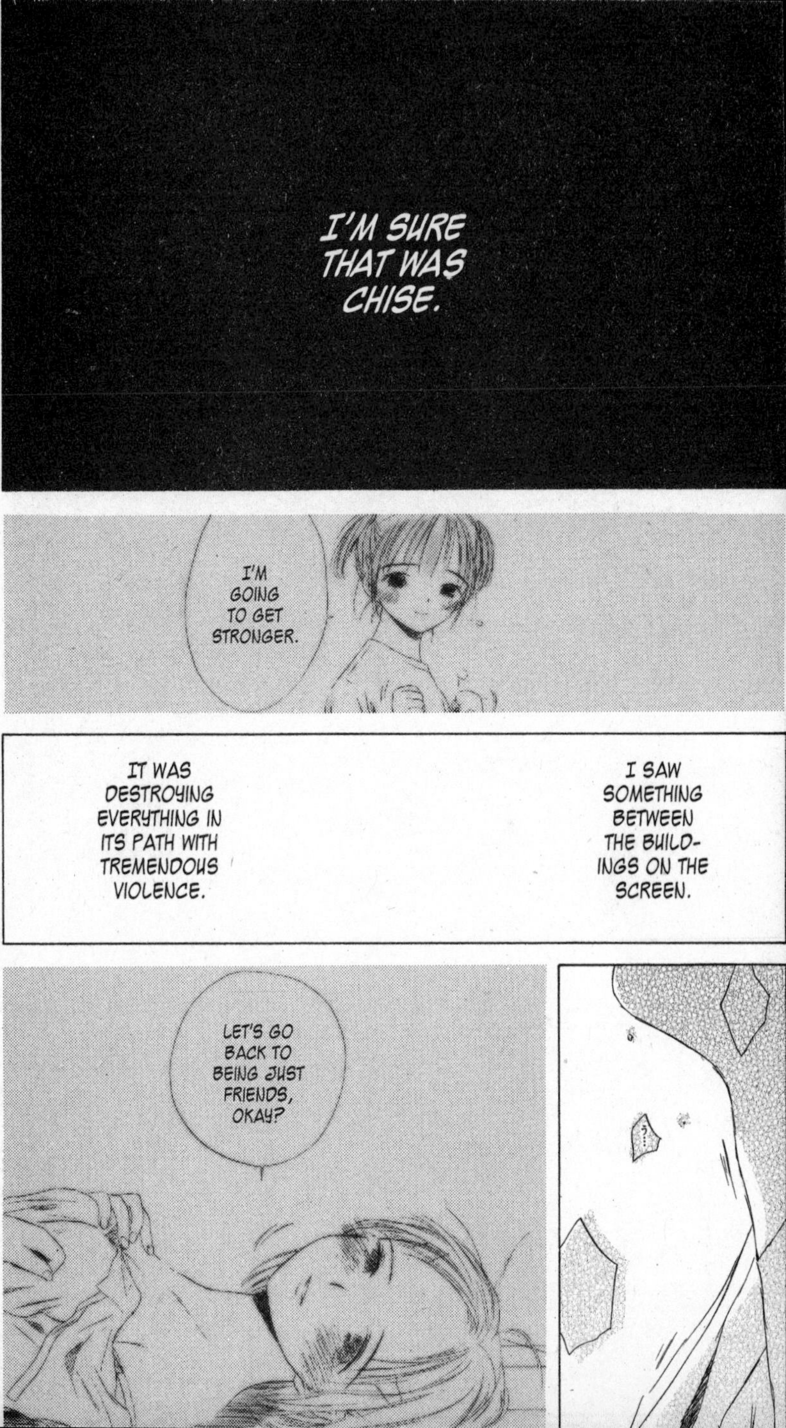
I'M SURE THAT WAS CHISE.
I'M GOING TO GET STRONGER.
I SAW SOMETHING BETWEEN THE BUILDINGS ON THE SCREEN.
IT WAS DESTROYING EVERYTHING IN ITS PATH WITH TREMENDOUS VIOLENCE.
LET'S GO BACK TO BEING JUST FRIENDS, OKAY?

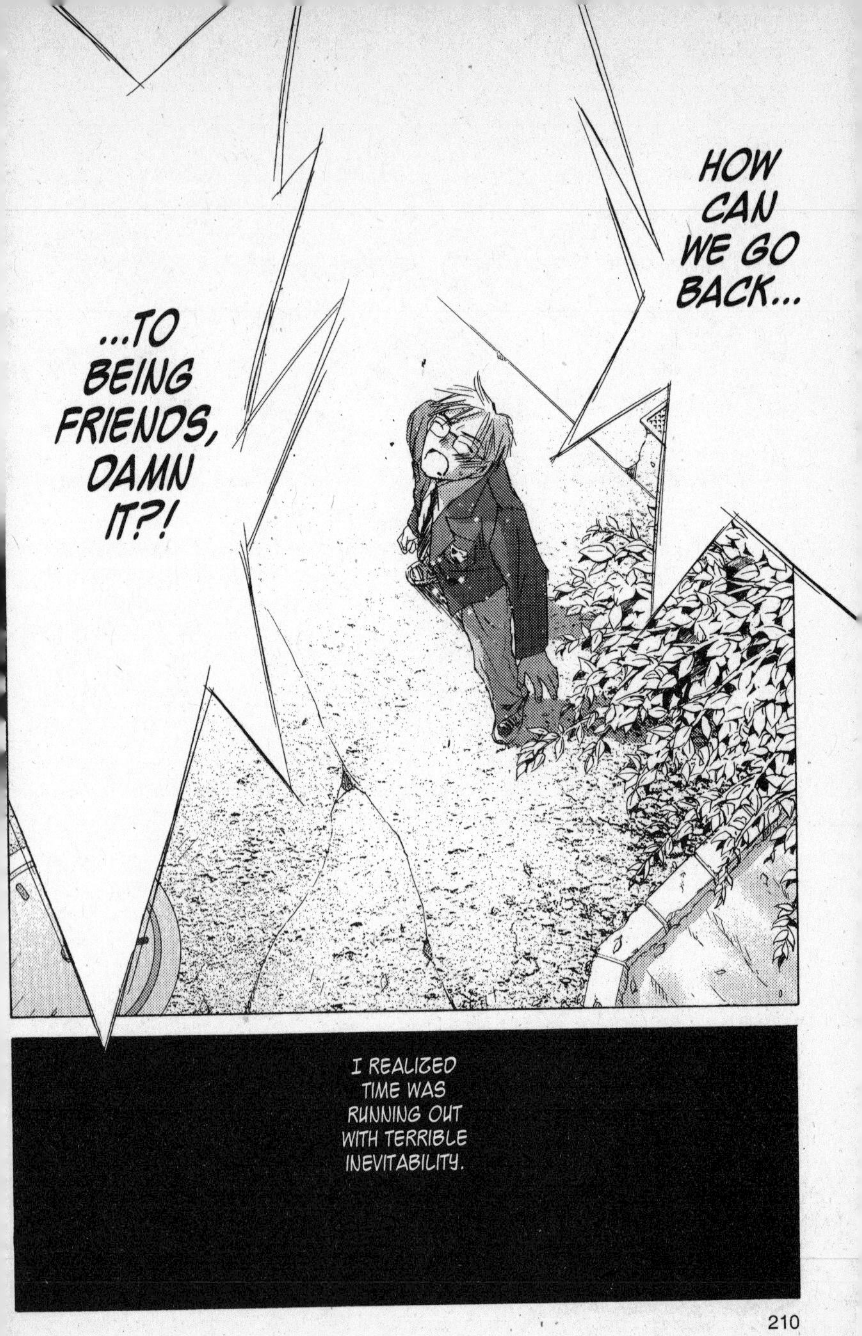
HOW CAN WE GO BACK...
...TO BEING FRIENDS, DAMN IT?!
I REALIZED TIME WAS RUNNING OUT WITH TERRIBLE INEVITABILITY.

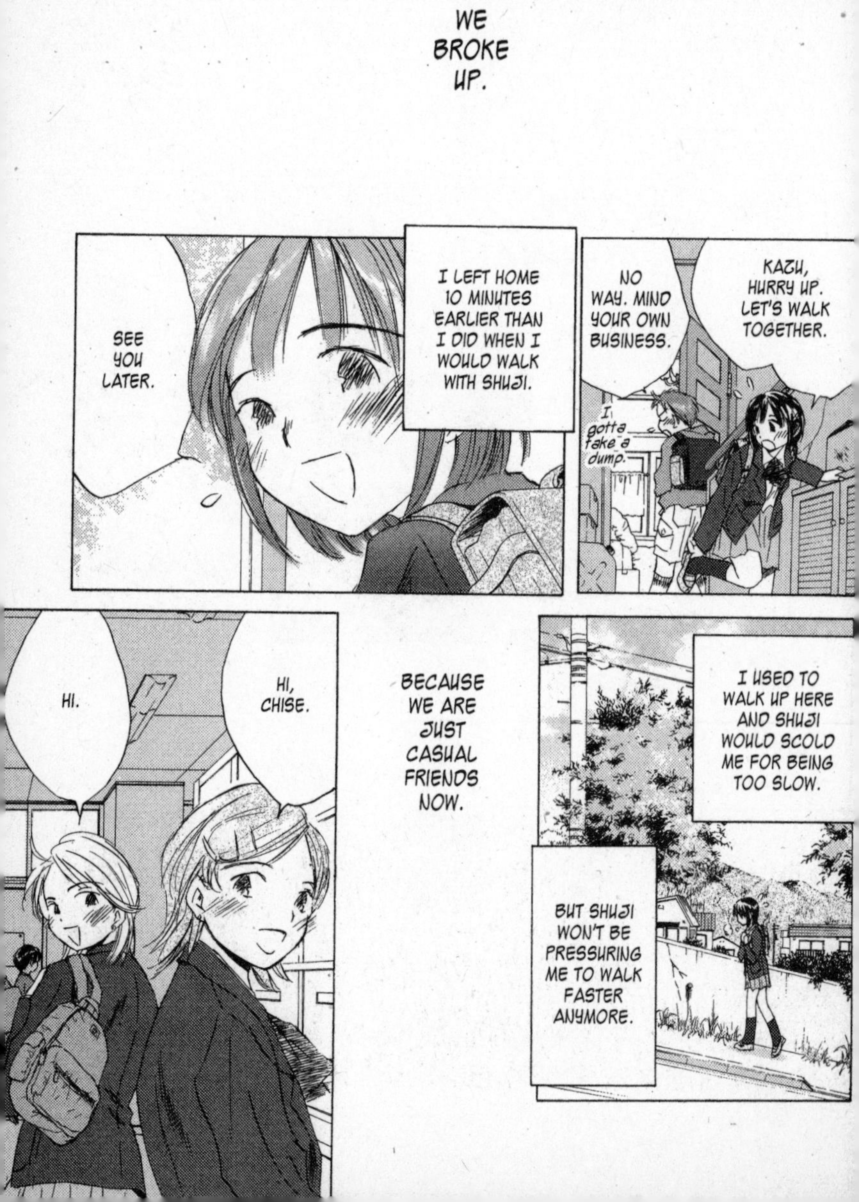
WE BROKE UP.
KAZU, HURRY UP. LET'S WALK TOGETHER.
NO WAY. MIND YOUR OWN BUSINESS.
I gotta take a dump.
I LEFT HOME 10 MINUTES EARLIER THAN I DID WHEN I WOULD WALK WITH SHUJI.
SEE YOU LATER.
I USED TO WALK UP HERE AND SHUJI WOULD SCOLD ME FOR BEING TOO SLOW.
BUT SHUJI WON'T BE PRESSURING ME TO WALK FASTER ANYMORE.
BECAUSE WE ARE JUST CASUAL FRIENDS NOW.
HI, CHISE.
HI.

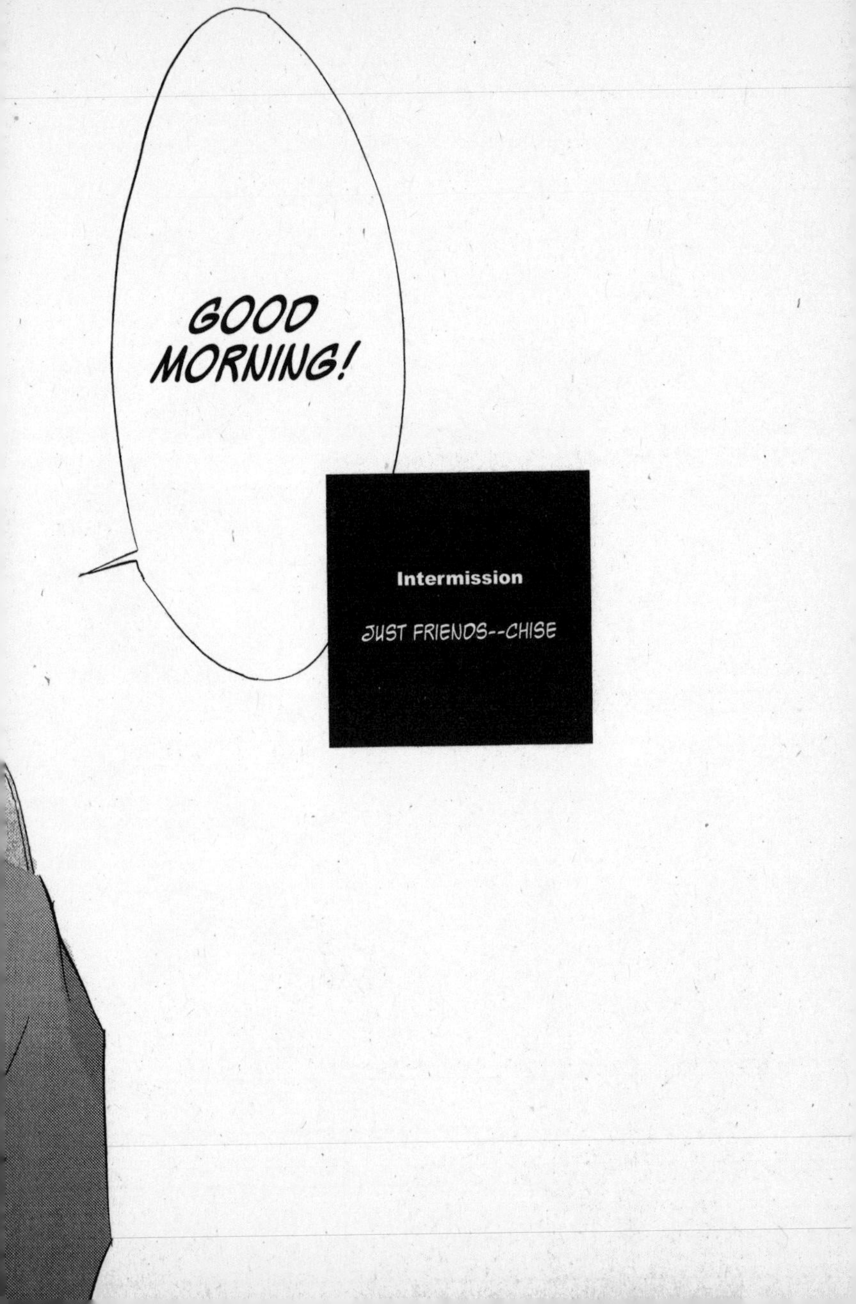
GOOD MORNING!
Intermission
JUST FRIENDS--CHISE

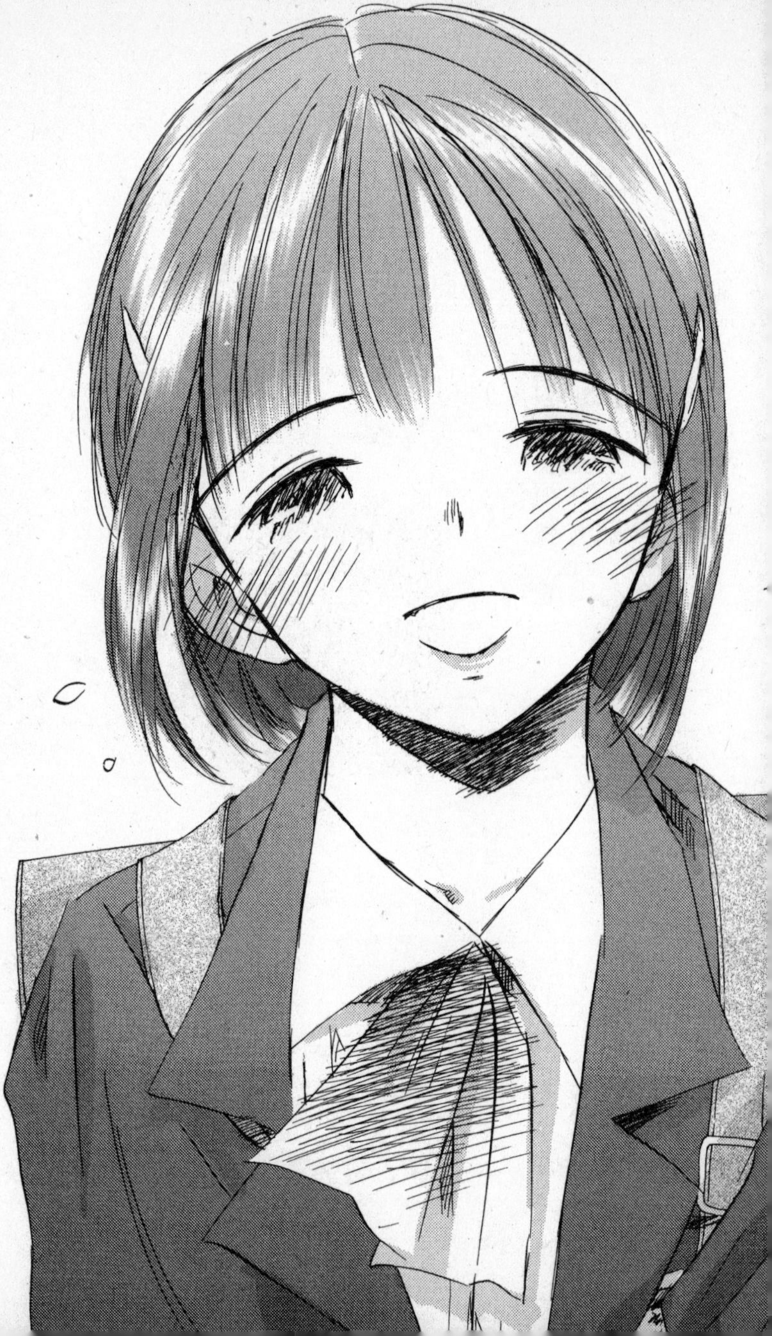

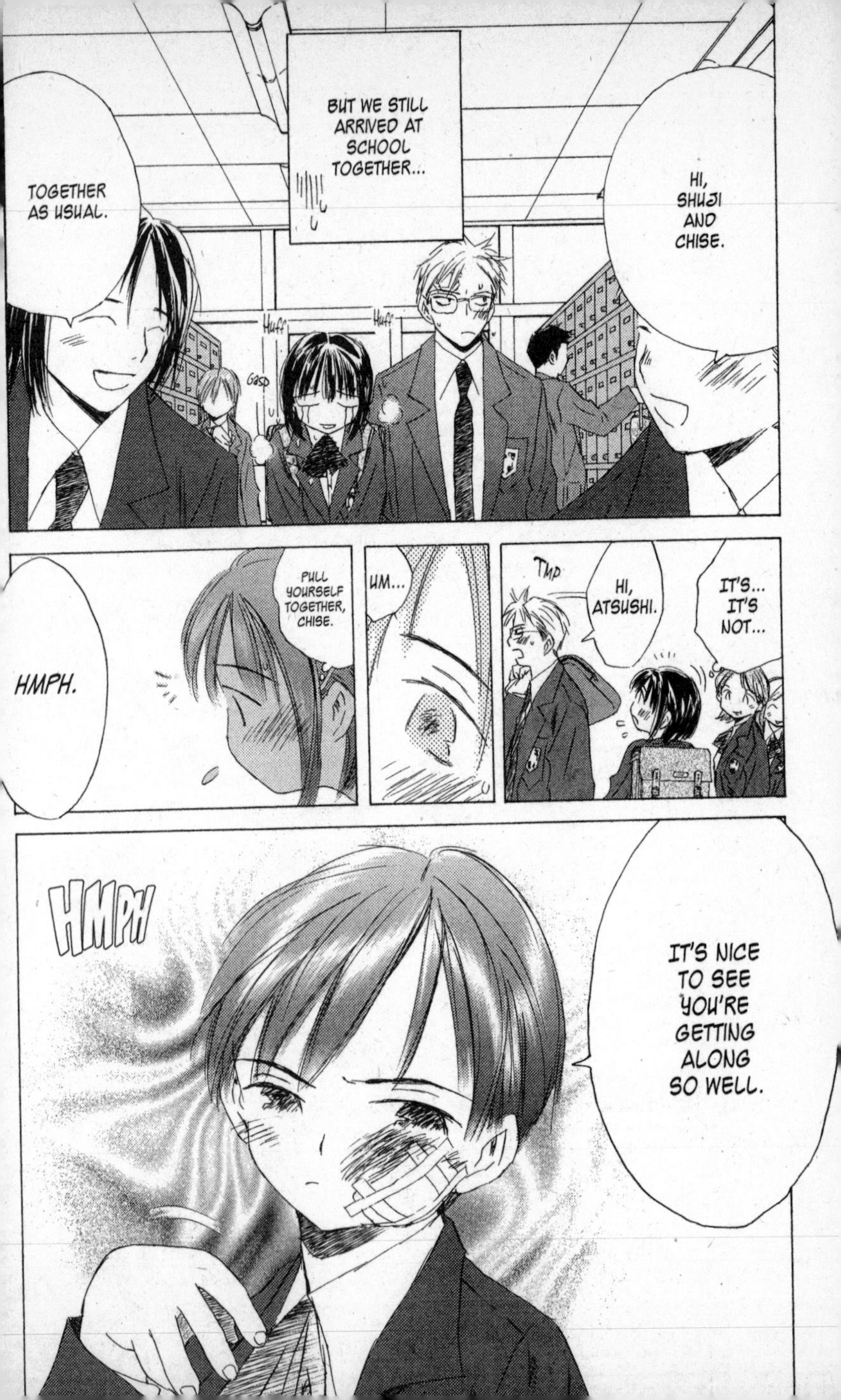
BUT WE STILL ARRIVED AT SCHOOL TOGETHER...
HI, SHUJI AND CHISE.
Huff
Huff
Gasp
TOGETHER AS USUAL.
IT'S... IT'S NOT...
HI, ATSUSHI.
TMP
UM...
PULL YOURSELF TOGETHER, CHISE.
HMPH.
IT'S NICE TO SEE YOU'RE GETTING ALONG SO WELL.
HMPH

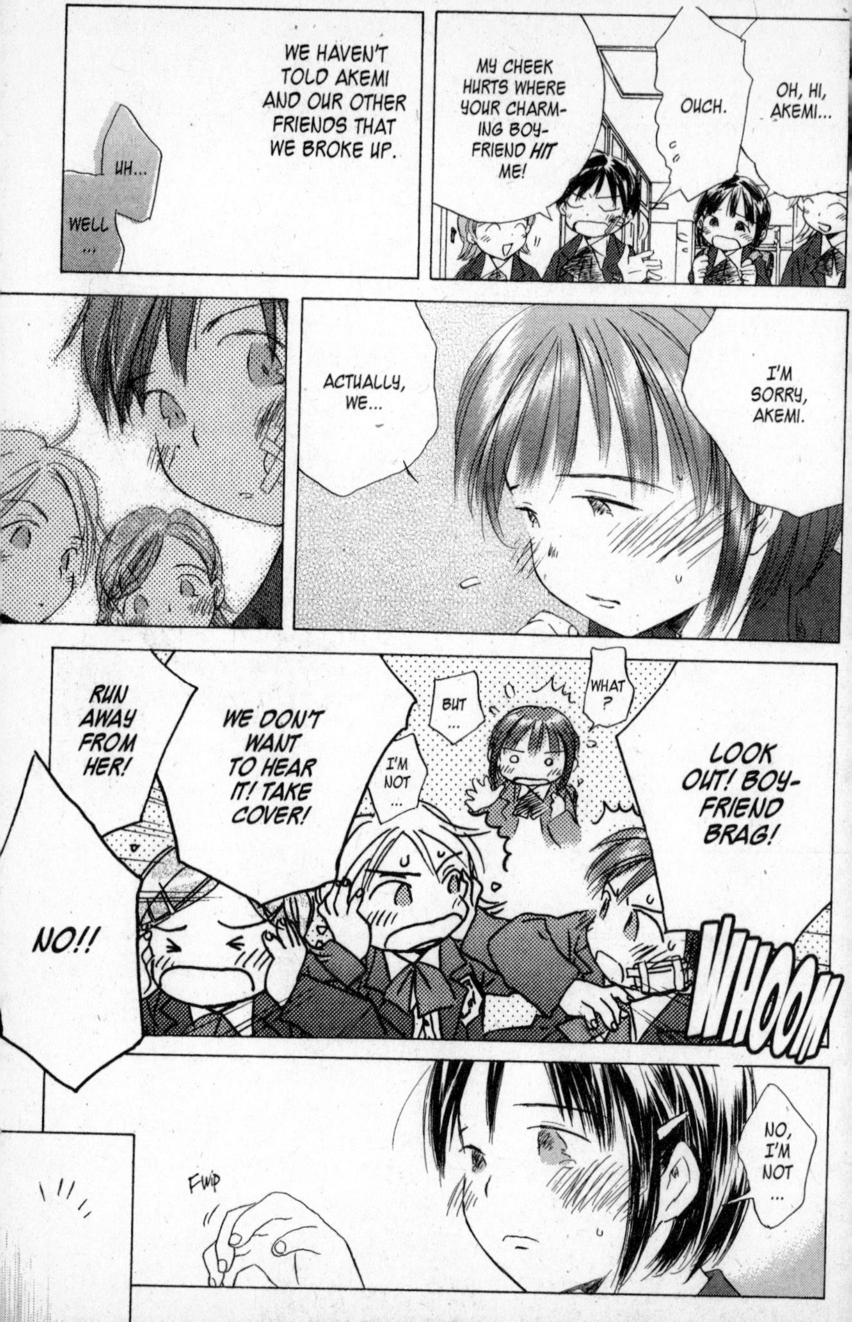
OH, HI, AKEMI...
OUCH.
MY CHEEK HURTS WHERE YOUR CHARMING BOYFRIEND HIT ME!
WE HAVEN'T TOLD AKEMI AND OUR OTHER FRIENDS THAT WE BROKE UP.
UH... WELL...
I'M SORRY, AKEMI.
ACTUALLY, WE...
LOOK OUT! BOYFRIEND BRAG!
WHAT?
BUT...
I'M NOT...
WE DON'T WANT TO HEAR IT! TAKE COVER!
RUN AWAY FROM HER!
WHOOM
NO!!
NO, I'M NOT...
FWIP

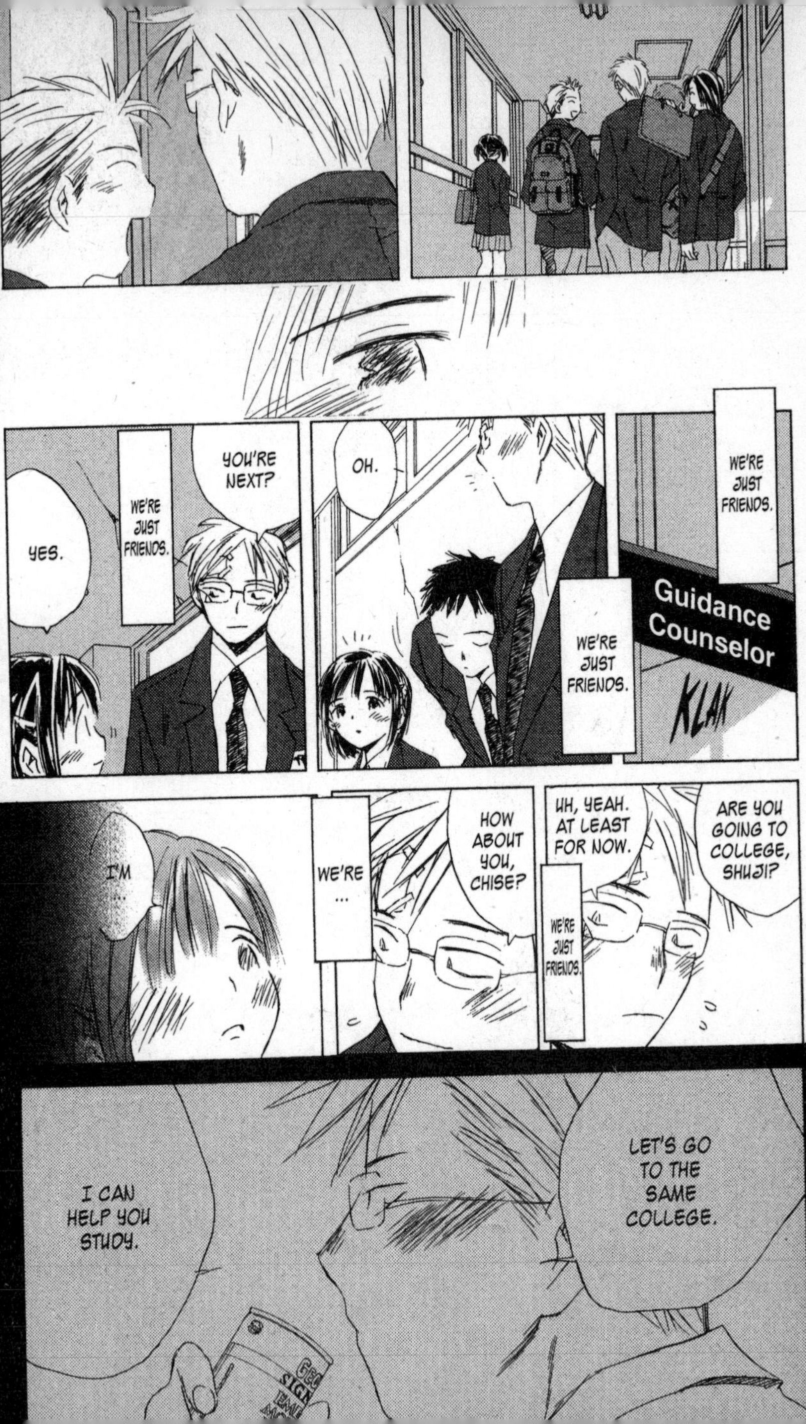
WE'RE JUST FRIENDS.
Guidance Counselor
KLAK
OH.
WE'RE JUST FRIENDS.
YOU'RE NEXT?
WE'RE JUST FRIENDS.
YES.
ARE YOU GOING TO COLLEGE, SHUJI?
UH, YEAH. AT LEAST FOR NOW.
WE'RE JUST FRIENDS.
HOW ABOUT YOU, CHISE?
WE'RE ...
I'M ...
LET'S GO TO THE SAME COLLEGE.
I CAN HELP YOU STUDY.

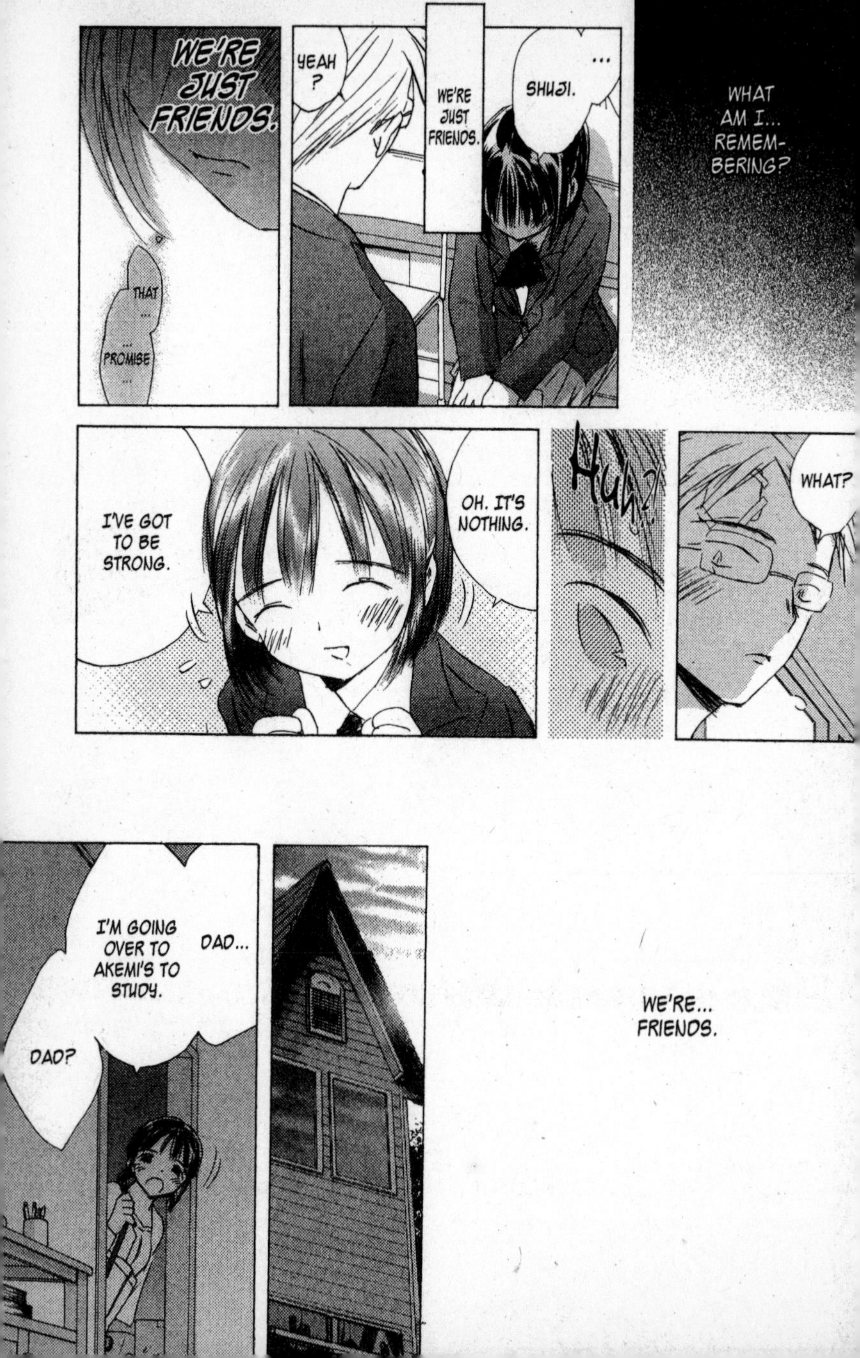
WHAT AM I... REMEMBERING?
...
SHUJI.
WE'RE JUST FRIENDS.
YEAH ?
WE'RE JUST FRIENDS.
THAT ... ... PROMISE ...
WHAT?
HUH?!
OH. IT'S NOTHING.
I'VE GOT TO BE STRONG.
WE'RE... FRIENDS.
DAD...
I'M GOING OVER TO AKEMI'S TO STUDY.
DAD?

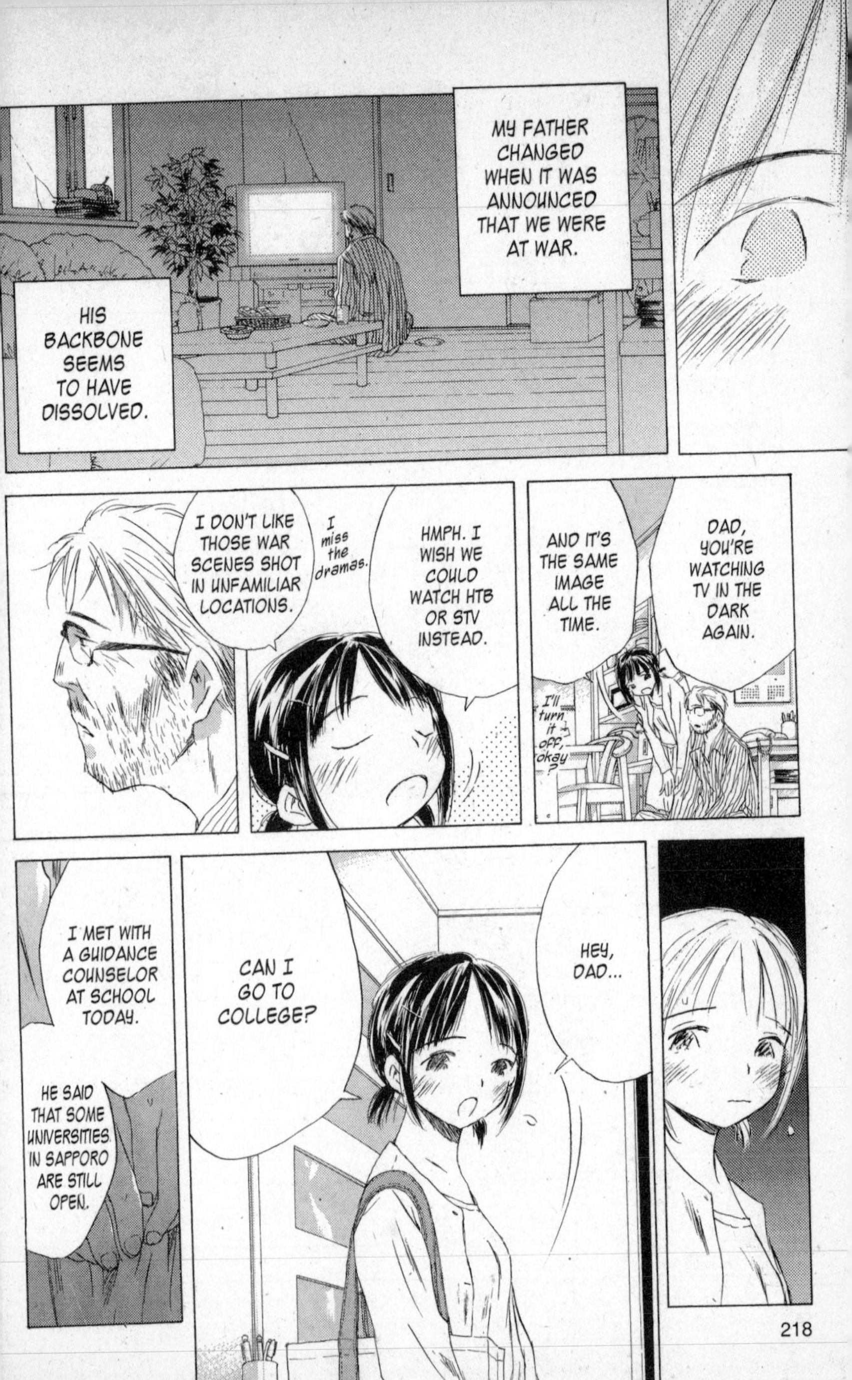
MY FATHER CHANGED WHEN IT WAS ANNOUNCED THAT WE WERE AT WAR.
HIS BACKBONE SEEMS TO HAVE DISSOLVED.
DAD, YOU'RE WATCHING TV IN THE DARK AGAIN.
AND IT'S THE SAME IMAGE ALL THE TIME.
I'll turn it off, okay?
HMPH. I WISH WE COULD WATCH HTB OR STV INSTEAD.
I miss the dramas.
I DON'T LIKE THOSE WAR SCENES SHOT IN UNFAMILIAR LOCATIONS.
HEY, DAD...
CAN I GO TO COLLEGE?
I MET WITH A GUIDANCE COUNSELOR AT SCHOOL TODAY.
HE SAID THAT SOME UNIVERSITIES IN SAPPORO ARE STILL OPEN.

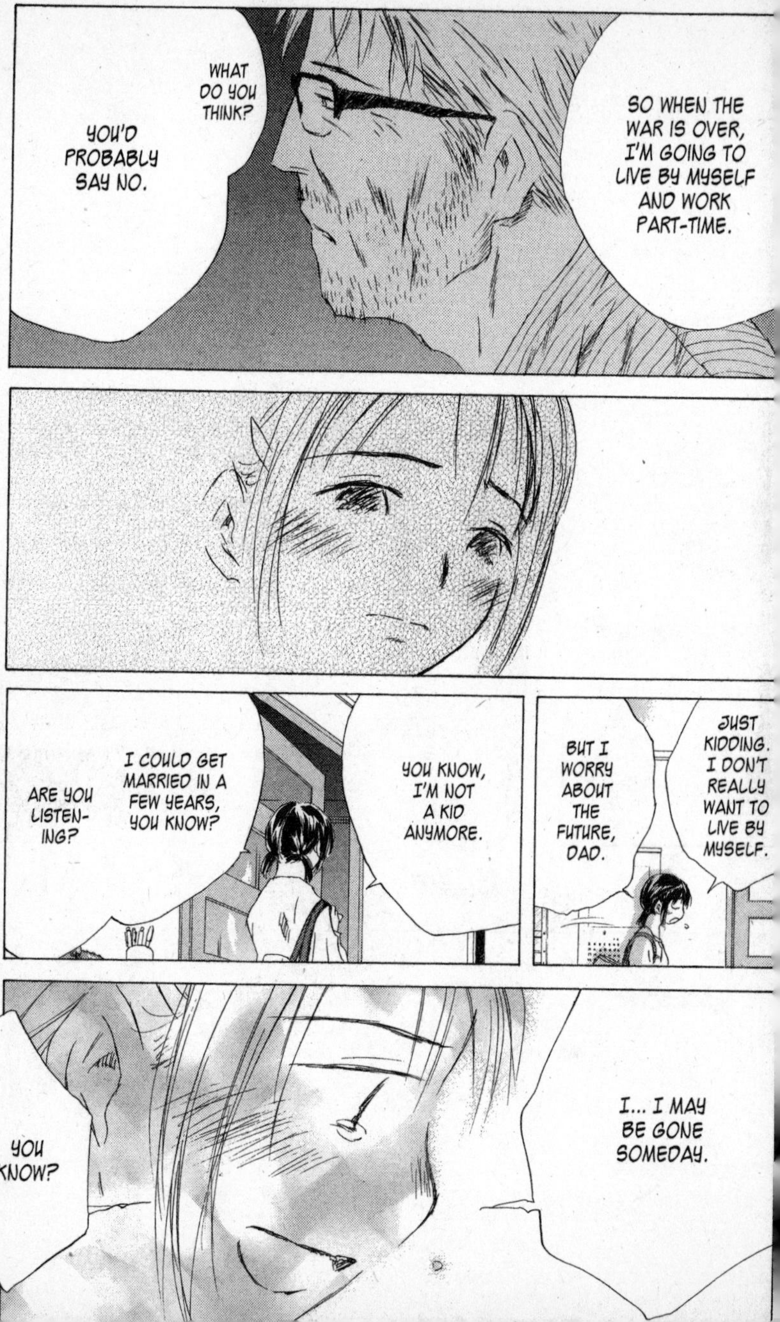
SO WHEN THE WAR IS OVER, I'M GOING TO LIVE BY MYSELF AND WORK PART-TIME.
WHAT DO YOU THINK?
YOU'D PROBABLY SAY NO.
JUST KIDDING. I DON'T REALLY WANT TO LIVE BY MYSELF.
BUT I WORRY ABOUT THE FUTURE, DAD.
YOU KNOW, I'M NOT A KID ANYMORE.
I COULD GET MARRIED IN A FEW YEARS, YOU KNOW?
ARE YOU LISTEN-ING?
I... I MAY BE GONE SOMEDAY.
YOU KNOW?

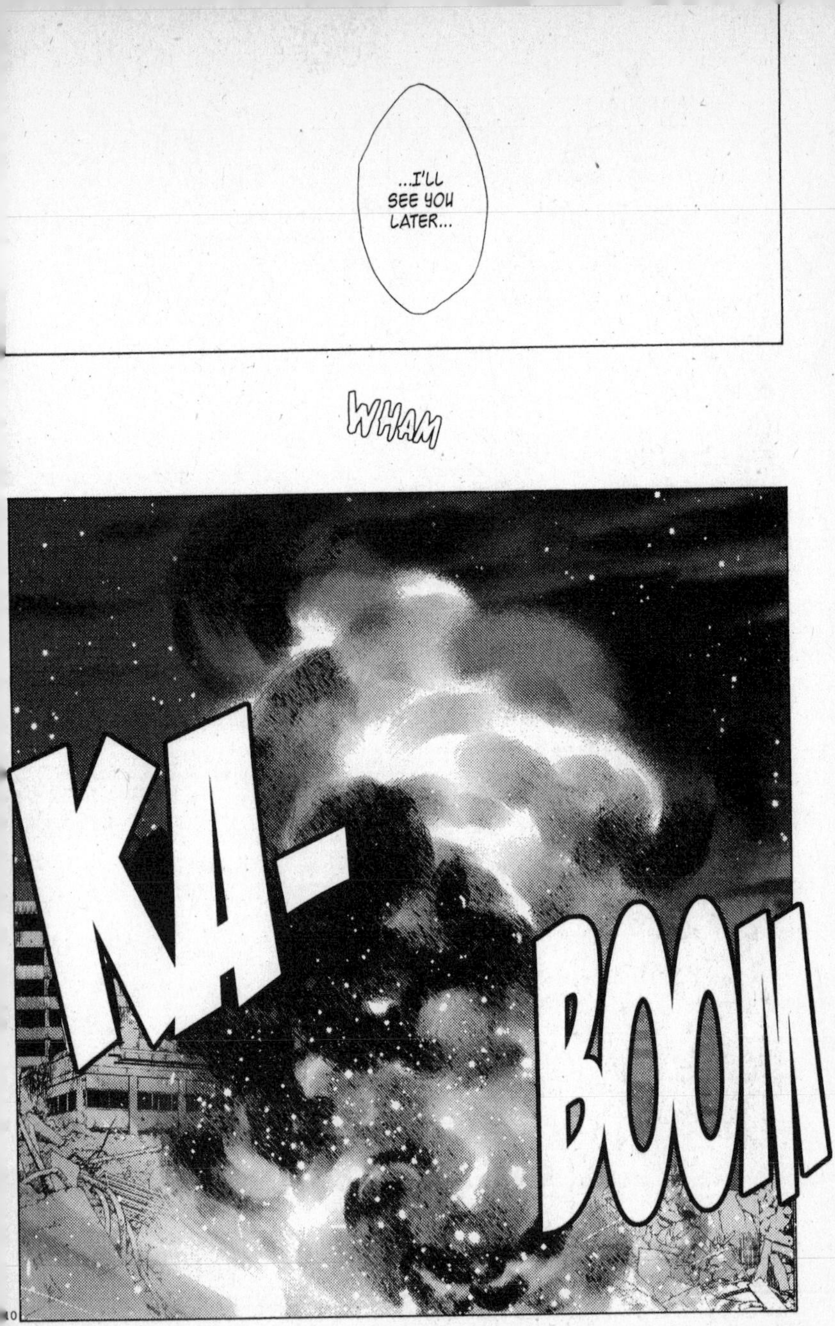
...I'LL SEE YOU LATER...
WHAM
KA-
BOOM

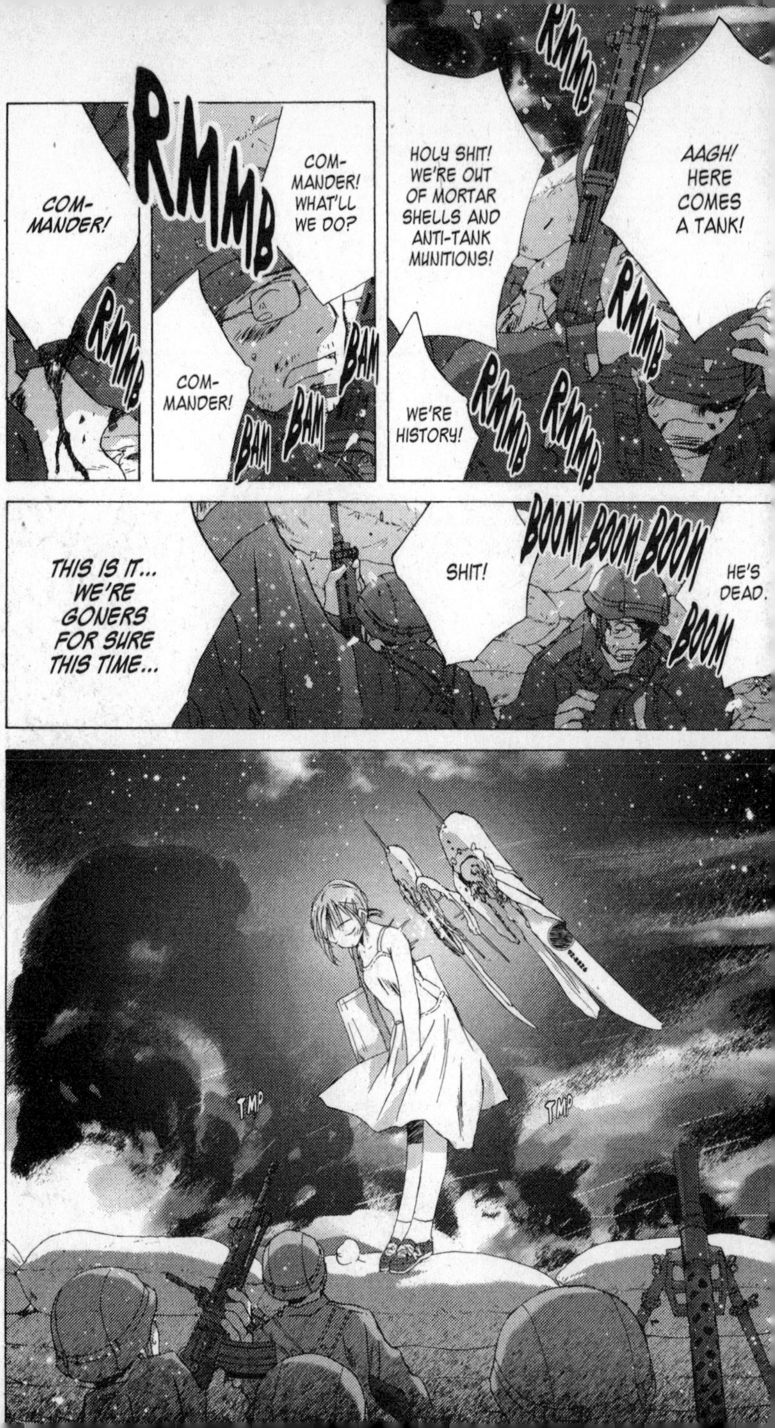

RMMB
AAGH! HERE COMES A TANK!
HOLY SHIT! WE'RE OUT OF MORTAR SHELLS AND ANTI-TANK MUNITIONS!
RMMB
RMMB
RMMB
WE'RE HISTORY!
RMMB
COM-MANDER! WHAT'LL WE DO?
BAM
BAM
COM-MANDER!
BAM
COM-MANDER!
RMMB
BOOM BOOM BOOM
HE'S DEAD.
BOOM
SHIT!
THIS IS IT... WE'RE GONERS FOR SURE THIS TIME...
TMP
TMP

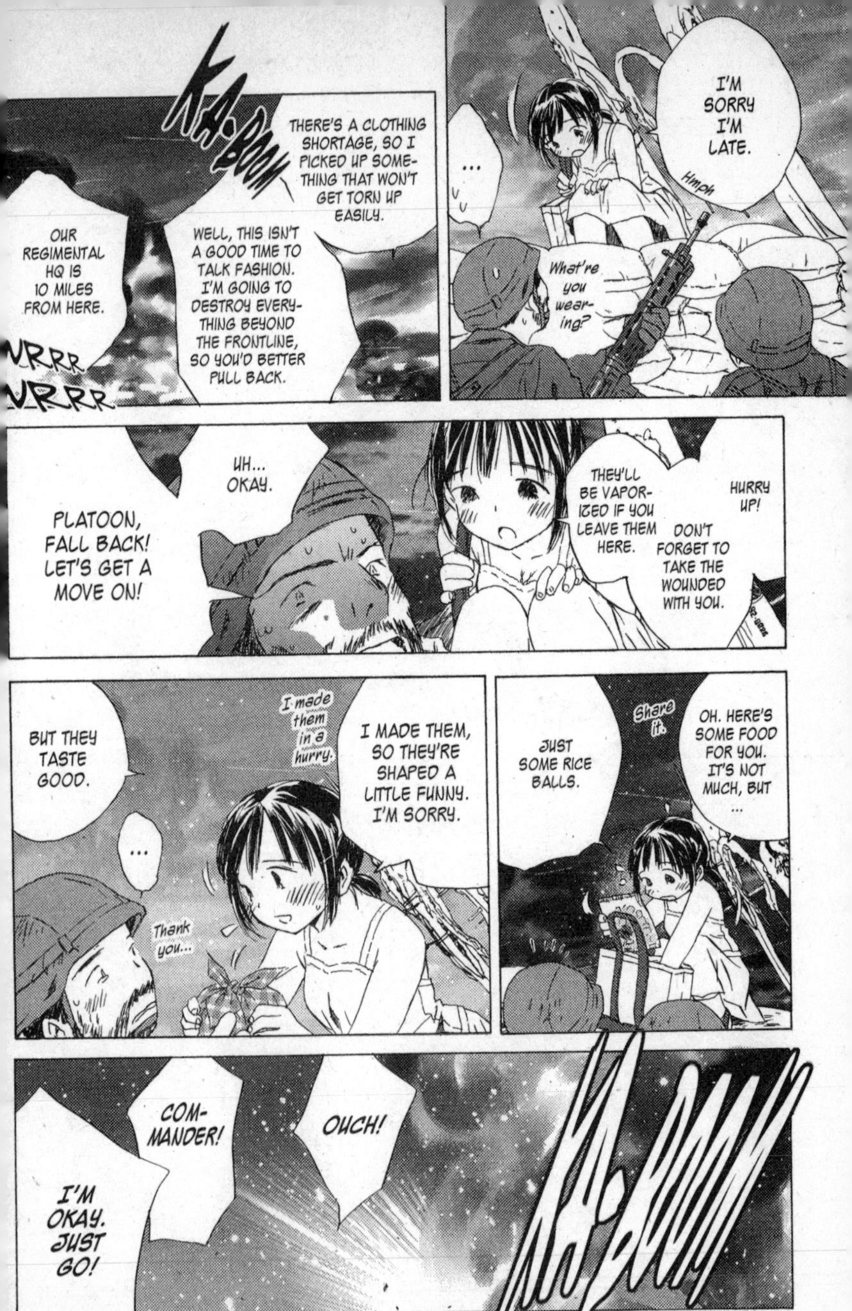
I'M SORRY I'M LATE.
Hmph
...
What're you wearing?
THERE'S A CLOTHING SHORTAGE, SO I PICKED UP SOMETHING THAT WON'T GET TORN UP EASILY.
KA-BOOM
WELL, THIS ISN'T A GOOD TIME TO TALK FASHION. I'M GOING TO DESTROY EVERYTHING BEYOND THE FRONTLINE, SO YOU'D BETTER PULL BACK.
OUR REGIMENTAL HQ IS 10 MILES FROM HERE.
VRRR
VRRR
HURRY UP!
DON'T FORGET TO TAKE THE WOUNDED WITH YOU.
THEY'LL BE VAPORIZED IF YOU LEAVE THEM HERE.
UH... OKAY.
PLATOON, FALL BACK! LET'S GET A MOVE ON!
OH. HERE'S SOME FOOD FOR YOU. IT'S NOT MUCH, BUT ...
Share it.
JUST SOME RICE BALLS.
I MADE THEM, SO THEY'RE SHAPED A LITTLE FUNNY. I'M SORRY.
I made them in a hurry.
BUT THEY TASTE GOOD.
...
Thank you...
OUCH!
COMMANDER!
I'M OKAY. JUST GO!

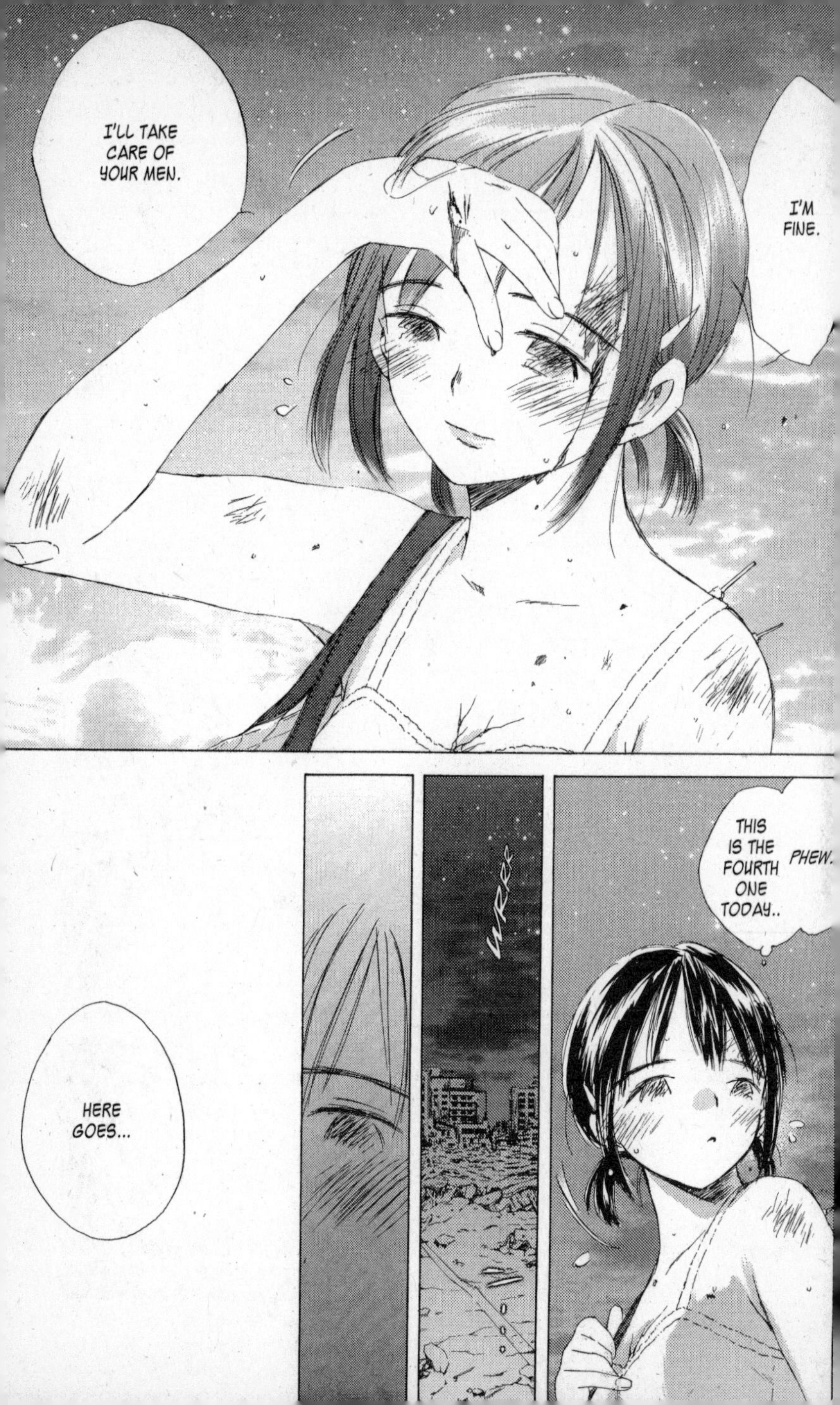
I'M FINE.
I'LL TAKE CARE OF YOUR MEN.
PHEW.
THIS IS THE FOURTH ONE TODAY..
WRRR
HERE GOES...

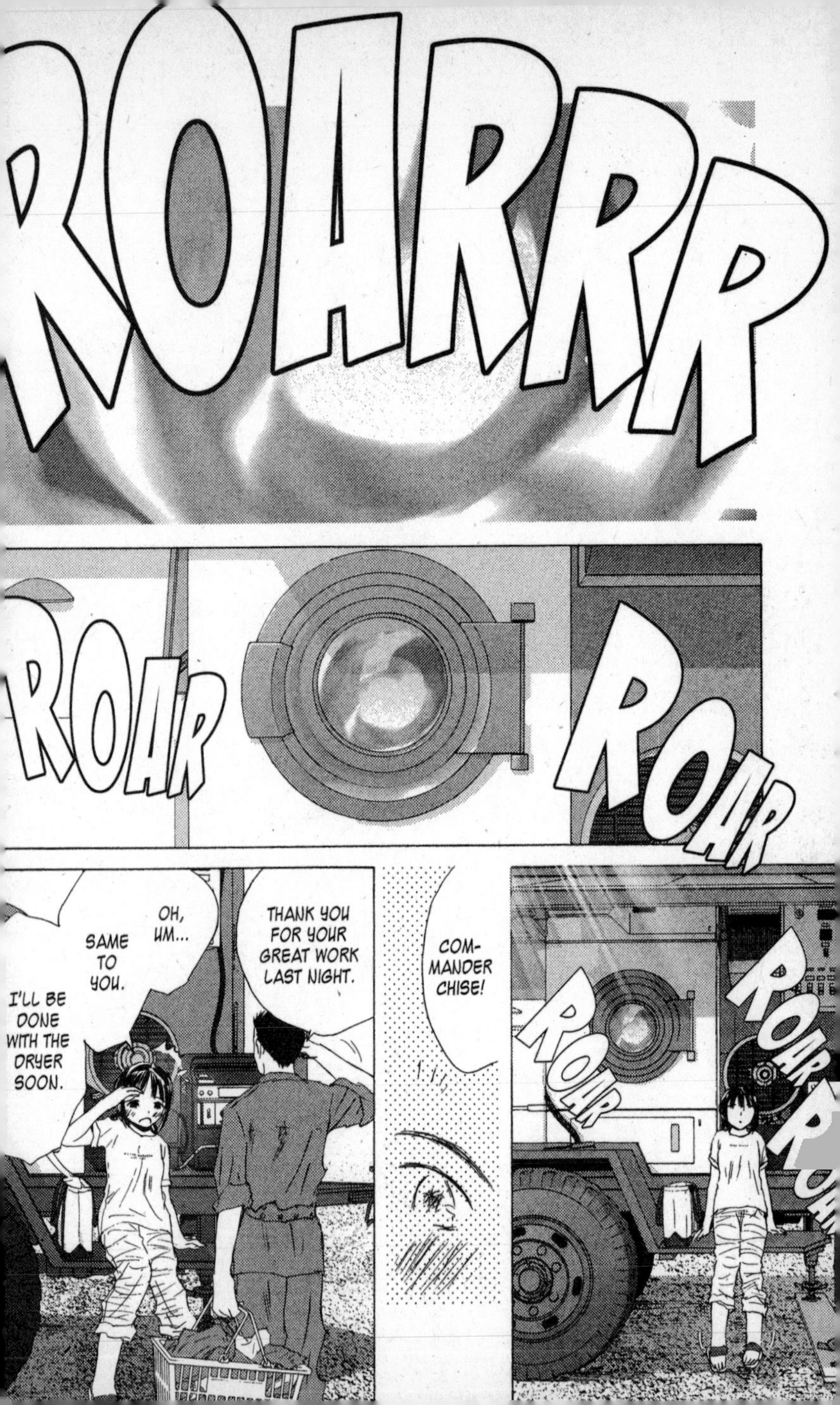
ROARRR
ROAR
ROAR
ROAR
ROAR
COM-MANDER CHISE!
THANK YOU FOR YOUR GREAT WORK LAST NIGHT.
OH, UM...
SAME TO YOU.
I'LL BE DONE WITH THE DRYER SOON.

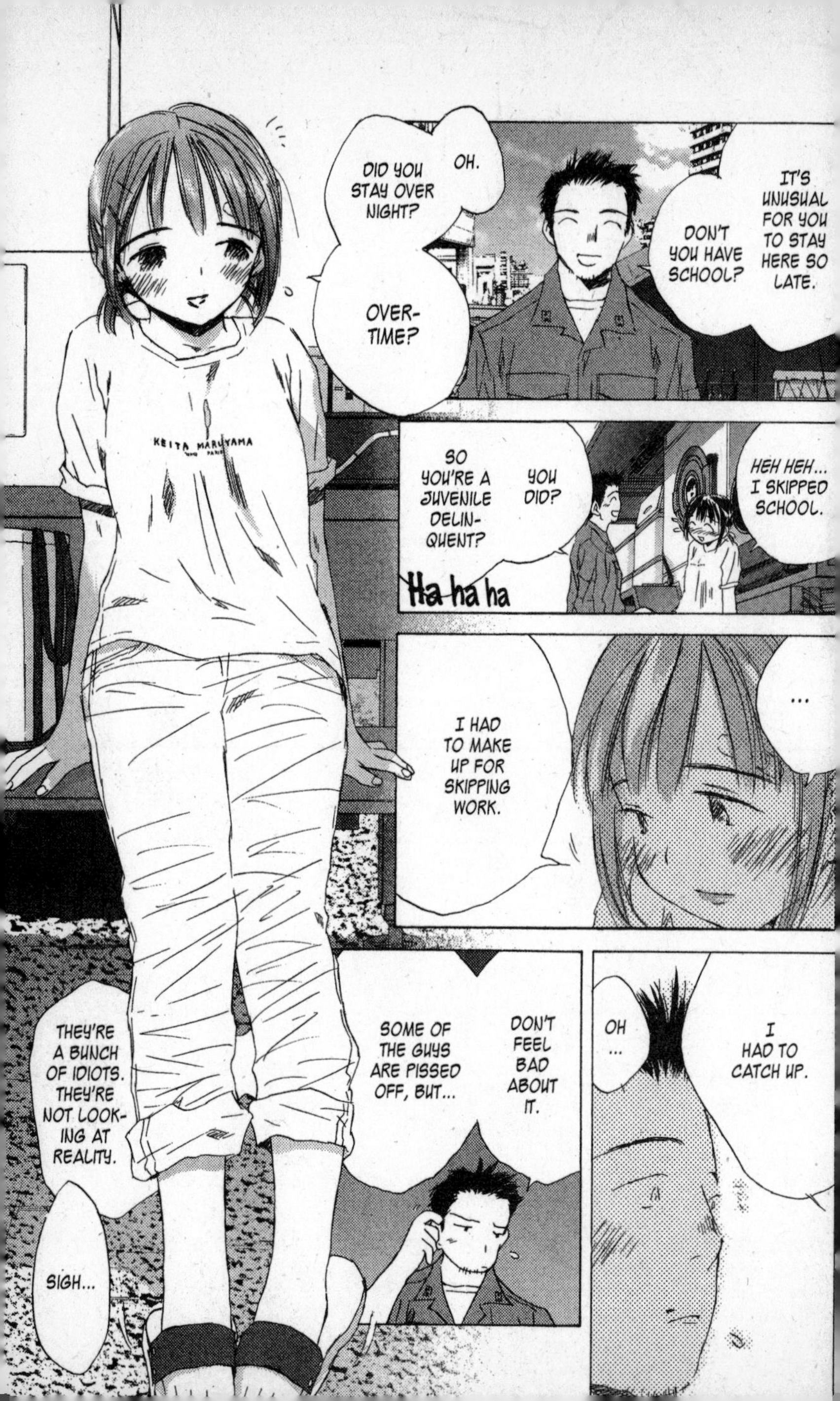
IT'S UNUSUAL FOR YOU TO STAY HERE SO LATE.
DON'T YOU HAVE SCHOOL?
OH.
DID YOU STAY OVER NIGHT?
OVER-TIME?
HEH HEH... I SKIPPED SCHOOL.
YOU DID?
SO YOU'RE A JUVENILE DELIN-QUENT?
Ha ha ha
...
I HAD TO MAKE UP FOR SKIPPING WORK.
I HAD TO CATCH UP.
OH ...
DON'T FEEL BAD ABOUT IT.
SOME OF THE GUYS ARE PISSED OFF, BUT...
THEY'RE A BUNCH OF IDIOTS. THEY'RE NOT LOOK-ING AT REALITY.
SIGH...
KEITA MARUYAMA

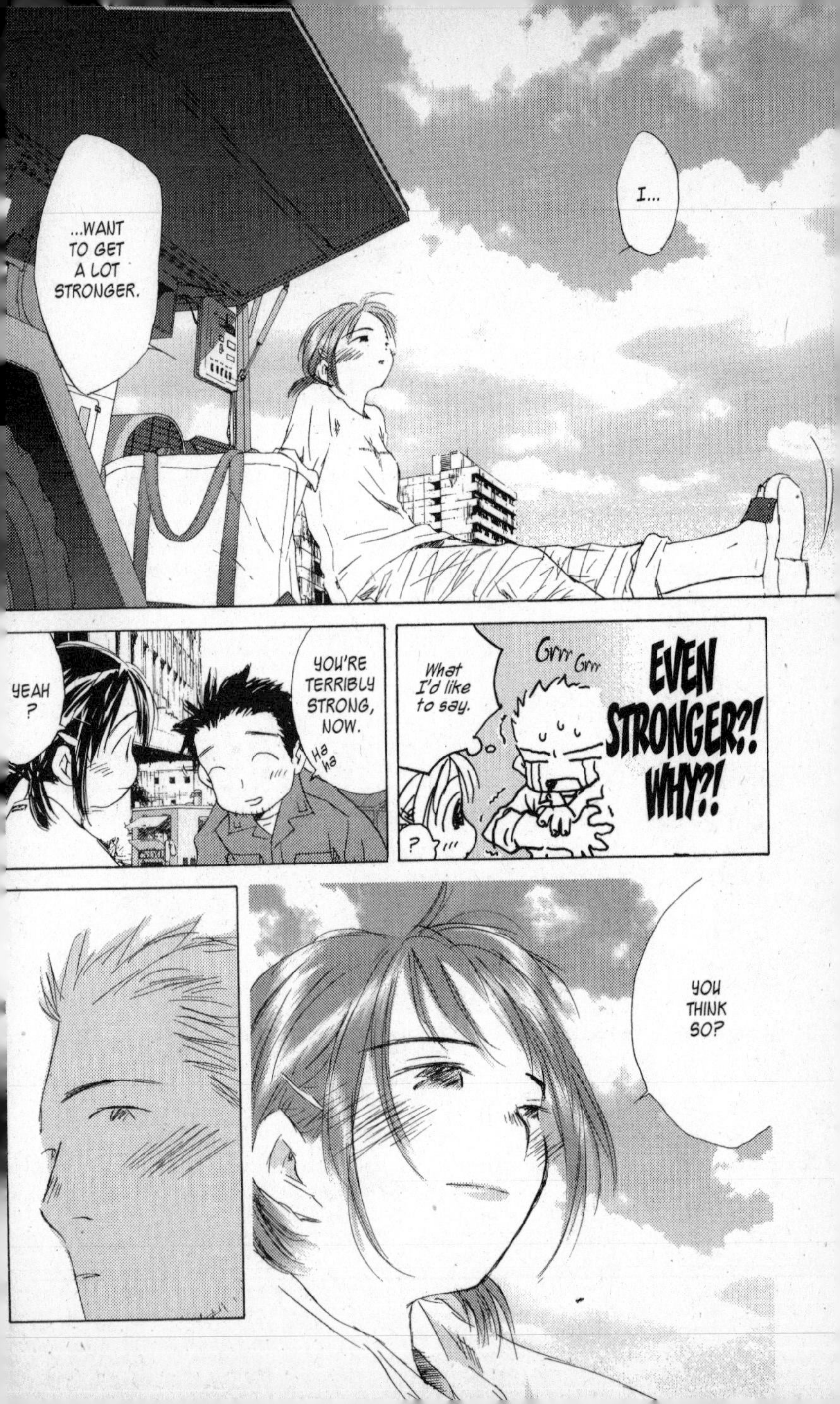
I...
...WANT TO GET A LOT STRONGER.
EVEN STRONGER?! WHY?!
Grrr Grrr
What I'd like to say.
?
YOU'RE TERRIBLY STRONG, NOW.
Ha ha
YEAH ?
YOU THINK SO?

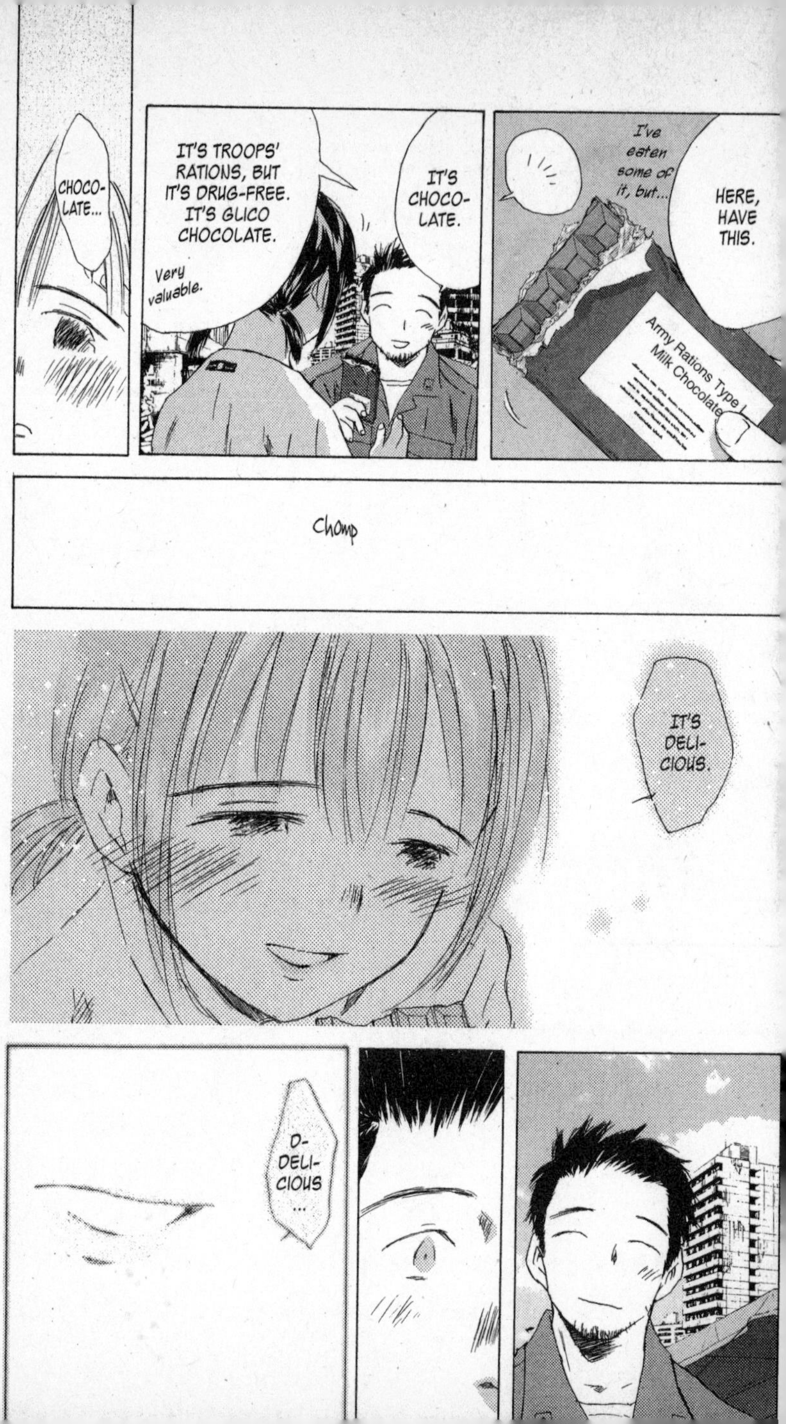
HERE, HAVE THIS.
I've eaten some of it, but...
Army Rations Type Milk Chocolate
IT'S CHOCO-LATE.
IT'S TROOPS' RATIONS, BUT IT'S DRUG-FREE. IT'S GLICO CHOCOLATE.
Very valuable.
CHOCO-LATE...
Chomp
IT'S DELI-CIOUS.
D-DELI-CIOUS...

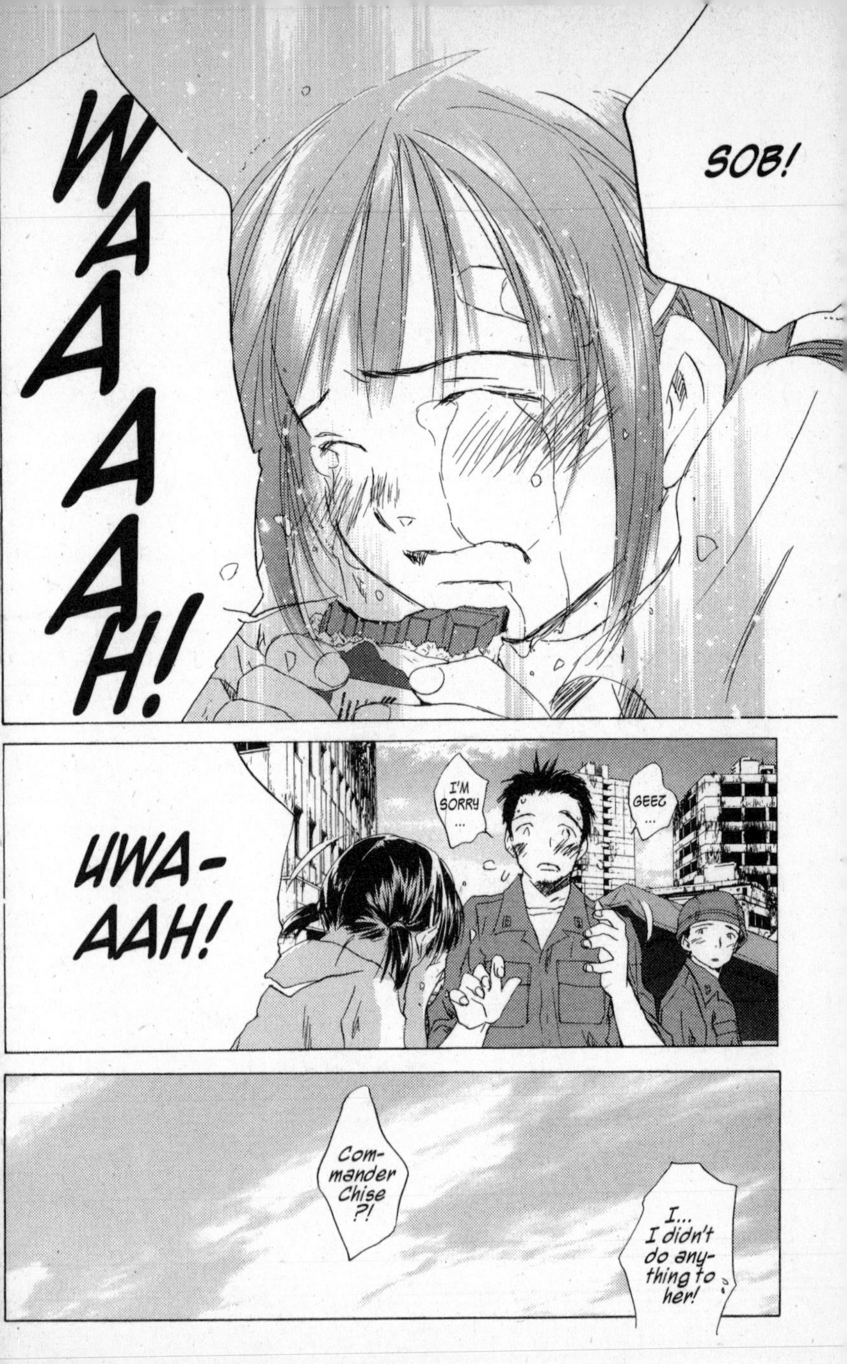
SOB!
WAAAAH!
GEEZ ...
I'M SORRY ...
UWA-AAH!
I... I didn't do anything to her!
Commander Chise ?!

I HAVEN'T CRIED LIKE THIS SINCE I BROKE UP WITH SHUJI.

I CAN'T BREATHE.

MY THROAT HURTS.

HOW EMBARRASSING
...

I CAN'T STOP CRYING.

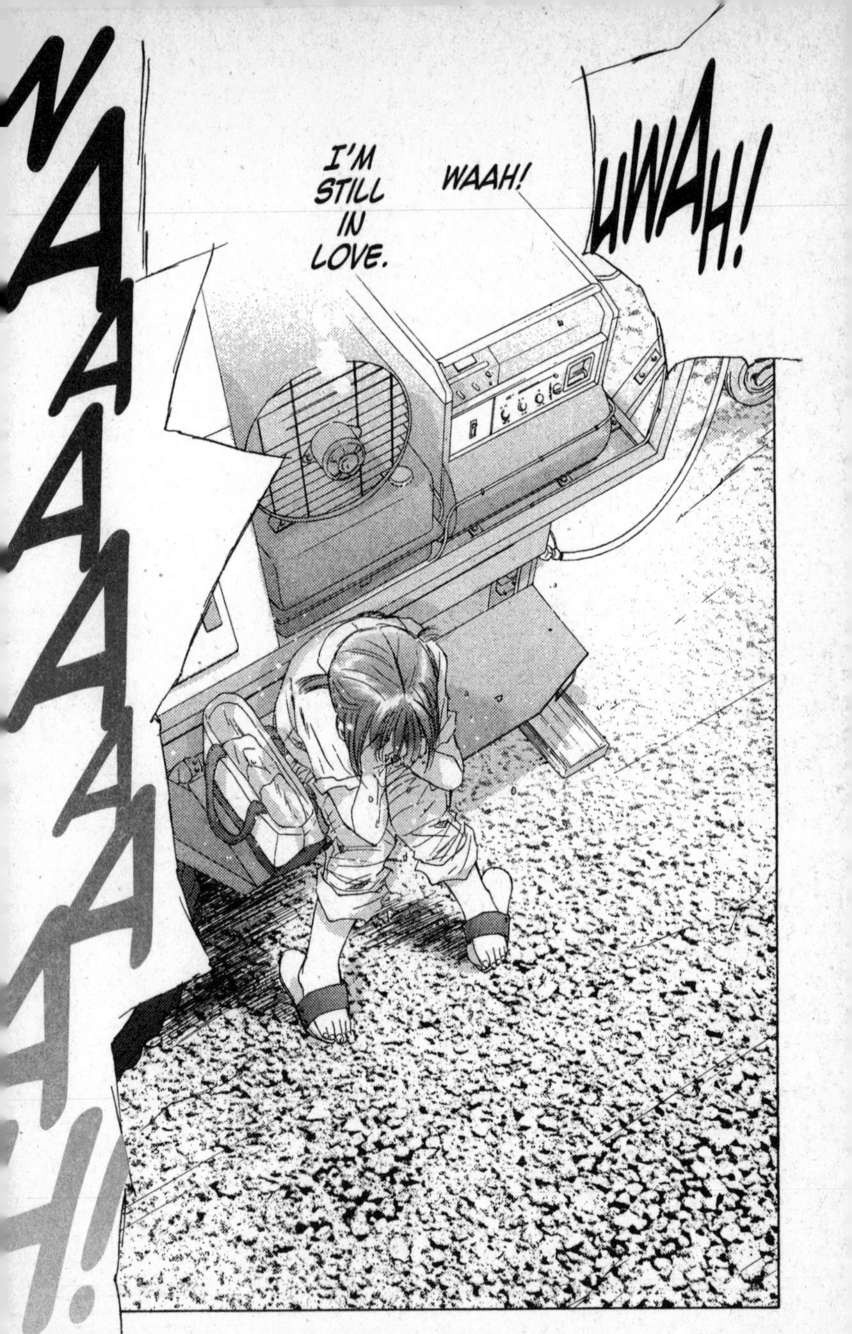
UWAH!
WAAH!
I'M STILL IN LOVE.
NAAAAAAAAH!!

最終兵器彼女

SAIKANO™

Volume 3

Story & Art by
Shin Takahash

Editor's Choice Edition

English Adaptation — Lance Caselm

Translation — Yuko Sawa

Touch-up & Lettering — Gia Cam L

Design — Izumi Eve

Editor — Eric Searlem

Managing Editor — Annette Rom

Director of Production — Noboru Watana

Editorial Director — Alvin

Sr. Director of Licensing & Acquisitions — Rika Inou

Vice President of Sales & Marketing — Liza Coppo

Executive Vice President of Editoria — Hyoe Nar

Publisher — Seiji Horibuc

Printed in the U.S.A.

Published by VIZ, LLC
P.O. Box 77010
San Francisco, CA 94107

Editor's Choice Edition
10 9 8 7 6 5 4 3 2 1
First printing December 2004

www.viz.com

RATED M FOR MATURE

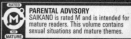

PARENTAL ADVISORY
SAIKANO is rated M and is intended for mature readers. This volume contains sexual situations and mature themes.